A COMPLETE HISTORY OF THE WORLD FIGURE SKATING CHAMPIONSHIPS

Ryan Stevens

Copyright © 2025 by Ryan Stevens

Print edition published 2025

Independently published
All rights reserved

Library and Archives Canada Cataloguing in Publication

Names: Stevens, Ryan, author
Title: A Complete History of the World Figure Skating Championships / Ryan Stevens
Description: Paperback edition | Ryan Stevens | Halifax, NS : Ryan Stevens, 2025.
Identifier: ISBN: 978-1-0691705-8-3
Subject: LCSH: Figure skating [GV.850.4] | BISAC: SPO023000   SPORTS & RECREATION/Winter Sports/Ice & Figure Skating | SPO019000 SPORTS & RECREATION/History

Every reasonable effort has been made to credit all source material included in this book.

If errors or omissions have occurred, they will be corrected in future editions provided written notification and supporting documentation has been received by the author.

All photos that appear within the book are public domain, fully licensed from Alamy or used with permission. Cover design by Stefan Prodanovic.

TABLE OF CONTENTS

Introduction	1
The Victorian Era	5
The Edwardian Era	17
The Pre-War Era	47
The Roaring Twenties	59
The Great Depression	85
The Age of Austerity	109
The Space Age	135
The Decade of Disco	167
The Decade of Decadence	201
The Age of Globalization	237
The Digital Revolution	307
The Pandemic	383
The New Normal	401
Appreciation	411
Author's Note	412
Other Books	413

GLOSSARY

ARG	Argentina
ARM	Armenia
AUS	Australia
AUT	Austria (Austria-Hungary until 1918)
AZE	Azerbaijan
BEL	Belgium
BIH	Bosnia and Herzegovina
BLS	Belarus
BRA	Brazil
BUL	Bulgaria
C/OSP	Compulsory Dances/Original Set Pattern
CAN	Canada
CCP	Compulsory Connected Program
CD	Compulsory Dance(s)
CD1	Compulsory Dance #1
CD2	Compulsory Dance #2
CDA	Compulsory Dance Qualifying Group "A"
CDB	Compulsory Dance Qualifying Group "B"
CF	Compulsory (School) Figures
CHN	China
CIS	Commonwealth of Independent States
CRO	Croatia
CYP	Cyprus
CZE	Czech Republic (Czechoslovakia until 1992)
DEN	Denmark
DQ	Disqualified
ESP	Spain
EST	Estonia

FIN	Finland
FD	Free Dance
FRA	France
FRG	Federal Republic of Germany (West Germany)
FS	Free Skating
FS1	Free Skating (1st round)
FS2	Free Skating (2nd round)
FSR	Figure Skating Federation of Russia
GDR	German Democratic Republic (East Germany)
GEO	Georgia
GER	Germany
GRB	Great Britain (United Kingdom)
GRE	Greece
HKG	Hong Kong
HUN	Hungary
IEV	Internationale Eislauf-Vereingung (also see ISU)
IND	India
IRL	Ireland
ISL	Iceland
ISR	Israel
ISU	International Skating Union
ITA	Italy
JPN	Japan
KAZ	Kazakhstan
KGZ	Kyrgyzstan
KOR	South Korea
LAT	Latvia
LIT	Lithuania
LUX	Luxembourg
MAS	Malaysia
MDA	Moldova

MEX	Mexico
MON	Monaco
MNE	Montenegro
NED	Netherlands
NOR	Norway
NZL	New Zealand
OD	Original Dance
OP	Original Program
OSP	Original Set Pattern Dance
PHI	Philippines
POL	Poland
PRI	Puerto Rico
PRK	North Korea
QR	Qualifying Round
QRA	Qualifying Round "A"
QRB	Qualifying Round "B"
RD	Rhythm Dance
ROM	Romania
RUS	Russia
S/F	Short Program/Free Skating
SAF	South Africa
SD	Short Dance
SF	Semi-Final
SFG	Special Figures
SRB	Serbia
SCG	Serbia and Montenegro
SGP	Singapore
SLO	Slovenia
SOV	Soviet Union
SUI	Switzerland
SVK	Slovakia
SWE	Sweden
(t)	Tie
THA	Thailand

TP	Technical Program
TPE	Chinese Taipei
TUR	Turkey
UKR	Ukraine
USA	United States of America
UZB	Uzbekistan
WD	Withdrew
WSF	World Skating Federation
YUG	Yugoslavia

INTRODUCTION

The World Figure Skating Championships have been around longer than airplanes, automobiles, computers, television and the internet, as well as Major League Baseball, the NHL and NFL. They existed before figure skating made its first appearance at the Summer Olympics in 1908 and they're still going strong over a century later. Remarkably, the World Championships have survived two World Wars, a devastating airplane crash and a global pandemic.

In the information age, you would think that finding detailed and accurate information about the World Championships online would be a cinch. As it turns out, much of the information that is available about this historic competition's early years is woefully incomplete and even, at times, inaccurate. If you rely on Wikipedia, which I really hope you don't, there wasn't a ladies competition at the World Championships until 1906, a pairs competition until 1908 or an ice dancing event until 1952. That's not exactly how things went down.

Before World War II, the International Skating Union largely left the organization of its Championships up to the countries that hosted them. At times, the World Championships for men, women and pairs were held in different cities, so organizers typically added additional events to the program to draw in more skaters and spectators. Anything to sell a ticket!

The World Championships for men might also consist of additional ladies and pairs events, competitions for junior skaters and obstacle races. The ladies event might be paired with speed skating races, waltzing competitions and even same-sex pairs events. The World Championships were a 'Wild West' of sorts until after World War II, when improvements in the governance of the ISU naturally led to the standardized competition we all know and love today.

Every book serves a unique purpose, but not everyone sees it that way. You can publish a fabulous book about baking delicious pies and there will still be people who complain that there weren't any recipes for cakes.. Believe it or not, there are even people who will complain that your book about pies isn't a racy "trope-filled" romance novel. I don't get it... but it's a thing.

Call me old-fashioned, but I believe every type of book has its own audience. This is a figure skating book for figure skating people.

Like cookbooks, dictionaries, encyclopedias and atlases, nonfiction historical reference books are valuable and important resources and that's what "A Complete History of the World Figure Skating" is – nothing more and certainly nothing less.

This was a daunting project to take on, but I trust that this collection of historical skating results, facts and firsts will prove a valuable and useful resource to anyone with an interest in the history of the best winter sport out there.

The history of figure skating matters and I hope this book will enlighten you as to how this historic competition has evolved and thrived over centuries and decades.

Henning Grenander, World Champion 1898. Public Domain / Skate Guard Collections

THE VICTORIAN ERA

1882 GREAT INTERNATIONAL SKATING TOURNAMENT
Vienna, Austria-Hungary, January 21-22, 1882

International Figure Skating Prize for Amateurs:

1. Leopold Frey (AUT)
2. Eduard Engelmann (AUT)
3. Axel Paulsen (NOR)
4. Anton Tuschl (AUT)
5. Franz Biberhofer (AUT)
6. Heinrich Jockl (AUT)
7. P.O. Aune (NOR)
8. Carl Werner (NOR)
9. Ernst von Stein (AUT)
WD. Franz Bellazi (AUT)
WD. F. Kostial (AUT)

International Figure Skating Prize for Professionals:

1. Callie C. Curtis (USA)
2. Edwin Paulsen (NOR)

Speed Skating (1600 meters):

1. Axel Paulsen (NOR)
2. P.O. Aune (NOR)
3. Carl Werner (NOR)
4. Carl Reinhard (GER)
5. F. Kistemann (AUT)
WD. Richard Kräuter (AUT)

Speed Skating (Wiener Eislaufverein Prize):

1. J. Leykauf (AUT)
2. Leopold Frey (AUT)
3. L. Schlesinger (AUT)
4. K. Buchmüller (AUT)
5. Richard Kräuter (AUT)
WD. E. Wernau (AUT)

Though not historically recognized as a World Championship, the Great International Skating Tournament in Vienna in 1882 was the first major international figure skating competition. The first prize was a gold medal worth 500 francs and a silver statuette of Jackson Haines. It was at this event that Norwegian speed skater Axel Paulsen debuted his namesake jump. Carl Werner, a Norwegian skater who participated in both the figure and speed skating events, was deaf and non-vocal.

Sources: Allgemeine Sport-Zeitung, January 26, 1882; Sydney Morning Herald, January 26, 1882

1890 WORLD FIGURE SKATING CHAMPIONSHIPS
St. Petersburg, Russia, February 15-17, 1890

Men's Compulsory Figures:

1(t). Alexei P. Lebedeff (RUS)
1(t). Louis Rubenstein (CAN)
2. Willi Dinstl (GER)
3(t). John Catani (FIN)
3(t). Rudolf Sundgren (FIN)
3(t). Carl Kaiser (AUT)
*. Ivar Hult (SWE)
*. W. Besch (RUS)
*. Baron I. Stackelberg (FIN)
*. O. Wollert (SWE)

Men's Special Figures:

1. Alexei P. Lebedeff (RUS)
2(t). Louis Rubenstein (CAN)
2(t). John Catani (FIN)
3. Carl Kaiser (AUT)
*. Ivar Hult (SWE)
*. W. Besch (RUS)
*. Baron I. Stackelberg (FIN)
*. O. Wollert (SWE)

Men's Free Skating:

1(t). Alexei P. Lebedeff (RUS)
1(t). John Catani (FIN)
2. Willi Dinstl (GER)
3. Carl Kaiser (AUT)
*. Ivar Hult (SWE)
*. W. Besch (RUS)
*. Baron I. Stackelberg (FIN)
*. O. Wollert (SWE)
WD. Louis Rubenstein (CAN)

Ladies Figure Skating:

1. A. Malmgren (FIN)
2. A.M. Druschinina (RUS)
3. T.T. Dybko (RUS)

Gentlemen's Pairs Skating:

1. Ivar Hult/Rudolf Sundgren (SWE/FIN)
2. I. Ketnitz/N. Krewing (RUS)

Ladies and Gentlemen's Pairs Skating:

1. A. Malmgren and I. Ketnitz (FIN/RUS)
2. Mrs. P. Dybko and Mr. F. Göhlich (RUS/POL)

3. Mrs. A. Drushinin and Mr. G. Janson (POL)

Speed Skating (536 meters):

1. I. Lindstedt (FIN)
2. Alexander Panschin (RUS)
3. P. Winogradoff (RUS)

Speed Skating (1609 meters):

1. Ad. Norseng (NOR)
2. Herr Lindstedt (NOR)
3. Th. Baltscheffski (FIN)
WD. Alexander Panschin (RUS)

Speed Skating (long distance):

1. Ad. Norseng (NOR)
2. I. Lindstedt (NOR)
3. Th. Baltscheffsky (FIN)
WD. Alexander Panschin (RUS)

Though not recognized historically as a World Championship, an international competition staged in Russia in 1890 to commemorate the founding of the Neva Skating Association (later the St. Petersburg Society Of Ice Skating Amateurs) was billed as a World Championship at the time it was held. This event was an important precursor to the ISU's official World Championships that would follow. There were three separate categories: compulsory figures, special figures and free skating. Gold, silver and bronze medals were awarded by the judges in each category, based on merit, and multiple medals of each colour could be awarded if the judges saw fit to do so.

Louis Rubenstein, who was Jewish, was harassed by Russian police while in St. Petersburg. He was only allowed to stay in the city and compete after producing a letter of introduction from the Governor General of Canada Lord Stanley, namesake of hockey's famous

Stanley Cup. Ivar Hult and Rudolf Sundgren gave a demonstration of hand-in-hand pairs skating. Willi Dinstl, Carl Kaiser and Rudolf Sundgren gave an exhibition as a trio.

Sources: Hufvudstadsbladet, February 15 and 17, 1890; Westra Finland, February 19, 1890; Kotka, February 22, 1890; Lappeenranta News, February 22, 1890; Reflections on the CFSA: A History of the Canadian Figure Skating Association 1887-1990, Teresa Moore and Sheila Robertson, 1993

1896 WORLD FIGURE AND SPEED SKATING CHAMPIONSHIPS
St. Petersburg, Russia, February 7-9, 1896

World Men's Figure Skating Championships:

	CF	FS
1. Gilbert Fuchs (GER)	1	1
2. Gustav Hügel (AUT)	2	2
3. Georg Sanders (RUS)	3	3
4. Nikolai Poduskov (RUS)	4	4

Men's Special Figures:

1. Georg Sanders (RUS)
2. Gilbert Fuchs (GER)
3. Gustav Hügel (AUT)
4. Nikolai Poduskov (RUS)

Men's Speed Skating (overall):

1. Jaap Eden (NED)
2. Gustaf Estlander (FIN)
3. Johan Wink (FIN)
4. Nikolay Fyodorov (RUS)
5. N. Obukhov (RUS)
6. K.A. Müller (RUS)
7. Wladimir Gumbin (RUS)
8. Aleksandr P. Pupikin (RUS)

9. Pyotr Kusminsky (RUS)
10. Eduard Vollenvejder (RUS)
11. A. Nikolayev (RUS)
12. Kh. Roos (RUS)
13. M. Pfeffer (RUS)
14. Julius Seyler (GER)

This event, held in St. Petersburg, Russia, included the first World Figure Skating Championships held under the auspices of the Internationale Eislauf-Vereingung (IEV/ISU). The men's competition consisted of compulsory figures and free skating. There was a separate competition for special figures, where skaters had to submit a diagram of a figure of their own creation in advance. The speed skating competition consisted of 4 races: 500, 1500, 5000 and 1000 meters.

Gilbert Fuchs made history as the first skater from Germany to win a gold medal in an official World Championship event. Fuchs, Gustav Hügel, Georg Sanders and Nikolai Poduskovmade history as the first skaters to represent Germany, Austria-Hungary and Russia in official World Championship events. Sanders was the first man to win a medal at an official World Championship event held in his home country.

Sources: Allgemeine Sport-Zeitung, February 16, 1896; Seventy-five years of European and World's championships in figure skating, ISU, 1970

1897 WORLD FIGURE AND SPEED SKATING CHAMPIONSHIPS
Stockholm, Sweden, February 13-14, 1897

World Men's Figure Skating Championships:

	SP	FS
1. Gustav Hügel (AUT)	1	3
2. Ulrich Salchow (SWE)	2	2
3. Johan Peter Lefstad (NOR)	3	4
4. Thiodolf Borgh (SWE)	5	1
5. Hugo Carlsson (SWE)	4	6

6. Oscar Holthe (NOR)	6	5

The Crown Prince of Sweden, later King Gustav V of Sweden, attended this event. Though injured, Gustav Hügel made history as the first Austrian skater to win a gold medal at the European Figure Skating Championships. Johan Peter Lefstad won Norway's first medal at the World Championships. Hügel's prizes for winning were a gold medal and a heavy silver jug.

Sources: Allgemeine Sport-Zeitung, March 7, 1897; Seventy-five years of European and World's championships in figure skating, ISU, 1970

1898 WORLD FIGURE SKATING CHAMPIONSHIPS
London, England, February 15, 1898

World Men's Figure Skating Championships:

	CF	FS
1. Henning Grenander (SWE)	3	1
2. Gustav Hügel (AUT)	1	2
3. Gilbert Fuchs (GER)	2	3
4. H. C. Holt (GRB)	4	4
WD. L. Wük (FIN)	-	-

National Skating Association's Challenge Shield for Combined Figure Skating (English Style):

1. C.E. Bell's Team - C.E. Bell/H.M. Morris/D. Mann/Robert Muirhead Hewett (GRB)
2. International Skating Club of Davos Team - J. Le Fleming/George K. Wood/H.B. Hawes/Evan Gwynne-Evans (SUI)
3. Ipswich Team - L.E. Pretty/Frank Pretty/Stanley Turner/S.A. Notcutt (GRB)
WD. Manchester Team (GRB)

Henning Grenander made history as the first skater from Scandinavia to win a gold medal at the World Figure Skating Championships. He was also the first skater to win a gold medal at the World Figure Skating Championships without winning the compulsory figures, which held a higher value than the free skating at the time.

H.C. Holt made history as the first skater to represent Great Britain at the World Figure Skating Championships.

Under the ISU regulations at that time, skaters or their federations were required to deposit an amount equal to their entry fee to protect the results. The German and Austrian Federation complied. However, both lodged a complaint stating that the Swedish judge and two British judges had scored Henning Grenander too favourably in the free skating, though he had stopped in his program which was not allowed. Although the silver and bronze medallists requested a review of the results, the ISU dismissed their protest.

The event marked the first time that an ISU Championship was held in the UK and the first time the World Championships were held in an indoor rink. His Royal Highness Prince Edward of Wales (later King Edward VII) and members of The Royal Family attended the competition at the National Skating Palace in London and a newspaper of the time remarked, "The assemblage was such as one expects to see at the opera house on a big night."

Sources: The Times, February 16, 1898; The Field: The Country Gentleman's Newspaper, February 17, 1898; The Penny Illustrated Paper, February 26, 1898; Outing: The Magazine of Amateur Sport and Pastime, April 1898; Seventy-five years of European and World's championships in figure skating, ISU, 1970

1899 WORLD FIGURE SKATING CHAMPIONSHIPS
Davos, Switzerland, February 12, 1899

World Men's Figure Skating Championships:

	CF	FS
1. Gustav Hügel (AUT)	2	1
2. Ulrich Salchow (SWE)	1	2

3. Edgar Syers (GRB) 3 3
WD. L. Dinn (GRB) - -
WD. H. Klein - pseudonym (SUI) - -

This event was originally scheduled to be held in Vienna, but it was moved to Davos because of a thaw. Edgar Syers made history as the first British skater to win a medal at the World Figure Skating Championships.

Sources: Allgemeine Sport-Zeitung, February 19, 1899; Seventy-five years of European and World's championships in figure skating, ISU, 1970

1900 WORLD FIGURE SKATING CHAMPIONSHIPS
Davos, Switzerland, February 10-11, 1900

World Men's Figure Skating Championships:

	CF	FS
1. Gustav Hügel (AUT)	2	1
2. Ulrich Salchow (SWE)	1	2
WD. George Wood (GRB)	-	-

Speed Skating (500 meters):

1. Peder Østlund (NOR)
2. Franz Wathén (FIN)
3. Jan Grève (NED)
WD. Eduard Vollenvejder (RUS)
WD. Georges de Stoppani (SUI)

Speed Skating (1000 meters):

1. Peder Østlund (NOR)
2. Jan Grève (NED)
3. Franz Wathén (FIN)
WD. Eduard Vollenvejder (RUS)

Speed Skating (1500 meters):

1. Peder Østlund (NOR)
2. Franz Wathén (FIN)
3. Jan Grève (NED)

Speed Skating (5000 meters):

1. Peder Østlund (NOR)
2. Jan Grève (NED)
3. Franz Wathén (FIN)

Speed Skating (10000 meters):

1. Peder Østlund (NOR)
2. Jan Grève (NED)
3. Franz Wathén (FIN)

Source: Allgemeine Sport-Zeiting, February 18, 1900; Seventy-five years of European and World's championships in figure skating, ISU, 1970

Gustav Hügel, *World Champion 1897 and 1899-1900*. *Public Domain / Skate Guard Collections*

Illustrations of skaters at the 1902 World Figure Skating Championships, including Ulrich Salchow and Madge Syers. Chronicle / Alamy Stock Photo.

THE EDWARDIAN ERA

1901 WORLD FIGURE AND SPEED SKATING CHAMPIONSHIPS
Stockholm, Sweden, February 10-11, 1901

World Men's Figure Skating Championships:

	CF	FS
1. Ulrich Salchow (SWE)	1	2
2. Gilbert Fuchs (GER)	2	1
WD. G. Hopp (RUS)	-	-
WD. Nikolay Panin-Kolomenkin (RUS)	-	-

World Speed Skating Championships (overall):

1. Franz Wathén (FIN)
2. Rudolf Gundersen (NOR)
3. Gustaf Sörman (SWE)
4. Martinus Lørdahl (NOR)
5. Walter Johansson (FIN)
6. Josef Jahnzon (SWE)
7. Jan Grève (NED)
8. Fredrik Sjöqvist (SWE)
9. David Jahrl (SWE)
10. Ernst Johansson (SWE)
11. Ernst Ehrnström (SWE)
12. Karl Olofsson (SWE)
13. Gösta Smitt (SWE)

International Men's Figure Skating Championships for the Nordiska Spelens prize):

1. Oscar Holthe (NOR)
2. Einar de Flon (SWE)
3. Martin Gordan (GER)
4. Dr. Kurt Dannenberg (GER)

5. John Depken (SWE)
6. Christian Soldan (SWE)

International Pairs Skating Championships for the Nordiska Spelens prize:

1. Christine von Szabo/Gustav Euler (AUT)
2. Madge Syers/Edgar Syers (GRB)
3. Hedwig Müller/Martin Gordan (GER)
*. Ada Borell/I. Harling (SWE)
*. Emmy Sjöberg/August Andersson (SWE)
*. Elna Montgomery/Erik Amundson (SWE)
*. Paula Nilsson/Per Thorén (SWE)
*. Signe Andersson/Ernst Ehrnström (SWE)

Gentlemen's Pairs Skating for the Nordiska Spelens prize:

1. Egron Wirström/Nils Rosenius (SWE)
2. E. Ehrnström/E. Nordling (SWE)
3. Walter Rosenberger/Per Thorén (SWE)
*. Edgar Syers/Martin Gordan (GRB/GER)
*. E. Höglund/Bror Meyer (SWE)
*. E. Bartholdy/Erik Amundson (SWE)

The World Figure Skating Championships were slated to be held in London, England, but as the country was in mourning following the death of Queen Victoria, the competition was moved to Stockholm, Sweden.

The on-ice events were held as part of a larger multi-sport festival called the Nordiska Spelens (Nordic Games), which also included skiing, ski jumping and equestrian events.

Sources: Programme, 1901 World Figure Skating Championships; Suomen Kansa, February 13, 1901; Neues Wiener Tagblatt, February 16, 1901; Wiborgsbladet, February 20, 1901; Allgemeine Sport-Zeitung, February 17, 1901; Suomen Urheilulehti, April 1, 1901; Seventy-five years of European and World's championships in figure skating, ISU, 1970

1902 WORLD FIGURE SKATING CHAMPIONSHIPS
London, England, February 10-17, 1902

World Men's Figure Skating Championships:

	CF	FS
1. Ulrich Salchow (SWE)	1	1
2. Madge Syers (GRB)	2	3
3. Martin Gordan (GER)	4	2
4. Horatio Tertuliano Torromé (GRB)	3	4

Pairs Skating:

1. Madge Syers/Edgar Syers (GRB)
2. Emmy Sjöberg/Christian Soldan (SWE)
3. Hedwig Weingartner/Martin Gordan (GER)

Valsing (Waltzing on Ice):

1. Gladys Duddell/French Brewster (GRB)
2. Miss Irby/W.F. Adams (GRB)
3. Miss Marshall/C.F. Clayton (GRB)

English Style - Challenge Cup (Combined Skating):

1. Frank G. Fedden - partnered by H.M. Morris (GRB)
2. Phyllis Squire - partnered by H.D. Hoffman (GRB)
3. H.M. Morris - partnered by Frank G. Fedden (GRB)

English Style - Individual (British Championships):

1. Frank G. Fedden (GRB)
2. Alan J. Davidson (GRB)

English Style - Team (British Championships):

1. H.D. Hoffman/Phyllis Squire/H.M. Morris/H.M. Elder (GRB)
2. Frank G. Fedden/George Wood/Alan J. Davidson/F.T. Leeming (GRB)

3. F.B.O. Hawes/A.W. Bristow/W.A. Russell/R. Moreland (GRB)

After being moved to Stockholm the year prior, London had its turn in hosting the World Figure Skating Championships, as part of a week-long celebration of figure skating and special events organized by the National Skating Association. The event was attended by King Edward VII and the Prince and Princess of Wales, later King George V and Queen Mary of Teck.

Figure skating was very much seen as a "gentleman's sport" and no one ever conceived the fact that a woman might consider entering. With the encouragement of her husband and pairs partner Edgar, Madge Syers entered the World Figure Skating Championships and made history as the first woman to win a medal. She was also the first woman to win a medal at a World Championship event held in her home country. Years later, ISU President Herbert J. Clarke claimed, "Salchow presented the Gold Medal he had won to Mrs. Syers, but the news of this was not made public. Many years afterwards I told Mrs. Salchow of this presentation; Mrs. Salchow replied that she knew now for the first time why her husband had only nine Gold Medals although he had won the World Championship ten times."

Eleven couples participated in the valsing on ice competition, but only the top 3 finishers were recorded. Though it would be decades before an official ice dancing competition would be held at the World Figure Skating Championships, this was the first instance ice dancing made an appearance at the event.

Sources: The Guardian, February 14, 1902; Daily Express, February 14, 1902; The Illustrated London News, February 22, 1902; The Illustrated Sporting and Dramatic News, February 22, 1902; Allgemeine Sport-Zeitung, February 23, 1902; Skating magazine, December 1952; Seventy-five years of European and World's championships in figure skating, ISU, 1970

1903 WORLD FIGURE SKATING CHAMPIONSHIPS
St. Petersburg, Russia, February 20-21, 1903

World Men's Figure Skating Championships:

	CF	FS
1. Ulrich Salchow (SWE)	1	1
2. Nikolay Panin-Kolomenkin (RUS)	2	3
3. Max Bohatsch (AUT)	4	2
4. Ernst Lassahn (GER)	5	4
WD. Gilbert Fuchs (GER)	3	-

Pairs Skating:

1. Christine von Szabo/Karl Euler (AUT)
2. Mizzi Bohatsch/Otto Bohatsch (AUT)
3. Frieda Bellinger/Gustav Stahlberg (GER)
4. Frau Antonewitsch/G. Hopp (RUS)
5. Frau Kauffmann/Herr Wessmann (RUS)

Men's Skating (Yusupov Prize):

	CF	FS
1. A.G. Rosz (RUS)	1	5
2. Karl A. Ollo (RUS)	3	1
3. Fedor Datlin (RUS)	2	3
4. Sakari Ilmanen (FIN)	4	2
5. R. Palmgren (SWE)	5	4
WD. A. Laumann (RUS)	-	

Sources: Helsingfors-Posten, February 23 and 24, 1903; Wiborgs Nyheter, February 25, 1903; Allgemeine Sport-Zeitung, March 8, 1903

1904 WORLD FIGURE SKATING CHAMPIONSHIPS
Berlin, Germany, January 23-24, 1904

World Men's Figure Skating Championships:

	CF	FS
1. Ulrich Salchow (SWE)	1	1

2. Heinrich Burger (GER)　　　　　　　　　　3　　2
3. Martin Gordan (GER)　　　　　　　　　　　2　　3
WD. Madge Syers (GRB)　　　　　　　　　　 -　　 -
WD. Karl Zenger (GER)

Pairs Skating (Jubilee Prize):

1. Madge Syers/Edgar Syers (GRB)
2. Christine von Szabo/Gustav Euler (AUT)
3. Else Müller/Herr Rasche (GER)
4. Fraulein Müller/Herr Müller (GER)

Men's Figure Skating (Jubilee Prize):

1. Anton Steiner (AUT)
2. H. Hofmann (GER)
3. Ernst Lassahn (GER)
4. Herr Barthel (AUT)
5. Eugen Dreyer (GER)

Pairs Skating (Internationales Paarlaufen):

1. Frau Beranek/Anton Beranek (AUT)
2. Frau Hofmann/H. Hofmann (GER)
3. Frieda Bellinger/Franz Zilly (AUT)
4. Fraulein Otto/Karl Gützlaff (GER)

Group Skating (Internationales Gruppenlaufen - Wanderpreis):

1. Berliner Schlittschuhclub - Else Müller/Fraulein Müller/Herr Müller/Herr Rasche (GER)
2. Münchener Eislauf-Verein - Frau Hofmann/Anna Hübler/Fraulein Birsch/Fraulein Rau (GER)

Junior Men's Figure Skating:

1. Max Rendschmidt (GER)
2. Herr Hagenow (GER)

3. Adolf Schmidt (GER)
4. Herr Richter (GER)
5. Herr Müller (GER)
6. Herr Lily (GER)
7. Herr Tietz (GER)

Speed Skating (500 meters):

1. Rudolf Gundersen (DEN)
2. Alfred Lauenberg (GER)
3. Emerich Wampetits (HUN)
4. Herr Christiani (NOR)
5. Herr Becker (NOR)
6. Herr Bannoff (GER)
WD. Schultze (GER)

Junior Speed Skating (500 meters):

1. Herr Schultze (GER)
2. Herr Schönemann (GER)
3. Béla Grof (HUN)
4. Herr Pape (GER)
5. Herr Arnold (GER)
6. Herr Waesch (GER)
7. Herr Tietz (GER)
8. Ferdinand Bölling (GER)

Speed Skating (1500 meters, Jubilee Prize):

1. Rudolf Gundersen (DEN)
2. Emerich Wampetits (HUN)
3. Alfred Lauenberg (GER)
DNQ. Herr Becker (NOR)
DNQ. Schultze (GER)
WD. Herr Christiani (NOR)
WD. Herr Bannoff (GER)

Sources: Neues Wiener Tagblatt, January 22, 26 and 27, 1904; Allgemeine

Sport-Zeitung, January 31, 1904; Seventy-five years of European and World's championships in figure skating, ISU, 1970

1905 WORLD FIGURE SKATING CHAMPIONSHIPS
Stockholm, Sweden, February 4-6, 1905

World Men's Figure Skating Championships:

	CF	FS
1. Ulrich Salchow (SWE)	1	2
2. Max Bohatsch (AUT)	2	1
3. Per Thorén (SWE)	3	3
4. Richard Johansson (SWE)	4	4
5. Martin Gordan (GER)	5	5

European Speed Skating Championships:

1. Johan Vikander (FIN)
2. Waldemar Ylander (FIN)
3. Franz Wathén (FIN)
4. Moje Öholm (SWE)
5. Birger Carlsson (SWE)
6. Olof Hofstedt (SWE)
7. Jean Pettersson (SWE)
8. Erik Thour (SWE)
9. Ejnar Sørensen (DEN)
10. Gotthard Thourén (SWE)
11. Nils Willnow (SWE)
12. Arvid Åberg (SWE)
13. Herman Söderbäck (SWE)
14. Anton Ryberg (SWE)
15. David Eriksson (SWE)
16. Erik Kullman (SWE)
17. Miltiades Mannó (HUN)
18. Carl Carlsson (SWE)
19. Henrik Morén (SWE)
20. Osvald Låstbom (SWE)
21. Richard Andersson (SWE)
22. Gösta Asp (SWE)

23. Arnold Protzen (GER)

Ladies Figure Skating (International Amateur Figure Skating Championships for the Nordiska Spelens pris):

1. Muriel Harrison (GRB)
2. Lili Kronberger (HUN)
3. Mrs. Kellie (GRB)
4. Elna Montgomery (SWE)
5. Bella McKinnan (GRB)
6. Helga Liljegren (SWE)
7. Anna Hamilton (SWE)
WD. Valborg Lindahl (SWE)
WD. Edith Behrens (SWE)

Pairs Skating (International Amateur Figure Skating Championships for the Nordiska Spelens pris):

1. Mizzi Bohatsch/Max Bohatsch (AUT)
2. Madge Syers/Edgar Syers (GRB)
3. Valborg Lindahl/Emil Lindahl (SWE)
4. Muriel Harrison/Ulrich Salchow (GRB/SWE)

Men (International Amateur Figure Skating Championships for the Nordiska Spelens pris):

	SF	FS
1. Bror Meyer (SWE)	1	2
2. Karl Axel Holmström (SWE)	4	1
3. Gustav Schönning (SWE)	2	5
4. Nils Rosenius (SWE)	3	3
5. Max Rendschmidt (GER)	5	4
6. Emil Höglund (SWE)	6	6
7. Birgir Eriksson (SWE)	7	7
8. Ivar von Feilitzen (SWE)	8	8

The on-ice events were held as part of a larger multi-sport festival called the Nordiska Spelens (Nordic Games), which also included skiing, ski jumping and equestrian events.

For the first time, a women's figure skating competition was held in conjunction with the ISU's World Figure Skating Championships. The first official ISU Championship for Ladies, later recognized as the World Championships for ladies, was not held until the following year. The 1905 winner, Muriel Harrison, has sadly received very little recognition for her historic achievement in 1905.

Sources: Allgemeine Sport-Zeitung, February 12, 1905; Scrapbook of programmes and newspaper clippings, 1905 Nordic Games, Sveriges Centralförening för Idrottens Främjande; Seventy-five years of European and World's championships in figure skating, ISU, 1970

1906 WORLD MEN'S FIGURE SKATING CHAMPIONSHIPS
Munich, Germany, February 3-4, 1906

World Men's Figure Skating Championships:

	CF	FS
1. Gilbert Fuchs (GER)	1	1
2. Heinrich Burger (GER)	4	2
3. Bror Meyer (SWE)	2	4
4. Karl Zenger (GER)	5	3
5. Per Thorén (SWE)	3	6
6. Anton Steiner (AUT)	6	5
7. Martin Gordan (GER)	7	7

German Men's Figure Skating Championships:

1. Heinrich Burger (GER)
2. Karl Zenger (GER)
3. Martin Gordan (GER)

German Speed Skating Championships:

1. Julius Seyler (GER)
2. Herr Becker (GER)
3. Herr Sulzberg (GER)

Pairs Skating:

1. Anna Hübler/Heinrich Burger (GER)
2. Käthchen Beer/Ludwig Niedermayer (GER)
3. Grete Pfeffer/Herr Pfeffer (GER)

Men's Figure Skating (Association Prize):

1. Max Rendschmidt (GER)
2. Erich Bartel (AUT)
3. Ludwig Niedermayer (GER)

Junior Men's Figure Skating:

1. Georg Velisch (GER)
2. Alois Wilschek (AUT)
3. Robert Sonder (GER)
4. Herr Bauer (GER)

Junior Ladies Figure Skating:

1. Elsa Rendschmidt (GER)
2. Anna Hübler (GER)

Junior Speed Skating (1000 meters):

1. Herr Sulzberg (GER)
2. Herr Braun (GER)
3. Herr Hollweck (GER)

Sources: Neues Wiener Tagblatt, February 5, 1906; Allgemeine Sport-Zeitung, February 11, 1906; Seventy-five years of European and World's championships in figure skating, ISU, 1970

1906 WORLD LADIES FIGURE SKATING CHAMPIONSHIPS
Davos, Switzerland, January 28-29, 1906

ISU Championship for Ladies (World Ladies Figure Skating Championships):

	CF	FS
1. Madge Syers (GRB)	1	1
2. Jenny Herz (AUT)	3	3(t)
3. Lili Kronberger (HUN)	4	2
4. Elsa Rendschmidt (GER)	5	3(t)
5. Dorothy Greenhough Smith (GRB)	2	5
WD. Anna Hübler (GER)	-	-

European Men's Figure Skating Championships:

	CF	FS
1. Ulrich Salchow (SWE)	1	1
2. Ernst Herz (AUT)	2	2
3. Per Thorén (SWE)	3	3
4. Bror Meyer (SWE)	4	6
5. Sándor Urbáry (HUN)	6	4
6. Max Rendschmidt (GER)	5	5
WD. Gilbert Fuchs (GER)	-	-
WD. Heinrich Burger (GER)	-	-
WD. J. Hunziker (SUI)	-	-

European Speed Skating Championships (500 meters):

1. Rudolf Gundersen (NOR)
2. Franz Schilling (AUT)
3. Coen de Koning (NED)
4. Steven George Ashe (GRB)
5. Albin Rochat (SUI)
6. Richard Muser (SUI)

European Speed Skating Championships (1500 meters):

1. Rudolf Gundersen (NOR)
2. Franz Schilling (AUT)
3. Coen de Koning (NED)
4. Steven George Ashe (GRB)
5. Richard Muser (SUI)
DNF. Albin Rochat (SUI)

European Speed Skating Championships (5000 meters)

1. Rudolf Gundersen (NOR)
2. Coen de Koning (NED)
3. Franz Schilling (AUT)
4. Steven George Ashe (GRB)
5. Richard Muser (SUI)
6. Albin Rochat (SUI)

European Speed Skating Championships (10000 meters):

1. Coen de Koning (NED)
2. Rudolf Gundersen (NOR)
3. Franz Schilling (AUT)
4. Steven George Ashe (GRB)
DNF. Richard Muser (SUI)
DNF. Albin Rochat (SUI)

European Speed Skating Championships (Final):

1. Rudolf Gundersen (NOR)
2. Coen de Koning (NED)
3. Franz Schilling (AUT)

Pairs Skating:

1. Madge Syers/Edgar Syers (GRB)
2. Anna Hübler/Heinrich Burger (GER)
3. Phyllis Johnson/James Henry Johnson (GRB)

4. Valborg Lindahl/Emil Lindahl (NOR)

Ladies Figure Skating (Internationales Damenlaufen) - Prize of the International Skating Club of Davos:

1. Elsa Rendschmidt (GER)
2. Jenny Herz (AUT)
3. Anna Hübler (GER)
4. Miss Harrington (GRB)
5. Miss Rossel (SUI)

The 1906 ISU Championship for Ladies, held in conjunction with that year's European Figure Skating Championships, was later recognized as the first official World Championships for ladies. As the women's suffrage movement gained momentum in England, Madge Syers made history as the first British skater to win a gold medal at the World Championships.

Sources: Feuille D'Avis de Lausanne, January 29, 1906; Neues Wiener Tagblatt, January 30, 1906; Der Bund, January 30, 1906; Allgemeine Sport-Zeitung, February 4, 1906; Seventy-five years of European and World's championships in figure skating, International Skating Union, 1970

1907 WORLD FIGURE SKATING CHAMPIONSHIPS
Vienna, Austria-Hungary, January 22, 1907

World Men's Figure Skating Championships:

		CF	FS
1. Ulrich Salchow (SWE)		1	3
2. Max Bohatsch (AUT)		2	1
3. Gilbert Fuchs (GER)		3	2
4. Per Thorén (SWE)		4	4
5. Heinrich Burger (GER)	5	5	
6. Martin Gordan (GER)		7	6
7. Martinus Lørdahl (NOR)		6	7

ISU Championship for Ladies (World Ladies Figure Skating Championships):

		CF	FS
1. Madge Syers (GRB)		1	1
2. Jenny Herz (GER)		2	2
3. Lili Kronberger (GER)	3	4	
4. Elsa Rendschmidt (GER)		5	3
5. Gwendolyn Lycett (GRB)		4	5

Pairs Skating Championships:

1. Anna Hübler/Heinrich Burger (GER)
2. Phyllis Johnson/James Henry Johnson (GRB)
3. Madge Syers/Edgar Syers (GRB)

Pairs Skating (B Class):

1. Helene Kuich/Karl Mejstrik (AUT)
2. Else Barthel/Alois Wilschek (AUT)

Men's Figure Skating (Karl von Korper Prize):

1. Max Rendschmidt (GER)
2. Fedor Datlin (RUS)
3. Gustav Schöning (SWE)
4. Alois Wilschek (AUT)
5. Oskar Hoppe (AUT)
6. Erich Gutleben (GER)

Speed Skating (500 meters):

1. Miltiades Mannó (HUN)
2. Andrea Péczely (HUN)
3. Franz Schilling (AUT)
4. Josef 'Pepi' Weiß-Pfändler (AUT)
5. Ludwig Haraszty (HUN)
6. Karl Levitzky (HUN)
7. Josef Sablatnig (AUT)

Speed Skating (1500 meters):

1. Miltiades Mannó (HUN)
2. Franz Schilling (AUT)
3. Ladislaus Schick (HUN)
4. Ludwig Haraszty (HUN)
5. Heinrich Weidinger (AUT)
6. Josef 'Pepi' Weiß-Pfändler (AUT)
7. Karl Levitzky (HUN)

Speed Skating (5000 meters):

1. Franz Schilling (AUT)
2. Ladislaus Schick (HUN)
3. Ludwig Haraszty (HUN)
4. Heinrich Weidinger (AUT)
5. Franz Sattler (AUT)
6. Josef Sablatnig (AUT)
7. Josef Brunner (AUT)
8. Ignaz Proksch (AUT)
9. Karl Levitzky (HUN)

The World Figure Championships in Vienna nearly relocated to Klagenfurt because of a thaw, but once the competitors and judges arrived, the temperature unexpectedly plummeted to minus twenty-six degrees Celsius. A blizzard struck, forcing skaters to compete in terrible conditions. Battling the cold, the band that provided music for the free skating events divided into two groups and played in shifts to prevent their instruments from freezing. Madge and Edgar Syers recalled, "The Championship of 1907 will long be remembered by those who took part in it owing to the suffering entailed on them by the intense cold which, accentuated by a bitter wind, was almost unbearable. Several times the benumbed skaters were forced to retire and restore the circulation to their hands and feet, and many of the competitors and judges were subsequently hors de combat as the result of this trying experience... The competition lasted far into the evening, the committee making the serious mistake of crowding far too many events into the limits of a brief winter day, thus inflicting on judges and competitors an unnecessary amount of pain and discomfort. The cold during the whole of the meeting was indescribable. Several persons were seriously frost bitten, and many others were quite overcome by the severe conditions. It cannot be said that the committee of the Vienna Club were ideal hosts. The competitors were left to their own devices during their stay, and located where no food, save a scanty breakfast, could be obtained, and where a bath was an almost unheard of luxury."

Sources: The Sportsman, January 26, 1907; Allgemeine Sport-Zeitung, January 27, 1907; Seventy-five years of European and World's championships in figure skating, ISU, 1970; The Book of Winter Sports, Madge and Edgar Syers, 1908

1908 WORLD MEN'S AND LADIES FIGURE SKATING CHAMPIONSHIPS
Troppau, Austria-Hungary, January 25-26, 1908

World Men's Figure Skating Championships:

		CF	FS
1. Ulrich Salchow (SWE)		1	2
2. Gilbert Fuchs (GER)		2	1
3. Heinrich Burger (GER)	3	3	

ISU Championship for Ladies (World Ladies Figure Skating Championships):

		CF	FS
1. Lili Kronberger (HUN)	1	1	
2. Elsa Rendschmidt (GER)		2	2

Pairs Skating:

1. Anna Hübler/Heinrich Burger (GER)
2. Grete Bartel/Alois Wilschek (AUT)
3. Helene Kuich/Karl Mejstrik (AUT)
4. Hedwig Müller/Otto Aigner (AUT)
5. Else Müller/George Müller (GER)

6. Julie Bernhart/Ewald Hellebrand (AUT)
7. Hilda Ballusek/Wilfried Jahn (AUT)

Men's Fours Skating:

1. Otto Aigner/Edgar Bareck/Oskar Hoppe/Leo Urban (AUT)

Men's Figure Skating (Internationales Seniorlaufen):

1. Alois Wilschek (AUT)
2. Oscar Hoppe (AUT)
3. Erich Gutleben (GER)
WD. Leo Scheu (AUT)
WD. Erich Bartel (AUT)
WD. Kurt Schmidt (GER)
WD. Anton Steiner (AUT)

Ladies Figure Skating (Internationales Damenlaufen):

1. Zsófia Méray-Horváth (HUN)
2. Anna Hübler (GER)
3. Helene Kuich (AUT)
4. Hedwig Müller (AUT)
5. Hermine Kunz (AUT)
6. Grete Bartel (AUT)
7. Angela Meixner (AUT)
8. Grete Strasilla (AUT)
9. Marie Ballusek (AUT)
10. Else Tomann (AUT)
11. Grete Janotta (AUT)
12. Julie Bernhart (AUT)

Junior Men's Figure Skating (International):

1. Ewald Hellebrand (AUT)
2. Andor Szende (HUN)
3. Otto Aigner (AUT)
4. George Müller (GER)

5. Leo Scheu (AUT)
6. Leo Urban (AUT)
7. Hubert Oppitz (AUT)
8. Karl Friedel (AUT)
9. Georg Hallana (GER)
WD. Alois Eschner (AUT)
WD. Adolf Harich (AUT)
WD. Wilfried Jahn (AUT)
WD. Karl Jüttner (GER)
WD. Leopold Szollás (HUN)

Sources: Allgemeine Sport-Zeitung, January 26 and February 2, 1908; Seventy-five years of European and World's championships in figure skating, International Skating Union, 1970

1908 WORLD PAIRS SKATING CHAMPIONSHIPS
St. Petersburg, Russia, February 16, 1908

World Pairs Skating Championships:

1. Anna Hübler/Heinrich Burger (GER)
2. Phyllis Johnson/James Henry Johnson (GRB)
3. Lidia Popova/Aleksandr Fischer (RUS)

Men's Figure Skating (Alexander Panschin Wanderpreis):

1. Nikolay Panin-Kolomenkin (RUS)
2. Ulrich Salchow (SWE)
3. Karl Ollo (RUS)
4. Fedor Datlin (RUS)
5. Heinrich Burger (GER)

Ladies Figure Skating:

1. Lili Kronberger (HUN)
2. Elsa Rendschmidt (GER)
3. Elna Montgomery (SWE)

Though pairs skating competitions had long been held in conjunction with the World Figure Skating Championships, the 1908 event in St. Petersburg was the first to be officially recognized as a World Championship event. Germany's Anna Hübler and Heinrich Burger won the first official title in this discipline. Russia's Lidia Popova and Aleksandr Fischer were the first pair to win a medal at a World Championship event held in their home country.

The men's competition in St. Petersburg consisted of special figures, compulsory figures and free skating. Ulrich Salchow won the free skating, but Panin-Kolomenkin's strength in the special figures (a Russian specialty that Salchow didn't excel at) earned him the overall title.

Sources: Nya Pressen, February 18, 1908; Seventy-five years of European and World's championships in figure skating, International Skating Union, 1970

1909 WORLD MEN'S AND PAIRS FIGURE SKATING CHAMPIONSHIPS
Stockholm, Sweden, February 7-8, 1909

World Men's Figure Skating Championships:

	CF	FS
1. Ulrich Salchow (SWE)	1	2
2. Per Thorén (SWE)	2	1
3. Ernst Herz (AUT)	3	4
4. Richard Johansson (SWE)	4	3
5. Fedor Datlin (RUS)	5	5

World Pairs Skating Championships:

1. Phyllis Johnson/James Henry Johnson (GRB)
2. Valborg Lindahl/Nils Rosenius (SWE)
3. Gertrud Ström/Richard Johansson (SWE)
4. Mimi Grømer/Karl Erikson (NOR)
5. Alexia Schøien/Yngvar Bryn (NOR)

Men's Figure Skating (International):

1. Karl Axel Holmström (SWE)
2. Ivar Wennerholm (SWE)
3. Martinus Lørdahl (NOR)
4. Martin Stixrud (NOR)
5. F. Mothander (SWE)
6. Max Rendschmidt (GER)
7. Andor Szende (HUN)

Junior Men's Figure Skating (International):

1. Gösta Sandahl (SWE)
2. Carl Sandahl (SWE)
3. Gillis Grafström (SWE)
4. Andreas Krogh (NOR)

Ladies Figure Skating (International):

1. Elsa Rendschmidt (GER)
2. Zsófia Méray-Horváth (HUN)
3. Elna Montgomery (SWE)

Speed Skating (500 meters):

1. Oskar Mathiesen (NOR)
2. Sigurd Mathisen (NOR)
3. Moje Öholm (SWE)
4. Eino Vanhala (FIN)
5. K. Louholla (FIN)
6. F. Wath (SWE)
7. Olof Hofstedt (SWE)
8. Magnus Johansen (NOR)

Speed Skating (1500 meters):

1. Oskar Mathiesen (NOR)
2. Sigurd Mathisen (NOR)

3. Moje Öholm (SWE)

Speed Skating (5000 meters):

1. Oskar Mathiesen (NOR)
2. O. Thorén (SWE)
3. O. Andersson (SWE)
4. Magnus Johansen (NOR)
5. Moje Öholm (SWE)

Speed Skating (10000 meters):

1. Oskar Mathiesen (NOR)
2. O. Thorén (SWE)
3. Moje Öholm (SWE)
4. O. Andersson (SWE)
6. Sigurd Mathisen (NOR)

Junior Speed Skating (500 meters):

1. Alexander Bäckström (FIN)

Sources: Helsingin Sanomat, February 12, 1909; The Field: The Country Gentleman's Newspaper, February 13, 1909; Hufvudstadsbladet, February 13, 1909; Allgemeine Sport-Zeitung, February 14 and 21, 1909

1909 WORLD LADIES FIGURE SKATING CHAMPIONSHIPS
Budapest, Hungary, January 23-24, 1909

ISU Championship for Ladies (World Ladies Figure Skating Championships):

	CF	FS
1. Lili Kronberger (HUN)	1	1
WD. Dorothy Greenhough Smith (GRB)	-	-

European Men's Figure Skating Championships:

	CF	FS
1. Ulrich Salchow (SWE)	1	2
2. Gilbert Fuchs (GER)	3	1
3. Per Thorén (SWE)	2	3
4. Karl Ollo (RUS)	4	4(t)
5. Sándor Urbáry (HUN)	5	4(t)
WD. Irving Brokaw (USA)	-	-
WD. Anton Steiner (AUT)	-	-

European Speed Skating Championships (500 meters):

1. Oskar Mathiesen (NOR)
2. Moje Öholm (SWE)
3. Thomas Bohrer (AUT)
4. Sigurd Mathisen (NOR)
5. Miltiades Mannó (HUN)
6. Franz Schilling (AUT)

European Speed Skating Championships (1500 meters):

1. Oskar Mathiesen (NOR)
2. Thomas Bohrer (AUT)
3. Moje Öholm (SWE)
4. Sigurd Mathisen (NOR)
5. Franz Schilling (AUT)

European Speed Skating Championships (5000 meters):

1. Thomas Bohrer (AUT)
2. Oskar Mathiesen (NOR)
3. Moje Öholm (SWE)
4. Sigurd Mathisen (NOR)
5. Franz Schilling (AUT)

European Speed Skating Championships (10000 meters):

1. Thomas Bohrer (AUT)
2. Oskar Mathiesen (NOR)
3. Moje Öholm (SWE)
4. Sigurd Mathisen (NOR)
WD. Franz Schilling (AUT)

Ladies Figure Skating (Seniorenkunstlaufen):

1. Jenny Herz (AUT)
2. Elsa Rendschmidt (GER)
3. Zsófia Méray-Horváth (HUN)
4. Anna Hübler (GER)
WD. Hermine Kunz (AUT)

Pairs Skating:

1. Anna Hübler/Heinrich Burger (GER)
2. Helene Kuich/Karl Mejstrik (AUT)
3. Ludovika Eilers/Walter Jakobsson (GER/FIN)
4. Hedwig Müller/George Müller (GER)
5. Elsa Lischka/Oskar Hoppe (AUT)
6. Fräulein Beranek/Anton Beranek (AUT)
7. Hedwig Winzer/Hugo Winzer (AUT)
8. Grete Bartel/Alois Wilschek (AUT)
WD. Fräulein Müller/O. Aigner (AUT)

Men's Figure Skating (International Senior Herrenkunst):

1. Andor Szende (HUN)
2. Walter Jakobsson (FIN)
3. Ludwig Richard (AUT)
*. Rudolf Beck (AUT)
*. Herr Wrobt (RUS)
*. Dr. Ernst Oppacher (AUT)
*. Oskar Hoppe (AUT)
*. Henryk J. Krukowicz-Przedrzymirski (RUS)

*. Heinrich Burger (GER)
*. Alois Wilschek (AUT)
*. E. Gutleben (GER)

*Skaters listed are the original entrants in this category. Records from the "Neues Wiener Tagblatt" noted that eight skaters actually competed, but only the top 3 finishers were noted.

Junior Men's Figure Skating:

1. Robert Sander (GER)
2. George Müller (GER)
3. B. Wrobel (AUT)
*. Dr. Ernst Oppacher (AUT)
*. Henryk J. Krukowicz-Przedrzymirski (RUS)
*. Sander - pseudonym
*. O. Aigner (AUT)
*. Herr Farkas (HUN)
*. Seitz - pseudonym
*. Herr Wrobt (RUS)
*. Herr Urban (AUT)
*. Herr Szollás (HUN)
*. Willy Böckl (AUT)

*Skaters listed are the original entrants in this category. Records from the "Neues Wiener Tagblatt" noted that eight skaters actually competed, but only the top 3 finishers were noted.

Junior Ladies Figure Skating:

1. Helene Fräter (HUN)
2. Hedwig Müller (GER)
3. Hermine Kunz (AUT)
*. Hedwig Winzer (AUT)
*. Grete Bartel (AUT)
*. Grete Strassila (AUT)
*. Elsa Lischka (AUT)
*. Fräulein Meixner (AUT)

*Skaters listed are the original entrants in this category. Records from the "Neues Wiener Tagblatt" noted that nine skaters actually competed, but only the top 3 finishers were noted.

In 1909, the ISU Championship for Ladies (World Ladies Figure Skating Championships) was held in conjunction with the European Figure and Speed Skating Championships.

Sources: Allgemeine Sport-Zeitung, January 24, 1909; Neues Wiener-Tagblatt, January 25, 1909; Pester Lloyd, January 25, 1909; Allgemeine Sport-Zeitung, January 31, 1909; Seventy-five years of European and World's championships in figure skating, International Skating Union, 1970

1910 WORLD MEN'S FIGURE SKATING CHAMPIONSHIPS
Davos, Switzerland, January 29-30, 1910

World Men's Figure Skating Championships:

	CF	FS
1. Ulrich Salchow (SWE)	1	2
2. Werner Rittberger (GER)	2	1
3. Andor Szende (HUN)	3	4
4. Per Thorén (SWE)	4	3

Pairs Skating (International):

1. Anna Hübler/Heinrich Burger (GER)
2. Ludovika Eilers/Walter Jakobsson (GER/FIN)
3. Hedwig Winzer/Hugo Winzer (GER)

Speed Skating (500 meters):

1. Oscar Mathisen (NOR)
2. Magnus Johansen (NOR)
3. Herr Weibel (SUI)
4. Wijnout Taconis (NED)
5. Coen de Koning (NED)

6. Charles Sabouret (FRA)
7. Herr Freytag (GER)
8. Martin Sæterhaug (NOR)
9. Adrien Maucort (FRA)
10. Louis Breteau (FRA)

Speed Skating (1500 meters):

1. Oscar Mathisen (NOR)
2. Martin Sæterhaug (NOR)
3. Magnus Johansen (NOR)
4. Wijnout Taconis (NED)
5. Coen de Koning (NED)
6. Herr Freytag (GER)
7. Charles Sabouret (FRA)
8. Adrien Maucort (FRA)
10. Louis Breteau (FRA)

Speed Skating (5000 meters):

1. Oskar Mathiesen (NOR)
2. Magnus Johansen (NOR)
3. Martin Sæterhaug (NOR)
4. Wijnout Taconis (NED)
5. Herr Weibel (SUI)
6. Herr Freytag (GER)
7. Charles Sabouret (FRA)
8. Coen de Koning (NOR)
9. Adrien Maucort (FRA)
10. Louis Breteau (FRA)

Speed Skating (10000 meters):

1. Oskar Mathiesen (NOR)
2. Martin Sæterhaug (NOR)
3. Magnus Johansen (NOR)
4. Wijnout Taconis
5. Coen de Koning (NOR)

6. Herr Weibel (SUI)
7. Charles Sabouret (FRA)
8. Herr Freytag (GER)
9. Adrien Maucort (FRA)
10. Louis Breteau (FRA)

Junior Speed Skating (500 meters):

1. Herr Kmel (SUI)
2. Herr Weibe (SUI)
3. Peyton Busberg (SUI)
4. Herr Freytag (GER)
5. C. von Hoffmann (AUT)
6. Charlie Morley (GRB)

Junior Speed Skating (1500 meters):

1. Herr Weibe (SUI)
2. Herr Kmel (SUI)
3. Charlie Morley (GRB)
4. Herr Freytag (GER)
5. C. von Hoffmann (AUT)

Sources: Royston Weekly News, January 28, 1910; Neue Zürcher Nachrichten, January 31, 1910; Seventy-five years of European and World's championships in figure skating, International Skating Union, 1970

1910 WORLD LADIES AND PAIRS FIGURE SKATING CHAMPIONSHIPS
Berlin, Germany, February 4, 1910

ISU Championship for Ladies (World Ladies Figure Skating Championships):

	CF	FS
1. Lili Kronberger (HUN)	1	1
2. Elsa Rendschmidt (GER)	2	2

World Pairs Skating Championships:

1. Anna Hübler/Heinrich Burger (GER)
2. Ludovika Eilers/Walter Jakobsson (GER/FIN)
3. Phyllis Johnson/James Henry Johnson (GRB)

Valsing (Waltzing on Ice):

1. Alice Rolle/Bruno Grauel (GER)
2. Fraulein Heimann/Herr Kroll (GER)

Junior Men's Figure Skating:

1. Alfons Zintl (GER)
2. Herr Bomhardt (GER)
3. Otto Mövius (GER)
4. F. Horn (GER)

Sources: Münchner neueste Nachrichten : Wirtschaftsblatt, alpine und Sport-Zeitung, February 8, 1910; Seventy-five years of European and World's championships in figure skating, International Skating Union, 1970

Phyllis and James Henry Johnson, World Champions 1909 and 1912. GL Archive / Alamy Stock Photo.

THE PRE-WAR ERA

1911 WORLD MEN'S FIGURE SKATING CHAMPIONSHIPS
Berlin, Germany, February 2-3, 1911

World Men's Figure Skating Championships:

	CF	FS
1. Ulrich Salchow (SWE)	1	1
2. Werner Rittberger (GER)	3	2
3. Fritz Kachler (AUT)	2	4
4. Andor Szende (HUN)	5	3
5. Richard Johansson (SWE)	4	5
6. Martin Stixrud (NOR)	6	6
7. Dunbar Poole (SWE)	7	7

Ladies Figure Skating:

1. Zsófia Méray-Horváth (HUN)
2. Grete Strasilla (AUT)

Pairs Skating:

1. Alice Rolle/Bruno Grauel (GER)
2. Else Weber/Heinrich Weber (GER)

Valsing (Waltzing on Ice):

1. Else Weber/Heinrich Weber (GER)
2. Alice Rolle/Bruno Grauel (GER)
3. Fraulein Lehmann/Herr Maerländer (GER)

Junior Men's Figure Skating (International):

1. Artur Vieregg (GER)
2. F. Horn (GER)

3. Erwin Schwarzböck (AUT)
4. Rudolf Kutzer (AUT)
5. Otto Mövius (GER)

Junior Men's Figure Skating (Berliner Schlittschuhklub Prize):

1. Artur Vieregg (GER)
2. F. Horn (GER)

Though he represented Sweden, as a member of the Stockholms Allmänna Skridskoklubb, Dunbar Poole made history as the first Australian skater to participate in the World Figure Skating Championships.

Sources: Allgemeine Sport-Zeitung, February 12 and March 5, 1911; Seventy-five years of European and World's championships in figure skating, International Skating Union, 1970

1911 WORLD LADIES AND PAIRS FIGURE SKATING CHAMPIONSHIPS
Vienna, Austria-Hungary, January 22, 1911

ISU Championship for Ladies (World Ladies Figure Skating Championships):

	CF	FS
1. Lili Kronberger (HUN)	1	1
2. Zsófia Méray-Horváth (HUN)	2	2
3. Ludovika Eilers (GER)	3	3

World Pairs Figure Skating Championships:

1. Ludovika (Eilers)/Walter Jakobsson (GER/FIN)

Men's Figure Skating:

1. Fritz Kachler (AUT)
2. Harald Rooth (SWE)
3. Walter Jakobsson (FIN)

4. Karl Mejstrik (AUT)
5. Josef Oppacher (AUT)
6. Alfons Zintl (GER)
7. Dr. Ernst Oppacher (AUT)
WD. Rudolf Kutzer (AUT)
WD. Andor Szende (HUN)
WD. Werner Rittberger (GER)

Junior Men's Figure Skating:

1. Artur Vieregg (GER)
2. Rudolf Kutzer (AUT)
3. Erwin Schwarzböck (AUT)
4. Anton Tranquillini (AUT)

Walter Jakobsson made history as the first Finnish-born skater to win a gold medal at the World Championships, with his German-born wife Ludovika Eilers.

Sources: Allgemeine Sport-Zeitung, January 22, January 29 and February 26, 1911; Neues Wiener Tagblatt, January 23, 1911; Seventy-five years of European and World's championships in figure skating, International Skating Union, 1970

1912 WORLD MEN'S AND PAIRS FIGURE SKATING CHAMPIONSHIPS
Manchester, England, February 16-17, 1912

World Men's Figure Skating Championships:

	CF	FS
1. Fritz Kachler (AUT)	1	4
2. Werner Rittberger (GER)	2	1
3. Andor Szende (HUN)	3	3
4. Harald Rooth (SWE)	4	2
5. Arthur Cumming (GRB)	5	5
6. Dunbar Poole (SWE)	6	6

World Pairs Skating Championships:

1. Phyllis Johnson/James Henry Johnson (GRB)
2. Ludovika Jakobsson/Walter Jakobsson (FIN)
3. Alexia Bryn/Yngvar Bryn (NOR)
4. Hedwig Winzer/Hugo Winzer (GER)
5. Anita del Monte/Louis Magnus (FRA)
6. Muriel Harrison/Basil Williams (GRB)
7. Mary Cadogan/Arthur Cumming (GRB)
8. Lois Lovett/Ernest Worsley (GRB)

Junior Men's Figure Skating:

1. Basil Williams (GRB)
2. Walter Hennig (GER)
3. Herbert James Clarke (GRB)
4. Lucien Trugard (FRA)
5. Kenneth Macdonald Beaumont (GRB)
6. H. Carver (GRB)
7. W.E. Kay (GRB)

Anita del Monte and Louis Magnus made history as the first skaters to represent France at the World Figure Skating Championships.

A special exhibition was given by Madge Syers, the first British skater to win a gold medal at the Olympics and World Figure Skating Championships.

Sources: The Guardian, January 27, 1912; The Manchester Guardian, February 19, 1912; Evening Gazette, February 19, 1912; The Daily Mirror, February 19, 1912; Allgemeine Sport-Zeitung, February 25, 1912; Seventy-five years of European and World's championships in figure skating, International Skating Union, 1970

1912 WORLD LADIES FIGURE SKATING CHAMPIONSHIPS
Davos, Switzerland, January 27-28, 1912

ISU Championship for Ladies (World Ladies Figure Skating Championships):

	CF	FS
1. Zsófia Méray-Horváth (HUN)	1	1
2. Dorothy Greenhough Smith (GRB)	4	2
3. Phyllis Johnson (GRB)	3	4
4. Gwendolyn Lycett (GRB)	2	6
5. Grete Strasilla (GER)	5	3
6. Mizzi Wellenreiter (AUT)	6	5
7. Ludovika Jakobsson (FIN)	7	7

Valsing (Waltzing on Ice):

1. Daphne Wrinch/H. Jensen (SUI)
2. Mary Cadogan/Arthur Cumming (GRB)
3. Gwendolyn Lycett/Louis Magnus (GRB/FRA)
4. Mlle. Roussel/Charles Sabouret (FRA)
5. Fraulein Vischer/Herr Biesenberger (GER)

Junior Men's Figure Skating:

1. Walter Hennig (GER)
2. Basil Williams (GRB)
3. Francis Pigueron (FRA)
4. Ernst Seitz (GER)
5. Charles Sabouret (FRA)
6. Felix Locher (SUI)

Speed Skating (Overall):

1. Thomas Bohrer (AUT)
2. Ejnar Sørensen (DEN)
3. J. Christiansen (NOR)
4. M. Kniel (SUI)

Junior Men's Speed Skating:

1. H. Hack (SUI)
2. J. Mulier (SUI)
3. Herr Fopp (SUI)
4. P. Müller (SUI)

Sources: La Suisse, January 29, 1912; Allgemeine Sport-Zeitung, February 4, 1912; Seventy-five years of European and World's championships in figure skating, International Skating Union, 1970

1913 WORLD MEN'S FIGURE SKATING CHAMPIONSHIPS
Vienna, Austria, February 23, 1913

World Men's Figure Skating Championships:

	CF	FS
1. Fritz Kachler (AUT)	1	1
2. Willy Böckl (AUT)	3	2
3. Andor Szende (HUN)	2	4
4. Ivan Malinin (RUS)	6	3
5. Dr. Ernst Oppacher (AUT)	4	6
6. Harald Rooth (SWE)	7	5
7. Werner Rittberger (GER)	5	7
8. Paul Metzner (GER)	8	8

Junior Men's Figure Skating (Wanderpreis des Training-Eisklubs):

1. Alfred Berger (AUT)
2. Karl Linsenmeyer (AUT)
3. Ferdinand Weber (AUT)
4. Wilhelm Czech (CZE)
5. J. von Farkas (HUN)
6. Dr. Heinrich Keller (AUT)
7. Leo Scheu (CZE)
8. Pál Jaross (HUN)
WD. Emil Pešek (CZE)

Sources: *Allgemeine Sport-Zeitung, February 23 and March 2, 1913;*
Seventy-five years of European and World's championships in figure skating,
ISU, 1970

1913 WORLD LADIES AND PAIRS FIGURE SKATING CHAMPIONSHIPS
Stockholm, Sweden, February 9-11, 1913

ISU Championship for Ladies (World Ladies Figure Skating Championships:

	CF	FS
1. Zsófia Méray-Horváth (HUN)	1	1
2. Phyllis Johnson (GRB)	2	5
3. Svea Norén (SWE)	3	4
4. Grete Strasilla (GER)	5	6
5. Anna Lisa Allardt (FIN)	6	2
6. Magda Mauroy (SWE)	4	7
7. Thea Frenssen (GER)	7	3
8. Lady Ursula Blackwood (GRB)	8	8

World Pairs Skating Championships:

1. Helene Engelmann/Karl Mejstrik (AUT)
2. Ludovika Jakobsson/Walter Jakobsson (FIN)
3. Christine von Szabo/Leo Horwitz (AUT)
4. Alexia Bryn/Yngvar Bryn (NOR)
5. Elly Svensson/Per Thorén (SWE)
6. Helfrid Palm/Agard Palm (SWE)
7. Mary Cadogan/Arthur Cumming (GRB)

Men's Figure Skating (Nordiska Spelens Prize):

1. Gösta Sandahl (SWE)
2. Harald Rooth (SWE)
3. Arthur Cumming (GRB)
4. Carl Sandahl (SWE)
5. Olof Hultgren (SWE)

Ladies Figure Skating (International):

1. Eva Lindahl (SWE)
2. Astrid Nordsveen (NOR)
3. Margit Johansen (NOR)
4. Irma Pagel (SWE)
5. Elly Svensson (SWE)

Speed Skating (500 meters):

1. Oskar Mathiesen (NOR)
2. Martin Sæterhaug (NOR)
3. Väinö Wickström (FIN)
4. Hening Olsen (NOR)
5. Otto Andersson (SWE)

Speed Skating (1500 meters):

1. Oskar Mathiesen (NOR)
2. Vasily Ippolitov (RUS)
3. Hening Olsen (NOR)

Speed Skating (5000 meters):

1. Vasily Ippolitov (RUS)
2. Oskar Mathiesen (NOR)
3. Herr Neidenow (RUS)

Speed Skating (10000 meters):

1. Vasily Ippolitov (RUS)
2. Oskar Mathiesen (NOR)
3. Herr Neidenow (RUS)

The on-ice events were held as part of a larger multi-sport festival called the Nordiska Spelens (Nordic Games), which also included skiing, ski jumping and equestrian events.

Svea Norén made history as the first woman from Scandinavia to win a medal in the ISU Championship for Ladies.

Sources: Allgemeine Sport-Zeitung, February 16, 1913; Scrapbook of programmes and newspaper clippings, 1913 Nordic Games, Sveriges Centralförening för Idrottens Främjande; Seventy-five years of European and World's championships in figure skating, ISU, 1970

1914 WORLD MEN'S FIGURE SKATING CHAMPIONSHIPS
Helsinki, Finland, February 21-22, 1914

World Men's Figure Skating Championships:

	CF	FS
1. Gösta Sandahl (SWE)	3	1
2. Fritz Kachler (AUT)	1	9
3. Willy Böckl (AUT)	4	3
4. Dr. Ernst Oppacher (AUT)	7	2
5. Andor Szende (HUN)	2	7
6. Ivan Malinin (RUS)	5	5(t)
7. Gillis Grafström (SWE)	6	8
8. Harald Rooth (SWE)	10	4
9. Richard Johansson (SWE)	9	5(t)
10. Erwin Schwarzböck (AUT)	8	10
11. Martin Stixrud (NOR)	11	12
12. Björnsson Schauman (FIN)	13	11
13. Sergei Vandervliet (RUS)	14	13
WD. Sakari Ilmanen (FIN)	12	-

Ladies Figure Skating:

1. Anna-Lisa Allardt (FIN)
2. Magda Mauroy (SWE)

Sources: Työmies, February 24, 1914; Suomen Urheilulehti, February 26, 1914; Seventy-five years of European and World's championships in figure skating, ISU, 1970

1914 WORLD LADIES AND PAIRS FIGURE SKATING CHAMPIONSHIPS
St. Moritz, Switzerland, January 24-25, 1914

ISU Championship for Ladies (World Ladies Figure Skating Championships:

	CF	FS
1. Zsófia Méray-Horváth (HUN)	1	1
2. Angela Hanka (GER)	2	4
3. Phyllis Johnson (GRB)	3	2
4. Thea Frenssen (GER)	6	3
5. Gisela Reichmann (AUT)	5	7
6. Anna Lisa Allardt (FIN)	4	6
7. Xenia Caesar (RUS)	7	5
8. Ramsay Salmon (SWE)	8	9
9. Hon. Irene Lawley (GRB)	9	8

World Pairs Skating Championships:

1. Ludovika Jakobsson/Walter Jakobsson (FIN)
2. Helene Engelmann/Karl Mejstrik (AUT)
3. Christine von Szabo/Leo Horwitz (AUT)
4. Thea Frenssen/Julius Vogel (GER)
5. Alexia Bryn/Yngvar Bryn (NOR)

Junior Men's Figure Skating:

1. Pál Jaross (HUN)
2. Kenneth Macdonald Beaumont (GRB)
3. Herbert James Clarke (GRB)

Sources: Allgemeine Sport-Zeitung, March 8, 1914; Seventy-five years of European and World's championships in figure skating, ISU, 1970

1915-1921
*EVENT NOT HELD**

*The World Figure Skating Championships were not held during

The Great War. While several nations still organized their own figure skating competitions, the ISU did not reconvene its Congresses until the spring of 1921. Benjamin T. Wright, a well-respected international judge and referee and ISU Historian, commented on the postponement:: "Why did it take so long? There is nothing specific in the record to explain the long delay of three years, except the chaotic state of Europe itself, with the defeat and break up of the Central European empires and the formation of new nations resulting from The Treaty of Versailles (signed at the end of June, 1919). In addition, a severe economic depression in Europe after the War had a direct effect on leisure type activities, such as sports."

Source: Skating Around the World: International Skating Union, the One Hundredth Anniversary History 1892 -1992, Benjamin T. Wright

Ethel Muckelt, ladies competitor in the World Championships in the 1920s and silver medallist in pairs at the 1924 World Championships. Smith Archive / Alamy Stock Photos.

THE ROARING 20s

1922 WORLD MEN'S AND LADIES FIGURE SKATING CHAMPIONSHIPS
Stockholm, Sweden, February 4-6, 1922

World Men's Figure Skating Championships:

	CF	FS
1. Gillis Grafström (SWE)	2	1
2. Fritz Kachler (AUT)	1	3
3. Willy Böckl (AUT)	3	2
4. Martin Stixrud (NOR)	4	4

ISU Championship for Ladies (World Ladies Figure Skating Championships):

	CF	FS
1. Herma Szabo (AUT)	1	1
2. Svea Norén (SWE)	2	2
3. Margot Moe (NOR)	3	3

Men's Figure Skating (Nordiska Spelens prize):

1. Lars Grafström (SWE)
2. Arne Lie (NOR)
3. Kaj af Ekström (SWE)
4. Martinus Lørdahl (NOR)
5. Tore Mothander (SWE)
WD. Gunnar Jakobsson (FIN)
WD. Nils Grafström (SWE)
WD. Rudolf Eilers (GER)
WD. Pierre Brunet (FRA)

Ladies Figure Skating (Nordiska Spelens prize):

1. Ilse Adametz (AUT)
2. Ragnvi Torslow (SWE)

3. Margit Edlund (SWE)
4. Anna-Lisa Collin (SWE)
5. Greta Nissen (SWE)
6. Alice Krayenbühl (DEN)
WD. Andrée Joly (FRA)

Pairs Skating:

1. H. Berghagen/Agard Palm (SWE)
2. Elna Henriksson/Kaj af Ekström (SWE)
3. Margit Edlund/Anders Palm (SWE)

Speed Skating (1500 meters):

1. Eric Blomgren (SWE)
2. Gustaf Andersson (SWE)
3. Axel Blomqvist (SWE)

Speed Skating (5000 meters):

1. Eric Blomgren (SWE)
2. Gustaf Andersson (SWE)
3. Karl Johansson (SWE)

Speed Skating (10000 meters):

1. Julius Skutnabb (FIN)
2. Ole Olsen (NOR)
3. Eric Blomgren (SWE)
4. Roald Morel Larsen (NOR)
5. Theodor Pedersen (NOR)
6. Gustaf Andersson (SWE)
7. Oscar Olsen (NOR)
8. Karl Johansson (SWE)
9. E. Augustsson (SWE)
10. Werner Eriksson (SWE)
11. S. Carlsson (SWE)

The on-ice events were held as part of a larger multi-sport festival called the Nordiska Spelens (Nordic Games), which also included skiing, ski jumping and equestrian events.

Herma Szabo made history as the first Austrian skater to win a gold medal in the ISU Championship for Ladies.

Sources: Scrapbook of programmes and newspaper clippings, 1922 Nordic Games, Sveriges Centralförening för Idrottens Främjande; Hufvudsbladet, February 6, 1922; Idrottsbladet, February 6, 1922; Dagens Nyheter, February 6, 1922; Seventy-five years of European and World's championships in figure skating, International Skating Union, 1970

1922 WORLD PAIRS SKATING CHAMPIONSHIPS
Davos, Switzerland, January 28-29, 1922

World Pairs Skating Championships:

1. Helene Engelmann/Alfred Berger (AUT)
2. Ludovika Jakobsson/Walter Jakobsson (FIN)
3. Margarete Metzner/Paul Metzner (GER)
4. Grete Weise/Georg Velisch (GER)
5. Alexia Bryn/Yngvar Bryn (NOR)

European Men's Figure Skating Championships:

	CF	FS
1. Willy Böckl (AUT)	1	3
2. Fritz Kachler (AUT)	2	4
3. Dr. Ernst Oppacher (AUT)	3	1
4. Werner Rittberger (GER)	5	2
5. Martin Stixrud (NOR)	4	5
6. Sakari Ilmanen (FIN)	6	7
7. Gunnar Jakobsson (FIN)	7	8
8. Artur Vieregg (GER)	9	6
9. Dr. Georges Gautschi (SUI)	8	9
10. Wilhelm Czech (CZE)	10	10

Speed Skating (500 meters):

1. Roald Morel Larsen (NOR)
2. Hellmut Kofler (AUT)
3. Alexander Spengler (SUI)
4. Herr Hermann (SUI)
5. Paul Bombig (AUT)

Speed Skating (1500 meters):

1. Roald Morel Larsen (NOR)
2. Paul Bombig (AUT)
3. Hellmut Kofler (AUT)
4. Alexander Spengler (SUI)
5. Herr Hermann (SUI)

Speed Skating (5000 meters):

1. Paul Bombig (AUT)
2. Hellmut Kofler (AUT)
3. Alexander Spengler (SUI)
4. Herr Hermann (SUI)

Speed Skating (10000 meters):

1. Roald Morel Larsen (NOR)
2. Paul Bombig (AUT)
3. Hellmut Kofler (AUT)
4. Alexander Spengler (SUI)
5. Herr Hermann (Davos)

In the aftermath of The Great War, the Club des Sports d'Hiver de Paris sent a letter instructing the French pairs team to withdraw from the Championships in protest of the ISU, because competitors whose countries were not members of the League of Nations were permitted to compete.

Sources: Neue Zürcher Zeitung, January 30 and February 3, 1922; Seventy-

five years of European and World's championships in figure skating, International Skating Union, 1970

1923 WORLD MEN'S AND LADIES FIGURE SKATING CHAMPIONSHIPS
Vienna, Austria, January 27-28, 1923

World Men's Figure Skating Championships:

	CF	FS
1. Fritz Kachler (AUT)	1	2
2. Willy Böckl (AUT)	2	4
3. Gösta Sandahl (SWE)	3	5
4. Dr. Ernst Oppacher (AUT)	4	1
5. Ludwig Wrede (AUT)	5	3
6. Artur Vieregg (GER)	6	6

ISU Championship for Ladies (World Ladies Figure Skating Championships):

	CF	FS
1. Herma Szabo (AUT)	1	1
2. Gisela Reichmann (AUT)	2	2
3. Svea Norén (SWE)	3	4
4. Ethel Muckelt (GRB)	4	3

Men's Figure Skating (International):

1. Jack Ferguson Page (GRB)
2. Emil von Bertanlaffy (AUT)
3. Karl Kronfuss (AUT)
4. Otto Preißecker (AUT)
5. Josef Slíva (CZE)
6. Gunnar Jakobsson (FIN)
7. Erwin Schwarzböck (AUT)
8. Robert Hönigschmidt (GER)
9. Wilhelm Czech (CZE)

Ladies Figure Skating:

1. Käthe Wulff (AUT)
2. Hildegard Thiel (AUT)
3. Mizzi Schilling (AUT)
4. Else Wilschek (AUT)

Pairs Skating:

1. Margrete Weiss/Georg Velisch (GER)
2. Lisl Meisner/Oscar Hoppe (AUT)
3. Elle May/Öskar May (AUT)
4. Grete Rosmus/Otto Preißecker (AUT)

Sources: Der Montag, January 29, 1923; Seventy-five years of European and World's championships in figure skating, International Skating Union, 1970

1923 WORLD PAIRS SKATING CHAMPIONSHIPS
Oslo, Norway, January 19-20, 1923

World Pairs Skating Championships:

1. Ludovika Jakobsson/Walter Jakobsson (FIN)
2. Alexia Bryn/Yngvar Bryn (NOR)
3. Elna Henrikson/Kaj af Ekström (SWE)
4. Margit Engebretse/Bjarne Engebretsen (NOR)
5. Randi Bakke/Christen Christensen (NOR

European Men's Figure Skating Championships:

	CF	FS
1. Willy Böckl (AUT)	1	1
2. Martin Stixrud (NOR)	2	3
3. Gunnar Jakobsson (FIN)	3	4
4. Kaj af Ekström (SWE)	4	2

Ladies Figure Skating:

1. Herma Szabo (AUT)
2. Margot Moe (NOR)
3. Ingrid Guldbransen (NOR)

Speed Skating (500 meters):

1. Roald Larsen (NOR)
2. Oscar Olsen (NOR)
3. Theodor Pedersen (NOR)
4. Harald Halvorsen (NOR)
5. Rolf Gihle (NOR)
6. Ole Olsen (NOR)
7. Knut Sundheim (NOR)
8. Hans Thoralf Hansen (NOR)
9. Fridtjof Paulsen (NOR)
10. Ernst Granstrom (NOR)
11. Markus Johansen (NOR)
12. Sigurd Moen (NOR)
13. Fr. Mikkelsen (NOR)

Speed Skating (1500 meters):

1. Roald Larsen (NOR)
2. Ole Olsen (NOR)
3. Fridtjof Paulsen (NOR)
4. Hans Thoralf Hanson (NOR)
5. Sigurd Moen (NOR)
6. Oscar Olsen (NOR)
7. Markus Johansen (NOR)
8. Harald Halvorsen (NOR)

Speed Skating (5000 meters):

1. Ole Olsen (NOR)
2. Roald Larsen (NOR)
3. Fridtjof Paulsen (NOR).

4. Sigurd Moen (NOR)
5. Oscar Olsen (NOR)
6. Rolf Gihle (NOR)
7. Harald Halvorsen (NOR)
8. Alfred Johansen (NOR)
9. Hans Thoralf Hanson (NOR)
10. Theodor Pedersen (NOR)

Speed Skating (10000 meters):

1. Ole Olsen (NOR)
2. Fridtjof Paulsen (NOR)
3. Sigurd Moen (NOR)
4. Roald Larsen (NOR)
5. Rolf Gihle (NOR)
6. Oscar Olsen (NOR)

Junior Speed Skating (500 meters):

1. Bernt Evenson (NOR)
2. Jacob Hansen (NOR)
3. Rolf S. Tandberg (NOR)
4. Einar Fredriksen (NOR)
5. Lorang Andresen (NOR)

Junior Speed Skating (1500 meters):

1. Eigil Hoel (NOR)
2. Jacob Hansen (NOR)
3. Bernt Evensen (NOR)
4. Rolf Larsen (NOR)

Sources: Aftenposten, January 20 and 22, 1923; Neue Zürcher Zeitung, February 3, 1922; Seventy-five years of European and World's championships in figure skating, International Skating Union, 1970

1924 WORLD MEN'S AND PAIRS FIGURE SKATING CHAMPIONSHIPS
Manchester, England, February 26-27, 1924

World Men's Figure Skating Championships:

	CF	FS
1. Gillis Grafström (SWE)	1	1
2. Willy Böckl (AUT)	2	2
3. Dr. Ernst Oppacher (AUT)	4	5
4. Jack Ferguson Page (GRB)	3	6
5. Ludwig Wrede (AUT)	5	3
6. Otto Preißecker (AUT)	6	4
7. Martin Stixrud (NOR)	7	-
8. Herbert J. Clarke (GRB)	8	-
WD. Werner Rittberger (GER)	-	-

World Pairs Figure Skating Championships:

1. Helene Engelmann/Alfred Berger (AUT)
2. Ethel Muckelt/Jack Ferguson Page (GRB)
3. Elna Henrikson/Kaj af Ekström (SWE)

Ladies Figure Skating:

1. Ethel Muckelt (GRB)
2. Cecil Smith (CAN)
3. Kathleen Shaw (GRB)
WD. Beatrix Loughran (USA)

Waltzing:

1. K. Lancashire/Henry C. Lowther (GRB)
2. Ethel Muckelt/Jack Ferguson Page (GRB)
3. Kathleen Lovett/Albert Proctor Burman (GRB)
*. Miss Magrath/Mr. MacDonald (GRB)
*. Miss Causton/W.E. Kay (GRB)
*. Miss Alexander/Herbert J. Clarke (GRB)

Tenstep:

1. K. Lancashire/Henry C. Lowther (GRB)
2. Ethel Muckelt/Jack Ferguson Page (GRB)
3. Miss Aspinall/Mr. Burwell (GRB)
*. Kathleen Lovett/Albert Proctor Burman (GRB)
*. Miss Magrath/Mr. MacDonald (GRB)
*. Miss Alexander/Herbert J. Clarke (GRB)

Cecil Smith made history as the first skater from Canada to participate in a figure skating competition held in conjunction with an ISU Championship.

Sources: The Guardian, February 26 and 27, 1924; Sports de neige et de glace, March 6, 1924; Wiener Sporttagblatt, March 11, 1924; Seventy-five years of European and World's championships in figure skating, International Skating Union, 1970

1924 WORLD LADIES FIGURE SKATING CHAMPIONSHIPS
Oslo, Norway, February 16-17, 1924

ISU Championship for Ladies (World Ladies Figure Skating Championships):

	CF	FS
1. Herma Szabo (GRB)	1	1
2. Ellen Brockhöft (GER)	2	2
3. Beatrix Loughran (USA)	3	4
4. Gisela Reichmann (AUT)	4	5
5. Sonja Henie (NOR)	6	3
6. Klara Johansen (NOR)	5	6
7. Ragnvi Torslow (SWE)	7	7

European Speed Skating Championships (overall):

1. Roald Morel Larsen (NOR)
2. Clas Thunberg (FIN)
3. Oskar Olsen (NOR)

4. Sigurd Moen (NOR)
5. Julius Skutnabb (FIN)
6. Ivar Ballangrud (NOR)
7. Sverre Aune (NOR)
8. Asbjørn Steffensen (NOR)
9. Ragnvald Olsen (NOR)
10. Harald Belewicz (FIN)
11. Eric Blomgren (SWE)
12. Harald Halvorsen (NOR)
13. Fridtjof Paulsen (NOR)
14. Rolf Reiersen (NOR)

Men's Figure Skating:

1. Zakken Johansen Jr. (NOR)
2. Jens Larsen (NOR)

Pairs Skating:

1. Randi Bakke/Christen Christensen (NOR)
2. Margit Engebretsen/Bjarne Engebretsen (NOR)
3. Fru Quinland/Rudi Zürig (DEN)

This was the final year that the ladies competition was styled as the "ISU Championship for Ladies". Following this 1924 event, the ladies event was billed as a World Championship and previous winners from 1906 onwards were recognized as World Champions.

Beatrix Loughran made history as the first American figure skater to participate and win a medal in the World Figure Skating Championships.

Sources: Dagens Nyt, February 18, 1924; Seventy-five years of European and World's championships in figure skating, International Skating Union, 1970; Skating Around the World: International Skating Union, the One Hundredth Anniversary History 1892-1992, Benjamin T. Wright

1925 WORLD MEN'S AND PAIRS FIGURE SKATING CHAMPIONSHIPS
Vienna, Austria, February 14-15, 1925

World Men's Figure Skating Championships:

	CF	FS
1. Willy Böckl (AUT)	2	1
2. Fritz Kachler (AUT)	1	3
3. Otto Preißecker (AUT)	3	2
4. Dr. Ernst Oppacher (AUT)	5	6
5. Josef Slíva (CZE)	6	5
6. Georges Gautschi (SUI)	4	7
7. Ludwig Wrede (AUT)	7	4

World Pairs Skating Championships:

1. Herma Szabo/Ludwig Wrede (AUT)
2. Andrée Joly/Pierre Brunet (FRA)
3. Lilly Scholz/Otto Kaiser (AUT)
4. Gisela Hochhaltinger/Georg Pamperl (AUT)
5. Else Hoppe/Oscar Hoppe (CZE)
WD. Milly Foerster/Hellmuth Jüngling (GER)

Men's Figure Skating (Preis des Wiener Eislauf-Vereines):

1. Dr. Ernst Oppacher (AUT)
2. Dr. Hugo Distler (AUT)
3. Pál Jaross (HUN)
4. Wilhelm Czech (CZE)
WD. Ludwig Wrede (AUT)
WD. Hellmuth Jüngling (GER)

Ladies Figure Skating (Gurschner-Preis):

1. Melitta Brunner (AUT)
2. Ilse Hornung (AUT)
3. Hildegard Thiel (AUT)
4. Gerda Hornung (AUT)

WD. Gisela Reichmann (AUT)
WD. Mizzi Schilling (AUT)

Source: Wiener Sporttagblatt, February 16, 1925; Seventy-five years of European and World's championships in figure skating, International Skating Union, 1970; Programme, 1925 World Figure Skating Championships

1925 WORLD LADIES FIGURE SKATING CHAMPIONSHIPS
Davos, Switzerland, January 31-February 1, 1925

World Ladies Figure Skating Championships:

	CF	FS
1. Herma Szabo (AUT)	1	1
2. Ellen Brockhöft (GER)	2	2
3. Elisabeth Böckel (GER)	4	4
4. Kathleen Shaw (GRB)	5	3
5. Ethel Muckelt (GRB)	3	5

Speed Skating (overall):

1. Otto Polacsek (AUT)
2. Herr Brot (NED)
3. Fritz Moser (AUT)
4. Herr Rolisana (NED)
5. Herr Hoftman (NED)
6. Herr Leicht (SUI)

Source: Journal du Jura, February 2, 1925; Seventy-five years of European and World's championships in figure skating, International Skating Union, 1970

1926 WORLD MEN'S AND PAIRS FIGURE SKATING CHAMPIONSHIPS
Berlin, Germany, February 13-14, 1926

World Men's Figure Skating Championships:

	CF	FS
1. Willy Böckl (AUT)	1	1
2. Otto Preißecker (AUT)	2	2
3. Jack Ferguson Page (GRB)	3	5
4. Werner Rittberger (GER)	4	3
5. Josef Slíva (CZE)	5	7
6. Ludwig Wrede (AUT)	6	4
7. Robert van Zeebroeck (BEL)	7	6
8. Arne Lie (NOR)	9	8
9. Paul Franke (GER)	8	9
WD. Gunnar Jakobsson (FIN)	-	-

World Pairs Skating Championships:

1. Andrée Joly/Pierre Brunet (FRA)
2. Lilly Scholz/Otto Kaiser (AUT)
3. Herma Szabo/Ludwig Wrede (AUT)
4. Gisela Hochhaltinger/Georg Pamperl (AUT)
5. Sonja Henie/Arne Lie (NOR)
6. Ethel Muckelt/Jack Ferguson Page (GRB)
7. Else Hoppe/Oskar Hoppe (CZE)
8. Ilse Kishauer/Herbert Haertel (GER)
9. Grete Weise/Georg Velisch (GER)
10. Margit Edlund/Anders Palm (SWE)

Men's Figure Skating (International):

1. Walter Jakobsson (FIN)
2. Pál Jaross (HUN)
3. Herbert Haertel (GER)

Ladies Figure Skating (International):

1. Ellen Brockhöft (GER)
2. Elisabeth Böckel (GER)
3. Hildegard Thiel (AUT)

Pairs Skating (International):

1. Ethel Muckelt/Jack Ferguson Page (GRB)
2. Else Flebbe/Bruno Grauel (GER)
3. Else Hoppe/Oskar Hoppe (CZE)

Valsing for the Berliner Zeitung Preis (Waltzing on Ice):

1. Ethel Muckelt/Jack Ferguson Page (GRB)
2. Else Flebbe/Bruno Grauel (GER)
3. Olga Schiffelers/Robert van Zeebroeck (BEL)
4. Fraulein Voges/Herr Hallania (CZE)
5. Frau Nelfe/Georg Mazke (CZE)

Junior Men's Figure Skating:

1. Karl Schäfer (AUT)
2. Leopold Maier-Labergo (GER)
3. Rudolf Práznovský (CZE)
4. Otto Gold (CZE)
5. Herr Frei (GER)

Junior Ladies Figure Skating:

1. Grete Kubitschek (AUT)
2. Else Flebbe (GER)
3. Libuše Veselá (CZE)

Andrée Joly and Pierre Brunet made history as the first French skaters to win gold medals at the World Figure Skating Championships. Robert van Zeebroeck made history as the first skater to represent Belgium at the World Championships.

Sources: Reichspost, February 13, 1926; Münchner neueste Nachrichten, February 15, 1926; Wiener Sporttagblatt, February 15, 1926; Sports de neige et de glace, March 1, 1926; Seventy-five years of European and World's championships in figure skating, International Skating Union, 1970

1926 WORLD LADIES FIGURE SKATING CHAMPIONSHIPS
Stockholm, Sweden, February 7-8, 1926

World Ladies Figure Skating Championships:

	CF	FS
1. Herma Szabo (AUT)	1	1(t)
2. Sonja Henie (NOR)	2	1(t)
3. Kathleen Shaw (GRB)	3	5
4. Elisabeth Böckel (GER)	5	3
5. Solveig Johansen (NOR)	6	4
6. Hildegard Thiel (AUT)	4	6
WD. Ellen Brockhöft (GER)	-	-

Pairs Skating:

1. Sonja Henie/Arne Lie (NOR)
2. Margit Edlund/Anders Palm (SWE)
3. Randi Bakke/Christen Christensen (NOR)

Sources: Uusi Suomi, February 9, 1926; Seventy-five years of European and World's championships in figure skating, International Skating Union, 1970

1927 WORLD MEN'S FIGURE SKATING CHAMPIONSHIPS
Davos, Switzerland, February 12-14, 1927

World Men's Figure Skating Championships:

	CF	FS
1. Willy Böckl (AUT)	1	2
2. Otto Preißecker (AUT)	2	3
3. Karl Schäfer (AUT)	5	1
4. Georges Gautschi (SUI)	3	4

5. Jack Ferguson Page (GRB)	4	5
6. Ludwig Wrede (AUT)	6	6
7. Herbert Haertel (GER)	7	7
8. Jean Henrion (FRA)	9	8
WD. Paul Franke (GER)	8	-

Pairs Skating:

1. Lilly Scholz/Otto Kaiser (AUT)
2. Ilse Kishauer/Ernst Gaste (GER)

Speed Skating (overall):

1. Alberts Rumba (LAT)
2. Zoltán Eötvös (HUN)
3. Teun Boot (NED)
4. Fritz Moser (AUT)
5. Herr Hofstman (NED)
6. Gerard Elema (NED)

The on-ice events were held as part of a larger multi-sport festival called the Davoser Eisfest, which also included alpine and cross country skiing, ski jumping, bobsled, relay races and military patrol events.

Sources: Neue Zürcher Zeitung, February 11, 1927; Seventy-five years of European and World's championships in figure skating, International Skating Union, 1970

1927 WORLD LADIES FIGURE SKATING CHAMPIONSHIPS
Oslo, Norway, February 19-20, 1927

World Ladies Figure Skating Championships:

	CF	FS
1. Sonja Henie (NOR)	1	1
2. Herma Szabo (AUT)	2	2
3. Karen Simensen (NOR)	3	3

4. Ellen Brockhöft (GER) 4 4

Sonja Henie made history as the first Norwegian skater to win a gold medal at the World Championships, but the judging in the ladies event was extremely controversial. The competition was held in Henie's home country, and three out of the five judges were from Norway. In both the figures and free skating, the three Norwegian judges voted as a bloc, placing Norwegian skater Sonja Henie ahead of reigning World Champion Herma Szabo. Similarly, the three Norwegian judges voted as a bloc, placing a largely-unknown Norwegian skater, Karen Simensen, ahead of Germany's Ellen Brockhöft in both the figures and free skating. This particularly egregious example of bloc judging led to the ISU's institution of a "one judge per country" rule.

Sources: Seventy-five years of European and World's championships in figure skating, International Skating Union, 1970; Skating Around the World: International Skating Union, the One Hundredth Anniversary History 1892 -1992, Benjamin T. Wright, 1992

1927 WORLD PAIRS SKATING CHAMPIONSHIPS
Vienna, Austria, January 22-23, 1927

World Pairs Skating Championships:

1. Herma Szabo/Ludwig Wrede (AUT)
2. Lilly Scholz/Otto Kaiser (AUT)
3. Else Hoppe/Oscar Hoppe (CZE)
4. Hansi Essert/Georg Pamperl (AUT)

European Men's Figure Skating Championships:

	CF	FS
1. Willy Böckl (AUT)	1	1
2. Dr. Hugo Distler (AUT)	2	3
3. Karl Schäfer (AUT)	4	2
4. Dr. Ernst Oppacher (AUT)	3	4
5. Paul Franke (GER)	5	5

International Men's Figure Skating:

1. Herbert Haertel (GER)
2. Josef Bernhauser (AUT)
3. Herr Schrötter (AUT)
4. Herr Friedel (CZE)
5. Rudolf Práznovský (CZE)
6. Walter Arian (AUT)
7. Herr Hönigschmidt (AUT)

Ladies Figure Skating (Jubiläums Preis):

1. Herma Szabo (AUT)
2. Fritzi Burger (AUT)
3. Melitta Brunner (AUT)
4. Elisabeth Böckel (GER)
5. Olga Schiffelers (AUT)

Ladies Figure Skating (Gurschner Preis):

1. Fritzi Burger (AUT)
2. Elli Winter (GER)
3. Melitta Brunner (AUT)
4. Fräulein Bernhardt (AUT)
5. Ilse Hornung (AUT)
6. Gerda Hornung (AUT)
7. Gerda Veit (GER)

Pairs Skating:

1. Ilse Kishauer/Ernst Gaste (GER)
2. Marie Schwendtbauer/Gustav Aichinger (GER)

Waltzing on Ice:

1. Minna Klingel/Willy Petter (AUT)
2. Fräulein Just/Eugen Richter (AUT)
3. Fräulein Pfeiffer/Karl Zwack (AUT)
4. Fräulein Fischl/Herr Bayerle (AUT)
5. Fräulein Samstag/Fritz Wächtler (AUT)
6. Trude Wintersteiner/Walter Malek (AUT)
7. Herta Baumgartner/Herr Kucharz (AUT)
8. Fräulein Brand/Herr Stöpf (GER)
9. Fräulein Wilpert/Herr Ludwig (GER)

Junior Ladies Figure Skating (Schönheitpreis):

1(t). Melitta Brunner (AUT)
1(t). Olga Schiffelers (AUT)

Sources: Illustrierte Kronen Zeitung, January 24, 1927; Neues Wiener Tagblatt, January 24, 1927; Seventy-five years of European and World's championships in figure skating, International Skating Union, 1970

1928 WORLD MEN'S FIGURE SKATING CHAMPIONSHIPS
Berlin, Germany, February 25-27, 1928

World Men's Figure Skating Championships

	CF	FS
1. Willy Böckl (AUT)	1	1(t)
2. Karl Schäfer (AUT)	3	1(t)
3. Dr. Hugo Distler (AUT)	2	7
4. Jack Ferguson Page (GRB)	5	4
5. Roger Turner (USA)	4	5
6. Ludwig Wrede (AUT)	7	3
7. Montgomery Wilson (CAN)	**6**	**6**
8. Paul Franke (GER)	8	8
9. Jack Eastwood (CAN)	**9**	**9**
10. Nathaniel Niles (USA)	10	10

Men's Figure Skating:

1. Markus Nikkanen (FIN)
2. Ernst Baier (GER)
3. Hugo Danzig (GER)

Ladies Figure Skating:

1. Fritzi Burger (AUT)
2. Melitta Brunner (AUT)
3. Ellen Brockhöft (GER)
4. Theresa Weld Blanchard (USA)

Pairs Skating:

1. Lilly Scholz/Otto Kaiser (AUT)
2. Melitta Brunner/Ludwig Wrede (AUT)
3. Ilse Kishauer/Ernst Gaste (GER)
4. Ilse Hoppe/Oskar Hoppe (CZE)

Ice Dancing (Tanz-Wettbewerb)

1. Frieda Staffa/Eugen Richter (AUT)
2. Trude Wintersteiner/Walter Malek (AUT)
3. Frau Strumling/Herr Strumling (GER)

Junior Men's Figure Skating:

1. Ernst Baier (GER)
2. Otto Gold (CZE)
3. Heinrich Nagel (GER)
4. Rudolf Práznovský (CZE)

Junior Ladies Figure Skating:

1. Lilly Weiller (AUT)
2. Grete Lainer (GER)
3. Annemarie Deitze (GER)

Montgomery Wilson and Jack Eastwood made history as the first skaters to represent Canada in the men's event at the World Figure Skating Championships since the event was an official ISU Championship.

Sources: Der Morgen, February 27, 1928; Grazer Tagblatt, February 27, 1928; Skating magazine, May 1928; Seventy-five years of European and World's championships in figure skating, International Skating Union, 1970

1928 WORLD LADIES AND PAIRS FIGURE SKATING CHAMPIONSHIPS
London, England, March 5-6, 1928

World Ladies Figure Skating Championships:

	CF	FS
1. Sonja Henie (NOR)	1	1
2. Maribel Vinson (USA)	2	3
3. Fritzi Burger (AUT)	4	2
4. Constance Wilson (CAN)	**5**	**4**
5. Melitta Brunner (AUT)	3	5
6. Kathleen Shaw (GRB)	6	6
WD. Cecil Smith (CAN)	-	-
WD. Rosalie Knapp (USA)	-	-

World Pairs Skating Championships:

1. Andrée Joly/Pierre Brunet (FRA)
2. Lilly Scholz/Otto Kaiser (AUT)
3. Melitta Brunner/Ludwig Wrede (AUT)
4. Ethel Muckelt/Jack Ferguson Page (GRB)
5. Beatrix Loughran/Sherwin Badger (USA)
6. Maude Smith/Jack Eastwood (CAN)
7. Theresa Weld Blanchard/Nathaniel Niles (USA)
8. Kathleen Lovett/Albert Proctor Burman (GRB)

Waltzing:

1. Kathleen Lovett/Jack Ferguson Page (GRB)
2. Maribel Vinson/Roger Turner (USA)
3. Dorothy Greenhough Smith/Conrad Rivett (GRB)

This star-studded figure skating competition featured the first pairs skaters from Canada and the United States. Constance Wilson and Maude Smith and Jack Eastwood made history as the first skaters to represent Canada in the ladies and pairs events at the World Figure Skating Championships.

The event was attended by King George V and Queen Mary of Teck, the Duke of York, Prince Henry and Princess Mary.

Sources: The Yorkshire Post, March 3 and 6, 1928; The Guardian, March 5 and 6, Seventy-five years of European and World's championships in figure skating, International Skating Union, 1970

1929 WORLD MEN'S FIGURE SKATING CHAMPIONSHIPS
London, England, March 4-5, 1929

World Men's Figure Skating Championships:

	CF	FS
1. Gillis Grafström (SWE)	1	2
2. Karl Schäfer (AUT)	2	1
3. Ludwig Wrede (AUT)	5	3
4. Jack Ferguson Page (GRB)	4	4
5. Dr. Hugo Distler (AUT)	6	5
6. Markus Nikkanen (FIN)	3	7
7. Ian Bowhill (GRB)	7	6

Ladies Figure Skating:

1. Fritzi Burger (AUT)
2. Melitta Brunner (AUT)
3. Kathleen Shaw (GRB)
4. Ashley Cowan (GRB)

Pairs Skating:

1. Melitta Brunner/Ludwig Wrede (AUT)
2. Ilse Kishauer/Ernst Gaste (GER)
3. Ethel Muckelt/Jack Ferguson Page (GRB)

Sources: The Guardian, March 5, 1929; Evening Express, March 6, 1929; Seventy-five years of European and World's championships in figure skating, International Skating Union, 1970

1929 WORLD LADIES AND PAIRS FIGURE SKATING CHAMPIONSHIPS
Budapest, Hungary, February 2-3, 1929

World Ladies Figure Skating Championships:

	CF	FS
1. Sonja Henie (NOR)	1	1
2. Fritzi Burger (AUT)	2	2
3. Melitta Brunner (AUT)	3	3
4. Ilse Hornung (AUT)	4	4
5. Grete Kubitschek (AUT)	5	6
6. Yvonne de Ligne (BEL)	6	5
WD. Libuše Veselá (CZE)	-	-

World Pairs Skating Championships:

1. Lilly Scholz/Otto Kaiser (AUT)
2. Melitta Brunner/Ludwig Wrede (AUT)
3. Olga Orgonista/Sándor Szalay (HUN)
4. Gisela Hochhaltinger/Otto Preißecker (AUT)
5. Emília Rotter/László Szollás (HUN)

6. Else Hoppe/Oskar Hoppe (CZE)
7. Maria Schwendtbauer/Gustav Aichinger (GER)

Sources: Sportkiadás, February 1, 1929; Seventy-five years of European and World's championships in figure skating, International Skating Union, 1970

Jack Dunn, silver medallist at the World Championships 1935. Smith Archive / Alamy Stock Photo.

THE GREAT DEPRESSION

1930 WORLD FIGURE SKATING CHAMPIONSHIPS
New York City, United States, February 3-5, 1930

World Men's Figure Skating Championships:

	CF	FS
1. Karl Schäfer (AUT	1	1
2. Roger Turner (USA)	2	2
3. Georges Gautschi (SUI)	4	4
4. Montgomery Wilson (CAN)	**3**	**5**
5. Ludwig Wrede (AUT)	5	3
6. Gail Borden (USA)	6(t)	6
7. James Lester Madden (USA)	6(t)	7
8. William Nagle (USA)	8	8
WD. Gillis Grafström (SWE)	-	-
WD. Ian Bowhill (GRB)	-	-

World Ladies Figure Skating Championships:

	CF	FS
1. Sonja Henie (NOR)	1	1
2. Cecil Smith (CAN)	**2**	**3**
3. Maribel Vinson (USA)	4	2
4. Constance Wilson Samuel (CAN)	**3**	**4**
5. Melitta Brunner (AUT)	5	5
6. Suzanne Davis (USA)	6	6

World Pairs Skating Championships:

1. Andrée Brunet/Pierre Brunet (FRA)
2. Melitta Brunner/Ludwig Wrede (AUT)
3. Beatrix Loughran/Sherwin Badger (USA)
4. Constance Wilson Samuel/Montgomery Wilson (CAN)
5. Isobel Rogers/Melville Rogers (CAN)

6. Theresa Weld Blanchard/Nathaniel Niles (USA)
7. Maude Smith/Jack Eastwood (CAN)
8. Edith Secord/Joseph K. Savage (USA)

The World Figure Skating Championships were held in North America for the first time and 11,000 spectators - the "strictly high hat and boiled shirt crowd" - showed up to watch at Madison Square Garden.

Dr. George Gautschi made history as the first Swiss skater to win a medal at the World Championships.

Cecil Smith made history as the first Canadian woman to win a medal at the World Championships. American skaters won medals in all three disciplines for the first time.

Sources: Brooklyn Eagle, January 29, 1930; Daily News (New York), February 6, 1930; Skating magazine, March 1930; Seventy-five years of European and World's championships in figure skating, International Skating Union, 1970

1931 WORLD FIGURE SKATING CHAMPIONSHIPS
Berlin, Germany, February 28-March 1, 1931

World Men's Figure Skating Championships:

	CF	FS
1. Karl Schäfer (AUT)	1	1
2. Roger Turner (USA)	4	3
3. Ernst Baier (GER)	8	2
4. Dr. Hugo Distler (AUT)	3	5
5. Leopold Maier-Labergo (GER)	5	6
6. Marcell Vadas (HUN)	6	9
7. Marcus Nikkanen (FIN)	2	10
8. Herbert Haertel (GER)	7	11
9. Pierre Brunet (FRA)	9	8
10. Rudolf Práznovský (CZE)	12	4
11. George E.B. Hill (USA)	11	13
12. Josef Slíva (CZE)	10	12

13. Theo Lass (GER)		13	7

World Ladies Figure Skating Championships:

	CF	FS
1. Sonja Henie (NOR)	1	1
2. Hilde Holovsky (AUT)	4	2
3. Fritzi Burger (AUT)	2	4
4. Maribel Vinson (USA)	3	3
5. Vivi-Anne Hultén (SWE)	5	5
6. Edel Randem (NOR)	7	7
7. Nanna Egedius (NOR)	8	6
8. Yvonne de Ligne (BEL)	6	8
9. Randi Gulliksen (NOR)	9	9

World Pairs Skating Championships:

1. Emília Rotter/László Szollás (HUN)
2. Olga Orgonista/Sándor Szalay (HUN)
3. Idi Papez/Karl Zwack (AUT)
4. Lilly Scholz-Gaillard/Willy Petter (AUT)
5. Maribel Vinson/George E.B. Hill (USA)
6. Else Hoppe/Oskar Hoppe (CZE)
7. Ilse Gaste/Ernst Gaste (GER)
8. Hansi Kast/Otto Kaiser (AUT)
9. Elisabeth Böckel/Otto Hayek (GER)

In the 1930s, skaters were at the mercy of the rink side bands at competitions. The free skating competitions at the World Figure Skating Championships in Berlin were actually delayed because the band didn't have the sheet music for the pieces of music several skaters requested. With larger than usual fields, the judging was particularly erratic. In an egregious example of national bias, the Czechoslovakian judge placed Josef Slíva, who finished second-to-last, in third place in the figures and first in free skating.

Emília Rotter and László Szollás made history as the first Hungarian skaters to win gold medals in the pairs event at the World Championships.

Sources: *Wiener Sporttagblatt*, February 28, 1931; *Wiener Montagblatt*, March 2, 1931; *Skating magazine*, May 1931; *Seventy-five years of European and World's championships in figure skating*, International Skating Union, 1970

1932 WORLD FIGURE SKATING CHAMPIONSHIPS
Montreal, Canada, February 18-20, 1932

World Men's Figure Skating Championships:

	CF	FS
1. Karl Schäfer (AUT)	1	1
2. Montgomery Wilson (CAN)	**2**	**2**
3. Ernst Baier (GER)	5	3
4. Marcus Nikkanen (FIN)	4	5
5. Roger Turner (USA)	3	6
6. James Lester Madden (USA)	6	4
7. Kazuyoshi Oimatsu (JPN)	8	7
8. Ryuichi Obitani (JPN)	7	9
9. Robin Lee (USA)	9	8
WD. Gillis Grafström (SWE)	-	-

World Ladies Figure Skating Championships:

	CF	FS
1. Sonja Henie (NOR)	1	1
2. Fritzi Burger (AUT)	2	3
3. Constance Wilson Samuel (CAN)	**4**	**2**
4. Maribel Vinson (USA)	5	4
5. Vivi-Anne Hultén (SWE)	3	5
6. Yvonne de Ligne (BEL)	6	6
7. Megan Taylor (GRB)	8	7
8. Cecilia Colledge (GRB)	7	8
9. Mollie Phillips (GRB)	9	9
10. Joan Dix (GRB)	11	11
11. Suzanne Davis (USA)	10	12
12. Margaret Bennett (USA)	13	10
13. Elizabeth Fisher (CAN)	**12**	**13**
14. Mary Littlejohn (CAN)	**14**	**14**

World Pairs Skating Championships:

1. Andrée Brunet/Pierre Brunet (FRA)
2. Emília Rotter/László Szollás (HUN)
3. Beatrix Loughran/Sherwin Badger (USA)
4. Olga Orgonista/Sándor Szalay (HUN)
5. **Frances Claudet/Chauncey Bangs (CAN)**
6. **Constance Wilson Samuel/Montgomery Wilson (CAN)**
7. **Maude Smith/Jack Eastwood (CAN)**
8. Theresa Weld Blanchard/Nathaniel Niles (USA)
9. **Isobel Rogers/Melville Rogers (CAN)**
WD. Grace Madden/James Lester Madden (USA)

For the first time, the World Figure Skating Championships were held in Canada. Montgomery Wilson won Canada's first medal in the men's event and Kazuyoshi Oimatsu and Ryuichi Obitani made history as the first Japanese skaters to participate in the event.

Sources: The Montreal Gaezette, February 17, 1932; Programme, 1932 World Figure Skating Championships; The Ottawa Journal, February 19, 1932; Seventy-five years of European and World's championships in figure skating, International Skating Union, 1970

1933 WORLD MEN'S FIGURE SKATING CHAMPIONSHIPS
Zürich, Switzerland, February 18-19, 1933

World Men's Figure Skating Championships:

	CF	FS
1. Karl Schäfer (AUT)	1	1
2. Ernst Baier (GER)	2	2
3. Marcus Nikkanen (FIN)	3	4(t)
4. Erich Erdös (AUT)	4	3
5. Herbert Haertel (AUT)	5	7
6. Edi Scholdan (AUT)	6	4(t)
7. Rudolf Práznovský (CZE)	10	6
8. Erwin Keller (SUI)	8	8
9. Jean Henrion (FRA)	7	9

10. Othmar Jordi (SUI)	9	10
WD. Benno Wellmann (GER)	-	-

Ladies Figure Skating:

1. Hilde Holovsky (AUT)
2. Grete Lainer (AUT)
3. Olly Holzmann (AUT)
4. Maxi Herber (GER)
5. Gerda Ibscher (GER)
6. Jeanine Garanger (FRA)
7. Paula Schmidt (GER)
WD. Liselotte Landbeck (AUT)
WD. Yvonne de Ligne (BEL)

Pairs Skating:

1. Idi Papez/Karl Zwack (AUT)
2. Hansi Kast/Otto Kaiser (AUT)
3. Mr. Anderson/Mrs. Anderson (GRB)
4. Fraulein Streuli/Erwin Keller (SUI)

Marcus Nikkanen made history as the first skater from Finland to win a medal in the men's event at the World Figure Skating Championships.

Sources: Neue Zürcher Zeitung, February 14 and 20, 1933; Seventy-five years of European and World's championships in figure skating, International Skating Union, 1970

1933 WORLD LADIES AND PAIRS FIGURE SKATING CHAMPIONSHIPS
Stockholm, Sweden, February 11-12, 1933

World Ladies Figure Skating Championships:

	CF	FS
1. Sonja Henie (NOR)	1	1
2. Vivi-Anne Hultén (SWE)	2	3

3. Hilde Holovsky (AUT)	4	2
4. Megan Taylor (GRB)	3	5
5. Cecilia Colledge (GRB)	5	6
6. Liselotte Landbeck (AUT)	6	4
7. Nanna Egedius (NOR)	8	8
8. Yvonne de Ligne (BEL)	7	9
9. Erna Andersen (NOR)	9	7

World Pairs Skating Championships:

1. Emília Rotter/László Szollás (HUN)
2. Idi Papez/Karl Zwack (AUT)
3. Randi Bakke/Christen Christensen (NOR)
4. Anna-Lisa Rydqvist/Einar Törsleff (SWE)
5. Dagmar von Kothen/Fred Ericson (SWE)

Sources: Turku Sanomat, February 13, 1933; Seventy-five years of European and World's championships in figure skating, International Skating Union, 1970

1934 WORLD MEN'S FIGURE SKATING CHAMPIONSHIPS
Stockholm, Sweden, February 16-18, 1934

World Men's Figure Skating Championships:

	CF	FS
1. Karl Schäfer (AUT)	1	1
2. Ernst Baier (GER)	2	4
3. Erich Erdös (AUT)	5	2
4. Marcus Nikkanen (FIN)	3	5
5. Dénes Pataky (HUN)	4	3
6. Graham Sharp (GRB)	6	7
7. Elemér Terták (HUN)	7	6
8. Gail Borden II (USA)	8	8

Ladies Figure Skating:

1. Megan Taylor (GRB)

2. Vivi-Anne Hultén (SWE)
3. Maribel Vinson (USA)
4. Liselotte Landbeck (AUT)
5. Grete Lainer (AUT)
6. Nanna Egedius (NOR)
7. Maxi Herber (GER)
8. Edith Michaelis (GER)
9. Erna Andersen (NOR)
10. Mollie Phillips (GRB)

Pairs Skating:

1. Emília Rotter/László Szollás (HUN)
2. Idi Papez/Karl Zwack (AUT)
3. Maxi Herber/Ernst Baier (GER)
4. Zofia Bilorówna/Tadeusz Kowalski (POL)
5. Randi Bakke/Christen Christensen (NOR)
6. Margit Josephson/Anders Palm (SWE)
7. Helene Michelson/Eduard Hiiop (EST)

Zofia Bilorówna and Tadeusz Kowalski made history as the first skaters to represent Poland in an official event at the World Figure Skating Championships.

Sources: Uusi Suomi, February 16, 1934; Der Tag, February 19, 1934; Wiener Sporttagblatt, February 19, 1934; Seventy-five years of European and World's championships in figure skating, International Skating Union, 1970

1934 WORLD LADIES FIGURE SKATING CHAMPIONSHIPS
Oslo, Norway, February 10-11, 1934

World Ladies Figure Skating Championships:

	CF	FS
1. Sonja Henie (NOR)	1	1
2. Megan Taylor (GRB)	2	3
3. Liselotte Landbeck (SWE)	4	2
4. Vivi-Anne Hultén (SWE)	5	5

5. Maribel Vinson (USA)	3	8
6. Grete Lainer (AUT)	7	6
7. Maxi Herber (GER)	10	4
8. Nanna Egedius (NOR)	6	10
9. Mollie Phillips (GRB)	9	7
10. Erna Andersen (NOR)	8	12
11. Edith Michaelis (GER)	11	9
12. Ester Bornstein (DEN)	12	11
13. Randi Gulliksen (NOR)	13	13

Pairs Skating:

1. Idi Papez/Karl Zwack (AUT)
2. Emília Rotter/László Szollás (HUN)
3. Maxi Herber/Ernst Baier (GER)
4. Randi Bakke/Christen Christensen (NOR)
5. Margit Josephson/Anders Palm (SWE)
6. Dagmar von Kothen/Fred Ericsson (SWE)
7. Anna-Lisa Rydqvist/Einar Törsleff (SWE)

Sources: Sportsmanden, February 12, 1934; Skating magazine, May 1934; Seventy-five years of European and World's championships in figure skating, International Skating Union, 1970

1934 WORLD PAIRS FIGURE SKATING CHAMPIONSHIPS
Helsinki, Finland, February 23, 1934

World Pairs Skating Championships:

1. Emília Rotter/László Szollás (HUN)
2. Idi Papez/Karl Zwack (AUT)
3. Maxi Herber/Ernst Baier (GER)
4. Zofia Bilorówna/Tadeusz Kowalski (POL)
5. Randi Bakke/Christen Christensen (NOR)
6. Margit Josephson/Anders Palm (SWE)

Men's Figure Skating:

1. Marcus Nikkanen (FIN)
2. Dénes Pataky (HUN)
3. Erich Erdös (AUT)
4. Alfred Hirv (EST)
5. Bertel Nikkanen (FIN)

Ladies Figure Skating:

1. Vivi-Anne Hultén (SWE)
2. Liselotte Landbeck (AUT)
3. Maribel Vinson (USA)
4. Nanna Egedius (NOR)
5. Grete Lainer (AUT)
6. Edith Michaelis (GER)
7. Erna Andersen (NOR)
8. Ilma Suuronen (FIN)
WD. Megan Taylor (GRB)

The Finnish Skating Federation filed a formal complaint with the ISU, claiming that Sonja Henie had demanded 100,000 Finnish marks to give an exhibition in Helsinki during the World Figure Skating Championships. Stockholm newspapers claimed she was in clear violation of the ISU's rules surrounding amateurism but because she was never paid the money, the ISU turned the other cheek. It was long rumoured that Henie's father would skirt the strict rules surrounding amateurism by accepting lavish gifts on Henie's behalf, then sell them for cash.

Sources: Aamulehti, February 23, 1934; Helsingin Sanomat, January 24, 1934; Wiener Sporttagblatt, February 19, 1934; Seventy-five years of European and World's championships in figure skating, International Skating Union, 1970; Reflections on Ice: A Diary of Ladies Figure Skating (documentary), 1998

1935 WORLD MEN'S AND PAIRS FIGURE SKATING CHAMPIONSHIPS
Budapest, Hungary, February 16-17, 1935

World Men's Figure Skating Championships:

	CF	FS
1. Karl Schäfer (AUT)	1	1
2. Jack Dunn (GRB)	5	2
3. Dénes Pataky (HUN)	2	3
4. Graham Sharp (GRB)	3	5
5. Marcus Nikkanen (FIN)	4	6
6. Elemér Terták (HUN)	6	4
7. Erich Erdös (AUT)	8	7
8. Ferenc Kertész (HUN)	7	8

World Pairs Figure Skating Championships:

1. Emília Rotter/László Szollás (HUN)
2. Ilse Pausin/Erich Pausin (AUT)
3. Lucy Gallo/Rezső Dillinger (HUN)
4. Piroska Szekrényessy/Attila Szekrényessy (HUN)
5. Zofia Bilorówna/Tadeusz Kowalski (POL)
6. Wally Hampel/Otto Weiß (GER)
7. Liese Kianek/Adolf Rosdol (AUT)
8. Barbara Chachlewska/Alfred Theuer (POL)

Ladies Figure Skating:

1. Vivi-Anne Hultén (SWE)
2. Liselotte Landbeck (AUT)
3. Grete Lainer (AUT)
4. Emmy Puzinger (AUT)
5. Nadine Szilassy (HUN)

Junior Men's Figure Skating:

1. Herbert Alward (AUT)
2. Béla Barcza-Rotter (HUN)

3. Kristóf Kállay (HUN)
4. Walter Grobert (POL)
5. Károly Katschnig (CZE)
6. Kurt Ronge (CZE)

Junior Ladies Figure Skating:

1. Hedy Stenuf (AUT)
2. Éva von Botond (HUN)
3. Gina von Botond (HUN)
4. Edith Ollé (HUN)
5. Klara Erdös (HUN)
6. Liesel Holbaum (CZE)
7. Maria Schweinburg (AUT)
8. Fritzi Gillard (AUT)
9. Martha Mayerhans (GER)
10. Anita Wägeler (AUT)
11. Erna Scheibert (POL)

Sources: Sportkiadas, February 17, 1935; Der Montag, February 18, 1935; Seventy-five years of European and World's championships in figure skating, International Skating Union, 1970

1935 WORLD LADIES FIGURE SKATING CHAMPIONSHIPS
Vienna, Austria, February 8-9, 1935

World Ladies Figure Skating Championships:

	SP	FS
1. Sonja Henie (NOR)	1	1
2. Cecilia Colledge (GRB)	2	4
3. Vivi-Anne Hultén (SWE)	4	2
4. Hedy Stenuf (AUT)	6	3
5. Gweneth Butler (GRB)	3	7
6. Herta Frey-Dexler (AUT)	7(t)	5
7. Nanna Egedius (NOR)	5	6
8. Helga Schrittwieser-Dietz (AUT)	7(t)	8
WD. Lisolette Landbeck (AUT)	-	-

WD. Bianca Schenk (AUT)	-	-
WD. Grete Lainer (AUT)	-	-
WD. Nadine Szilassy (HUN)	-	-
WD. Maxi Herber (GER)	-	-

Though many previous World Figure Skating Championships had included exhibition performances, the 1935 event in Vienna was one of the first to include a full exhibition gala show following the competition. A newspaper report noted that "the show... was almost a bigger success than the [competition]. The skaters were freer, less depressed by the worry over their rating and also were able to incorporate riskier figures into their programs." Guest performers included Karl Schäfer, Jack Dunn and Ilse and Erich Pausin.

Sources: Wiener Sporttagblatt, February 9 and 11, 1935; Skating magazine, March 1935; Seventy-five years of European and World's championships in figure skating, International Skating Union, 1970

1936 WORLD FIGURE SKATING CHAMPIONSHIPS
Paris, France, February 21-29, 1936

World Men's Figure Skating Championships:

	CF	FS
1. Karl Schäfer (AUT)	1	1
2. Graham Sharp (GRB)	2	4
3. Felix Kaspar (AUT)	4	3
4. Jack Dunn (GRB)	5	2
5. Montgomery Wilson (CAN)	**3**	**6**
6. Dénes Pataky (HUN)	6	5
7. Leopold Linhart (AUT)	10	7
8. Robin Lee (USA)	7	10
9. Herbert Alward (AUT)	8	9
10. Freddy Mésot (BEL)	9	8
11. Erle Reiter (USA)	11	13
12. Jean Henrion (FRA)	14	11
13. Toshikazu Katayama (JPN)	13	12
14. Lucian Büeler (SUI)	12	16
15. Kazuyoshi Oimatsu (JPN)	15	14

	CF	FS
16. Zenjiro Watanabe (JPN)	16	17
17. Tsugio Hasegawa (JPN)	17	15

World Ladies Figure Skating Championships:

	CF	FS
1. Sonja Henie (NOR)	1	1
2. Megan Taylor (GRB)	2	4
3. Vivi-Anne Hultén (SWE)	3	2
4. Emmy Puzinger (AUT)	6	3
5. Gweneth Butler (GRB)	4	12
6. Victoria Lindpaintner (GER)	5	6
7. Mollie Phillips (GRB)	8	5
8. Mia Macklin (GRB)	7	7
9. Pamela Prior (GRB)	9	10
10. Etsuko Inada (JPN)	10	8
11. Yvonne de Ligne (BEL)	11	13
12. Gladys Jagger (GRB)	13	11
13. Audrey Peppe (USA)	16	9
14. Gaby Clericetti (FRA)	12	14
15. Jacqueline Vaudecrane (FRA)	15	15
16. Pamela Stephany (GRB)	14	17
17. Jeanine Garanger (FRA)	17	16

World Pairs Skating Championships:

1. Maxi Herber/Ernst Baier (GER)
2. Ilse Pausin/Erich Pausin (AUT)
3. Violet Cliff/Leslie Cliff (GRB)
4. Louise Bertram/Stewart Reburn (CAN)
5. Maribel Vinson/George E.B. Hill (USA)
6. Grace Madden/James Lester Madden (USA)
WD. Piroska Szekrényessy/Attila Szekrényessy (HUN)
WD. Audrey Garland/Fraser Sweatman (CAN)
WD. Rosemarie Stewart/Ernest Yates (GRB)
WD. Louise Contamine/Robert Verdun (BEL)

Ladies Speed Skating:

1. Kit Klein (USA)
2. Hattie Donaldson Briggs (CAN)
3. Minako Taki (JPN)
4. Colette Remondeau (FRA)
5. Maria Oréfice (FRA)
6. Taeko Kitani (JPN)
7. Choko Yanase (JPN)
8. Yasuko Kawanami (JPN)

Hockey:

1. Français Volants (FRA/CAN)
2. Chamonix Hockey Club (FRA)

A hockey game was scheduled to take place after the men's free skate. In a boorish display, one of the French hockey teams interrupted the competition by standing by the boards and shouting "Hockey!" and booing during Robin Lee's performance.
Sources: L'Auto-vélo, February 23, 1936; Le Petit Parisien, February 24, 1936; L'Écho des sports, February 25, 1936; Skating magazine, April 1936; Seventy-five years of European and World's championships in figure skating, International Skating Union, 1970

1937 WORLD MEN'S FIGURE SKATING CHAMPIONSHIPS
Vienna, Austria, February 12-13, 1937

World Men's Figure Skating Championships:

	CF	FS
1. Felix Kaspar (AUT)	1	1
2. Graham Sharp (GRB)	2	3
3. Elemér Terták (HUN)	3	5
4. Herbert Alward (AUT)	4	4
5. Freddie Tomlins (GRB)	7	2
6. Leopold Linhart (AUT)	6	6
7. Marcus Nikkanen (FIN)	5	10

8. Freddy Mésot (BEL)	8	8
9. Emil Ratzenhofer (AUT)	10	7
10. Lucian Büeler (SUI)	9	11
11. Jaroslav Sadílek (CZE)	11	9

Ladies Figure Skating (Jubilaums-Preis):

	CF	FS
1. Emmy Puzinger (AUT)	1	1
2. Hanne Niernberger (AUT)	2	2
3. Martha Mayerhans (GER)	3	4
4. Eva Nyklová (CZE)	8	3
5. Audrey Peppe (USA)	9	5
6. Eva Resinger (AUT)	7	6
7. Bianca Schenk (AUT)	4	7
8. Anita Wägeler (AUT)	5	8
9. Maria Schweinburg (AUT)	6	9
WD. Liselotte Verdun-Landbeck (BEL)	-	-
WD. Nadine Szilassy (HUN)	-	-
WD. Lydia Veicht (GER)	-	-

Pairs Skating:

1. Ilse Pausin/Erich Pausin (AUT)
2. Erika Bass/Béla Barcza-Rotter (HUN)
3. Eva Tusak/Dr. Zoltan Balázs (CZE)
4. Liese Kianek/Adolf Rosdol (AUT)
5. Hildegard Faulhaber/Dr. Karl Eigel (AUT)
6. Helga Branowitzer/Herr Beloschek (GER)

Sources: Wiener Sporttagblatt, February 9 and 15, 1937; Der Tag, February 13, 1937; Seventy-five years of European and World's championships in figure skating, International Skating Union, 1970

1937 WORLD LADIES AND PAIRS FIGURE SKATING CHAMPIONSHIPS
London, England, March 1-2, 1937

World Ladies Figure Skating Championships:

	CF	FS
1. Cecilia Colledge (GRB)	1	1
2. Megan Taylor (GRB)	2	2
3. Vivi-Anne Hultén (SWE)	3	4
4. Hedy Stenuf (FRA)	5	3
5. Emmy Puzinger (AUT)	4	5
6. Hanne Niernberger (AUT)	7	6
7. Belita Jepson-Turner (GRB)	8	7
8. Gladys Jagger (GRB)	9	9
9. Martha Mayerhans (GER)	10	11
10. Angela Anderes (SUI)	11	10
11. Victoria Lindpaintner (GER)	6	12
12. Audrey Peppe (USA)	12	8
WD. Vera Hrubá (CZE)	-	-
WD. Jacqueline Bossoutrot-Vaudecrane (FRA)	-	-
WD. Gaby Clericetti (FRA)	-	-

World Pairs Skating Championships:

1. Maxi Herber/Ernst Baier (GER)
2. Ilse Pausin/Erich Pausin (AUT)
3. Violet Cliff/Leslie Cliff (GRB)
4. Piroska Szekrényessy/Attila Szekrényessy (HUN)
5. Inge Koch/Günther Noack (GER)
6. Anna Cattaneo/Ercole Cattaneo (ITA)
7. Stephanie Kalus/Erwin Kalus (POL)
8. Feda Kalenčíková/Karel Globar (CZE)

Anna and Ercole Cattaneo made history as the first Italian skaters to participate in the World Figure Skating Championships.

Sources: Daily News (London), February 23, 1937; The Daily Telegraph, March 2, 1937; Seventy-five years of European and World's championships in figure skating, International Skating Union, 1970

1938 WORLD MEN'S AND PAIRS FIGURE SKATING CHAMPIONSHIPS
Berlin, Germany, February 18-19, 1938

World Men's Figure Skating Championships:

	CF	FS
1. Felix Kaspar (AUT)	1	1
2. Graham Sharp (GRB)	2	3
3. Herbert Alward (AUT)	3	6
4. Horst Faber (GER)	4	4
5. Freddie Tomlins (GRB)	8	2
6. Elemér Terták (HUN)	5	5
7. Edi Rada (AUT)	6	8
8. Günther Lorenz (GER)	7	7
9. Robert van Zeebroeck (BEL)	10	9
10. Per Cock-Clausen (DEN)	9	10

World Pairs Skating Championships:

1. Maxi Herber/Ernst Baier (GER)
2. Ilse Pausin/Erich Pausin (AUT)
3. Inge Koch/Günther Noack (GER)
4. Violet Cliff/Leslie Cliff (GRB)
5. Piroska Szekrényessy/Attila Szekrényessy (HUN)
6. Pierette Dubois/Paul Dubois SUI)
7. Elisabeth Roth/Bruno Walter (GER)
8. Gisela Grätz/Otto Weiß (GER)
9. Hildegard Faulhaber/Dr. Karl Eigel (AUT)
10. Anna Cattaneo/Ercole Cattaneo (ITA)
11. Liese Kianek/Adolf Rosdol (AUT)
12. Stephanie Kalusz/Erwin Kalusz (POL)
13. A. Wächter/Fritz Lesk (CZE)

Ladies Figure Skating (Preis der Stadt Berlin):

1. Hedy Stenuf (USA)
2. Hanne Niernberger (AUT)
3. Emmy Puzinger (AUT)
4. Lydia Veicht (GER)
5. Gladys Jagger (AUT)
6. Angela Anderes (SUI)
7. Nadine Szilassy (HUN)
8. Anita Wägeler (AUT)
WD. Gerti Nathansky (AUT)

Ice Dancing:

1. Trude Wagner/Franz Staniek (AUT)
2. Edith Winkelmann/Walter Löhner (AUT)
3. Jutta Stöhr/Fritz Hackl (AUT)
4. Erna Bauer/Josef Kröpfl (AUT)
5. Fraulein Kraupa/Herr Mänar (AUT)

Junior Men's Figure Skating:

1. Ulrich Kohn (GER)
2. Erich Zeller (GER)
3. Alexander Balisch (AUT)

Junior Ladies Figure Skating:

1. Herta Wächtler (AUT)
2. Anita Wägeler (AUT)
3. Gerti Nathansky (AUT)
4. Lucy Merz (GER)
5. Sophie Schmidt (GER)
6. Erna Scheibert (POL)
7. Martha Bruchowcr (CZE)
8. Gertha Böttcher (GER)
9. Jiřina Stachova (CZE)

Junior Pairs Skating:

1. Liselotte Roth/Bruno Walter (GER)
2. Hildegard Faulhaber/Dr. Karl Eigel (AUT)
3. Erika Bass/Béla Barcza-Rotter (HUN)
4. Stefania Kalusz/Erwin Kalusz (POL)
5. Fraulein Dolavos/Herr Wachtl (CZE)
6. Fraulein Dufold/Herr Hofer (GER)
7. Fraulein Nofe/Herr Nofe (GER)

Sources: Neues Wiener Tagblatt, February 18, 21 and 22, 1938; Neue Freie Presse, February 21, 1938; Der Tag, February 21, 1938; Seventy-five years of European and World's championships in figure skating, International Skating Union, 1970

1938 WORLD LADIES FIGURE SKATING CHAMPIONSHIPS
Stockholm, Sweden, February 4-5, 1938

World Ladies Figure Skating Championships:

	CF	FS
1. Megan Taylor (GRB)	2	1
2. Cecilia Colledge (GRB)	1	2
3. Hedy Stenuf (USA)	3	6
4. Gladys Jagger (GRB)	4	5
5. Lydia Veicht (GER)	6	3
6. Hanne Niernberger (AUT)	5	7
7. Daphne Walker (GRB)	8	4
8. Gerd Helland-Bjørnstad (NOR)	9	9
9. Gunnel Ericson (SWE)	11	8(t)
10. Britta Råhlén (SWE)	12	8(t)
11. Anne-Marie Sæther (NOR)	10	10
WD. Emmy Puzinger (AUT)	7	-

Sources: Neue Zürcher Nachrichten, February 7, 1938; Seventy-five years of European and World's championships in figure skating, International Skating Union, 1970

1939 WORLD MEN'S AND PAIRS FIGURE SKATING CHAMPIONSHIPS
Budapest, Hungary, February 17-19, 1939

World Men's Figure Skating Championships:

	CF	FS
1. Graham Sharp (GRB)	1	2
2. Freddie Tomlins (GRB)	3	1
3. Horst Faber (GER)	2	3
4. Edi Rada (GER)	6	4
5. Herbert Alward (HUN)	4	7
6. Elemér Terták (HUN)	5	6
7. Kristóf Kállay (HUN)	9	5
8. Franz Loichinger (GER)	7	8
9. Per Cock-Clausen (DEN)	8	9
10. Max Bindea (ROM)	10	11
11. Dr. Alfred Hirv (EST)	11	10
WD. Tony Austin (GRB)	-	-
WD. Emil Ratzenhofer (GER)	-	-
WD. Roman Turuşanco (ROM)	-	-

World Pairs Skating Championships:

1. Maxi Herber/Ernst Baier (GER)
2. Ilse Pausin/Erich Pausin (GER)
3. Inge Koch/Günther Noack (GER)
4. Piroska Szekrényessy/Attila Szekrényessy (HUN)
5. Violet Cliff/Leslie Cliff (GRB)
6. Pierette Dubois/Paul Dubois (SUI)
7. Nadine Szilassy/Ferenc Kertész (HUN)
8. Erika Bass/Béla Barcza-Rotter (HUN)
9. Stephanie Kalusz/Erwin Kalusz (POL)
10. Silva Palme/Paul Schwab (YUG)
WD. Anna Cattaneo/Ercole Cattaneo (ITA)
WD. Ileana Moldován/Alfred Eisenbeisser-Fieraru (ROM)
WD. Fraulein Guber/Berthold Henkert (ROM)

Ladies Figure Skating (Jubilaums Preis):

1. Daphne Walker (GRB)
2. Hanne Niernberger (GER)
3. Éva von Botond (HUN)
4. Herta Wächtler (GER)
5. Györgi von Botond (HUN)
6. Emmi Pollak (GER)
7. Anita Wägeler (GER)
WD. Gladys Jagger (GRB)
WD. Emmy Puzinger (GER)
WD. Martha Musilek (GER)
WD. Eva Reisinger (GER)
WD. Liesl Wohlbaum (CZE)

Ice Dancing:

1. Trude Wagner/Fritz Staniek (GER)
2. Jutta Stöhr/Fritz Hackl (GER)
3. Kato Székely/József Parády (HUN)
4. Erna Bauer/Josef Kröpfl (GER)
WD. Edith Winkelmann/Walter Löhner (GER)
WD. Fraulein Bonkowszki/Rudolf Plaschke (GER)

Following The Anschluss in March of 1938, skaters from annexed Austria competed under the flag of Nazi Germany.

Dr. Alfred Hirv, Max Bindea and Silva Palme and Paul Schwab made history as the first skaters to represent Estonia, Romania and Yugoslavia in official events at the World Figure Skating Championships.

Sources: Sportkiadas, February 11, 18 and 19, 1939; Völkischer Beobachter, February 20, 1939; Seventy-five years of European and World's championships in figure skating, International Skating Union, 1970

1939 WORLD LADIES FIGURE SKATING CHAMPIONSHIPS
Prague, Czechoslovakia, February 11-12, 1939

World Ladies Figure Skating Championships:

		CF	FS
1.	Megan Taylor (GRB)	1	1
2.	Hedy Stenuf (USA)	4	2
3.	Daphne Walker (GRB)	2	3
4.	Lydia Veicht (GER)	3	5
5.	Eva Nyklová (CZE)	5	7
6.	Emmy Puzinger (GER)	6	6
7.	Martha Musilek (GER)	8	4
8.	Gladys Jagger (GRB)	7	9
9.	Gerd Helland-Bjørnstad (NOR)	9	11
10.	Anne-Marie Sæther (NOR)	10	12
11.	Anita Wägeler (GER)	11	13
12.	Turid Helland-Bjørnstad (NOR)	13	8
13.	Britta Råhlén (SWE)	14	10
14.	Jacqueline Bossoutrot-Vaudecrane (FRA)	12	14
15.	Zdeňka Porgesová (CZE)	15	15
WD.	Cecilia Colledge (GRB)	-	-
WD.	Hanne Niernberger (GER)	-	-
WD.	Herta Wächtler (GER)	-	-
WD.	Ileana Moldován (ROM)	-	-
WD.	Angela Anderes (SUI)	-	-

Source: Programme, 1939 World Figure Skating Championships; Seventy-five years of European and World's championships in figure skating, International Skating Union, 1970

1940-1946
EVENT NOT HELD*

*The World Figure Skating Championships were cancelled during World War II. Some countries held national competitions intermittently or in altered formats, due to many skating club members serving in the military or being involved with war work.

Though World War II ended in 1945, the World Championships did not resume until 1947, as Europe was still recovering from the war and there was not enough time to make appropriate arrangements.

Source: Skating Around the World: International Skating Union, the One Hundredth Anniversary History 1892 -1992, Benjamin T. Wright

Alain Giletti, Hayes Alan Jenkins and Jimmy Grogan at the 1954 World Championships. NTB / Alamy Stock Photo.

THE AGE OF AUSTERITY

1947 WORLD FIGURE SKATING CHAMPIONSHIPS
Stockholm, Sweden, February 13-17, 1947

World Men's Figure Skating Championships:

	CF	FS
1. Hans Gerschwiler (SUI)	1	2
2. Dick Button (USA)	2	1
3. Arthur Apfel (GRB)	4	3
4. Vladislav Čáp (CZE)	3	4
5. Per Cock-Clausen (DEN)	5	5

World Ladies Figure Skating Championships:

	CF	FS
1. Barbara Ann Scott (CAN)	**1**	**1**
2. Daphne Walker (GRB)	2	2
3. Gretchen Van Zandt Merrill (GRB)	3	4
4. Eileen Seigh (USA)	11	3
5. Jeannette Altwegg (GRB)	4	8
6. Janette Ahrens (USA)	9	5
7. Alena Vrzáňová (CZE)	7	6
8. Bridget Shirley Adams (GRB)	5	9
9. Britta Råhlén (SWE)	10	7
10. Jiřína Nekolová (CZE)	6	11
11. Jill Hood-Linzee (GRB)	8	10
12. Patricia Malony (AUS)	12	12
13. Gun Ericson (SWE)	13	13
14. Liv Borg (NOR)	14	14
15. Ingeborg Nilsson (NOR)	16	15
16. Leena Pietilä (FIN)	15	16
17. Kristi Linna (FIN)	17	18
18. Liisa Helanterä (FIN)	18	19
19. Harriet Pantanenius (FIN)	19	17

WD. Marilyn Ruth Take (CAN) - -
WD. Marion Davies (GRB) - -
WD. Barbara Wyatt (GRB) - -
WD. Marit Henie (NOR) - -
WD. Jadwiga Dąbrowska (POL) - -
WD. Anna Bursche-Lindnerowa (POL) - -

World Pairs Skating Championships:

1. Micheline Lannoy/Pierre Baugniet (BEL)
2. Karol Kennedy/Peter Kennedy (USA)
3. Suzanne Diskeuve/Edmond Verbustel (BEL)
4. Winnie Silverthorne/Dennis Silverthorne (GRB)
5. Britta Råhlén/Bo Mothander (SWE)
6. Doris Schubach/Walter Noffke (USA)
7. Denise Faoylle/Guy Pigier (FRA)
8. Běla Zachova/Jaroslav Zach (CZE)
9. Margot Walle/Allan Fjeldheim (NOR)
10. Denise Favart/Jacques Favart (FRA)
11. Marit Henie/Erling Bjerkhoel (NOR)

The ISU only invited countries that were "not under the control of foreign forces" to participate in the first World Figure Skating Championships, excluding Germany, Austria and Japan, which were all under full or partial occupation by Allied Forces. The first post-war World Championships were held in Sweden, a country that remained neutral throughout the War.

Micheline Lannoy and Pierre Baugniet made history as the first Belgian skaters to win gold medals at the World Championships.

Australia was represented in the ladies event for the first time. Barbara Ann Scott made history as the first Canadian and North American skater to win a gold medal at the World Championships. Though he represented Great Britain, Arthur Apfel made history as the first South African-born skater to win a medal in the World Championships.

Sources: *Skating World magazine*, March 1947; *Skating magazine*, April 1947; *Seventy-five years of European and World's championships in figure skating*, International Skating Union, 1970; *Skating Around the World: International Skating Union, the One Hundredth Anniversary History 1892 -1992*, Benjamin T. Wright

1948 WORLD FIGURE SKATING CHAMPIONSHIPS
Davos, Switzerland, February 11-15, 1948

World Men's Figure Skating Championships:

	CF	FS
1. Dick Button (USA)	2	1
2. Hans Gerschwiler (SUI)	1	3
3. Ede Király (HUN)	3	4
4. Johnny Lettengarver (USA)	5	2
5. Jimmy Grogan (USA)	9	5
6. Graham Sharp (GRB)	6	7
7. Hellmut Seibt (AUT)	8	10
8. Hellmut May (AUT)	7	12
9. Wally Distelmeyer (CAN)	**12**	**6**
10. Vladislav Čáp (CZE)	11	8
11. Fernand Leemans (BEL)	10	9
12. Zdeněk Fikar (CZE)	13	11
13. Per Cock-Clausen (DEN)	14	13
WD. Edi Rada (AUT)	4	-

World Ladies Figure Skating Championships:

	CF	FS
1. Barbara Ann Scott (CAN)	**1**	**1**
2. Eva Pawlik (AUT)	3	2
3. Jiřína Nekolová (CZE)	4	4
4. Jeannette Altwegg (GRB)	2	5
5. Alena Vrzáňová (CZE)	5	3
6. Yvonne Sherman (USA)	7	9
7. Martha Bachem-Musilek (AUT)	11	7
8. Bridget Shirley Adams (GRB)	6	18
9. Andrea Kékesy (HUN)	15	6
10. Dagmar Lerchová (CZE)	12	12

11. Mária Saáry (HUN)	10	11
12. Marilyn Ruth Take (CAN)	**9**	**13**
13. Suzanne Morrow (CAN)	**8**	**17**
14. Maja Hug (SUI)	13	15
15. Marion Davies (GRB)	14	10
16. Barbara Wyatt (GRB)	16	16
17. Beryl Bailey (GRB)	17	14
18. Jacqueline du Bief (FRA)	19	8
19. Jill Hood-Linzee (GRB)	18	19
20. Lotti Höner (SUI)	20	20

World Pairs Skating Championships:

1. Micheline Lannoy/Pierre Baugniet (BEL)
2. Andrea Kékesy/Ede Király (HUN)
3. Suzanne Morrow/Wally Distelmeyer (CAN)
4. Karol Kennedy/Peter Kennedy (USA)
5. Yvonne Sherman/Robert Swenning (USA)
6. Winnie Silverthorne/Dennis Silverthorne (GRB)
7. Marianna Nagy/László Nagy (HUN)
8. Jennifer Nicks/John Nicks (GRB)
9. Blažena Knittlová/Karel Vosátka (CZE)
10. Luny Unold/Hans Kuster (SUI)
11. Herta Ratzenhofer/Emil Ratzenhofer (AUT)
12. Jean Thompson/Robert S. Ogilvie (GRB)
13. Susi Giebisch/Helmut Seibt (AUT)
14. Eliane Steinemann/André Calame (SUI)
WD. Denise Favart/Jacques Favart (FRA)

Austrian skaters were permitted to compete in the World Figure Skating Championships, but German and Japanese skaters remained banned from participating.

Barbara Ann Scott made history as the first North American skater to win back-to-back World titles. Suzanne Morrow and Wally Distelmeyer made history as the first Canadian skaters to win medals in the pairs event at the World Championships.

Sources: *Wiener Kurier, February 13, 1948; Skating magazine, April 1948; Skating World magazine, March 1948; Seventy-five years of European and World's championships in figure skating, International Skating Union, 1970*

1949 WORLD FIGURE SKATING CHAMPIONSHIPS
Paris, France, February 16-18, 1949

World Men's Figure Skating Championships:

	CF	FS
1. Dick Button (USA)	1	1
2. Ede Király (HUN)	3	2
3. Edi Rada (AUT)	2	3
4. Jimmy Grogan (USA)	5	4
5. Hellmut Seibt (AUT)	4	5
6. Hayes Alan Jenkins (USA)	6	6
7. Austin Holt (USA)	7	8
8. Carlo Fassi (ITA)	8	7
9. Per Cock-Clausen (DEN)	9	9
10. Jean Vives (FRA)	10	10

World Ladies Figure Skating Championships:

	CF	FS
1. Alena Vrzáňová (CZE)	1	1
2. Yvonne Sherman (USA)	3	2
3. Jeannette Altwegg (GRB)	4	3
4. Jiřina Nekolová (CZE)	6	9
5. Bridget Shirley Adams (GRB)	5	11
6. Andra McLaughlin (USA)	11	6
7. Virginia Baxter (USA)	13	4
8. Dagmar Lerchová (CZE)	9	8
9. Jacqueline du Bief (FRA)	16	5
10. Barbara Wyatt (GRB)	10	12
11. Helen Uhl (USA)	8	13
12. Valda Osborn (GRB)	12	10
13. Beryl Bailey (GRB)	14	7
14. Lilly Fuchs (AUT)	7	15
15. Liliane Madaule (FRA)	17	14
WD. Eva Pawlik (AUT)	2	-

WD. Joan Lister (GRB) 15 -

World Pairs Skating Championships:

1. Andrea Kékesy/Ede Király (HUN)
2. Karol Kennedy/Peter Kennedy (USA)
3. Anne Davies/Carleton Hoffner Jr. (USA)
4. Marianna Nagy/László Nagy (HUN)
5. Herta Ratzenhofer/Emil Ratzenhofer (AUT)
6. Jennifer Nicks/John Nicks (GRB)
7. Běla Zachova/Jaroslav Zach (CZE)
8. Eliane Steinemann/André Calame (SUI)
9. Elly Stärck/Harry Gareis (AUT)
10. Denise Favart/Jacques Favart (FRA)
11. Suzanne Gheldorf/Jacques Rénard (BEL)
12. Pamela Davis/Peter Scholes (GRB)

Sources: Skating World magazine, March 1949; The Skater magazine, May 1949; Seventy-five years of European and World's championships in figure skating, International Skating Union, 1970

1950 WORLD FIGURE SKATING CHAMPIONSHIPS
London, England, March 6-8, 1950

World Men's Figure Skating Championships:

	CF	FS
1. Dick Button (USA)	1	1
2. Ede Király (HUN)	2	2
3. Hayes Alan Jenkins (USA)	4	3
4. Hellmut Seibt (AUT)	3	5
5. Austin Holt (USA)	5	6
6. Michael Carrington (GRB)	6	4
7. Reg Park (AUS)	8	7
8. Roger Wickson (CAN)	**7**	**8**
9. Per Cock-Clausen (DEN)	9	9
WD. Zdeněk Fikar (CZE)	-	-
WD. Carlo Fassi (ITA)	-	-
WD. Jimmy Grogan (USA)	-	-

World Ladies Figure Skating Championships:

	CF	FS
1. Álena Vrzáňová (CZE)	1	1
2. Jeannette Altwegg (GRB)	2	4
3. Yvonne Sherman (USA)	3	7
4. Suzanne Morrow (CAN)	**4**	**5**
5. Sonya Klopfer (USA)	6	2
6. Jacqueline du Bief (FRA)	5	3
7. Virginia Baxter (USA)	10	6
8. Jiřina Nekolová (ISU)	7	14
9. Marlene Smith (CAN)	**9**	**8**
10. Barbara Wyatt (GRB)	8	10
11. Andra McLaughlin (USA)	12	9
12. Dagmar Lerchová (CZE)	11	12
13. Valda Osborn (GRB)	13	13
14. Beryl Bailey (GRB)	14	11
WD. Alexandra Černá (CZE)	-	-
WD. Miroslava Náchodská (CZE)	-	-
WD. Miloslava Tůmová (CZE)	-	-

World Pairs Skating Championships:

1. Karol Kennedy/Peter Kennedy (USA)
2. Jennifer Nicks/John Nicks (GRB)
3. Marianna Nagy/László Nagy (HUN)
4. Eliane Steinemann/André Calame (SUI)
5. Suzanne Gheldorf/Jacques Rénard (BEL)
6. Elly Stärck/Harry Gareis (AUT)
7. Marlene Smith/Donald Gilchrist (CAN)
8. Joan Waterhouse/Gordon Holloway (GRB)
9. Liliane de Becker/Edmond Verbustel (BEL)
10. Irene Maguire/Walter Muehlbronner (USA)
11. Sybil Cooke/Robert S. Hudson (GRB)
12. Denise Favart/Jacques Favart (FRA)
WD. Soňa Balunová/Miloslav Balun (CZE)

International Ice Dancing Competition:

1. Lois Waring/Michael McGean (USA)
2. Sybil Cooke/Robert S. Hudson (GRB)
3. Irene Maguire/Walter Muehlbronner (USA)
4. Julie Barrett/Bill Barrett (USA)
5. Carmel Bodel/Ed Bodel (USA)
6. Joan Chessman/George Bellchambers (GRB)

Karol and Peter Kennedy made history as the first Americans to win the pairs event at the World Figure Skating Championships.

Álena Vrzáňová and Ede Király made international headlines when they defected from behind the Iron Curtain after winning medals in London. Having already defected from Czechoslovakia, Jiřina Nekolová received permission to compete under the sanction of the ISU.

The ice dance event consisted of four compulsory dances and a three-minute free dance.

Sources: Programme, 1950 World Figure Skating Championships; Skating World magazine, April 1950; Skating magazine, May 1950; Seventy-five years of European and World's championships in figure skating, International Skating Union, 1970

1951 WORLD FIGURE SKATING CHAMPIONSHIPS
Milan, Italy, February 23-25, 1951

World Men's Figure Skating Championships:

	CF	FS
1. Dick Button (USA)	1	1
2. Jimmy Grogan (USA)	2	2
3. Hellmut Seibt (AUT)	3	4
4. Hayes Alan Jenkins (USA)	4	3
5. Dudley Richards (USA)	5	5
6. Carlo Fassi (ITA)	6	6
7. Don Laws (USA)	8	7

8. Michael Carrington (GRB)	7	8
9. William Lewis (CAN)	**9**	**10**
10. Freimut Stein (FRG)	10	9
11. Ryusuke Arisaka (JPN)	11	11

World Ladies Figure Skating Championships:

	CF	FS
1. Jeannette Altwegg (GRB)	1	5
2. Jacqueline du Bief (FRA)	2	1
3. Sonya Klopfer (USA)	5	2
4. Suzanne Morrow (CAN)	**3**	**4**
5. Barbara Wyatt (GRB)	4	12
6. Tenley Albright (USA)	8	3
7. Andra McLaughlin (USA)	6	6
8. Margaret Anne Graham (USA)	7	7
9. Valda Osborn (GRB)	9	9
10. Gundi Busch (GER)	13	8
11. Frances Dorsey (USA)	12	13
12. Helga Dudzinski (FRG)	14	10
13. Betty Hiscock (CAN)	**11**	**14**
14. Erika Kraft (FRG)	15	11
15. Susi Wirz (SUI)	10	15
16. Lotte Schwenk (AUT)	18	16
17. Yolande Jobin (SUI)	16	19
18. Ghislaine Köpf (SUI)	17	20
19. Yvonne Sugden (GRB)	20	17
20. Inge Jell (FRG)	22	18
21. Etsuko Inada (JPN)	19	21
22. Lidy Stoppelman (NED)	21	22
23. Grete Dunst (AUT)	23	23

World Pairs Skating Championships:

1. Ria Baran/Paul Falk (FRG)
2. Karol Kennedy/Peter Kennedy (USA)
3. Jennifer Nicks/John Nicks (GRB)
4. Eliane Steinemann/André Calame (SUI)
5. Inge Minor/Hermann Braun (FRG)

6. Marlies Schrör/Hans Schwarz (FRG)
7. Silvia Grandjean/Michel Grandjean (SUI)
8. Janet Gerhauser/John Nightingale (USA)
9. Silva Palme/Marko Lajović (YUG)
10. Elly Stärck/Harry Gareis (AUT)
11. Anne Holt/Austin Holt (USA)
12. Elizabeth Williams/John McCann (GRB)

International Ice Dancing Competition:

1. Jean Westwood/Lawrence Demmy (GRB)
2. Joan Dewhirst/John Slater (GRB)
3. Lois Waring/Michael McGean (USA)
4. Carol Ann Peters/Danny Ryan (USA)
5. Virginia Hoyns/Donald Jacoby (USA)
6. Suzanne Gheldorf/Jacques Rénard (BEL)
7. Catharina Odink/Jacobus Odink (NED)
8. Trude Leitner/Rudolf Gregorin (AUT)
9. Albertina Brown/Nigel Brown (SUI)
10. Pauline Haffner/Herbert Huber (AUT)
11. Ilse Reitmayer/Willy Behringer (AUT)
12. Helga Binder/Edwin Führich (AUT)

Italy played host to the World Figure Skating Championships for the first time. German and Japanese skaters were permitted to compete for the first time since the end of World War II.

29-year-old Donald Gilchrist, the Canadian judge in the men's, ladies and pairs event, was believed to be the youngest judge ever at the World Championships at the time.

The power went out during the ladies school figures and five skaters had to perform their bracket-change-bracket in the dark.

Lidy Stoppelman made history as the first skater to represent The Netherlands at the World Figure Skating Championships.

Sources: Skating magazine, April and May 1951; Skating World magazine,

April 1951; Seventy-five years of European and World's championships in figure skating, International Skating Union, 1970

1952 WORLD FIGURE SKATING CHAMPIONSHIPS
Paris, France, February 27-March 1, 1952

World Men's Figure Skating Championships:

	CF	FS
1. Dick Button (USA)	1	1
2. Jimmy Grogan (USA)	4	3
3. Hayes Alan Jenkins (USA)	5	2
4. Hellmut Seibt (AUT)	2	4
5. Dudley Richards (USA)	3	6
6. Carlo Fassi (ITA)	6	5
7. Peter Firstbrook (CAN)	**7**	**7**
8. Alain Giletti (FRA)	9	8
9. Martin Felsenreich (AUT)	8	9
10. Adrian Swan (AUS)	10	10
11. François Pache (SUI)	11	11

World Ladies Figure Skating Championships:

	CF	FS
1. Jacqueline du Bief (FRA)	1	1
2. Sonya Klopfer (USA)	3	3
3. Virginia Baxter (USA)	5	2
4. Suzanne Morrow (CAN)	**6**	**5**
5. Barbara Wyatt (GRB)	4	9
6. Gundi Busch (FRG)	10	4
7. Marlene Smith (CAN)	**8**	**6**
8. Valda Osborn (GRB)	7	7
9. Erica Batchelor (GRB)	9	10
10. Vevi Smith (CAN)	**11**	**11**
11. Helga Dudzinski (FRG)	13	8
12. Patricia Devries (GRB)	12	13
13. Eva Weidler (AUT)	15	12
14. Annelies Schilhan (AUT)	18	14
15. Nancy Hallam-Burley (AUS)	16	15
16. Ghislaine Kopf (SUI)	14	16

17. Lidy Stoppelman (NED)	17	17
18. Yolande Jobin (SUI)	19	20
19. Gweneth Molony (AUS)	20	18
20. Doris Zerbe (SUI)	21	19
21. Liliane de Becker (BEL)	22	22
22. Nicole Vanderberghe (BEL)	23	21
WD. Tenley Albright (USA)	2	-

World Pairs Skating Championships:

1. Ria Baran/Paul Falk (FRG)
2. Karol Kennedy/Peter Kennedy (USA)
3. Jennifer Nicks/John Nicks (GRB)
4. **Frances Dafoe/Norris Bowden (CAN)**
5. Janet Gerhauser/John Nightingale (USA)
6. Silvia Grandjean/Michel Grandjean (SUI)
7. Sissy Schwarz/Kurt Oppelt (AUT)
8. Caryl Johns/Jack B. Jost (USA)
9. Jacqueline Mason/Mervyn Bower (AUS)
10. Peri Horne/Raymond Lockwood (GRB)

World Ice Dancing Championships:

	CD	FD
1. Jean Westwood/Lawrence Demmy (GRB)	1	1
2. Joan Dewhirst/John Slater (GRB)	2	2
3. Carol Ann Peters/Danny Ryan (USA)	4	3
4. Carmel Bodel/Ed Bodel (USA)	3	4
5. Lydia Boon/Aadrian van Dam (NED)	5	5
6. Ilse Reitmayer/Hans Kutschera (AUT)	6	6
7. Catharina Odink/Jacobus Odink (NED)	7	9
8. Albertina Brown/Nigel Brown (SUI)	8	8
9. Pauline Haffner/Herbert Huber (AUT)	9	7

Though several ice dancing competitions had sporadically been held in conjunction with the World Figure Skating Championships, the 1952 event was the first to be officially recognized as a World Championship by the ISU. Jean Westwood and Lawrence Demmy made history as the first British ice dance team to win an official

World title.

Jacqueline du Bief made history as the first French singles skater to win a World title. U.S. skaters swept the podium for the first time in the men's event.

Dick Button made history as the first skater to land a triple jump (triple loop) at the World Championships.

Sources: Skating magazine, May 1952; Seventy-five years of European and World's championships in figure skating, International Skating Union, 1970; Stilwandel im Eiskunstlauf: Eine Ästhetikund Kulturgeschichte: Eine Ästhetik- und Kulturgeschichte, Dr. Matthias Hampe, 1994

1953 WORLD FIGURE SKATING CHAMPIONSHIPS
Davos, Switzerland, February 8-15, 1953

World Men's Figure Skating Championships:

	CF	FS
1. Hayes Alan Jenkins (USA)	2	1
2. Jimmy Grogan (USA)	1	3
3. Carlo Fassi (ITA)	3	6
4. Ronnie Robertson (USA)	7	2
5. Alain Giletti (FRA)	5	4
6. Dudley Richards (USA)	6	5
7. Peter Firstbrook (CAN)	**4**	**8**
8. Peter Dunfield (CAN)	**8**	**7**
9. Michael Booker (GRB)	9	9
10. Freimut Stein (FRG)	10	10
11. Kurt Oppelt (AUT)	13	11
12. Hubert Köpfler (SUI)	11	12
13. György Czakó (HUN)	14	13
WD. Klaus Loichinger (FRG)	12	-
WD. Martin Felsenreich (AUT)	15	-

World Ladies Figure Skating Championships:

	CF	FS
1. Tenley Albright (USA)	1	1

2. Gundi Busch (FRG)	2	3
3. Valda Osborn (GRB)	3	5
4. Carol Heiss (USA)	5	2
5. Suzanne Morrow (CAN)	**4**	**4**
6. Vevi Smith (CAN)	**6**	**10**
7. Margaret Anne Graham (USA)	7	7
8. Yvonne Sugden (GRB)	8	6
9. Erica Batchelor (GRB)	10	12
10. Ann Robinson (GRB)	9	13
11. Annelies Schilhan (AUT)	12	9
12. Mary Kenner (CAN)	**13**	**8**
13. Elaine Skevington (GRB)	11	14
14. Rosi Pottinger (FRG)	18	11
15. Doris Zerbe (SUI)	16	17
16. Miggs Dean (USA)	17	16
17. Yolande Jobin (SUI)	15	19
18. Eszter Jurek (HUN)	20	15
19. Lidy Stoppelman (NED)	19	18
WD. Helga Dudzinski (FRG)	14	-
WD. Sissy Schwarz (AUT)	-	-

World Pairs Skating Championships:

1. Jennifer Nicks/John Nicks (GRB)
2. Frances Dafoe/Norris Bowden (CAN)
3. Marianna Nagy/László Nagy (HUN)
4. Silvia Grandjean/Michel Grandjean (SUI)
5. Peri Horne/Raymond Lockwood (GRB)
6. Sissy Schwarz/Kurt Oppelt (AUT)
7. Jane Higson/Robert S. Hudson (GRB)
8. Éva Szöllősi/Gábor Vida (HUN)
9. Eva Neeb/Karl Probst (FRG)
10. Charlotte Michiels/Gaston van Ghelder (BEL)

World Ice Dancing Championships:

	CD	FD
1. Jean Westwood/Lawrence Demmy (GRB)	1	1
2. Joan Dewhirst/John Slater (GRB)	2	2

3. Carol Ann Peters/Danny Ryan (USA)	3	3
4. Nesta Davies/Paul Thomas (GRB)	5	4
5. Virginia Hoyns/Donald Jacoby (USA)	4	6
6. Lydia Boon/Aadrian van Dam (NED)	6	7
7. Carmel Bodel/Ed Bodel (USA)	7	5
8. Albertina Brown/Nigel Brown (SUI)	8	9
9. Helga Binder/Edwin Führich (AUT)	10	8
10. Catharina Odink/Jacobus Odink (NED)	9	12
11. Lucia Fischer/Rudolf Zorn (AUT)	11	11
12. Luise Lehner/Hans Kutschera (AUT)	12	10

Mollie Phillips made history as the first woman to serve as a referee at the World Figure Skating Championships. Carlo Fassi made history as the first Italian skater to win a medal at the World Championships. Tenley Albright made history as the first American winner of the ladies event. Jennifer and John Nicks made history as the first British winners of the pairs event. For the first time, ISU Dance Tests were held during the World Championships.

Sources: Skating magazine, April 1953; Seventy-five years of European and World's championships in figure skating, International Skating Union, 1970

1954 WORLD FIGURE SKATING CHAMPIONSHIPS
Oslo, Norway, February 16-19, 1954

World Men's Figure Skating Championships:

	CF	FS
1. Hayes Alan Jenkins (USA)	1	1
2. Jimmy Grogan (USA)	2	4
3. Alain Giletti (FRA)	3	5
4. David Jenkins (USA)	4	2
5. Ronnie Robertson (USA)	5	3
6. Michael Booker (GRB)	6	9
7. Charles Snelling (CAN)	**7**	**7**
8. Peter Dunfield (CAN)	**8**	**11**
9. Norbert Felsinger (AUT)	9	10
10. Douglas Court (CAN)	**10**	**6**
11. Alain Calmat (FRA)	11	8

World Ladies Figure Skating Championships:

		CF	FS
1.	Gundi Busch (FRG)	2	1
2.	Tenley Albright (USA)	1	2
3.	Erica Batchelor (GRB)	3	3
4.	**Barbara Gratton (CAN)**	**4**	**4**
5.	Frances Dorsey (USA)	5	5
6.	Yvonne Sugden (GRB)	7	6
7.	Hanna Eigel (AUT)	9	7
8.	**Carole Jane Pachl (CAN)**	**10**	**9**
9.	**Ann Johnston (CAN)**	**8**	**10**
10.	**Sonja Currie (CAN)**	**11**	**11**
11.	Margaret Anne Graham (USA)	6	8
12.	Ingrid Wendl (AUT)	12	12
13.	Rosi Pettinger (FRG)	14	13
14.	Erika Rücker (FRG)	13	14
15.	Miggs Dean (USA)	16	15
16.	Clema Cowley (GRB)	15	16
17.	Fiorella Negro (ITA)	17	17
18.	Ally Lundström (SWE)	20	18
19.	Gun Ericson-Mothander (SWE)	18	19
20.	Ingeborg Nilsson (NOR)	19	20
WD.	Carol Heiss (USA)	-	-

World Pairs Skating Championships:

1. Frances Dafoe/Norris Bowden (CAN)
2. Silvia Grandjean/Michel Grandjean (SUI)
3. Sissy Schwarz/Kurt Oppelt (AUT)
4. Carole Ann Ormaca/Robin Greiner (USA)
5. Margaret Anne Graham/Hugh Graham Jr. (USA)
6. Alice Zettel/Klaus Loichinger (FRG)
7. Inge Minor/Hermann Braun (FRG)
8. Jane Higson/Robert S. Hudson (GRB)
9. Britta Lindmark/Ulf Berendt (SWE)
10. Bjørg Skjælaaen/Johannes Thorsen (NOR)

World Ice Dancing Championships:

	CD	FD
1. Jean Westwood/Lawrence Demmy (GRB)	1	1
2. Nesta Davies/Paul Thomas (GRB)	2	2
3. Carmel Bodel/Ed Bodel (USA)	3	3
4. Barbara Radford/Raymond Lockwood (GRB)	4	4
5. Virginia Hoyns/Donald Jacoby (USA)	5	5
6. Phyllis Forney/Martin Forney (USA)	6	6
7. Edith Peikert/Hans Kutschera (AUT)	7	7

Frances Dafoe and Norris Bowden made history as the first Canadian team to win a gold medal in the pairs event at the World Figure Skating Championships. Silvia and Michel Grandjean won Switzerland's first medal in the pairs event.

Gundi Busch made history as the first skater from West Germany to win a gold medal in the ladies event.

The ISU Gold Dance Test was conducted for the first time during the event. The first two teams to pass it were Jean Westwood and Lawrence Demmy and Virginia Hoyns and Donald Jacoby.

Skaters competed in freezing temperatures and drank brandy in the dressing room after they skated to warm up.

Sources: Bergens Tidende, February 19, 1954; Arbeiderbladet, February 19, 1954; Bergens Arbeiderblad, February 20, 1954; Arbeiderbladet, February 20, 1954; Skating magazine, April 1954; Seventy-five years of European and World's championships in figure skating, International Skating Union, 1970; Interview with Frances Dafoe, The Manleywoman SkateCast, April 3, 2012

1955 WORLD FIGURE SKATING CHAMPIONSHIPS
Vienna, Austria, February 15-18, 1955

World Men's Figure Skating Championships:

	CF	FS
1. Hayes Alan Jenkins (USA)	1	3

2. Ronnie Robertson (USA)	3	1
3. David Jenkins (USA)	4	2
4. Alain Giletti (FRA)	2	9
5. Karol Divín (CZE)	7	4
6. Michael Booker (GRB)	6	6
7. Norbert Felsinger (AUT)	5	11
8. Charles Snelling (CAN)	**8**	**10**
9. Alain Calmat (FRA)	10	5
10. Hugh Graham Jr. (USA)	9	7
11. István Szenes (HUN)	14	8
12. Hans Müller (SUI)	12	13
13. Tilo Gutzeit (FRG)	11	14
14. Edward Brian Tuck (GRB)	13	12

World Ladies Figure Skating Championships:

	CF	FS
1. Tenley Albright (USA)	1	1
2. Carol Heiss (USA)	5	2
3. Hanna Eigel (AUT)	2	6
4. Ingrid Wendl (AUT)	3	5
5. Erica Batchelor (GRB)	4	7
6. Carole Jane Pachl (CAN)	**7**	**8**
7. Patricia Firth (USA)	9	4
8. Yvonne Sugden (GRB)	6	9
9. Ann Johnston (CAN)	**8**	**12**
10. Catherine Machado (USA)	12	3
11. Rosi Pettinger (FRG)	14	11
12. Dawn Hunter (AUS)	11	19
13. Ilse Musyl (AUT)	13	15
14. Dagmar Lerchová-Řeháková (CZE)	20	10
15. Joan Haanappel (NED)	18	14
16. Fiorella Negro (ITA)	15	17
17. Alice Fischer (SUI)	17	20
18. Miroslava Náchodská (CZE)	19	18
19. Maryvonne Huet (FRA)	16	21
20. Erika Rücker (FRG)	21	16
21. Sjoukje Dijkstra (NED)	22	13
WD. Hanna Walter (AUT)	10	-

World Pairs Skating Championships:

1. **Frances Dafoe/Norris Bowden (CAN)**
2. Sissy Schwarz/Kurt Oppelt (AUT)
3. Marianna Nagy/László Nagy (HUN)
4. Carole Ann Ormaca/Robin Greiner (USA)
5. **Barbara Wagner/Robert Paul (CAN)**
6. Věra Suchánková/Zdeněk Doležal (CZE)
7. Marika Kilius/Franz Ningel (FRG)
8. Lucille Ash/Sully Kothmann (USA)
9. Alice Zettel/Klaus Loichinger (USA)
10. Liesl Ellend/Konrad Lienert (AUT)
11. Éva Szöllősi/Gábor Vida (HUN)
12. Vivien Higson/Robert S. Hudson (GRB)

World Ice Dancing Championships:

	CD	FD
1. Jean Westwood/Lawrence Demmy (GRB)	1	1
2. Pamela Weight/Paul Thomas (GRB)	2	2
3. Barbara Radford/Raymond Lockwood (GRB)	3	3
4. Carmel Bodel/Ed Bodel (USA)	4	4
5. Joan Zamboni/Roland Junso (USA)	5	5
6. Phyllis Forney/Martin Forney (USA)	6	6
7. Fanny Besson/Jean Paul Guhel (FRA)	7	7
8. Sigrid Knake/Günther Koch (FRG)	8	9
9. Lucia Fischer/Rudolf Zorn (AUT)	11	8
10. Bona Giammona/Giancarlo Sioli (ITA)	9	10
11. Lindis Johnston/Jeffrey Johnston (CAN)	**10**	**11**
12. Catharina Odink/Jacobus Odink (NED)	14	13
13. Claude Weinstein/Claude Lambert (FRA)	12	12
14. Edith Peikert/Hans Kutschera (AUT)	13	14
15. Luise Lehner/Georg Lenitz (AUT)	15	15

Tenley Albright made history as the first World Champion in the ladies event to reclaim a World title after losing it the year prior.

The pairs competition and three of the four compulsory dances were skated outdoors during a heavy snowstorm. Heavy winds plagued the men's school figures.

British ice dance teams took the top three spots, achieving the first podium sweep by a single country in the discipline. Siblings Lindis and Jeffrey Johnston made history as the first Canadian ice dancers to compete at the World Championships.

Ronnie Robertson made history as the first skater to perform a triple Salchow jump at the World Figure Skating Championships.

Sources: Independent (Long Beach, CA), October 30, 1955; Skating magazine, April 1955; Seventy-five years of European and World's championships in figure skating, International Skating Union, 1970

1956 WORLD FIGURE SKATING CHAMPIONSHIPS
Garmisch-Partenkirchen, West Germany, February 16-19, 1956

World Men's Figure Skating Championships:

	CF	FS
1. Hayes Alan Jenkins (USA)	1	2
2. Ronnie Robertson (USA)	2	1
3. David Jenkins (USA)	3	3
4. Charles Snelling (CAN)	**4**	**4**
5. Michael Booker (GRB)	5	6
6. Karol Divín (CZE)	6	5
7. Alain Calmat (FRA)	7	8
8. Norbert Felsinger (AUT)	8	11
9. Tilo Gutzeit (FRG)	9	7
10. François Pache (SUI)	10	10
11. Allan Ganter (AUS)	15	12
12. Hans-Jürgen Bäumler (FRG)	14	9
13. Hans Müller (SUI)	12	13
14. Hanno Ströher (AUT)	11	14
15. Darío Villalba Flórez (ESP)	16	16
16. Charles Keeble (AUS)	17	15
WD. Manfred Schnelldorfer (FRG)	13	-
WD. Alain Giletti (FRA)	-	-

World Ladies Figure Skating Championships:

	CF	FS
1. Carol Heiss (USA)	1	1
2. Tenley Albright (USA)	2	2
3. Ingrid Wendl (AUT)	3	3
4. Yvonne Sugden (GRB)	4	4
5. Hanna Eigel (AUT)	5	7
6. Catherine Machado (USA)	6	5
7. Hanna Walter (AUT)	9	8
8. Erica Batchelor (GRB)	7	11
9. Ann Johnston (CAN)	**8**	**9**
10. Mary Ann Dorsey (USA)	10	13
11. Joan Haanappel (NED)	11	10
12. Dianne C.R. Peach (GRB)	13	12
13. Fiorella Negro (ITA)	15	16
14. Emma Giardini (ITA)	12	20
15. Jindra Kramperová (CZE)	17	14
16. Sjoukje Dijkstra (NED)	16	18
17. Carine Borner (SUI)	18	17
18. Ilse Musyl (AUT)	14	21
19. Alice Fischer (SUI)	19	19
20. Ina Bauer (CZE)	21	5
21. Jana Dočekalová (CZE)	20	15
WD. Carole Jane Pachl (CAN)	-	-
WD. Rosi Pettinger (FRG)	-	-

World Pairs Skating Championships:

1. Sissy Schwarz/Kurt Oppelt (AUT)
2. Frances Dafoe/Norris Bowden (CAN)
3. Marika Kilius/Franz Ningel (FRG)
4. Carole Ann Ormaca/Robin Greiner (USA)
5. Barbara Wagner/Robert Paul (CAN)
6. Lucille Ash/Sully Kothmann (USA)
7. Joyce Coates/Anthony Holles (GRB)
8. Liesl Ellend/Konrad Lienert (AUT)
9. Carolyn Krau/Rodney Ward (GRB)
10. Eva Neeb/Karl Probst (FRG)

11. Jacqueline Mason/Mervyn Bower (AUS)

World Ice Dancing Championships:

	CD	FD
1. Pamela Weight/Paul Thomas (GRB)	1	1
2. June Markham/Courtney Jones (GRB)	2	2
3. Barbara Thompson/Gerard Rigby (GRB)	5	4
4. Joan Zamboni/Roland Junso (USA)	3	6
5. Fanny Besson/Jean Paul Guhel (FRA)	6	3
6. Carmel Bodel/Ed Bodel (USA)	4	7
7. Sidney Arnold/Franklin Nelson (USA)	7	8
8. Sigrid Knake/Günther Koch (FRG)	8	5
9. Lindis Johnston/Jeffrey Johnston (CAN)	**9**	**11**
10. Gerda Wohlgemuth/Hannes Burkhardt (FRG)	10	12
11. Edith Peikert/Hans Kutschera (AUT)	11	10
12. Bona Giammona/Giancarlo Sioli (ITA)	13	9
13. Lucia Fischer/Rudolf Zorn (AUT)	12	14
14. Catharina Odink/Jacobus Odink (NED)	14	13
15. A. Giuggiolini/G. Ceccattini (ITA)	15	16
16. Rita Paucka/Peter Kwiet (FRG)	16	15
17. M-G. Locatelli/V. Toncelli (ITA)	17	17

Temperatures dipped as low as minus twenty-seven degrees, causing brittle ice conditions. Skaters had to bundle up to compete and many suffered frostbite.

Highlights from the World Figure Skating Championships were broadcast on BBC television for the first time.

Darío Villalba Flórez made history as the first skater from Spain to compete at the World Championships.

Sources: Berner Tagwacht, February 20, 1956; Neue Zürcher Nachrichten, February 20, 1956; Skating magazine, May 1956; Protocol, 1956 World Figure Skating Championships; BBC Programme Index; Seventy-five years of European and World's championships in figure skating, International Skating Union, 1970

1957 WORLD FIGURE SKATING CHAMPIONSHIPS
Colorado Springs, United States, February 26-March 2, 1957

World Men's Figure Skating Championships:

	CF	FS
1. David Jenkins (USA)	1	1
2. Tim Brown (USA)	2	3
3. Charles Snelling (CAN)	**3**	**2**
4. Alain Giletti (FRA)	6	4
5. Tommy Moore (USA)	5	6
6. Norbert Felsinger (AUT)	4	8
7. Donald Jackson (CAN)	**10**	**5**
8. Robert Brewer (USA)	7	10
9. Alain Calmat (FRA)	8	7
10. Michael Booker (GRB)	9	9
11. Manfred Schnelldorfer (FRG)	12	11
12. Hubert Köpfler (SUI)	11	15
13. Yukio Nishikura (JPN)	13	13
14. Hideo Sugita (JPN)	15	12
15. Kazuo Ōhashi (JPN)	14	16
16. Charles Keeble (AUS)	17	14
17. William Cherrell (AUS)	16	17

World Ladies Figure Skating Championships:

	CF	FS
1. Carol Heiss (USA)	1	1
2. Hanna Eigel (AUT)	3	4
3. Ingrid Wendl (AUT)	2	7
4. Carole Jane Pachl (CAN)	**4**	**5**
5. Claralyn Lewis (USA)	6	3
6. Hanna Walter (AUT)	5	11
7. Joan Schenke (USA)	8	9
8. Nancy Heiss (USA)	10	6
9. Erica Batchelor (USA)	11	10
10. Karen Dixon (CAN)	**7**	**14**
11. Ina Bauer (FRG)	19	2
12. Sjoukje Dijkstra (NED)	14	12
13. Joan Haanappel (NED)	16	8

14. Margaret Crosland (CAN)	**12**	**13**
15. Ilse Musyl (AUT)	9	15
16. Emma Giardini (ITA)	13	18
17. Junko Ueno (JPN)	15	19
18. Carla Tichatschek (ITA)	17	17
19. Yūko Araki (JPN)	20	16
20. Alice Fischer (SUI)	18	20
WD. Eszter Jurek (HUN)	-	-
WD. Helga Zöllner (HUN)	-	-

World Pairs Skating Championships:

1. Barbara Wagner/Robert Paul (CAN)
2. Marika Kilius/Franz Ningel (FRG)
3. Maria Jelinek/Otto Jelinek (CAN)
4. Nancy Rouillard/Ron Ludington (USA)
5. Joyce Coates/Anthony Holles (GRB)
WD. Marianna Nagy/László Nagy (HUN)
WD. Liesl Ellend/Konrad Lienert (AUT)

World Ice Dancing Championships:

	CD	FD
1. June Markham/Courtney Jones (GRB)	1	1
2. Geraldine Fenton/William McLachlan (CAN)	**2**	**2**
3. Sharon McKenzie/Bert Wright (USA)	3	3
4. Joan Zamboni/Roland Junso (USA)	4	4
5. Barbara Thompson/Gerard Rigby (GRB)	6	5
6. Kay Morris/Michael Robinson (GRB)	5	6
7. Carmel Bodel/Ed Bodel (USA)	7	7
8. Beverley Orr/Hugh Smith (CAN)	**8**	**8**
9. Sigrid Knake/Günther Koch (FRG)	9	9
10. Christiane Elien/Claude Lambert (FRA)	10	10
11. Edith Peikert/Hans Kutschera (AUT)	11	11
WD. Fanny Besson/Jean Paul Guhel (FRA)	-	-

The event had a 'Wild West' theme. Skaters were greeted by a cowboy on horseback performing rope tricks. When ISU officials and judges arrived in Colorado Springs, greeters dramatically drew guns from their holsters and fired several rounds in salute. A voice from the plane loudly exclaimed, "My God, they've shot the judges!"

Spoiler alert: the judges were fine! In fact, Pierrette Paquin Devine made history as the first Canadian woman to serve as a judge at the World Figure Skating Championships. Devine was the youngest Canadian woman to be appointed a World judge and the Canadian Figure Skating Assciation's only French-Canadian international judge.

Geraldine Fenton and William McLachlan won Canada's first medals in ice dancing at the World Championships and Americans Sharon McKenzie and Bert Wright made history as the first ice dance team to win a medal at a World Championship event in their home country.

Sources: Letter from Manfred Schnelldorfer to his parents, February 1957; Skating World magazine, April 1957; Skating magazine, March and May 1957; Protocol, 1957 World Figure Skating Championships; Seventy-five years of European and World's championships in figure skating, International Skating Union, 1970

Peggy Fleming, World Champion 1966-1968. Everett Collection Inc / Alamy Stock Photo.

THE SPACE AGE

1958 WORLD FIGURE SKATING CHAMPIONSHIPS
Paris, France, February 13-15, 1958

World Men's Figure Skating Championships:

	CF	FS
1. David Jenkins (USA)	2	1
2. Tim Brown (USA)	1	10
3. Alain Giletti (FRA)	3	7
4. Donald Jackson (CAN)	**9**	**2**
5. Alain Calmat (FRA)	6	5
6. Karol Divín (CZE)	4	9
7. Tilo Gutzeit (FRG)	5	8
8. Michael Booker (GRB)	8	11
9. Eddie Collins (CAN)	**12**	**3**
10. Robert Brewer (USA)	10	12
11. Charles Snelling (CAN)	**11**	**4**
12. Tommy Moore (USA)	13	6
13. Norbert Felsinger (AUT)	7	15
14. Hans-Jürgen Bäumler (FRG)	15	13
15. Manfred Schnelldorfer (FRG)	14	17
16. Peter Jonas (AUT)	17	19
17. Lev Mikhailov (SOV)	20	16
18. François Pache (SWE)	16	20
19. Per Kjølberg (NOR)	18	18
20. Valentin Zakharov (SOV)	22	14
21. Igor Persiantsev (SOV)	19	21
22. William Cherrell (AUS)	21	22
23. Charles Keeble (AUS)	23	23

World Ladies Figure Skating Championships:

	CF	FS
1. Carol Heiss (USA)	1	1
2. Ingrid Wendl (AUT)	2	2
3. Hanna Walter (AUT)	3	4

4. Ina Bauer (FRG)	8	3
5. Dianne C.R. Peach (GRB)	5	13
6. Nancy Heiss (USA)	4	9
7. Patricia Pauley (GRB)	10	7
8. Joan Haanappel (NED)	6	16
9. Carol Wanek (USA)	9	12
10. Claralyn Lewis (USA)	7	15
11. Karin Frohner (AUT)	13	10
12. Regine Heitzer (AUT)	15	5
13. Margaret Crosland (CAN)	**12**	**11**
14. Dany Rigoulot (FRA)	14	14
15. Sonia Snelling (CAN)	**16**	**6**
16. Sjoukje Dijkstra (NED)	11	17
17. Jindra Kramperová (CZE)	19	8
18. Corinne Altmann (FRA)	20	18
19. Petra Damm (FRG)	18	22
20. Carla Tichatschek (ITA)	17	20
21. Anna Galmarini (ITA)	21	24
22. Nicole Erdos (FRA)	25	19
23. Nicole Hassler (FRA)	23	23
24. Liliane Crosa (SUI)	24	21
25. Lois Thomson (AUS)	26	25
26. Rita Müller (SUI)	22	28
27. Grete Borgen (NOR)	27	26
28. Karin Dehle (NOR)	28	27
29. Gunhild Frylén (SWE)	29	29

World Pairs Skating Championships:

1. Barbara Wagner/Robert Paul (CAN)
2. Věra Suchánková/Zdeněk Doležal (CZE)
3. Maria Jelinek/Otto Jelinek (CAN)
4. Joyce Coates/Anthony Holles (GRB)
5. Nancy Ludington/Ronald Ludington (USA)
6. Marika Kilius/Hans-Jürgen Bäumler (FRG)
7. Marianna Nagy/László Nagy (HUN)
8. Nina Zhuk/Stanislav Zhuk (SOV)
9. Mary Watson/John Jarmon (USA)

10. Liesl Ellend/Konrad Lienert (AUT)
11. Eszter Jurek/Miklós Kucharovits (HUN)
12. Carolyn Krau/Rodney Ward (GRB)
13. Ludmila Belousova/Oleg Protopopov (SOV)
14. Agneta Wale/Kristian Wale (SWE)
15. Ingeborg Nilsson/Reidar Børjeson (NOR)

World Ice Dancing Championships:

	CD	FD
1. June Markham/Courtney Jones (GRB)	1	1
2. Geraldine Fenton/William McLachlan (CAN)	**2**	**4**
3. Andree Anderson/Donald Jacoby (USA)	3	3
4. Kay Morris/Michael Robinson (GRB)	4	6
5. Barbara Thompson/Gerard Rigby (GRB)	5	2
6. Christiane Guhel/Jean Guhel (FRA)	6	5
7. Beverley Orr/Hugh Smith (CAN)	**7**	**7**
8. Claire O'Neil/J.J. Bejshak (USA)	8	8
9. Lucia Zorn/Rudolf Zorn (AUT)	9	13
10. Rita Paucka/Peter Kwiet (FRG)	10	12
11. Catharina Odink/Jacobus Odink (NED)	11	10
12. Annick de Trentinian/Jacques Mer (FRA)	12	9
13. A. Giuggiolini/G. Ceccattini (ITA)	13	11
14. Petra Steigerwald/Hannes Burkhardt (FRG)	15	14
15. Ludovica Boccacci/Giancarlo Sioli (ITA)	14	16
16. M-G. Toncelli/Vinicio Toncelli (ITA)	16	15

Though Russian skaters competed at the World Figure Skating Championships before The Great War, the 1958 World Championships marked the first time the Soviet Union sent a small team.

Sources: Skating World magazine, March and April 1958; Protocol, 1958 World Figure Skating Championships; Seventy-five years of European and World's championships in figure skating, ISU, 1970

1959 WORLD FIGURE SKATING CHAMPIONSHIPS
Colorado Springs, United States, February 24-28, 1959

World Men's Figure Skating Championships:

	CF	FS
1. David Jenkins (USA)	2	1
2. Donald Jackson (CAN)	**4**	**2**
3. Tim Brown (USA)	1	5
4. Alain Giletti (FRA)	3	3
5. Karol Divín (CZE)	6	4
6. Tilo Gutzeit (FRG)	7	7
7. Alain Calmat (FRA)	9	9
8. Bradley Lord (USA)	8	8
9. Norbert Felsinger (AUT)	5	10
10. Eddie Collins (CAN)	**11**	**6**
11. Robert Brewer (USA)	10	11
12. David Clements (GRB)	12	12
13. Hubert Köpfler (SUI)	13	13

World Ladies Figure Skating Championships:

	CF	FS
1. Carol Heiss (USA)	1	1
2. Hanna Walter (AUT)	2	6
3. Sjoukje Dijkstra (NED)	3	3
4. Ina Bauer (FRG)	6	2
5. Barbara Ann Roles (USA)	4	7
6. Lynn Finnegan (USA)	9	4
7. Regine Heitzer (AUT)	8	8
8. Nancy Heiss (USA)	7	10
9. Anna Galmarini (ITA)	10	5
10. Sandra Tewkesbury (CAN)	**13**	**9**
11. Margaret Crosland (CAN)	**11**	**13**
12. Sonia Snelling (CAN)	**14**	**11**
13. Carla Tichatschek (ITA)	15	12
13. Yuko Araki (JPN)	12	14
WD. Joan Haanappel (AUT)	5	-

World Pairs Skating Championships:

1. Barbara Wagner/Robert Paul (CAN)
2. Marika Kilius/Hans-Jürgen Bäumler (FRG)
3. Nancy Ludington/Ron Ludington (USA)
4. Maria Jelinek/Otto Jelinek (CAN)
5. Margret Göbl/Franz Ningel (FRG)
6. Maribel Yerxa Owen Jr./Dudley Richards (USA)
7. Gayle Freed/Karl Freed (USA)
8. Diana Hinko/Heinz Döpfl (AUT)

World Ice Dancing Championships:

	CD	FD
1. Doreen Denny/Courtney Jones (GRB)	1	1
2. Andree Anderson/Donald Jacoby (USA)	2	2
3. Geraldine Fenton/William McLachlan (CAN)	**3**	**3**
4. Margie Ackles/Chuck Phillips Jr. (USA)	4	4
5. Ann Martin/Eddie Collins (CAN)	**5**	**6**
6. Christiane Guhel/Jean Paul Guhel (FRA)	6	5
7. Kay Morris/Michael Robinson (GRB)	7	7
8. Svata Staroba/Mirek Staroba (CAN)	**8**	**9**
9. Judy Lamar/Ron Ludington (USA)	9	8

Sources: Skating magazine, May 1959; Seventy-five years of European and World's championships in figure skating, ISU, 1970

1960 WORLD FIGURE SKATING CHAMPIONSHIPS
Vancouver, Canada, March 1-5, 1960

World Men's Figure Skating Championships:

	CF	FS
1. Alain Giletti (FRA)	1	2
2. Donald Jackson (CAN)	**2**	**1**
3. Alain Calmat (FRA)	3	3
4. Norbert Felsinger (AUT)	4	4
5. Tilo Gutzeit (FRG)	5	6
6. Bradley Lord (USA)	6	8
7. Manfred Schnelldorfer (FRG)	7	7

	CF	FS
8. Donald McPherson (CAN)	8	5
9. Gregory Kelley (USA)	9	10
10. Peter Jonas (AUT)	11	9
11. Louis Stong (CAN)	**12**	**11**
12. Nobuo Sato (JPN)	14	13
13. Hubert Köpfler (SUI)	10	16
14. Robin Jones (GRB)	13	14
15. David Clements (GRB)	15	15
16. Tim Spencer (AUS)	16	12
17. William Cherrell (AUS)	17	17
WD. David Jenkins (USA)	-	-
WD. Karol Divín (CZE)	-	-
WD. Tim Brown (USA)	-	-
WD. Robert Brewer (USA)	-	-

World Ladies Figure Skating Championships:

	CF	FS
1. Carol Heiss (USA)	1	1
2. Sjoukje Dijkstra (NED)	2	2
3. Barbara Ann Roles (USA)	3	3
4. Regine Heitzer (AUT)	5	4
5. Joan Haanappel (NED)	4	9
6. Jana Dočekalová-Mrázková (CZE)	9	5
7. Wendy Griner (CAN)	**6**	**8**
8. Karin Frohner (AUT)	8	6
9. Laurence Owen (USA)	7	7
10. Anna Galmarini (ITA)	11	10
11. Dany Rigoulot (FRA)	10	11
12. Nicole Hassler (FRA)	13	12
13. Sonia Snelling (CAN)	**12**	**13**
14. Miwa Fukuhara (JPN)	14	14
15. Shirra Kenworthy (CAN)	**15**	**19**
16. Junko Ueno (JPN)	18	17
17. Bärbel Martin (FRG)	19	15
18. Ursel Barkey (FRG)	20	18
19. Fränzi Schmidt (SUI)	22	16
20. Carolyn Krau (GRB)	16	21
21. Liliane Crosa (SUI)	21	20

22. Carla Tichatschek (ITA)	17	22
23. Beverly Helmore (AUS)	24	23
24. Mary Lynette Wilson (AUS)	23	24
WD. Ina Bauer (FRG)	-	-
WD. Patricia Pauley (GRB)	-	-

World Pairs Figure Skating Championships:

1. Barbara Wagner/Robert Paul (CAN)
2. Maria Jelinek/Otto Jelinek (CAN)
3. Marika Kilius/Hans-Jürgen Bäumler (FRG)
4. Margret Göbl/Franz Ningel (FRG)
5. Nina Zhuk/Stanislav Zhuk (SOV)
6. Nancy Ludington/Ron Ludington (USA)
7. Diana Hinko/Heinz Döpfl (AUT)
8. Ludmila Belousova/Oleg Protopopov (RUS)
9. Rita Blumenberg/Werner Mensching (FRG)
10. Maribel Yerxa Owen Jr./Dudley Richards (USA)
11. Debbi Wilkes/Guy Revell (CAN)
12. Ila Ray Hadley/Ray Hadley Jr. (USA)
WD. Jacqueline Mason/Mervyn Bower (AUS)

World Ice Dancing Championships:

	CD	FD
1. Doreen Denny/Courtney Jones (GRB)	1	1
2. V. Thompson/W. McLachlan (CAN)	**2**	**2**
3. Christiane Guhel/Jean Paul Guhel (FRA)	3	4
4. Margie Ackles/Chuck Phillips Jr. (USA)	4	3
5. Marilyn Meeker/Larry Pierce (USA)	5	5
6. Ann Martin/Gilles Vanasse (CAN)	**6**	**8**
7. Svata Staroba/Mirek Staroba (CAN)	**7**	**9**
8. Yvonne Littlefield/Roger Campbell (USA)	8	6
9. Rita Paucka/Peter Kwiet (FRG)	9	7

The World Figure Skating Championships returned to Canada for the first time since before World War II.

Alain Giletti made history as the first skater from France to win a gold medal in the men's event.

For the first time, the World Championships were broadcast on television in North America.
The event also marked the first time that the number of entries per country per discipline was limited to three by the ISU.

Christiane and Jean Paul Guhel won France's first medal in ice dancing at the World Championships.

Sources: Skating World magazine, April 1960; Skating magazine, May 1960; Programme, 1960 World Figure Skating Championships; Seventy-five years of European and World's championships in figure skating, ISU, 1970

1961
EVENT NOT HELD*

*The entire U.S. figure skating team, along with coaches, judges, officials and family members, tragically perished iwhen Sabena Flight 548 crashed in Belgium, enroute to the 1961 World Figure Skating Championships in Prague, Czechoslovakia. The Czechoslovakian organizers of the event were insistent that the event continued as planned despite the tragedy, but the ISU made the decision to cancel the Championships as "a sign of mourning for our sports comrades".

In Memory:

Bradley Richard Lord - 1939-1961
Maribel Vinson Owen - 1911-1961
Maribel Yerxa Owen Jr. - 1940-1961
Laurence Rochon Owen - 1944-1961
Dudley Shaw Richards - 1932-1961
Diane Carol Sherbloom - 1942-1961
Dallas Larry Pierce - 1936-1961
Gregory Eric Kelley - 1944-1961
Nathalie Kelley - 1932-1961
Stephanie Westerfeld - 1943-1961

Sharon Lee Westerfeld - 1935-1961
Ila Ray Hadley - 1942-1961
Ray Ellis Hadley Jr. - 1943-1961
Alvah Lynn 'Linda' Hadley - 1929-1961
Roger Hunter Campbell - 1942-1961
Ann Brownloe Campbell - 1905-1961
Dona Lee Carrier - 1940-1961
Douglas Alexander Ramsay - 1944-1961
Rhode Lee Michelson - 1943-1961
William Homes Hickox - 1942-1961
Laurie Jean Hickox - 1945-1961
Patricia Barbara (Major) Dineen - 1935-1961
Robert Francis Dineen - 1937-1961
William Robert Kipp - 1932-1961
Daniel Charles Ryan - 1929-1961
Eduard Wilhelm 'Edi' Scholdan - 1910-1961
James Edward Scholdan - 1949-1961
Carl William Swallender - 1908-1961
Harold Hartshorne Sr. - 1891-1961
Louisa Hartshorne - 1903-1961
Edward 'Eddie' LeMaire - 1924-1961
Richard Osborn LeMaire - 1947-1961
Deane Everett McMinn - 1916-1961
Walter Sidney Powell – 1879-1961

May they rest in peace, skating in the sky.

Source: Indelible Tracings: The Story of the 1961 U.S. World Figure Skating Team, Patricia Shelley Bushman, 2010

1962 WORLD FIGURE SKATING CHAMPIONSHIPS
Prague, Czechoslovakia, March 14-17, 1962

World Men's Figure Skating Championships:

	CF	FS
1. Donald Jackson (CAN)	2	1
2. Karol Divín (CZE)	1	4
3. Alain Calmat (FRA)	3	3

4. **Donald McPherson (CAN)**	5	2
5. Manfred Schnelldorfer (FRG)	4	6
6. Monty Hoyt (USA)	6	13
7. Emmerich Danzer (AUT)	8	7
8. Scott Ethan Allen (USA)	10	5
9. Peter Jonas (AUT)	7	12
10. Nobuo Sato (JPN)	9	8
11. Bodo Bockenauer (FRG)	13	9
12. Robin Jones (GRB)	12	11
13. Sepp Schönmetzler (FRG)	15	10
14. Valeri Meshkov (SOV)	11	15
15. Per Kjølberg (NOR)	17	14
16. Károly Újlaky (HUN)	14	18
17. Robert Dureville (FRA)	16	16
18. Alain Trouillet (FRA)	18	17

World Ladies Figure Skating Championships:

	CF	FS
1. Sjoukje Dijkstra (NED)	1	1
2. **Wendy Griner (CAN)**	2	3
3. Regine Heitzer (AUT)	3	8
4. **Petra Burka (CAN)**	4	2
5. Barbara Ann Roles Pursley (USA)	5	4
6. Nicole Hassler (FRA)	7	7
7. Jana Dočekalová-Mrázková (CZE)	9	5
8. Karin Frohner (AUT)	6	14
9. Miwa Fukuhara (JPN)	8	13
10. Lorraine Hanlon (USA)	10	15
11. Jacqueline Harbord (GRB)	12	12
12. Helli Sengstschmid (AUT)	16	6
13. Eva Grožajová (CZE)	11	11
14. Fränzi Schmidt (SUI)	15	10
15. Karin Gude (FRG)	14	16
16. Vicky Fisher (USA)	13	21
17. Ann-Margreth Frei (SWE)	21	9
18. Sandra Brugnera (ITA)	17	18
19. Helga Zöllner (HUN)	18	19
20. Tatiana Nemtsova (SOV)	20	17

21. Gaby Seyfert (GDR)   19   20

World Pairs Skating Championships:

1. **Maria Jelinek/Otto Jelinek (CAN)**
2. Ludmila Protopopov/Oleg Protopopov (RUS)
3. Margret Göbl/Franz Ningel (FRG)
4. **Debbi Wilkes/Guy Revell (CAN)**
5. Milada Kubíková/Jaroslav Votruba (CZE)
6. **Gertrude Desjardins/Maurice Lafrance (CAN)**
7. Gerda Johner/Rüdi Johner (SUI)
8. Dorothyann Nelson/Pieter Kollen (USA)
9. Irene Müller/Hans-Georg Dallmer (GDR)
10. Judianne Fotheringill/Jerry Fotheringill (USA)
11. Valerie Hunt/Peter Burrows (GRB)
12. Diana Hinko/Bernhard Henhappel (AUT)
13. Mieko Ōiwa/Yutaka Dōke (JPN)
WD. Marika Kilius/Hans-Jürgen Bäumler (FRG)

World Ice Dancing Championships:

	CD	FD
1. Eva Romanová/Pavel Roman (CZE)	2	1
2. Christiane Guhel/Jean Paul Guhel (FRA)	1	3
3. V. Thompson/W. McLachlan (CAN)	**3**	**2**
4. Linda Shearman/Michael Phillips (GRB)	5	5
5. Paulette Doan/Kenneth Ormsby (CAN)	**4**	**4**
6. Donna Mitchell/John Mitchell (CAN)	**6**	**7**
7. Dorothyann Nelson/Pieter Kollen (USA)	7	6
8. Yvonne Littlefield/Peter Betts (USA)	8	8
9. Mary Parry/Roy Mason (GRB)	9	10
10. Györgyi Korda/Pál Vásárhelyi (HUN)	12	9
11. Helga Burkhardt/Hannes Burkhardt (FRG)	11	13
12. Olga Gilardi/Germano Ceccattini (ITA)	15	11
13. Marlyse Fornachon/Charly Pichard (SUI)	10	12
14. Armelle Flichy/Pierre Brun (FRA)	13	15
15. Christel Trebesiner/Georg Felsinger (AUT)	16	16
16. Gabriele Rauch/Rudi Matysik (FRG)	14	17
17. Keiko Kaneko/Mikio Takeuchi (JPN)	17	14

Donald Jackson made history as the first Canadian skater to win a gold medal in the men's event at the World Championships. Jackson also landed the first triple Lutz ever performed at an ISU Championship.

Eva Romanová and Pavel Roman made history as the first Czechoslovakian team to win gold medals in the ice dance event.

Skaters from East Germany (the German Democratic Republic) competed in the World Championships for the first time.

Sources: Skating magazine, May 1962; Seventy-five years of European and World's championships in figure skating, ISU, 1970

1963 WORLD FIGURE SKATING CHAMPIONSHIPS
Cortina d'Ampezzo, Italy, February 28-March 3, 1963

World Men's Figure Skating Championships:

	CF	FS
1. Donald McPherson (CAN)	4	1
2. Alain Calmat (FRA)	3	2
3. Manfred Schnelldorfer (FRG)	1	5
4. Karol Divín (CZE)	2	7
5. Scott Ethan Allen (USA)	5	3
6. Peter Jonas (AUT)	6	8
7. Sepp Schönmetzler (FRG)	9	4
8. Donald Knight (CAN)	8	10
9. Emmerich Danzer (AUT)	11	6
10. Nobuo Sato (JPN)	10	9
11. Monty Hoyt (USA)	7	14
12. Robert Dureville (FRA)	14	13
13. Hugo Dümmler (FRG)	13	12
14. Jenő Ébert (HUN)	17	11
15. William Neale (CAN)	16	15
16. Valeri Meshkov (SOV)	15	16
17. Giordano Abbondati (ITA)	12	17
18. Malcolm Cannon (GRB)	18	19
19. Wouter Touledo (NED)	19	18

World Ladies Figure Skating Championships:

	CF	FS
1. Sjoukje Dijkstra (NED)	1	1
2. Regine Heitzer (AUT)	2	5
3. Nicole Hassler (FRA)	3	2
4. Wendy Griner (CAN)	**4**	**7**
5. Petra Burka (CAN)	**6**	**3**
6. Miwa Fukuhara (JPN)	9	8
7. Inge Paul (FRG)	12	4
8. Jana Dočekalová-Mrázková (CZE)	10	6
9. Helli Sengstschmid (AUT)	8	9
10. Lorraine Hanlon (USA)	7	13
11. Diana Clifton-Peach (GRB)	5	17
12. Ingrid Ostler (AUT)	14	12
13. Karen Howland (USA)	11	16
14. Fränzi Schmidt (SUI)	18	11
15. Eva Grožajová (CZE)	13	15
16. Ann-Margreth Frei (SWE)	20	10
17. Junko Ueno (JPN)	16	19
18. Sandra Brugnera (ITA)	19	14
19. Christine Haigler (USA)	15	23
20. Shirra Kenworthy (CAN)	**17**	**21**
21. Zsuzsa Szentmiklóssy (HUN)	22	20
22. Karin Dehle (NOR)	21	24
23. Tatiana Nemtsova (SOV)	23	18
24. Elżbieta Kościk (POL)	24	22

World Pairs Skating Championships:

1. Marika Kilius/Hans-Jürgen Bäumler (FRG)
2. Ludmila Belousova/Oleg Protopopov (SOV)
3. Tatiana Zhuk/Aleksandr Gavrilov (SOV)
4. Gertrude Desjardins/Maurice Lefrance (CAN)
5. Milada Kubíková/Jaroslav Votruba (CZE)
6. Gerda Johner/Rüdi Johner (SUI)
7. Judianne Fotheringill/Jerry Fotheringill (USA)
8. Vivian Joseph/Ronald Joseph (USA)

9. Patti Gustafson/Pieter Kollen (USA)
10. Sonja Pfersdorf/Günther Matzdorf (FRG)
11. Linda Ward/Neil Carpenter (CAN)
12. Gunilla Lindberg/Gunnar de Shàrengrad (SWE)
WD. Debbi Wilkes/Guy Revell (CAN)

World Ice Dancing Championships:

	CD	FD
1. Eva Romanová/Pavel Roman (CZE)	2	1
2. Linda Shearman/Michael Phillips (GRB)	1	2
3. Paulette Doan/Kenneth Ormsby (CAN)	**3**	**3**
4. Janet Sawbridge/David Hickinbottom (GRB)	4	4
5. Donna Mitchell/John Mitchell (CAN)	**5**	**5**
6. Mary Parry/Roy Mason (GRB)	6	8
7. Sally Schantz/Stanley Urban (USA)	7	6
8. Lorna Dyer/John Carrell (USA)	8	7
9. Györgyi Korda/Pál Vásárhelyi (HUN)	11	9
10. Carole Forrest/Kevin Lethbridge (CAN)	**10**	**10**
11. Marlyse Fornachon/Charly Pichard (SUI)	12	11
12. Armelle Flichy/Pierre Brun (FRA)	13	14
13. Helga Burkhardt/Hannes Burkhardt (FRG)	15	15
14. Jitka Babická/Jaromír Holan (CZE)	14	13
15. Christel Trebesiner/Georg Felsinger (AUT)	17	12
16. Ghislaine Houdas/Francis Gamichon (FRA)	16	17
17. Yvonne Littlefield/Peter Betts (USA)	9	18
18. M-G. Toncelli/V. Toncelli (ITA)	18	16

The Italian organizers of the World Figure Skating Championships faced considerable criticism for their organization of the event. Free skating events started as late at 9:30 PM, with some skaters performing after midnight. Temperatures were freezing cold after dusk and the ice in the open-air rink was hard and brittle, resulting in many falls.

Sources: Skating magazine, May 1963; Seventy-five years of European and World's championships in figure skating, ISU, 1970

1964 WORLD FIGURE SKATING CHAMPIONSHIPS
Dortmund, West Germany, February 25-March 1, 1964

World Men's Figure Skating Championships:

	CF	FS
1. Manfred Schnelldorfer (FRG)	1	2
2. Alain Calmat (FRA)	3	4
3. Karol Divín (CZE)	2	9
4. Scott Ethan Allen (USA)	4	5
5. Emmerich Danzer (AUT)	5	3
6. Tommy Litz (USA)	8	1
7. Peter Jonas (AUT)	6	8
8. Nobuo Sato (JPN)	7	10
9. Donald Knight (CAN)	**10**	**7**
10. Sepp Schönmetzler (FRG)	11	6
11. Monty Hoyt (USA)	9	12
12. Charles Snelling (CAN)	**13**	**11**
13. Robert Dureville (FRA)	12	15
14. Patrick Péra (FRA)	14	16
15. Valeri Meshkov (SOV)	18	13
16. Hugo Dümmler (FRG)	17	17
17. Ondrej Nepela (CZE)	20	14
18. Hywel Evans (GRB)	16	18
19. Wouter Toledo (NED)	19	19
WD. Giordano Abbondati (ITA)	15	-
WD. Günter Zöller (GDR)	-	-

World Ladies Figure Skating Championships:

	CF	FS
1. Sjoukje Dijkstra (NED)	1	1
2. Regine Heitzer (AUT)	2	8
3. Petra Burka (CAN)	**3**	**2**
4. Nicole Hassler (FRA)	6	4
5. Christine Haigler (USA)	4	17
6. Miwa Fukuhara (JPN)	7	5
7. Peggy Fleming (USA)	5	10
8. Sally-Anne Stapleford (GRB)	8	13
9. Tina Noyes (USA)	10	6

10. Shirra Kenworthy (CAN)	9	12
11. Wendy Griner (CAN)	**11**	**11**
12. Helli Sengstschmid (AUT)	16	3
13. Kumiko Okawa (JPN)	15	7
14. Inge Paul (FRG)	13	15
15. Uschi Keszler (FRG)	14	9
16. Hana Mašková (CZE)	17	14
17. Astrid Czermak (AUT)	12	20
18. Zsuzsa Almássy (HUN)	18	16
19. Sandra Brugnera (ITA)	19	19
20. Ann-Margreth Frei (SWE)	21	18
21. Christine van de Putte (BEL)	20	21
WD. Gaby Seyfert (GDR)	-	-

World Pairs Skating Championships:

	CCP	FS
1. Marika Kilius/Hans-Jürgen Bäumler (FRG)	2	1
2. Ludmila Belousova/Oleg Protopopov (SOV)	1	2
3. Debbi Wilkes/Guy Revell (CAN)	**3**	**3**
4. Vivian Joseph/Ronald Joseph (USA)	4	4
5. Sonja Pfersdorf/Günther Matzdorf (FRG)	5	5
6. Tatiana Zhuk/Aleksandr Gavrilov (SOV)	7	6
7. Cynthia Kauffman/Ronald Kauffman (USA)	6	9
8. J. Fotheringill/J. Fotheringill (USA)	8	7
9. Sigrid Riechmann/Wolfgang Danne (FRG)	11	8
10. Agnesa Wlachovská/Peter Bartosiewicz (CZE)	9	10
11. Gerlinde Schönbauer/Wilhelm Bietak (AUT)	13	11
12. Mária Csordás/László Kondi (HUN)	10	12
13. Tatiana Sharanova/Alexandr Gorelik (SOV)	12	13
WD. Brigitte Wokoeck/Heinz-Ulrich Walther (GDR)	-	-
WD. Margit Senf/Peter Göbel (GDR)	-	-

World Ice Dancing Championships:

	CD	FD
1. Eva Romanová/Pavel Roman (CZE)	1	1
2. Paulette Doan/Kenneth Ormsby (CAN)	**3**	**2**
3. Janet Sawbridge/David Hickinbottom (GRB)	2	3
4. Yvonne Suddick/Roger Kennerson (GRB)	4	5

5. Lorna Dyer/John Carrell (USA)	5	6
6. Carole MacSween/Robert Munz (USA)	6	4
7. Carole Forrest/Kevin Lethbridge (CAN)	**7**	**7**
8. Darlene Streich/Charles Fetter (USA)	8	8
9. Györgyi Korda/Pál Vásárhelyi (HUN)	10	9
10. Jitka Babická/Jaromír Holan (CZE)	11	11
11. Marilyn Crawford/Blair Armitage (CAN)	**9**	**12**
12. Christel Trebesiner/Georg Felsinger (AUT)	14	10
13. Diane Towler/Bernard Ford (GRB)	13	14
14. Gabriele Rauch/Rudi Matysik (FRG)	12	15
15. Brigitte Martin/Francis Gamichon (FRA)	15	13
16. Jopie Wolff/Nico Wolff (NED)	16	16

For the first time, a computer was used to calculate the results at the World Figure Skating Championships. The software was developed by an IBM systems engineer from Stuttgart named Ulrich Barth.

The East German team withdrew from the World Figure Skating Championships in protest, after the event's West German organizers stated that East German skaters would be announced as representatives of the Deutscher Eislauf-Verband (Communist German's Skating Association) instead of "Deutschland Ost" (East Germany). West Germany's Manfred Schnelldorfer became the first skater from East, West or unified Germany to win a gold medal in the men's event since the Edwardian era.

Tommy Litz made history as the first skater to land a triple toe-loop at the World Championships.

For the first time, the pairs event featured two segments. In addition to the free skating program, teams performed a 2.5-minute compulsory connecting program.

Courtney Jones, Peri Horne and Joan (Dewhirst) and John Slater gave demonstrations of three new compulsory dances.

Sources: L'impartial, February 27, 1964; Journal du Jura, February 28, 1964; Skating magazine, May 1964; Seventy-five years of European and

World's championships in figure skating, ISU, 1970; Skating In America: The 75th Anniversary History of The United States Figure Skating Association, Benjamin T. Wright, 1996; A Spectator's Guide to Figure Skating, Debbi Wilkes, 1997

1965 WORLD FIGURE SKATING CHAMPIONSHIPS
Colorado Springs, United States, March 2-7, 1965

World Men's Figure Skating Championships:

	CF	FS
1. Alain Calmat (FRA)	1	1
2. Scott Ethan Allen (USA)	4	2
3. Donald Knight (CAN)	**2**	**4**
4. Nobuo Sato (JPN)	5	3
5. Emmerich Danzer (AUT)	3	5
6. Gary Visconti (USA)	6	6
7. Wolfgang Schwarz (AUT)	7	10
8. Peter Jonas (AUT)	10	8
9. Peter Krick (FRG)	8	11
10. Robert Dureville (FRA)	9	13
11. Sepp Schönmetzler (FRG)	11	9
12. Jay Humphry (CAN)	**15**	**7**
13. Tim Wood (USA)	13	12
14. Giordano Abbondati (ITA)	12	14
15. Patrick Péra (FRA)	14	16
16. Ondrej Nepela (CZE)	19	15
17. Sergei Chetverukhin (SOV)	17	17
18. Günter Zöller (GDR)	18	18
19. Jenő Ébert (HUN)	20	19
20. Hywel Evans (GRB)	16	20

World Ladies Figure Skating Championships:

	CF	FS
1. Petra Burka (CAN)	**1**	**1**
2. Regine Heitzer (AUT)	3	4
3. Peggy Fleming (USA)	4	2
4. Christine Haigler (USA)	2	6
5. Gaby Seyfert (GDR)	8	3

6. Miwa Fukuhara (JPN)	5	10
7. Valerie Jones (CAN)	**6**	**5**
8. Nicole Hassler (FRA)	7	9
9. Helli Sengstschmid (AUT)	10	7
10. Tina Noyes (USA)	13	8
11. Diana Clifton-Peach (GRB)	9	14
12. Kumiko Okawa (JPN)	11	13
13. Hana Mašková (CZE)	15	11
14. Gloria Tatton (CAN)	**12**	**15**
15. Sandra Brugnera (ITA)	16	12
16. Angelika Wagner (FRG)	14	18
17. Elena Slepova (SOV)	17	16
18. Zsuzsa Szentmiklóssy (HUN)	18	17
WD. Zsuzsa Almássy (HUN)	-	-
WD. Sally-Anne Stapleford (GRB)	-	-

World Pairs Skating Championships:

	CCP	FS
1. Ludmila Belousova/Oleg Protopopov (SOV)	1	1
2. Vivian Joseph/Ronald Joseph (USA)	3	2
3. Tatiana Zhuk/Aleksandr Gorelik (SOV)	4	3
4. Gerda Johner/Rüdi Johner (SUI)	2	6
5. Sonja Pfersdorf/Günther Matzdorf (FRG)	5	5
6. Cynthia Kauffman/Ronald Kauffman (USA)	6	4
7. Tatiana Tarasova/Georgi Proskurin (SOV)	7	7
8. Irene Müller/Hans-Georg Dallmer (GDR)	8	9
9. Joanne Heckert/Gary Clark (USA)	9	8
10. Gerlinde Schönbauer/Willy Bietak (AUT)	11	10
11. Margot Glockshuber/Wolfgang Danne (FRG)	13	11
12. Alexis Shields/Chris Shields (CAN)	**12**	**12**
13. Ingrid Bodendorff/Volker Waldeck (FRG)	14	13
14. S. Huehnergard/P. Huehnergard (CAN)	**10**	**14**

World Ice Dancing Championships:

	CD	FD
1. Eva Romanová/Pavel Roman (CZE)	1	1
2. Janet Sawbridge/David Hickinbottom (GRB)	2	3
3. Lorna Dyer/John Carrell (USA)	3	4

4. Diane Towler/Bernard Ford (GRB)	5	2
5. Kristin Fortune/Dennis Sveum (USA)	4	5
6. Yvonne Suddick/Roger Kennerson (GRB)	6	6
7. Susan Urban/Stanley Urban (USA)	7	7
8. Carole Forrest/Kevin Lethbridge (CAN)	**8**	**9**
9. Brigitte Martin/Francis Gamichon (FRA)	9	10
10. Györgyi Korda/Pál Vásárhelyi (HUN)	11	8
11. Lynn Matthews/Bryon Topping (CAN)	**10**	**13**
12. Christel Trebesiner/Georg Felsinger (AUT)	12	11
13. Gabriele Rauch/Rudi Matysik (FRG)	13	12
14. Annerose Baier/Eberhard Rüger (GDR)	14	14

Ludmila Belousova and Oleg Protopopov made history as the first team from the Soviet Union to win gold medals in the pairs event at the World Figure Skating Championships.

Sources: The Rocky Mountain News, March 2, 1965; Skating magazine, May 1965; Seventy-five years of European and World's championships in figure skating, ISU, 1970

1966 WORLD FIGURE SKATING CHAMPIONSHIPS
Davos, Switzerland, February 22-27, 1966

World Men's Figure Skating Championships:

	CF	FS
1. Emmerich Danzer (AUT)	1	1
2. Wolfgang Schwarz (AUT)	2	5
3. Gary Visconti (USA)	4	2
4. Scott Ethan Allen (USA)	3	3
5. Nobuo Sato (JPN)	5	4
6. Patrick Péra (FRA)	6	6
7. Donald Knight (CAN)	**7**	**8**
8. Ondrej Nepela (CZE)	8	12
9. Giordano Abbondati (ITA)	10	9
10. Jay Humphry (CAN)	**11**	**10**
11. Charles Snelling (CAN)	**13**	**11**
12. Billy Chapel (USA)	14	7
13. Robert Dureville (FRA)	9	15

14. Ralph Borghard (GDR)	12	14
15. Jenő Ébert (HUN)	17	13
16. Günter Anderl (AUT)	18	16
17. Valeri Meshkov (SOV)	15	18
18. Malcolm Cannon (GRB)	16	20
19. Tsuguhiko Kozuka (JPN)	20	17
20. Bodo Bockenauer (FRG)	19	19
21. Hans-Jürg Studer (SUI)	21	21
WD. Peter Krick (FRG)	-	-
WD. Jan Ullmark (SWE)	-	-

World Ladies Figure Skating Championships:

	CF	FS
1. Peggy Fleming (USA)	1	2
2. Gaby Seyfert (GDR)	3	1
3. Petra Burka (CAN)	**2**	**3**
4. Valerie Jones (CAN)	**4**	**8**
5. Nicole Hassler (FRA)	5	6
6. Hana Mašková (CZE)	10	5
7. Zsuzsa Almássy (HUN)	7	9
8. Miwa Fukuhara (JPN)	6	7
9. Tina Noyes (USA)	13	4
10. Kumiko Okawa (JPN)	9	10
11. Uschi Keszler (FRG)	12	11
12. Pamela Schneider (USA)	8	12
13. Sally-Anne Stapleford (GRB)	11	18
14. Elisabeth Mikula (AUT)	14	15
15. Roberta Laurent (CAN)	**15**	**14**
16. Elisabeth Nestler (AUT)	16	13
17. Elena Shcheglova (SOV)	17	16
18. Pia Zürcher (SUI)	18	17
19. Beate Richter (GDR)	19	19
20. Martina Clausner (GDR)	20	20
WD. Britt Elfving (SWE)	-	-

World Pairs Skating Championships:

	CCP	FS
1. Ludmila Belousova/Oleg Protopopov (SOV)	1	2

2. Tatiana Zhuk/Aleksandr Gorelik (SOV)	2	1
3. Cynthia Kauffman/Ronald Kauffman (USA)	5	3
4. Margot Glockshuber/Wolfgang Danne (FRG)	3	4
5. Sonja Pfersdorf/Günther Matzdorf (FRG)	6	5
6. Gudrun Hauss/Walter Häfner (FRG)	7	6
7. Irene Müller/Hans-Georg Dallmer (GDR)	4	7
8. Monique Mathys/Yves Ällig (SUI)	9	8
9. H. Steiner/H-U. Walther (GDR)	10	9
10. Agnesa Wlachovská/Peter Bartosiewicz (CZE)	8	11
11. Susie Behrens/Roy Wagelein (USA)	11	10
12. Mónika Szabó/Péter Szabó (SUI)	12	12
13. S. Huehnergard/P. Huehnergard (CAN)	**15**	**13**
14. Gerlinde Schönbauer/Willy Bietak (AUT)	13	14
15. Mária Csordás/László Kondi (HUN)	14	15

World Ice Dancing Championships:

	CD	FD
1. Diane Towler/Bernard Ford (GRB)	1	1
2. Kristin Fortune/Dennis Sveum (USA)	2	3
3. Lorna Dyer/John Carrell (USA)	3	2
4. Yvonne Suddick/Roger Kennerson (GRB)	4	4
5. Brigitte Martin/Francis Gamichon (FRA)	6	5
6. Janet Sawbridge/Jon Lane (GRB)	5	8
7. Gabriele Rauch/Rudi Matysik (FRG)	8	7
8. Jitka Babická/Jaromír Holan (CZE)	7	9
9. Carole Forrest/Kevin Lethbridge (CAN)	**9**	**10**
10. Lyudmila Pakhomova/Viktor Ryzhkin (SOV)	11	6
11. Susan Urban/Stanley Urban (USA)	10	14
12. Gail Snyder/Wayne Palmer (CAN)	**14**	**12**
13. Annerose Baier/Eberhard Rüger (GDR)	13	13
14. Susanna Carpani/Sergio Pirelli (ITA)	15	11
15. Edit Mató/Károly Csanádi (HUN)	12	16
16. C. Trebesiner/H. Rothkappel (AUT)	16	15

The second-to-last World Figure Skating Championships held outdoors was plagued by extremely poor ice conditions, fluctuating temperatures, rain, snow and high winds. Though the weather outside was frightful, Pierre Brunet, a former World Champion and long-time coach, asserted the conditions hardly compared to those at the 1948 Winter Olympic Games in St. Moritz, Switzerland.

Sources: The Spokesman Review, February 22, 1966; Skating World magazine, April 1966; Winter Sports magazine, May 1966; Skating magazine, May 1966; Seventy-five years of European and World's championships in figure skating, ISU, 1970

1967 WORLD FIGURE SKATING CHAMPIONSHIPS
Vienna, Austria, February 28-March 4, 1967

World Men's Figure Skating Championships:

	CF	FS
1. Emmerich Danzer (AUT)	2	1
2. Wolfgang Schwarz (AUT)	1	2
3. Gary Visconti (USA)	5	3
4. Donald Knight (CAN)	**3**	**8**
5. Scott Ethan Allen (USA)	4	4
6. Ondrej Nepela (CZE)	7	6
7. Patrick Péra (FRA)	6	7
8. Peter Krick (FRG)	8	10
9. Tim Wood (USA)	10	5
10. Robert Dureville (FRA)	9	11
11. Günter Zöller (GDR)	11	13
12. Jay Humphry (CAN)	**13**	**9**
13. Sergei Chetverukhin (SOV)	12	16
14. Marian Filc (CZE)	14	12
15. Günter Anderl (AUT)	15	17
16. Michael Williams (GRB)	16	14
17. Tsuguhiko Kozuka (JPN)	17	15
18. Masato Tamura (JPN)	18	20
19. Tony Berntler (SUI)	19	18
20. Daniel Höner (SUI)	20	19

World Ladies Figure Skating Championships:

	CF	FS
1. Peggy Fleming (USA)	1	1
2. Gaby Seyfert (GDR)	3	3

3. Hana Mašková (CZE)	5	2
4. Valerie Jones (CAN)	**2**	**6**
5. Kumiko Okawa (JPN)	6	4
6. Sally-Anne Stapleford (GRB)	4	13
7. Tina Noyes (USA)	8	5
8. Jennie Welsh (USA)	12	8
9. Trixi Schuba (AUT)	10	9
10. Roberta Laurent (CAN)	**9**	**10**
11. Monika Feldmann (FRG)	11	12
12. Karen Magnussen (CAN)	**14**	**7**
13. Rita Trapanese (ITA)	17	15
14. Martina Clausner (GDR)	15	17
15. Elena Shcheglova (SOV)	21	11
16. Marie Víchová (CZE)	20	14
17. Micheline Joubert (FRA)	19	16
18. Sylvaine Duban (FRA)	13	20
19. Beate Richter (GDR)	18	18
20. Charlotte Walter (SUI)	16	19
21. Zsuzsa Szentmiklóssy (HUN)	22	21
22. Katjuša Derenda (YUG)	23	22
WD. Miwa Fukuhara (JPN)	7	-
WD. Myung-su Chang (KOR)	-	-

World Pairs Skating Championships:

	CCP	FS
1. Ludmila Belousova/Oleg Protopopov (SOV)	1	1
2. Margot Glockshuber/Wolfgang Danne (FRG)	2	2
3. Cynthia Kauffman/Ronald Kauffman (USA)	3	3
4. Gudrun Hauss/Walter Häfner (FRG)	4	4
5. H. Steiner/H-U. Walther (GDR)	5	5
6. Tamara Moskvina/Alexei Mishin (SOV)	6	7
7. Susie Behrens/Roy Wagelein (USA)	8	6
8. Tatiana Sharanova/Anatoli Yevdokimov (SOV)	7	8
9. Brigitte Weise/Michael Brychcy (GDR)	9	10
10. Bohunka Šrámková/Jan Šrámek (CZE)	10	9
11. Marianne Streifler/Herbert Wiesinger (FRG)	12	13
12. Evelyne Schneider/Willy Bietak (AUT)	13	11
13. Betty Lewis/Richard Gilbert (USA)	17	12

14. Janina Poremska/Piotr Szczypa (POL)	14	14
15. Monique Mathys/Yves Ällig (SUI)	11	15
16. Mónika Szabó/Péter Szabó (SUI)	16	16
17. Anci Dolenc/Mitja Sketa (YUG)	18	18
18. Betty McKilligan/John McKilligan (CAN)	**15**	**19**
19. Dana Fialová/Milos Man (CZE)	19	17

World Ice Dancing Championships:

	CD	FD
1. Diane Towler/Bernard Ford (GRB)	1	1
2. Lorna Dyer/John Carrell (USA)	2	2
3. Yvonne Suddick/Malcolm Cannon (GRB)	3	3
4. Janet Sawbridge/Jon Lane (GRB)	4	4
5. Brigitte Martin/Francis Gamichon (FRA)	5	6
6. Joni Graham/Don Phillips (CAN)	**6**	**7**
7. Irina Grishkova/Viktor Ryzhkin (SOV)	8	5
8. Judy Schwomeyer/James Sladky (USA)	7	8
9. Alma Davenport/Roger Berry (USA)	9	9
10. Angelika Buck/Erich Buck (FRG)	10	10
11. Jitka Babická/Jaromír Holan (CZE)	12	12
12. Annerose Baier/Eberhard Rüger (GDR)	11	13
13. L. Pakhomova/A.Gorshkov (SOV)	14	11
14. Edit Mató/Károly Csanádi (HUN)	13	16
15. Heide Mezger/Herbert Rothkappel (AUT)	16	15
16. Judy Henderson/John Bailey (CAN)	**15**	**17**
17. Dana Novotná/Jaroslav Hainz (CZE)	18	14
18. Susanna Carpani/Sergio Pirelli (ITA)	17	18

For the final time, the free skating events at the World Figure Skating Championships were held in an open-air rink. The men's and ladies compulsory figures were held in a covered rink. Skaters contended with torrential rain, high winds and poor ice conditions.

The event marked the centennial anniversary of the Wiener Eislaufverein and the 75th anniversary of the ISU.

Sources: Winter Sports magazine, May 1967; Skating magazine, May 1967; Seventy-five years of European and World's championships in figure skating,

International Skating Union, 1970

1968 WORLD FIGURE SKATING CHAMPIONSHIPS
Geneva, Switzerland, February 27-March 3, 1968

World Men's Figure Skating Championships:

	CF	FS
1. Emmerich Danzer (AUT)	2	1
2. Tim Wood (USA)	1	2
3. Patrick Péra (FRA)	3	7
4. Scott Ethan Allen (USA)	4	5
5. Gary Visconti (USA)	5	3
6. Ondrej Nepela (CZE)	6	6
7. Jay Humphry (CAN)	**8**	**4**
8. Peter Krick (FRG)	7	12
9. Sergei Chetverukhin (SOV)	10	8
10. David McGillivray (CAN)	**12**	**11**
11. Günter Zöller (GDR)	9	9
12. Philippe Pélissier (FRA)	11	13
13. Michael Williams (GRB)	14	10
14. Tsuguhiko Kozuka (JPN)	13	14
15. Marián Filc (CZE)	16	15
16. Giordano Abbondati (ITA)	15	17
17. Reinhard Ketterer (FRG)	18	16
18. Günter Anderl (AUT)	17	18
19. Jenő Ébert (HUN)	20	19
20. Daniel Höner (SUI)	19	20

World Ladies Figure Skating Championships:

	CF	FS
1. Peggy Fleming (USA)	1	1
2. Gaby Seyfert (GDR)	2	2
3. Hana Mašková (CZE)	4	3
4. Trixi Schuba (AUT)	3	10
5. Kumiko Okawa (JPN)	5	5
6. Tina Noyes (USA)	6	6
7. Karen Magnussen (CAN)	**9**	**4**
8. Zsuzsa Almássy (HUN)	10	8

9. Janet Lynn (USA)	12	7
10. Elena Shcheglova (SOV)	11	11
11. Monika Feldmann (GDR)	8	12
12. Patricia Dodd (GRB)	7	15
13. Linda Carbonetto (CAN)	**18**	**9**
14. Marie Víchová (CZE)	19	13
15. Elisabeth Nestler (AUT)	14	16
16. Charlotte Walter (SUI)	17	14
17. Martina Clausner (GDR)	13	20
18. Kazumi Yamashita (JPN)	15	17
19. Haruko Ishida (JPN)	16	18
20. Sonja Morgenstern (GDR)	21	19
21. Mary-Ellen Holland (AUS)	20	21
22. Margaret Betts (SAF)	22	22

World Pairs Skating Championships:

	CCP	FS
1. Ludmila Belousova/Oleg Protopopov (SOV)	1	1
2. Tatiana Zhuk/Aleksandr Gorelik (SOV)	2	2
3. Cynthia Kauffman/Ronald Kauffman (USA)	5	3
4. Tamara Moskvina/Alexei Mishin (SOV)	4	4
5. H. Steiner/H-U. Walther (GDR)	3	5
6. Gudrun Hauss/Walter Häfner (FRG)	6	7
7. Bohunka Šrámková/Jan Šrámek (CZE)	9	6
8. Sandi Sweitzer/Roy Wagelein (USA)	8	8
9. Irene Müller/Hans-Georg Dallmer (GDR)	7	10
10. Liana Drahová/Peter Bartosiewicz (CZE)	17	9
11. JoJo Starbuck/Ken Shelley (USA)	13	11
12. Marianne Streifler/Herbert Wiesinger (FRG)	11	12
13. Betty McKilligan/John McKilligan (CAN)	**15**	**13**
14. Brigitte Weise/Michael Brychcy (GDR)	16	14
15. Mónika Szabó/Péter Szabó (SUI)	14	15
16. Janina Poremska/Piotr Szczypa (POL)	12	16
17. Glenda O'Shea/Brian O'Shea (SAF)	18	17
WD. Margot Glockshuber/Wolfgang Danne (FRG)	10	-

World Ice Dancing Championships:

	CD	FD
1. Diane Towler/Bernard Ford (GRB)	1	1
2. Yvonne Suddick/Malcolm Cannon (GRB)	2	3
3. Janet Sawbridge/Jon Lane (GRB)	3	2
4. Judy Schwomeyer/James Sladky (USA)	4	6
5. Irina Grishkova/Viktor Ryzhkin (SOV)	5	5
6. L. Pakhomova/A. Gorshkov (SOV)	6	4
7. Vicki Camper/Eugene Heffron (USA)	7	8
8. Angelika Buck/Erich Buck (FRG)	9	7
9. Joni Graham/Don Phillips (CAN)	**8**	**10**
10. Annerose Baier/Eberhard Rüger (GDR)	10	9
11. Edit Mató/Károly Csanádi (HUN)	11	12
12. Milena Tůmová/Josef Pešek (CZE)	13	11
13. Donna Taylor/Bruce Lennie (CAN)	**12**	**13**
14. Susanna Carpani/Sergio Pirelli (ITA)	14	14
15. Claude Couste/Jean-Pierre Noullet (FRA)	15	15

Sources: Skating magazine, May 1968; 100th Anniversary 1892-1992 - International Skating Union: Results 1968-1991 Figure Skating Championships, Elemér Terták, Benjamin T. Wright, Beat Häsler, 1992, courtesy World Figure Skating Museum & Hall of Fame

1969 WORLD FIGURE SKATING CHAMPIONSHIPS
Colorado Springs, United States, February 25-March 2, 1969

World Men's Figure Skating Championships:

	CF	FS
1. Tim Wood (USA)	1	1
2. Ondrej Nepela (CZE)	2	6
3. Patrick Péra (FRA)	3	5
4. Gary Visconti (USA)	4	4
5. John Misha Petkevich (USA)	7	2
6. Jay Humphry (CAN)	**5**	**3**
7. Günter Zöller (GDR)	6	10
8. Sergei Chetverukhin (SOV)	8	9
9. Marián Filc (CZE)	9	7
10. David McGillvray (CAN)	**13**	**8**

11. Yuri Ovchinnikov (SOV)	12	11
12. Philippe Pélissier (FRA)	11	13
13. Tsuguhiko Kozuka (JPN)	14	14
14. Jacques Mrozek (FRA)	16	12
15. Günter Anderl (AUT)	15	16
16. Reinhard Ketterer (FRG)	17	15
17. Klaus Grimmelt (FRG)	18	17
WD. Haig Oundjian (GRB)	10	-

World Ladies Figure Skating Championships:

	CF	FS
1. Gaby Seyfert (GDR)	2	1
2. Trixi Schuba (AUT)	1	6
3. Zsuzsa Almássy (HUN)	3	4
4. Julie Lynn Holmes (USA)	4	2
5. Janet Lynn (USA)	5	5
6. Linda Carbonetto (CAN)	**9**	**3**
7. Elisabeth Nestler (AUT)	6	7
8. Patricia Dodd (GRB)	7	14
9. Eileen Zillmer (FRG)	8	12
10. Elena Shcheglova (SOV)	12	8
11. Kazumi Yamashita (JPN)	13	10
12. Elisabeth Mikula (AUT)	10	11
13. Rita Trapanese (ITA)	11	13
14. Galina Grzhibovskaya (SOV)	16	9
15. Charlotte Walter (SUI)	14	15
16. Keiko Miyagawa (JPN)	17	16
17. Janet Schwarz (AUS)	18	17
WD. Sonja Morgenstern (GDR)	15	-
WD. Karen Magnussen (CAN)	**-**	**-**
WD. Hana Mašková (CZE)	-	-
WD. Vanessa Jackson (SAF)	-	-

World Pairs Skating Championships:

	SP	FS
1. Irina Rodnina/Alexei Ulanov (SOV)	1	1
2. Tamara Moskvina/Alexei Mishin (SOV)	3	2
3. Ludmila Belousova/Oleg Protopopov (SOV)	2	3

4. Cynthia Kauffman/Ronald Kauffman (USA)	4	5
5. H. Steiner/H-U. Walther (GDR)	5	6
6. JoJo Starbuck/Ken Shelley (USA)	7	4
7. Gudrun Hauss/Walter Häfner (FRG)	6	7
8. Melissa Militano/Mark Militano (USA)	10	8
9. Brunhilde Baßler/Eberhard Rausch (FRG)	8	9
10. Anna Forder/Richard Stephens (CAN)	**9**	**10**
11. Monique Szabo/Pierre Szabo (FRA)	11	11
12. Linda Bernard/Raymond Wilson (GRB)	13	12
13. Evelyne Schneider/Willy Bietak (AUT)	14	13
WD. Liana Drahová/Peter Bartosiewicz (CZE)	12	-
WD. Glenda O'Shea/Brian O'Shea (SAF)	-	-

World Ice Dancing Championships:

	C/OSP	FD
1. Diane Towler/Bernard Ford (GRB)	1	1
2. L. Pakhomova/A. Gorshkov (SOV)	2	2
3. Judy Schwomeyer/James Sladky (USA)	3	3
4. Janet Sawbridge/Jon Lane (GRB)	4	4
5. Angelika Buck/Erich Buck (FRG)	5	5
6. Annerose Baier/Eberhard Rüger (GDR)	6	6
7. Susan Getty/Roy Bradshaw (GRB)	7	7
8. Dana Holanová/Jaromír Holan (CZE)	8	8
9. Debbie Gerken/Raymond Tiedemann (USA)	9	13
10. Joan Bitterman/Brad Hislop (USA)	10	10
11. Donna Taylor/Bruce Lennie (CAN)	**11**	**9**
12. Mary Church/Tom Falls (CAN)	**13**	**12**
13. Ilona Berecz/István Sugár (HUN)	12	14
14. Tatiana Zoitiuk/Viacheslav Zhigalin (SOV)	14	11
15. Edeltraud Rotty/Joachim Iglowstein (FRG)	15	15

Soviet teams swept the podium in the pairs event at the World Figure Skating Championships for the first time.

The pairs compulsory connected program was rebranded as the short program and the OSP (original set pattern dance) was added to the ice dance competition.

Sources: Protocol, 1969 World Figure Skating Championships; 100th Anniversary 1892-1992 - International Skating Union: Results 1968-1991 Figure Skating Championships, Elemér Terták, Benjamin T. Wright, Beat Häsler, 1992, courtesy World Figure Skating Museum & Hall of Fame

Ondrej Nepela, World Champion 1971-1973 and Trixi Schuba, World Champion 1971-1972. Keystone Press / Alamy Stock Photo.

THE DECADE OF DISCO

1970 WORLD FIGURE SKATING CHAMPIONSHIPS
Ljubljana, Yugoslavia, March 3-8, 1970

World Men's Figure Skating Championships:

	CF	FS
1. Tim Wood (USA)	2	1
2. Ondrej Nepela (CZE)	1	3
3. Günter Zöller (GDR)	3	5
4. Patrick Péra (FRA)	4	6
5. John Misha Petkevich (USA)	5	2
6. Sergei Chetverukhin (SOV)	6	4
7. Sergei Volkov (SOV)	7	10
8. Ken Shelley (USA)	8	9
9. Haig Oundjian (GRB)	10	7
10. Jan Hoffmann (GDR)	11	11
11. David McGillivray (CAN)	**12**	**8**
12. Günter Anderl (AUT)	9	14
13. Toller Cranston (CAN)	**15**	**12**
14. Zdeněk Pazdírek (CZE)	14	17
15. Jacques Mrozek (FRA)	16	13
16. László Vajda (HUN)	17	15
17. Klaus Grimmelt (FRG)	18	16
18. Jozef Žídek (CZE)	19	18
19. Didier Gailhaguet (FRA)	20	19
20. Yutaka Higuchi (JPN)	21	20
21. Zoran Matas (YUG)	22	21
WD. Daniel Höner (SUI)	13	-

World Ladies Figure Skating Championships:

	CF	FS
1. Gaby Seyfert (GDR)	2	1
2. Trixi Schuba (AUT)	1	7
3. Julie Lynn Holmes (USA)	3	5
4. Karen Magnussen (CAN)	**7**	**3**

5. Zsuzsa Almássy (HUN)	5	4
6. Janet Lynn (USA)	8	2
7. Dawn Glab (USA)	6	10
8. Rita Trapanese (ITA)	9	6
9. Patricia Dodd (GRB)	4	13
10. Cathy Lee Irwin (CAN)	**13**	**8**
11. Sonja Morgenstern (GDR)	14	9
12. Elena Shcheglova (SOV)	11	12
13. Charlotte Walter (SUI)	12	16
14. Yelena Aleksandrova (SOV)	16	11
15. Eileen Zillmer (FRG)	10	17
16. Kazumi Yamashita (JPN)	17	15
17. Ľudmila Bezáková (CZE)	18	14
18. Frances Waghorn (GRB)	15	19
19. Simone Gräfe (GDR)	19	20
20. Judith Beyer (FRG)	20	18
21. Wilfriede Reiter (AUT)	21	21

World Pairs Skating Championships:

	SP	FS
1. Irina Rodnina/Alexei Ulanov (SOV)	1	1
2. Lyudmila Smirnova/Andrey Suraikin (SOV)	2	2
3. H. Walther/H-U. Walther (GDR)	3	3
4. Galina Karelina/Georgi Proskurin (SOV)	4	4
5. JoJo Starbuck/Ken Shelley (USA)	5	5
6. Almut Lehmann/Herbert Wiesinger (FRG)	6	6
7. Manuela Groß/Uwe Kagelmann (GDR)	7	7
8. Melissa Militano/Mark Militano (USA)	10	8
9. Brunhilde Baßler/Eberhard Rausch (FRG)	8	9
10. Janina Poremska/Piotr Szczypa (POL)	11	10
11. Monique Szabo/Pierre Szabo (FRA)	13	11
12. Dana Fialová/Josef Tůma (CZE)	9	12
13. Evelyne Schneider/Willy Bietak (AUT)	15	13
14. Sandra Bezic/Val Bezic (CAN)	**14**	**14**
15. Mary Petrie/Robert McAvoy (CAN)	**12**	**15**
16. Kotoe Nagasawa/Hiroshi Nagakubo (JPN)	16	16
17. Helena Gazvoda/Silvo Švejger (YUG)	17	17
WD. Annette Kansy/Axel Salzmann (GDR)	18	-

World Ice Dancing Championships:

	C/OSP	FD
1. L. Pakhomova/A. Gorshkov (SOV)	2	1
2. Judy Schwomeyer/James Sladky (USA)	1	2
3. Angelika Buck/Erich Buck (FRG)	3	3
4. Tatiana Zoitiuk/Viacheslav Zhigalin (SOV)	5	4
5. Susan Getty/Roy Bradshaw (GRB)	4	5
6. Annerose Baier/Eberhard Rüger (GDR)	7	6
7. Janet Sawbridge/Peter Dalby (GRB)	6	8
8. Elena Zharkova/Gennadi Karponosov (SOV)	8	7
9. Debbie Ganson/Brad Hislop (USA)	9	9
10. Anne Millier/Harvey Millier III (USA)	11	10
11. Diana Skotnická/Martin Skotnický (CZE)	12	11
12. Ilona Berecz/István Sugár (HUN)	10	14
13. Teresa Weyna/Piotr Bojańczyk (POL)	13	13
14. Mary Church/David Sutton (CAN)	**14**	**12**
15. Světlana Marinovová/Miloš Buršík (CZE)	15	15
16. Anne-Claude Wolfers/Roland Mars (FRA)	16	16
17. Brigitte Scheijbal/Kurt Jaschek (AUT)	17	17
18. A. Wiesner/H-J. Wiesner (FRG)	18	18

Yugoslavia played host to the World Figure Skating Championships for the first time.

Lyudmila Pakhomova and Aleksandr Gorshkov made history as the first Soviet team to win a gold medal in ice dance at the World Championships. Angelika and Erich Buck won West Germany's first medal in ice dancing at the World Championships.

Sources: Skating magazine, May 1970; Protocol, 1970 World Figure Skating Championships; 100th Anniversary 1892-1992 - International Skating Union: Results 1968-1991 Figure Skating Championships, Elemér Terták, Benjamin T. Wright, Beat Häsler, 1992, courtesy World Figure Skating Museum & Hall of Fame

1971 WORLD FIGURE SKATING CHAMPIONSHIPS
Lyon, France, February 23-28, 1971

World Men's Figure Skating Championships:

	CF	FS
1. Ondrej Nepela (CZE)	1	1
2. Patrick Péra (FRA)	2	3
3. Sergei Chetverukhin (SOV)	3	8
4. Jan Hoffmann (GDR)	4	2
5. John Misha Petkevich (USA)	5	4
6. Haig Oundjian (GRB)	6	7
7. Yuri Ovchinnikov (SOV)	7	9
8. Ken Shelley (USA)	9	5
9. Gordon McKellen Jr. (USA)	11	10
10. Didier Gailhaguet (FRA)	10	11
11. Toller Cranston (CAN)	**15**	**6**
12. Günter Anderl (AUT)	8	14
13. Jacques Mrozek (FRA)	14	12
14. John Curry (GRB)	13	13
15. Daniel Höner (SUI)	12	16
16. Jozef Žídek (CZE)	18	15
17. Zdeněk Pazdírek (CZE)	17	19
18. Stefano Bargauan (ITA)	16	18
19. Klaus Grimmelt (FRG)	21	17
20. Yutaka Higuchi (JPN)	19	20
21. György Fazekas (ROM)	20	21

World Ladies Figure Skating Championships:

	CF	FS
1. Trixi Schuba (AUT)	1	7
2. Julie Lynn Holmes (USA)	2	5
3. Karen Magnussen (CAN)	**4**	**2**
4. Janet Lynn (USA)	5	1
5. Rita Trapanese (ITA)	3	8
6. Sonja Morgenstern (GDR)	9	3
7. Zsuzsa Almássy (HUN)	6	4
8. Charlotte Walter (SUI)	8	14
9. Christine Errath (GDR)	13	6

10. Suna Murray (USA)	14	9
11. Yelena Aleksandrova (SOV)	10	13
12. Patricia Dodd (GRB)	7	16
13. Kazumi Yamashita (JPN)	12	11
14. Ľudmila Bezáková (CZE)	11	15
15. Jean Scott (GRB)	15	10
16. Diane Hall (CAN)	**19**	**12**
17. Anita Johansson (SWE)	16	18
18. Judith Beyer (FRG)	20	17
19. Ruth Hutchinson (CAN)	**17**	**20**
20. Sonja Balun (AUT)	22	19
21. Joëlle Cartaux (FRA)	18	22
22. Cinzia Frosio (ITA)	21	21

World Pairs Skating Championships:

	SP	FS
1. Irina Rodnina/Alexei Ulanov (SOV)	2	1
2. Lyudmila Smirnova/Andrei Suraikin (SOV)	1	2
3. JoJo Starbuck/Ken Shelley (USA)	3	3
4. Manuela Groß/Uwe Kagelmann (GDR)	4	4
5. Almut Lehmann/Herbert Wiesinger (FRG)	5	5
6. Melissa Militano/Mark Militano (USA)	7	6
7. Annette Kansy/Axel Salzmann (GDR)	8	7
8. Galina Karelina/Georgi Proskurin (SOV)	6	8
9. Sandra Bezic/Val Bezic (CAN)	**9**	**9**
10. Grażyna Osmańska/Adam Brodecki (POL)	11	10
11. Barbara Brown/Douglas Berndt (USA)	12	11
12. Brunhilde Baßler/Eberhard Rausch (FRG)	10	12
13. Linda Connolly/Colin Taylforth (GRB)	13	13
14. Florence Cahn/Jean-Roland Racle (FRA)	14	14
15. Kotoe Nagasawa/Hiroshi Nagakubo (JPN)	17	15
16. Karin Künzle/Christian Künzle (SUI)	18	16
17. Teresa Skrzek/Piotr Szczypa (POL)	16	17
WD. Evelyne Schneider/Willy Bietak (AUT)	15	-

World Ice Dancing Championships:

	C/OSP	FS
1. L. Pakhomova/A. Gorshkov (SOV)	1	1
2. Angelika Buck/Erich Buck (FRG)	3	2
3. Judy Schwomeyer/James Sladky (USA)	2	3
4. Susan Getty/Roy Bradshaw (GRB)	4	4
5. Tatiana Zoitiuk/Viacheslav Zhigalin (SOV)	5	5
6. Janet Sawbridge/Peter Dalby (GRB)	6	7
7. Hilary Green/Glyn Watts (GRB)	10	8
8. Elena Zharkova/Gennadi Karponosov (SOV)	7	6
9. Anne Millier/Harvey Millier III (USA)	9	10
10. Mary Karen Campbell/Johnny Johns (USA)	8	9
11. Louise Lind/Barry Soper (CAN)	**11**	**11**
12. Diana Skotnická/Martin Skotnický (CZE)	13	12
13. Anne-Claude Wolfers/Roland Mars (FRA)	12	13
14. Teresa Weyna/Piotr Bojańczyk (POL)	14	14
15. Ilona Berecz/István Sugár (HUN)	15	16
16. Matilde Ciccia/Lamberto Ceserani (ITA)	16	15
17. Tatiana Grossen/Alessandro Grossen (SUI)	17	17
18. Astrid Kopp/Axel Kopp (FRG)	18	18
19. A. Wiesner/H-J. Wiesner (FRG)	19	19
20. B. Scheijbal/W. Leschetizky (AUT)	20	20

Janet Lynn won the ladies free skate with an astonishing performance, but the media hoopla surrounding her loss in Lyon somewhat tarnished the event for all the top four finishers. Following the competition, Associated Press reporter Harvey Hudson claimed, "Boos and whistles of derision broke out from the crowd when Miss Schuba went to the victory stand. The same voices of disapproval broke out again while all three medal winners were in the center of the ice. When Miss Lynn appeared at rinkside a bedlam of cheering broke out and the crowd chanted 'Lynn, Lynn, Lynn.' Miss Schuba was disheartened by the display." Interrogated following her loss, Schuba shrugged and aptly said, "I didn't get any special benefit from the rules. The rules weren't made for me." Canadian writers viewed the situation following Lynn's loss a little differently. Author David Young asserted, "The producers of ABC television twisted the facts to suit their own purposes, and perpetrated a fraud on the American viewers. As the crowd applauded for the three medallists, the television camera focused on another unauthorized podium where Janet Lynn, who had finished fourth, was standing. The announcer explained that Janet had completely won the hearts of the French audience, and that all the applause was for her. Trixi, in what should have been the moment of her greatest triumph after years of hard and heart-breaking work, had to be consoled instead by the two other winners. It was a blatant example of the media moulding an event to suit the image which suited it best, and a great many people were extremely upset by the incident, including the U.S. team manager Charles DeMore, who later apologized for the whole thing, although he had nothing to do with it." Janet Lynn later recalled that the situation was "very embarrassing."

Sources: The Vancouver Sun, March 1, 1971; Skating magazine, May 1971; Peace + Love, Janet Lynn and Dean Merrill, 1973; The Golden Age of Canadian Figure Skating, David Young, 1984; 100th Anniversary 1892-1992 - International Skating Union: Results 1968-1991 Figure Skating Championships, Elemér Terták, Benjamin T. Wright, Beat Häsler, 1992, courtesy World Figure Skating Museum & Hall of Fame

1972 WORLD FIGURE SKATING CHAMPIONSHIPS
Calgary, Canada, March 7-11, 1972

World Men's Figure Skating Championships:

	CF	FS
1. Ondrej Nepela (CZE)	1	3
2. Sergei Chetverukhin (SOV)	2	2
3. Vladimir Kovalev (SOV)	3	5
4. John Misha Petkevich (USA)	5	4
5. Toller Cranston (CAN)	**9**	**1**
6. Jan Hoffmann (GDR)	4	9
7. Ken Shelley (USA)	7	6
8. Gordon McKellen Jr. (USA)	10	8
9. John Curry (GRB)	6	7
10. Sergei Volkov (SOV)	8	10
11. Jacques Mrozek (FRA)	11	11

	CF	FS
12. Zdeněk Pazdírek (CZE)	14	12
13. Didier Gailhauguet (FRA)	12	13
14. Josef Schneider (AUT)	13	15
15. Yutaka Higuchi (JPN)	16	14
16. Jozef Žídek (CZE)	17	16
17. Stefano Bargauan (ITA)	15	17
18. Harald Kuhn (FRG)	19	18
19. Pekka Leskinen (FIN)	18	19
WD. Haig Oundjian (GRB)	-	-

World Ladies Figure Skating Championships:

	CF	FS
1. Trixi Schuba (AUT)	1	9
2. Karen Magnussen (CAN)	**2**	**2**
3. Janet Lynn (USA)	3	1
4. Zsuzsa Almássy (HUN)	4	6
5. Sonja Morgenstern (GDR)	6	3
6. Jean Scott (GRB)	5	10
7. Dorothy Hamill (USA)	8	5
8. Suna Murray (USA)	7	7
9. Cathy Lee Irwin (CAN)	**9**	**8**
10. Christine Errath (GDR)	11	4
11. Ľudmila Bezáková (CZE)	10	13
12. Karin Iten (SUI)	12	16
13. Gerti Schanderl (FRG)	15	11
14. Cinzia Frosio (ITA)	13	12
15. Daria Prychun (CAN)	**14**	**14**
16. Marie-Claude Bierre (FRA)	17	15
17. Dianne de Leeuw (NED)	16	19
18. Myung-su Chang (KOR)	18	18
19. Sharon Burley (AUS)	19	21
20. Shuko Takeyama (JPN)	20	20
21. Marina Sanaya (SOV)	21	17
WD. Charlotte Walter (SUI)	-	-

World Pairs Skating Championships:

	SP	FS
1. Irina Rodnina/Alexei Ulanov (SOV)	1	1
2. Lyudmila Smirnova/Andrei Suraikin (SOV)	2	3
3. JoJo Starbuck/Ken Shelley (USA)	6	2
4. Manuela Groß/Uwe Kagelmann (GDR)	3	4
5. Almut Lehmann/Herbert Wiesinger (FRG)	4	5
6. Irina Chernyaeva/Vasili Blagov (SOV)	5	6
7. Annette Kansy/Axel Salzmann (GDR)	7	7
8. Sandra Bezic/Val Bezic (CAN)	**8**	**8**
9. Melissa Militano/Mark Militano (USA)	10	9
10. Corinna Halke/Eberhard Rausch (FRG)	11	10
11. Mary Petrie/John Hubbell (CAN)	**13**	**11**
12. Grażyna Osmańska/Adam Brodecki (POL)	9	12
13. Gabriele Cieplik/Reinhard Ketterer (FRG)	12	13
14. Barbara Brown/Douglas Berndt (USA)	14	14
15. Linda Connolly/Colin Taylforth (GRB)	15	15

World Ice Dancing Championships:

	C/OSP	FD
1. L. Pakhomova/A. Gorshkov (SOV)	1	1
2. Angelika Buck/Erich Buck (FRG)	2	2
3. Judy Schwomeyer/James Sladky (USA)	3	3
4. Janet Sawbridge/Peter Dalby (GRB)	4	4
5. Tatiana Zoitiuk/Viacheslav Zhigalin (SOV)	5	5
6. Hilary Green/Glyn Watts (GRB)	6	6
7. Anne Millier/Harvey Millier III (USA)	7	7
8. Elena Zharkova/Gennadi Karponosov (SOV)	8	8
9. Louise Lind/Barry Soper (CAN)	**9**	**9**
10. Mary Karen Campbell/Johnny Johns (USA)	10	10
11. Diana Skotnická/Martin Skotnický (CZE)	11	11
12. Anne-Claude Wolfers/Roland Mars (FRA)	12	13
13. Teresa Weyna/Piotr Bojańczyk (POL)	13	12
14. Sylvia Fuchs/Michael Fuchs (FRG)	14	14
15. Astrid Kopp/Axel Kopp (FRG)	15	15
16. Keiko Achiwa/Yasuhiro Noto (JPN)	16	16

Irina Rodnina and Alexei Ulanov made history, receiving the first two 6.0's ever awarded in the pairs short program at the World Figure Skating Championships - one for technical merit and and one for artistic impression.

Myung-su Chang made history as the first skater to represent South Korea at the Wold Championships. Keiko Achiwa and Yasuhiro Noto made history as the first Japanese ice dance team to compete in the World Championships.

Another first in Calgary was the introduction of a rotating starting list in the ice dance event. After each compulsory dance, the groups of skaters rotated, ensuring that no team consistently faced the perceived disadvantage of skating in the first or second group.

Trixi Schuba, one of the greatest specialists in school figures of all time, made history as the first skater to give a demonstration of figures in an exhibition gala at the World Figure Skating Championships. Schuba demonstrated an outside eight, outside three, double three, bracket and loop. Schuba's unorthodox choice of exhibition wasn't a statement. She injured herself during the competition, and would have been forced to withdraw from the gala had she not come up with the idea of demonstrating her specialty.

Sources: Skating magazine, May 1972; Protocol, 1972 World Figure Skating Championships; Programme, 1972 World Figure Skating Championships; 100th Anniversary 1892-1992 - International Skating Union: Results 1968-1991 Figure Skating Championships, Elemér Terták, Benjamin T. Wright, Beat Häsler, 1992, courtesy World Figure Skating Museum & Hall of Fame

1973 WORLD FIGURE SKATING CHAMPIONSHIPS
Bratislava, Czechoslovakia, February 26-March 3, 1973

World Men's Figure Skating Championships:

	CF	SP	FS
1. Ondrej Nepela (CZE)	1	2	2
2. Sergei Chetverukhin (SOV)	2	3	1

3. Jan Hoffmann (GDR)	3	7	6
4. John Curry (GRB)	4	8	7
5. Toller Cranston (CAN)	**6**	**1**	**5**
6. Yuri Ovchinnikov (SOV)	8	5	3
7. Gordon McKellen Jr. (USA)	5	4	8
8. Ron Shaver (CAN)	**12**	**6**	**4**
9. Jacques Mrozek (FRA)	9	10	11
10. Zdeněk Pazdírek (CZE)	10	12	9
11. Daniel Höner (SUI)	7	11	12
12. Robert Bradshaw (USA)	13	9	10
13. László Vajda (HUN)	11	14	13
14. Minoru Sano (JPN)	14	13	14
15. Erich Reifschneider (FRG)	15	15	16
16. Igor Lisovski (SOV)	18	17	17
17. Bernd Wunderlich (GDR)	20	18	15
18. Miroslav Šoška (CZE)	17	16	18
19. Robert Rubens (CAN)	**19**	**19**	**19**
20. Günther Hilgarth (AUT)	16	20	21
21. Jacek Tascher (POL)	23	23	20
22. Rolando Bragaglia (ITA)	22	21	22
23. György Fazekas (ROM)	21	24	24
24. Silvo Švejger (YUG)	24	22	23

World Ladies Figure Skating Championships:

	CF	SP	FS
1. Karen Magnussen (CAN)	**1**	**1**	**2**
2. Janet Lynn (USA)	2	12	1
3. Christine Errath (GDR)	5	2	5
4. Dorothy Hamill (USA)	8	3	4
5. Jean Scott (GRB)	4	10	11
6. Karin Iten (SUI)	3	14	14
7. Liana Drahová (CZE)	9	9	6
8. Sonja Morgenstern (GDR)	10	5	7
9. Juli McKinstry (USA)	12	7	9
10. Lynn Nightingale (CAN)	**15**	**4**	**3**
11. Maria McLean (GRB)	7	11	13
12. Cathy Lee Irwin (CAN)	**11**	**13**	**10**
13. Gerti Schanderl (FRG)	14	6	8

14. Anett Pötzsch (GDR)	13	8	12
15. Dianne de Leeuw (NED)	6	15	16
16. Marina Sanaya (SOV)	23	16	15
17. Emi Watanabe (JPN)	18	23	17
18. Marie-Claude Bierre (FRA)	16	18	22
19. Cinzia Frosio (ITA)	19	19	19
20. Lise-Lotte Öberg (SWE)	21	17	18
21. Sharon Burley (AUS)	20	20	21
22. Hannele Koskinen (FIN)	27	22	20
23. Grażyna Dudek (POL)	26	21	23
24. Helena Gazvoda (YUG)	25	26	24
25. Myung-su Chang (KOR)	17	28	27
26. Bente Tverran (NOR)	24	27	26
27. Ágnes Erős (HUN)	28	24	25
WD. Susanne Altura (AUT)	22	25	-
WD. Sonja Balun (AUT)	-	-	-
WD. Zsuzsa Homolya (HUN)	-	-	-

World Pairs Skating Championships:

	SP	FS
1. Irina Rodnina/Aleksandr Zaitsev (SOV)	1	1
2. Lyudmila Smirnova/Alexei Ulanov (SOV)	2	2
3. Manuela Groß/Uwe Kagelmann (GDR)	3	3
4. Almut Lehmann/Herbert Wiesinger (FRG)	6	5
5. Romy Kermer/Rolf Österreich (GDR)	4	4
6. Sandra Bezic/Val Bezic (CAN)	**7**	**6**
7. Irina Chernyaeva/Vasili Blagov (SOV)	5	7
8. Melissa Militano/Mark Militano (USA)	8	8
9. Marian Murray/Glenn Moore (CAN)	**9**	**9**
10. Karin Künzle/Christian Künzle (SUI)	11	10
11. Ilona Urbanová/Aleš Zach (CZE)	10	11
12. Corinna Halke/Eberhard Rausch (FRG)	12	12
13. Gale Fuhrman/Joel Fuhrman (USA)	15	13
14. Florence Cahn/Jean-Roland Racle (FRA) 13	14	
15. Ursula Nemec/Michael Nemec (AUT)	16	15
16. Teresa Skrzek/Piotr Szczypa (POL)	14	16

World Ice Dancing Championships:

	C/OSP	FD
1. L. Pakhomova/A. Gorshkov (SOV)	1	1
2. Angelika Buck/Erich Buck (FRG)	2	2
3. Hilary Green/Glyn Watts (GRB)	3	3
4. Janet Sawbridge/Peter Dalby (GRB)	4	6
5. Tatiana Zoitiuk/Viacheslav Zhigalin (SOV)	5	4
6. Mary Karen Campbell/Johnny Johns (USA)	6	7
7. Irina Moiseeva/Andrei Minenkov (SOV)	7	5
8. Diana Skotnická/Martin Skotnický (CZE)	8	8
9. Louise Soper/Barry Soper (CAN)	**9**	**9**
10. Anne Millier/Harvey Millier III (USA)	10	11
11. Matilde Ciccia/Lamberto Ceserani (ITA)	12	10
12. Rosalind Druce/David Barker (GRB)	11	13
13. Krisztina Regőczy/András Sallay (HUN)	13	12
14. Halina Gordon/Wojciech Bańkowski (POL)	14	15
15. Barbara Berezowski/David Porter (CAN)	**15**	**14**
16. Anne-Claude Wolfers/Roland Mars (FRA)	16	16
17. Christina Henke/Udo Dönsdorf (FRG)	17	17
18. B. Scheijbal/W. Leschetizky (AUT)	18	18

The men's and ladies short program made their debut at the World Figure Skating Championships, tipping the scales to give strong free skaters an advantage they didn't have before. The launch of the singles short program wasn't exactly a roaring success. Some medal contenders fumbled, while other skaters didn't perform all the required elements and weren't marked down appropriately. There was also a criticism that marks for artistic impression were too generous, as skaters didn't have enough time to showcase "composition and style."

A series of unusual incidents occurred in the pairs event. Americans Melissa and Mark Militano stopped their program twice. First, there was a problem with their music speed. The second time, they found a blue elastic band with a metal pin on the ice. When they brought the wire to the referee, they learned that it was the fourth piece that had been brought to them. Mark Militano stormed off the ice to the dressing room in protest, shouting, "I'm not skating on garbage!"

Officials believed the wires were being thrown on the ice intentionally by audience members. An announcement was made that if the projectiles continued, the arena would be cleared. The Militanos reskated their program a third time. Later, Irina Rodnina and Aleksandr Zaitsev's music mysteriously stopped during their performance. It was blamed on a mechanical failure. They ignored the referee's waves to stop their program and opted to continue their performance, without any music. After much discussion by ISU officials, Rodnina and Zaitsev were awarded first-place marks by every judge. This incident resulted in a rule change, which clearly stated that skaters must stop when instructed to do so by a referee.

Sources: Batavia Daily News, March 1, 1973; Knickerbocker News Union Star, March 1, 1973; The New York Times, March 1, 1973; Winnipeg Tribune, March 2, 1973; Skating magazine, May 1973; 100th Anniversary 1892-1992 - International Skating Union: Results 1968-1991 Figure Skating Championships, Elemér Terták, Benjamin T. Wright, Beat Häsler, 1992, courtesy World Figure Skating Museum & Hall of Fame; Skating Around the World: International Skating Union, the One Hundredth Anniversary History 1892 -1992, Benjamin T. Wright

1974 WORLD FIGURE SKATING CHAMPIONSHIPS
Munich, West Germany, March 5-10, 1974

World Men's Figure Skating Championships:

	CF	SP	FS
1. Jan Hoffmann (GDR)	1	5	2
2. Sergei Volkov (SOV)	2	3	7
3. Toller Cranston (CAN)	8	1	1
4. Vladimir Kovalev (SOV)	3	4	4
5. Ron Shaver (CAN)	7	2	3
6. Gordon McKellen Jr. (USA)	5	7	5
7. John Curry (GRB)	4	6	9
8. Minoru Sano (JPN)	11	8	6
9. Zdeněk Pazdírek (CZE)	9	10	10
10. Didier Gailhaguet (FRA)	6	11	12
11. László Vajda (HUN)	10	9	11
12. Terry Kubicka (USA)	15	15	8

13. Bernd Wunderlich (GDR)	13	12	14
14. Erich Reifschneider (FRG)	14	13	13
15. Robert Rubens (CAN)	**20**	**14**	**15**
16. Ronald Koppelent (AUT)	18	17	16
17. Miroslav Šoška (CZE)	12	16	21
18. Pekka Leskinen (FIN)	16	18	19
19. Jacek Tascher (POL)	21	20	17
20. Rolando Bragaglia (ITA)	19	19	20
21. Glyn Jones (GRB)	25	21	18
22. Gilles Beyer (FRA)	22	22	23
23. Thomas Öberg (SWE)	23	23	22
24. György Fazekas (ROM)	17	25	25
25. William Schober (AUS)	24	24	24
26. Silvio Švajger (YUG)	26	26	26

World Ladies Figure Skating Championships:

	CF	SP	FS
1. Christine Errath (GDR)	2	1	2
2. Dorothy Hamill (USA)	5	2	1
3. Dianne de Leeuw (NED)	4	5	4
4. Gerti Schanderl (FRG)	11	4	3
5. Karin Iten (SUI)	1	14	17
6. Lynn Nightingale (CAN)	**12**	**3**	**5**
7. Kath Malmberg (USA)	7	8	10
8. Juli McKinstry (USA)	6	9	7
9. Liana Drahová (CZE)	9	6	6
10. Marion Weber (GDR)	8	10	8
11. Anett Pötzsch (GDR)	10	7	9
12. Maria McLean (GRB)	3	12	13
13. Barbara Terpenning (CAN)	**13**	**11**	**11**
14. Gail Keddie (GRB)	17	16	14
15. Emi Watanabe (JPN)	19	17	12
16. Sonja Balun (AUT)	16	13	15
17. Cinzia Frosio (ITA)	13	15	16
18. Lyudmila Bakonina (SOV)	18	18	19
19. Hana Knapová (CZE)	20	19	18
20. Myung-su Chang (KOR)	15	20	20
21. Evelyne Reusser (SUI)	21	21	23

22. Grażyna Dudek (POL)	24	23	21
23. Eva Hansson (SWE)	25	22	24
24. Marie-Hélène Panet (FRA)	23	25	25
25. Helena Gazvoda (YUG)	28	24	22
26. Sharon Burley (AUS)	22	27	27
27. Susan Broman (FIN)	26	26	26
28. Liv Egelund (NOR)	27	28	28
WD. Sonja Morgenstern (GDR)	-	-	-

World Pairs Figure Skating Championships:

	SP	FS
1. Irina Rodnina/Aleksandr Zaitsev (SOV)	1	1
2. Lyudmila Smirnova/Alexei Ulanov (SOV)	2	2
3. Romy Kermer/Rolf Österreich (GDR)	3	3
4. Manuela Groß/Uwe Kagelmann (GDR)	4	4
5. Sandra Bezic/Val Bezic (CAN)	**5**	**5**
6. Irina Vorobieva/Alexander Vlasov (SOV)	6	6
7. Karin Künzle/Christian Künzle (SUI)	7	7
8. Melissa Militano/Johnny Johns (USA)	8	8
9. Corinna Halke/Eberhard Rausch (FRG)	9	9
10. Tai Babilonia/Randy Gardner (USA)	10	10
11. Katja Schubert/Knut Schubert (GDR)	11	11
12. Grażyna Kostrzewińska/Adam Brodecki (POL)	12	12
13. Florence Cahn/Jean-Roland Racle (FRA)	14	13
14. Ursula Nemec/Michael Nemec (AUT)	13	14
15. Linda McCafferty/Colin Tayforth (GRB)	16	15
16. Ilona Urbanová/Ales Zach (CZE)	15	16
17. Petra Schneider/Bogdan Pulcer (FRG)	17	17
18. Kathy Hutchinson/Jamie McGrigor (CAN)	**18**	**18**

World Ice Dancing Championships:

	C/OSP	FD
1. L. Pakhomova/A. Gorshkov (SOV)	1	1
2. Hilary Green/Glyn Watts (GRB)	2	2
3. Natalia Linichuk/Gennadi Karponosov (SOV)	3	3
4. Irina Moiseeva/Andrei Minenkov (SOV)	5	4
5. Janet Sawbridge/Peter Dalby (GRB)	4	5
6. Krisztina Regőczy/András Sallay (HUN)	6	6

7. Colleen O'Connor/Jim Millns (USA)	7	7
8. Matilde Ciccia/Lamberto Ceserani (ITA)	8	9
9. Louise Soper/Barry Soper (CAN)	**9**	**8**
10. Teresa Weyna/Piotr Bojańczyk (POL)	10	10
11. Janet Thompson/Warren Maxwell (GRB)	11	11
12. Diana Skotnická/Martin Skotnický (CZE)	13	12
13. Anne Millier/Harvey Millier III (USA)	12	15
14. Gerda Bühler/Mathis Bächi (SUI)	14	13
15. Barbara Berezowski/David Porter (CAN)	**15**	**14**
16. Sylvia Fuchs/Michael Fuchs (FRG)	16	16
17. Eva Peštová/Jiři Pokorný (CZE)	17	17
18. Nicole Rinsant/Dirk Beyer (FRG)	18	18
19. B. Scheijbal/W. Leschetizky (AUT)	19	19

Jan Hoffmann made history as the first East German skater to win a gold medal in the men's event at the World Figure Skating Championships.

One of the highlights of the event was a special ceremony put together by the organizers, featuring the largest gathering of past World Champions in history. The oldest was West Germany's own Anna (Hübler) Horn, who won the first official ISU World Championships in pairs skating in 1908.

Sources: Skating magazine, May 1974; 100th Anniversary 1892-1992 - International Skating Union: Results 1968-1991 Figure Skating Championships, Elemér Terták, Benjamin T. Wright, Beat Häsler, 1992, courtesy World Figure Skating Museum & Hall of Fame

1974 WORLD FIGURE SKATING CHAMPIONSHIPS
Colorado Springs, United States, March 4-8, 1975

World Men's Figure Skating Championships:

	CF	SP	FS
1. Sergei Volkov (SOV)	1	6	4
2. Vladimir Kovalev (SOV)	3	4	3
3. John Curry (GRB)	2	2	5
4. Toller Cranston (CAN)	**4**	**3**	**2**

5. Gordon McKellen Jr. (USA)	5	5	7
6. Yuri Ovchinnikov (SOV)	9	1	6
7. Terry Kubicka (USA)	11	7	1
8. Ron Shaver (CAN)	**6**	**9**	**9**
9. László Vajda (HUN)	8	10	10
10. Minoru Sano (JPN)	10	8	8
11. Zdeněk Pazdírek (CZE)	7	12	17
12. Robin Cousins (GRB)	15	11	11
13. Didier Gailhaguet (FRA)	12	13	14
14. Bernd Wunderlich (GDR)	13	16	15
15. Ronald Koppelent (AUT)	16	14	12
16. Mitsuru Matsumura (JPN)	17	17	13
17. František Pechar (CZE)	14	15	18
18. Robert Rubens (CAN)	**18**	**18**	**16**
19. Gilles Beyer (FRA)	19	19	21
20. Paul Cechmanek (LUX)	20	21	20
21. William Schober (AUS)	22	20	19
22. Flemming Söderquist (DEN)	21	22	22
WD. Hermann Schulz (GDR)	-	-	-

World Ladies Figure Skating Championships:

	CF	SP	FS
1. Dianne de Leeuw (NED)	1	1	2
2. Dorothy Hamill (USA)	5	6	1
3. Christine Errath (GDR)	6	2	4
4. Wendy Burge (USA)	8	5	3
5. Kath Malmberg (USA)	4	4	10
6. Isabel de Navarre (FRG)	3	7	8
7. Lynn Nightingale (CAN)	**13**	**3**	**5**
8. Anett Pötzsch (GDR)	10	10	7
9. Susanna Driano (ITA)	11	9	6
10. Marion Weber (GDR)	7	17	12
11. Liana Drahová (CZE)	9	12	14
12. Kim Alletson (CAN)	**14**	**11**	**9**
13. Emi Watanabe (JPN)	17	13	11
14. Gerti Schanderl (FRG)	15	8	13
15. Lyudmila Bakonina (SOV)	21	16	15
16. Sonja Balun (AUT)	12	20	19

17. Dagmar Lurz (FRG)	20	14	16
18. Hana Knapová (CZE)	24	19	17
19. Marie-Claude Bierre (FRA)	25	15	18
20. Gail Keddie (GRB)	16	22	23
21. Karin Iten (SUI)	2	27	27
22. Hyo-jean Yun (KOR)	23	18	21
23. Evi Köpfli (SUI)	19	21	24
24. Michelle Haider (SUI)	22	25	20
25. Sharon Burley (AUS)	18	23	26
26. Anne-Marie Verlaan (NED)	26	24	25
27. Sophie Verlaan (NED)	27	26	22

World Pairs Figure Skating Championships:

	SP	FS
1. Irina Rodnina/Aleksandr Zaitsev (SOV)	1	1
2. Romy Kermer/Rolf Österreich (GDR)	2	2
3. Manuela Groß/Uwe Kagelmann (GDR)	4	3
4. Irina Vorobieva/Aleksandr Vlasov (SOV)	3	4
5. Marina Leonidova/Vladimir Bogolyubov (SOV)	6	5
6. Melissa Militano/Johnny Johns (USA)	5	7
7. Kerstin Stolfig/Veit Kempe (GDR)	7	6
8. Karin Künzle/Christian Künzle (SUI)	9	8
9. Corinna Halke/Eberhard Rausch (FRG)	8	9
10. Tai Babilonia/Randy Gardner (USA)	10	10
11. Candy Jones/Don Fraser (CAN)	**11**	**11**
12. Ursula Nemec/Michael Nemec (AUT)	13	12
13. Grażyna Kostrzewińska/Adam Brodecki (POL)	12	13
14. Kathy Hutchinson/Jamie McGrigor (CAN)	**14**	**14**
WD. Sandra Bezic/Val Bezic (CAN)	-	-
WD. Rijana Hartmannová/Petr Starec (CZE)	-	-

World Ice Dancing Championships:

	C/OSP	FS
1. Irina Moiseeva/Andrei Minenkov (SOV)	2	1
2. Colleen O'Connor/Jim Millns (USA)	1	2
3. Hilary Green/Glyn Watts (GRB)	4	3
4. Natalia Linichuk/Gennadi Karponosov (SOV)	3	4
5. Matilde Ciccia/Lamberto Ceserani (ITA)	5	5

6. Krisztina Regőczy/András Sallay (HUN)	6	6
7. Teresa Weyna/Piotr Bojańczyk (POL)	8	8
8. Janet Thompson/Warren Maxwell (GRB)	7	9
9. Barbara Berezowski/David Porter (CAN)	**9**	**7**
10. Eva Peštová/Jiři Pokorný (CZE)	10	10
11. Kay Barsdell/Kenneth Foster (GRB)	11	11
12. Judi Genovesi/Kent Weigle (USA)	12	12
13. Susan Carscallen/Eric Gillies (CAN)	**13**	**13**
14. Halina Gordon/Wojciech Bańkowski (POL)	14	14
WD. L. Pakhomova/A. Gorshkov (SOV)	-	-

Sergei Volkov made history as the first Soviet singles skater to win a gold medal at the World Figure Skating Championships.

Paul Cechmanek made history as the first skater from Luxembourg to compete at the event.

Sources: Colorado Springs Gazette-Telegraph, March 3, 1975; The Daily Herald-Tribune, March 4, 1975; Skating magazine, May 1975; 100th Anniversary 1892-1992 - International Skating Union: Results 1968-1991 Figure Skating Championships, Elemér Terták, Benjamin T. Wright, Beat Häsler, 1992, courtesy World Figure Skating Museum & Hall of Fame

1976 WORLD FIGURE SKATING CHAMPIONSHIPS
Göteborg, Sweden, March 2-7, 1976

World Men's Figure Skating Championships:

	CF	SP	FS
1. John Curry (GRB)	2	3	1
2. Vladimir Kovalev (SOV)	1	5	4
3. Jan Hoffmann (GDR)	3	2	3
4. Toller Cranston (CAN)	**5**	**1**	**2**
5. David Santee (USA)	4	7	7
6. Terry Kubicka (USA)	7	4	5
7. Minoru Sano (JPN)	6	6	6
8. Igor Bobrin (SOV)	8	10	9
9. Robin Cousins (GRB)	14	8	8
10. Pekka Leskinen (FIN)	10	11	13

11. Konstantin Kokora (SOV)	11	12	10
12. Mitsuru Matsumura (JPN)	13	9	11
13. Christophe Boyadjian (FRA)	12	13	15
14. Zdeněk Pazdírek (CZE)	9	15	16
15. Grzegorz Głowania (POL)	20	14	12
16. Ted Barton (CAN)	**17**	**17**	**14**
17. Kenneth Polk (CAN)	**15**	**16**	**18**
18. Glyn Jones (GRB)	19	20	17
19. Gerd-Walter Gräbner (FRG)	18	19	19
20. Thomas Öberg (SWE)	16	18	20
21. Flemming Söderquist (DEN)	21	21	21

World Ladies Figure Skating Championships:

	CF	SP	FS
1. Dorothy Hamill (USA)	2	1	1
2. Christine Errath (GDR)	4	2	2
3. Dianne de Leeuw (NED)	3	3	4
4. Anett Pötzsch (GDR)	5	6	5
5. Linda Fratianne (USA)	6	5	3
6. Isabel de Navarre (FRG)	1	7	12
7. Lynn Nightingale (CAN)	**7**	**4**	**8**
8. Wendy Burge (USA)	8	8	6
9. Dagmar Lurz (FRG)	9	10	7
10. Susanna Driano (ITA)	10	9	10
11. Elena Vodorezova (SOV)	15	12	9
12. Kim Alletson (CAN)	**13**	**11**	**11**
13. Karena Richardson (GRB)	14	13	14
14. Grażyna Dudek (POL)	17	15	15
15. Denise Biellmann (SUI)	21	18	13
16. Claudia Kristofics-Binder (AUT)	16	19	16
17. Emi Watanabe (JPN)	11	16	18
18. Eva Ďurišinová (CZE)	18	17	17
19. Hyo-jean Yun (KOR)	12	22	20
20. Niina Kyöttinen (FIN)	22	14	21
21. Lise-Lotte Öberg (SWE)	19	20	19
22. Sharon Burley (AUS)	20	21	22
23. Bente Larsen (NOR)	25	23	23
24. Stella Bristing (DEN)	24	24	24

25. Gay Le Comte (NZL)　　　　　　　23　　25　　25

World Pairs Skating Championships:

	SP	FS
1. Irina Rodnina/Aleksandr Zaitsev (SOV)	1	1
2. Romy Kermer/Rolf Österreich (GDR)	2	2
3. Irina Vorobieva/Aleksandr Vlasov (SOV)	3	3
4. Manuela Groß/Uwe Kagelmann (GDR)	4	4
5. Tai Babilonia/Randy Gardner (USA)	5	6
6. Nadezhda Gorshkova/Evgeni Shevalovski (SOV)	6	5
7. Kerstin Stolfig/Veit Kempe (GDR)	7	7
8. Corinna Halke/Eberhard Rausch (FRG)	8	8
9. Alice Cook/Bill Fauver (USA)	9	9
10. Ingrid Spieglová/Alan Spiegl (CZE)	10	10
11. Ursula Nemec/Michael Nemec (AUT)	11	11
12. Candy Jones/Don Fraser (CAN)	**12**	**12**
13. Gabriele Beck/Jochen Stahl (FRG)	13	13

World Ice Dancing Championships:

	C/OSP	FD
1. L. Pakhomova/A. Gorshkov (SOV)	1	1
2. Irina Moiseeva/Andrei Minenkov (SOV)	2	2
3. Colleen O'Connor/Jim Millns (USA)	3	3
4. Krisztina Regőczy/András Sallay (HUN)	4	4
5. Natalia Linichuk/Gennadi Karponosov (SOV)	5	5
6. Janet Thompson/Warren Maxwell (GRB)	6	6
7. Barbara Berezowski/David Porter (CAN)	**9**	**8**
8. Eva Peštová/Jiři Pokorný (CZE)	8	9
9. Teresa Weyna/Piotr Bojańczyk (POL)	7	7
10. Susan Carscallen/Eric Gillies (CAN)	**10**	**10**
11. Kay Barsdell/Kenneth Foster (USA)	11	11
12. Susi Handschmann/Peter Handschmann (AUT)	12	12
13. Judi Genovesi/Kent Weigle (USA)	13	13
14. Stefania Bertele/Walter Cecconi (ITA)	14	14
15. Isabella Rizzi/Luigi Freroni (ITA)	15	15
16. Marie-Joëlle Michel/Frédéric Garcin (FRA)	16	16
17. Elżbieta Wegrzyk/Andrzej Alberciak (POL)	17	18
18. Susan Kelley/Andrew Stroukoff (USA)	18	17

19. Gabriele Schäfer/Robert Dietz (FRG)   19   19

Terry Kubicka made history as the first skater to perform a backflip at the World Figure Skating Championships. The ISU banned the backflip for decades afterwards, stating it was an acrobatic stunt with "no aesthetic value".

Gay Le Comte made history as the first skater to represent New Zealand at the World Championships.
Sources: Skating magazine, April and May 1976; 100th Anniversary 1892-1992 - International Skating Union: Results 1968-1991 Figure Skating Championships, Elemér Terták, Benjamin T. Wright, Beat Häsler, 1992, courtesy World Figure Skating Museum & Hall of Fame; Historical Dictionary of Figure Skating, James R. Hines, 2011

1977 WORLD FIGURE SKATING CHAMPIONSHIPS
Tokyo, Japan, March 1-6, 1977

World Men's Figure Skating Championships:

	CF	SP	FS
1. Vladimir Kovalev (SOV)	1	2	3
2. Jan Hoffmann (GDR)	2	1	2
3. Minoru Sano (JPN)	6	4	1
4. David Santee (USA)	4	9	5
5. Charles Tickner (USA)	5	3	7
6. Ron Shaver (CAN)	**9**	**8**	**6**
7. Yuri Ovchinnikov (SOV)	7	6	8
8. Mitsuru Matsumura (JPN)	15	11	4
9. Scott Cramer (USA)	8	10	9
10. Pekka Leskinen (FIN)	3	12	11
11. Konstantin Kokora (SOV)	11	7	10
12. Ronald Koppelent (AUT)	14	14	13
13. Kurt Kürzinger (FRG)	13	13	14
14. Brian Pockar (CAN)	**16**	**15**	**12**
15. Jean-Christophe Simond (FRA)	12	16	15
16. William Schober (AUS)	17	17	16
17. Soo-bong Han (KOR)	18	18	17
WD. Robin Cousins (GRB)	10	5	-

World Ladies Figure Skating Championships:

	CF	SP	FS
1. Linda Fratianne (USA)	4	1	2
2. Anett Pötzsch (GDR)	1	6	3
3. Dagmar Lurz (FRG)	2	3	8
4. Barbie Smith (USA)	5	4	7
5. Wendy Burge (USA)	7	2	4
6. Susanna Driano (ITA)	3	7	9
7. Elena Vodorezova (SOV)	13	5	1
8. Lynn Nightingale (CAN)	**8**	**9**	**5**
9. Marion Weber (GDR)	6	12	10
10. Denise Biellmann (SUI)	12	8	6
11. Claudia Kristofics-Binder (AUT)	9	10	12
12. Emi Watanabe (JPN)	11	11	13
13. Heather Kemkaran (CAN)	**14**	**13**	**11**
14. Garnet Ostermeier (FRG)	10	14	14
15. Karena Richardson (GRB)	19	16	15
16. Susan Broman (FIN)	15	15	16
17. Robyn Burley (AUS)	16	18	17
18. Maria-Claude Bierre (FRA)	17	17	18
19. Franca Bianconi (ITA)	21	20	19
20. Hyun-joo Lee (KOR)	18	21	21
21. Lotta Crispin (SWE)	20	19	20

World Pairs Skating Championships:

	SP	FS
1. Irina Rodnina/Aleksandr Zaitsev (SOV)	1	1
2. Irina Vorobieva/Aleksandr Vlasov (SOV)	2	2
3. Tai Babilonia/Randy Gardner (USA)	3	3
4. Marina Cherkasova/Sergei Shakhrai (SOV)	4	4
5. Manuela Mager/Uwe Bewersdorf (GDR)	5	5
6. Ingrid Spieglová/Alan Spiegl (CZE)	6	6
7. Gail Hamula/Frank Sweiding (USA)	7	7
8. Susanne Scheibe/Andreas Nischwitz (FRG)	8	9
9. Sheryl Franks/Michael Botticelli (USA)	9	8
10. Sherri Baier/Robin Cowan (CAN)	**11**	**10**
11. Gabriele Beck/Jochen Stahl (FRG)	10	11
12. Elizabeth Cain/Peter Cain (AUS)	13	12

13. Kyoko Hagiwara/Sumio Murata (JPN)	12	13

World Ice Dancing Championships:

	C/OSP	FS
1. Irina Moiseeva/Andrei Minenkov (SOV)	1	1
2. Janet Thompson/Warren Maxwell (GRB)	2	2
3. Natalia Linichuk/Gennadi Karponosov (SOV)	4	3
4. Krisztina Regőczy/András Sallay (HUN)	3	4
5. Marina Zoueva/Andrei Vitman (SOV)	5	5
6. Susan Carscallen/Eric Gillies (CAN)	**6**	**7**
7. Kay Barsdell/Kenneth Foster (GRB)	7	6
8. Liliana Řeháková/Stanislav Drastich (CZE)	9	8
9. Judi Genovesi/Kent Weigle (USA)	8	9
10. Lorna Wighton/John Dowding (CAN)	**10**	**10**
11. Isabella Rizzi/Luigi Freroni (ITA)	11	11
12. Susan Kelley/Andrew Stroukoff (USA)	13	12
13. Susi Handschmann/Peter Handschmann (AUT)	12	13
14. Misa Kage/Masanori Takeda (JPN)	14	14

Under the leadership of Tsuneyoshi Takeda, the National Skating Union of Japan played host to the first World Figure Skating Championships held in Asia. Minoru Sano won the men's free skate and made history as the first skater from Japan to win a medal at the World Championships.

The competition wasn't a raging success behind the scenes. The original Organizing Committee was fired several months before the Championships and ten members of the replacement committee walked out just before the event started. The rink at Yoyogi National Stadium, which was built over the swimming pool used at the 1964 Summer Olympics, was filthy and the ice conditions were extremely poor. A failed attempt to paint the ice blue resulted in mauve and grey streaked ice. A very expensive emergency repainting job yielded black ice, which was unpopular with skaters and television crews alike.

Marina Cherkasova and Sergei Shakhrai made history as the first team to successfully complete a quadruple twist lift at the World

Figure Skating Championships.

Sources: The Guardian, March 1, 1977; Press-Republican, March 2, 1977; The Patriot News, March 3, 1977; Skating magazine, April and May 1977; Skating Around the World: International Skating Union, the One Hundredth Anniversary History 1892 -1992, Benjamin T. Wright; 100th Anniversary 1892-1992 - International Skating Union: Results 1968-1991 Figure Skating Championships, Elemér Terták, Benjamin T. Wright, Beat Häsler, 1992, courtesy World Figure Skating Museum & Hall of Fame; Historical Dictionary of Figure Skating, James R. Hines, 2011

1978 WORLD FIGURE SKATING CHAMPIONSHIPS
Ottawa, Canada, March 7-12, 1978

World Men's Figure Skating Championships:

	CF	SP	FS
1. Charles Tickner (USA)	3	3	2
2. Jan Hoffmann (GDR)	2	1	3
3. Robin Cousins (GRB)	4	2	1
4. Vladimir Kovalev (SOV)	1	7	6
5. Igor Bobrin (SOV)	6	5	5
6. David Santee (USA)	5	4	8
7. Fumio Igarashi (JPN)	8	6	4
8. Mitsuru Matsumura (JPN)	9	8	11
9. Mario Liebers (GDR)	7	11	12
10. Brian Pockar (CAN)	**12**	**10**	**9**
11. Scott Hamilton (USA)	11	9	10
12. Vern Taylor (CAN)	**15**	**12**	**7**
13. Konstantin Kokora (SOV)	10	13	13
14. Rudi Cerne (FRG)	13	14	14
15. Gilles Beyer (FRA)	14	15	15
16. Brian Meek (AUS)	16	16	16
17. Soo-bong Han (KOR)	17	17	17
WD. Yuri Ovchinnikov (SOV)	-	-	-

World Ladies Figure Skating Championships:

	CF	SP	FS
1. Anett Pötzsch (GDR)	1	2	3
2. Linda Fratianne (USA)	3	1	1
3. Susanna Driano (ITA)	4	6	6
4. Dagmar Lurz (FRG)	2	10	7
5. Denise Biellmann (SUI)	16	3	2
6. Elena Vodorezova (SOV)	13	4	5
7. Lisa-Marie Allen (USA)	14	5	4
8. Emi Watanabe (JPN)	6	13	8
9. Priscilla Hill (USA)	5	8	10
10. Carola Weißenberg (GDR)	9	7	9
11. Karena Richardson (GRB)	12	11	11
12. Heather Kemkaran (CAN)	**10**	**9**	**14**
13. Claudia Kristofics-Binder (AUT)	11	12	15
14. Kristiina Wegelius (FIN)	7	16	13
15. Natalia Strelkova (SOV)	15	15	12
16. Danielle Rieder (SUI)	8	14	18
17. Cathie MacFarlane (CAN)	**17**	**17**	**20**
18. Astrid Jansen in de Wal (NED)	22	19	16
19. Karin Riediger (FRG)	18	20	19
20. Bodil Olsson (SWE)	21	18	17
21. Robyn Burley (AUS)	20	21	21
22. Young-soon Choo (KOR)	19	22	22
23. Katie Symmonds (NZL)	23	23	23
WD. Garnet Ostermeier (FRG)	-	-	-
WD. Renata Baierová (CZE)	-	-	-
WD. Franca Bianconi (ITA)	-	-	-

World Pairs Skating Championships:

	SP	FS
1. Irina Rodnina/Aleksandr Zaitsev (SOV)	1	1
2. Manuela Mager/Uwe Bewersdorf (GDR)	2	2
3. Tai Babilonia/Randy Gardner (USA)	4	3
4. Marina Cherkasova/Sergei Shakhrai (SOV)	3	4
5. Sabine Baeß/Tassilo Thierbach (GDR)	5	5
6. Ingrid Spieglová/Alan Spiegl (CZE)	6	6
7. Marina Pestova/Stanislav Leonovich (SOV)	7	7

8. Susanne Scheibe/Andreas Nischwitz (FRG)	8	8
9. Sheryl Franks/Michael Botticelli (USA)	9	9
10. Gail Hamula/Frank Sweiding (USA)	10	10
11. Lee-Ann Jackson/Paul Mills (CAN)	**13**	**11**
12. Sabine Fuchs/Xavier Videau (FRA)	12	12
13. Gabriele Beck/Jochen Stahl (FRG)	14	13
14. Elizabeth Cain/Peter Cain (AUS)	16	14
15. Kyoko Hagiwara/Sumio Murata (JPN)	15	15
WD. Sherri Baier/Robin Cowan (CAN)	**11**	-
WD. Kerstin Stolfig/Veit Kempe (GDR)	-	-

World Ice Dancing Championships:

	C/OSP	FD
1. Natalia Linichuk/Gennadi Karponosov (SOV)	1	1
2. Irina Moiseeva/Andrei Minenkov (SOV)	2	2
3. Krisztina Regőczy/András Sallay (HUN)	3	3
4. Janet Thompson/Warren Maxwell (GRB)	4	4
5. Liliana Řeháková/Stanislav Drastich (CZE)	5	6
6. Lorna Wighton/John Dowding (CAN)	**6**	**5**
7. Marina Zoueva/Andrei Vitman (SOV)	7	7
8. Carol Fox/Richard Dalley (USA)	8	8
9. Stacey Smith/John Summers (USA)	9	9
10. Susi Handschmann/Peter Handschmann (AUT)	11	10
11. Jayne Torvill/Christopher Dean (GRB)	10	11
12. P. Fletcher/M. de la Penotiere (CAN)	**12**	**12**
13. Stefania Bertele/Walter Cecconi (ITA)	13	13
14. Henriette Fröschl/Christian Steiner (FRG)	14	14
15. Muriel Boucher/Yves Malatier (FRA)	15	15
16. Michiko Abe/Nozomi Sakai (JPN)	16	16
WD. Kay Barsdell/Kenneth Foster (GRB)	-	-

For the first time, the defending men's, ladies and ice dancing champions lost their titles in the same year at the World Figure Skating Championships. Vern Taylor was credited as the first skater to land a triple Axel jump at the World Championships. Susanna Driano won Italy's first medal in the ladies event at the World Championships.

The ISU made the unprecedented decision to ban all Soviet judges from officiating at international competitions for a full year, citing persistent national bias exhibited over the last four seasons. This landmark ruling highlighted a pervasive issue within international figure skating during the 1970s. ISU historian Benjamin T. Wright noted, "The rule in question [by which the Soviets were banned] provided that if the Judges of a Member had proved to be unsatisfactory or incompetent for several years, although the Member had been warned, it would lose the right to nominate judges for Championships. The theory behind the rule... is that since the Member is responsible for the training and knowledge of its Judges, it is also responsible for their performance."

The ISU also placed a "temporary restriction of not taking part in ISU Championships" on the South African Ice Skating Association, barring South African skaters from participating due to the country's apartheid policies.

Sources: The Montreal Gazette, March 8, 1978; The Ottawa Citizen, March 13, 1978; Skating magazine, April and May 1978; Programme, 1978 World Figure Skating Championships; 100th Anniversary 1892-1992 - International Skating Union: Results 1968-1991 Figure Skating Championships, Elemér Terták, Benjamin T. Wright, Beat Häsler, 1992, courtesy World Figure Skating Museum & Hall of Fame

1979 WORLD FIGURE SKATING CHAMPIONSHIPS
Vienna, Austria, March 13-18, 1979

World Men's Figure Skating Championships:

	CF	SP	FS
1. Vladimir Kovalev (SOV)	2	1	4
2. Robin Cousins (GRB)	5	3	1
3. Jan Hoffmann (GDR)	1	5	3
4. Charles Tickner (USA)	4	4	2
5. Scott Cramer (USA)	8	2	6
6. Fumio Igarashi (JPN)	10	8	5
7. Jean-Christophe Simond (FRA)	6	12	7
8. David Santee (USA)	3	13	10

9. Mitsuru Matsumura (JPN)	11	10	8
10. Igor Bobrin (SOV)	7	11	12
11. Konstantin Kokora (SOV)	12	6	13
12. Hermann Schulz (GDR)	13	9	11
13. Brian Pockar (CAN)	**14**	**7**	**14**
14. Mario Liebers (GDR)	9	14	15
15. Vern Taylor (CAN)	**20**	**15**	**9**
16. Norbert Schramm (FRG)	15	16	19
17. Thomas Öberg (SWE)	18	17	16
18. Helmut Kristofics-Binder (AUT)	16	20	18
19. Jozef Sabovčík (CZE)	17	18	20
20. Christopher Howarth (GRB)	21	19	17
21. William Schober (AUS)	19	22	21
22. Matjaž Krušec (YUG)	22	21	22

World Ladies Figure Skating Championships:

	CF	SP	FS
1. Linda Fratianne (USA)	3	1	1
2. Anett Pötzsch (GDR)	1	5	3
3. Emi Watanabe (JPN)	4	2	4
4. Dagmar Lurz (FRG)	2	4	8
5. Denise Biellmann (SUI)	11	10	2
6. Lisa-Marie Allen (USA)	8	7	5
7. Claudia Kristofics-Binder (AUT)	5	6	9
8. Susanna Driano (ITA)	6	3	14
9. Carola Weißenberg (GDR)	9	21	7
10. Kristiina Wegelius (FIN)	7	8	18
11. Carrie Rugh (USA)	12	11	11
12. Sanda Dubravčić (YUG)	21	9	6
13. Natalia Strelkova (SOV)	14	20	15
14. Debbie Cottrill (GRB)	10	16	20
15. Karin Riediger (FRG)	15	12	16
16. Renata Baierová (CZE)	18	15	13
17. Petra Ernert (FRG)	19	19	12
18. Kira Ivanova (SOV)	29	13	10
19. Janet Morrissey (CAN)	**17**	**17**	**17**
20. Reiko Kobayashi (JPN)	13	18	21
21. Jeanne Chapman (NOR)	16	14	19

22. Anita Siegfried (SUI)	22	28	24
23. Astrid Jansen in de Wal (NED)	23	24	26
24. Franca Bianconi (ITA)	26	23	22
25. Bodil Olsson (SWE)	30	26	23
26. Corinne Wyrsch (SUI)	24	22	28
27. Myo-sil Kim (PRK)	27	25	25
28. Belinda Coulthard (AUS)	25	27	27
29. Katie Symmonds (NZL)	28	29	29
30. Hea-sook Shin (KOR)	29	30	31
31. Gloria Mas Gil (ESP)	31	31	30

World Pairs Skating Championships:

	SP	FS
1. Tai Babilonia/Randy Gardner (USA)	1	1
2. Marina Cherkasova/Sergei Shakhrai (SOV)	2	2
3. Sabine Baeß/Tassilo Thierbach (GDR)	4	3
4. Irina Vorobieva/Igor Lisovski (SOV)	3	4
5. Marina Pestova/Stanislav Leonovich (SOV)	5	5
6. Vicki Heasley/Robert Wagenhoffer (USA)	6	6
7. Cornelia Haufe/Kersten Bellmann (GDR)	7	10
8. Christina Riegel/Andreas Nischwitz (FRG)	9	8
9. Sheryl Franks/Michael Botticelli (USA)	8	9
10. Kerstin Stolfig/Veit Kempe (GDR)	11	7
11. Barbara Underhill/Paul Martini (CAN)	**10**	**11**
12. Gabriele Beck/Jochen Stahl (FRG)	14	12
13. Elizabeth Cain/Peter Cain (AUS)	12	13
14. Kyoko Hagiwara/Hisao Ozaki (JPN)	13	14

World Ice Dancing Championships:

	C/OSP	FD
1. Natalia Linichuk/Gennadi Karponosov (SOV)	1	1
2. Krisztina Regőczy/András Sallay (HUN)	2	2
3. Irina Moiseeva/Andrei Minenkov (SOV)	3	3
4. Liliana Řeháková/Stanislav Drastich (CZE)	4	4
5. Janet Thompson/Warren Maxwell (GRB)	5	5
6. Lorna Wighton/John Dowding (CAN)	**6**	**6**
7. Susi Handschmann/Peter Handschmann (AUT)	7	7
8. Jayne Torvill/Christopher Dean (GRB)	8	8

9. Stacey Smith/John Summers (USA)	9	10
10. Natalia Bestemianova/Andrei Bukin (SOV)	11	9
11. Carol Fox/Richard Dalley (USA)	10	11
12. Henriette Fröschl/Christian Steiner (FRG)	12	12
13. Karen Barber/Nicky Slater (GRB)	13	13
14. Anna Pisánská/Jiří Musil (CZE)	14	14
15. P. Fletcher/M. de la Penotiere (CAN)	**15**	**15**
16. Martine Olivier/Yves Tarayre (FRA)	16	16
17. Jindra Holá/Karol Foltán (CZE)	18	17
18. Gabriella Remport/Sándor Nagy (HUN)	17	18
19. Yumiko Kage/Tadayuki Takahashi (JPN)	19	19
20. Claudia Koch/Peter Schübl (AUT)	20	20

Tai Babilonia made history as the first biracial skater to win a gold medal at the World Figure Skating Championships. Babilonia and partner Randy Gardner were the first Americans to win the pairs event at the World Championships in 29 years.

Emi Watanabe made history as the first Japanese skater to win a medal in the ladies event at the World Championships. Myo-sil Kim made history as the first skater to represent the Democratic People's Republic of Korea (North Korea) at the World Championships.

Hungary suspended Visa requirements for border crossings the day of the free dance, allowing hundreds of Hungarians to come to Vienna to cheer on Krisztina Regőczy and András Sallay.

Sources: Skating magazine, May 1979; 100th Anniversary 1892-1992 - International Skating Union: Results 1968-1991 Figure Skating Championships, Elemér Terták, Benjamin T. Wright, Beat Häsler, 1992, courtesy World Figure Skating Museum & Hall of Fame

Katarina Witt, World Champion 1984-1985 and 1987-1988. PCN Photography / Alamy Stock Photo.

Jayne Torvill and Christopher Dean. World Champions 1981-1984. Photo courtesy Paul Dean, Ice Skate magazine. Used with permission.

THE DECADE OF DECADENCE

1980 WORLD FIGURE SKATING CHAMPIONSHIPS
Dortmund, West, Germany, March 11-16, 1980

World Men's Figure Skating Championships:

	CF	SP	FS
1. Jan Hoffmann (GDR)	1	2	2
2. Robin Cousins (GRB)	5	1	1
3. Charles Tickner (USA)	3	7	3
4. David Santee (USA)	2	3	6
5. Scott Hamilton (USA)	8	5	4
6. Mitsuru Matsumura (JPN)	9	6	5
7. Igor Bobrin (SOV)	6	4	8
8. Fumio Igarashi (JPN)	13	10	7
9. Brian Pockar (CAN)	**10**	**9**	**10**
10. Hermann Schulz (GDR)	7	8	11
11. Rudi Cerne (FRG)	12	11	9
12. Mario Liebers (GDR)	11	12	12
13. Jean-Christophe Simond (FRA)	4	14	16
14. Alexandr Fadeev (SOV)	16	15	14
15. Grzegorz Filipowski (POL)	18	13	13
16. Jozef Sabovčík (CZE)	14	16	15
17. William Schober (AUS)	19	19	17
18. Helmut Kristofics-Binder (AUT)	17	20	19
19. Thomas Öberg (SWE)	15	18	20
20. Eric Krol (BEL)	21	17	18
21. Miljan Begović (YUG)	20	21	21
22. Zhili Wang (CHN)	22	22	22

World Ladies Figure Skating Championships:

	CF	SP	FS
1. Anett Pötzsch (GDR)	1	6	2
2. Dagmar Lurz (FRG)	2	4	5

3. Linda Fratianne (USA)	4	3	1
4. Emi Watanabe (JPN)	5	2	3
5. Claudia Kristofics-Binder (AUT)	3	7	9
6. Denise Biellmann (SUI)	10	1	6
7. Lisa-Marie Allen (USA)	8	5	8
8. Kristiina Wegelius (FIN)	6	11	12
9. Debbie Cottrill (GRB)	9	8	14
10. Katarina Witt (GDR)	20	9	7
11. Elaine Zayak (USA)	22	10	4
12. Sanda Dubravčić (YUG)	12	12	11
13. Carola Weißenberg (GDR)	13	14	13
14. Tracey Wainman (CAN)	**21**	**17**	**10**
15. Sonja Stanek (AUT)	16	22	16
16. Renata Baierová (CZE)	23	19	15
17. Susan Broman (FIN)	17	16	18
18. Anne-Sophie de Kristoffy (FRA)	14	21	19
19. Christina Riegel (FRG)	18	26	17
20. Yoko Yakushi (JPN)	25	18	21
21. Reiko Kobayashi (JPN)	19	25	22
22. Anita Siegfried (SUI)	26	23	20
23. Bodil Olsson (SWE)	28	24	23
24. Belinda Coulthard (AUS)	27	27	24
25. Rudina Pasveer (NED)	24	28	26
26. Barbara Toffolo (ITA)	30	29	27
27. Hanne Gamborg (DEN)	29	31	25
28. Hea-sook Shin (KOR)	31	32	28
29. Zhiying Liu (CHN)	32	30	29
WD. Danielle Rieder (SUI)	7	13	-
WD. Elena Vodorezova (SOV)	11	15	-
WD. Karin Riediger (FRG)	15	20	-
WD. Susanna Driano (ITA)	-	-	-

World Pairs Skating Championships:

	SP	FS
1. Marina Cherkasova/Sergei Shakhrai (SOV)	1	1
2. Manuela Mager/Uwe Bewersdorf (GDR)	2	2
3. Marina Pestova/Stanislav Leonovich (SOV)	3	3
4. Sabine Baeß/Tassilo Thierbach (GDR)	4	4

5. Christina Riegel/Andreas Nischwitz (FRG)	6	5
6. Veronika Pershina/Marat Akbarov (SOV)	5	7
7. Kitty Carruthers/Peter Carruthers (USA)	8	6
8. Ingrid Spieglová/Alan Spiegl (CZE)	7	8
9. Cornelia Haufe/Kersten Bellmann (GDR)	9	10
10. Sheryl Franks/Michael Botticelli (USA)	10	11
11. Barbara Underhill/Paul Martini (CAN	11	9
12. Yukiko Okabe/Takashi Mura (JPN)	12	13
13. Susan Garland/Robert Daw (GRB)	13	12
14. Elizabeth Cain/Peter Cain (AUS)	14	14
15. Bo Luan/Bin Yao (CHN)	15	15

World Ice Dancing Championships:

	C/OSP	FD
1. Krisztina Regőczy/András Sallay (HUN)	2	1
2. Natalia Linichuk/Gennadi Karponosov (SOV)	1	3
3. Irina Moiseeva/Andrei Minenkov (SOV)	3	2
4. Jayne Torvill/Christopher Dean (GRB)	4	4
5. Lorna Wighton/John Dowding (CAN)	**5**	**6**
6. Judy Blumberg/Michael Seibert (USA)	6	5
7. N. Karamysheva/R. Sinitsyn (SOV)	7	7
8. Stacey Smith/John Summers (USA)	8	8
9. Henriette Fröschl/Christian Steiner (FRG)	9	9
10. Karen Barber/Nicky Slater (GRB)	10	10
11. Jana Beránková/Jan Barták (CZE)	11	11
12. Nathalie Hervé/Pierre Béchu (FRA)	12	12
13. Marie McNeil/Rob McCall (CAN)	**13**	**13**
14. Jindra Holá/Karol Foltán (CZE)	14	15
15. Noriko Sato/Tadeyuki Takahashi (JPN)	15	14
16. Gabriella Remport/Sándor Nagy (HUN)	16	16
17. Paola Casalotti/Sergio Ceserani (ITA)	17	17

Krisztina Regőczy and András Sallay made history as the first Hungarian team to capture gold medals in the ice dance event at the World Figure Skating Championships.

Zhili Wang, Zhiying Liu and Bo Luan and Bin Yao made history as the first skaters from China to participate in the World

Championships.

Grzegorz Filipowski made history as the first skater to land a triple/triple combination at the World Championships.

Sources: Skating magazine, April and May 1980; 100th Anniversary 1892-1992 - International Skating Union: Results 1968-1991 Figure Skating Championships, Elemér Terták, Benjamin T. Wright, Beat Häsler, 1992, courtesy World Figure Skating Museum & Hall of Fame; ; The BBC Book of Skating, Sandra Stevenson, 1984

1981 WORLD FIGURE SKATING CHAMPIONSHIPS
Hartford, United States, March 3-8, 1981

World Men's Figure Skating Championships:

	CF	SP	FS
1. Scott Hamilton (USA)	4	1	1
2. David Santee (USA)	2	3	3
3. Igor Bobrin (SOV)	5	4	2
4. Fumio Igarashi (JPN)	6	2	4
5. Jean-Christophe Simond (FRA)	1	5	6
6. Brian Orser (CAN)	**9**	**6**	**5**
7. Norbert Schramm (FRG)	7	7	7
8. Brian Pockar (CAN)	**3**	**8**	**11**
9. Vladimir Kotin (SOV)	10	10	10
10. Robert Wagenhoffer (USA)	14	12	8
11. Grzegorz Filipowski (POL)	8	11	12
12. Jozef Sabovčík (CZE)	11	9	13
13. Falko Kirsten (GDR)	15	14	9
14. Thomas Öberg (SWE)	12	13	14
15. Takashi Mura (JPN)	17	15	15
16. Bruno Watschinger (AUT)	13	16	17
17. Christopher Howarth (GRB)	18	18	16
18. Michael Pasfield (AUS)	19	17	18
19. Todd Sand (DEN)	20	19	19
20. Zhaoxiao Xu (CHN)	21	20	20
WD. Miljan Begović (YUG)	-	-	-

World Ladies Figure Skating Championships:

	CF	SP	FS
1. Denise Biellmann (SUI)	4	2	1
2. Elaine Zayak (USA)	7	3	2
3. Claudia Kristofics-Binder (AUT)	1	6	5
4. Debbie Cottrill (GRB)	2	8	4
5. Katarina Witt (GDR)	11	1	3
6. Kristiina Wegelius (FIN)	3	5	7
7. Priscilla Hill (USA)	5	10	9
8. Carola Paul (GDR)	16	7	6
9. Karin Riediger (FRG)	9	14	8
10. Tracey Wainman (CAN)	**6**	**15**	**10**
11. Sanda Dubravčić (YUG)	8	12	12
12. Kira Ivanova (SOV)	13	4	13
13. Manuela Ruben (FRG)	17	9	11
14. Anne-Sophie de Kristoffy (FRA)	15	11	16
15. Karen Wood (GRB)	18	16	14
16. Andrea Rohm (AUT)	14	18	17
17. Reiko Kobayashi (JPN)	10	13	22
18. Catarina Lindgren (SWE)	19	20	15
19. Corinne Wyrsch (SUI)	20	22	18
20. Sonja Stanek (AUT)	12	19	24
21. Masako Kato (JPN)	21	23	19
22. Editha Dotson (BEL)	23	17	21
23. Päivi Nieminen (FIN)	25	21	20
24. Vicki Maree Holland (AUS)	26	26	23
25. Rudina Pasveer (NED)	22	27	26
26. Lisa Coppola (ITA)	27	24	25
27. Hanne Gamborg (DEN)	24	25	27
28. Hye-kyung Lim (KOR)	28	28	28
29. Rosario Esteban (ESP)	30	31	29
30. Denyse Adam (NZL)	29	30	30
31. Zhenghua Bao (CHN)	31	29	31
WD. Anett Pötzsch (GDR)	-	-	-

World Pairs Skating Championships:

	SP	FS
1. Irina Vorobieva/Igor Lisovski (SOV)	1	1
2. Sabine Baeß/Tassilo Thierbach (GDR)	2	2
3. Christina Riegel/Andreas Nischwitz (FRG)	4	3
4. Marina Cherkasova/Sergei Shakhrai (SOV)	3	4
5. Kitty Carruthers/Peter Carruthers (USA)	7	5
6. Veronika Pershina/Marat Akbarov (SOV)	5	6
7. Barbara Underhill/Paul Martini (CAN)	**10**	**7**
8. Susan Garland/Robert Daw (GRB)	8	8
9. Birgit Lorenz/Knut Schubert (GDR)	6	9
10. Lea Ann Miller/Bill Fauver (USA)	9	10
11. Bo Luan/Bin Yao (CHN)	11	11

World Ice Dancing Championships:

	C/OSP	FD
1. Jayne Torvill/Christopher Dean (GRB)	1	1
2. Irina Moiseeva/Andrei Minenkov (SOV)	2	2
3. Natalia Bestemianova/Andrei Bukin (SOV)	4	3
4. Judy Blumberg/Michael Seibert (USA)	3	4
5. Olga Volozhinskaya/Aleksandr Svinin (SOV)	6	5
6. Carol Fox/Richard Dalley (USA)	5	6
7. Karen Barber/Nicky Slater (USA)	7	7
8. Nathalie Hervé/Pierre Béchu (FRA)	9	8
9. Jana Beránková/Jan Barták (CZE)	8	9
10. Birgit Goller/Peter Klisch (FRG)	10	10
11. Wendy Sessions/Stephen Williams (GRB)	11	11
12. Kelly Johnson/Kris Barber (CAN)	**13**	**12**
13. Marie McNeil/Robert McCall (CAN)	**12**	**13**
14. Judit Péterfy/Csaba Bálint (HUN)	14	14
15. Elisabetta Parisi/Roberto Pelizzola (ITA)	15	15
16. Noriko Sato/Tadayuki Takahashi (JPN)	17	16
17. Gabriella Remport/Sándor Nagy (HUN)	16	17
18. Maria Kniffer/Manfed Hübler (AUT)	19	18
19. Karen Mankovich/Douglas Mankovich (BEL)	18	21
20. Marianne van Bommel/Wayne Deweyert (NED)	21	19
21. Petra Born/Rainer Schönborn (FRG)	20	20
WD. Natalia Linichuk/Gennadi Karponosov (SOV)	-	-

The 6.0 judging system was reworked by the ISU, with each segment of the competition judged separately, factored and totaled to determine the final placements.

Denise Biellmann made history as the first skater from Switzerland to win a gold medal in the ladies event at the World Figure Skating Championships.

Foreshadowing a major trend in the years to come, there was a significant presence of skaters representing countries where they were not born. The ISU's criteria at the time was a six-month period of residence in the country a skater represented and approval of the sponsor country. Americans Todd Sand, Lisa Coppola, Editha Dotson and Karen and Douglas Mankovich represented Denmark, Italy and Belgium. Canadians Marianne van Bommel and Wayne Deweyert represented The Netherlands.

Sources: The Hartford Courant, February 27, March 3 and March 5, 1981; The Guardian, March 3, 1981; The Record, March 6, 1981; Skating magazine, May 1981; Canadian Skater magazine, May/June 1981; 100th Anniversary 1892-1992 - International Skating Union: Results 1968-1991 Figure Skating Championships, Elemér Terták, Benjamin T. Wright, Beat Häsler, 1992, courtesy World Figure Skating Museum & Hall of Fame

1982 WORLD FIGURE SKATING CHAMPIONSHIPS
Copenhagen, Denmark, March 9-14, 1982

World Men's Figure Skating Championships:

	CF	SP	FS
1. Scott Hamilton (USA)	2	1	1
2. Norbert Schramm (FRG)	6	2	2
3. Brian Pockar (CAN)	**5**	**7**	**4**
4. Brian Orser (CAN)	**12**	**3**	**3**
5. Jean-Christophe Simond (FRA)	1	8	8
6. Robert Wagenhoffer (USA)	9	4	5
7. Igor Bobrin (SOV)	4	9	6
8. David Santee (USA)	3	16	7
9. Fumio Igarashi (JPN)	8	14	9

10. Alexandr Fadeev (SOV)	15	6	10
11. Vladimir Kotin (SOV)	11	12	12
12. Takashi Mura (JPN)	14	11	11
13. Grzegorz Filipowski (POL)	10	13	13
14. Philippe Paulet (FRA)	7	15	15
15. Rudi Cerne (FRG)	16	5	14
16. Jozef Sabovčík (CZE)	13	10	16
17. Didier Monge (FRA)	19	17	17
18. Mitsuru Matsumura (JPN)	18	18	18
19. Lars Åkesson (SWE)	17	20	21
20. Thomas Hlavik (AUT)	21	19	20
21. Mark Pepperday (GRB)	27	25	19
22. Todd Sand (DEN)	22	21	25
23. Bruno Delmaestro (ITA)	24	28	22
24. Richard Furrer (SUI)	25	23	24
25. Miljan Begović (YUG)	20	24	29
26. Michael Pasfield (AUS)	26	22	27
27. Zhaoxiao Xu (CHN)	30	29	23
28. Eric Krol (BEL)	23	27	28
29. Edward van Campen (NED)	28	26	26
30. Fernando Soria (ESP)	29	30	30

World Ladies Figure Skating Championships:

	CF	SP	FS
1. Elaine Zayak (USA)	4	10	1
2. Katarina Witt (GDR)	9	1	2
3. Claudia Kristofics-Binder (AUT)	1	9	4
4. Claudia Leistner (FRG)	14	2	3
5. Elena Vodorezova (SOV)	5	3	8
6. Rosalynn Sumners (USA)	11	4	5
7. Vikki de Vries (USA)	8	7	6
8. Kay Thomson (CAN)	**6**	**6**	**9**
9. Kristiina Wegelius (FIN)	2	5	12
10. Debbie Cottrill (GRB)	3	8	17
11. Carola Paul (GDR)	13	12	10
12. Janina Wirth (GDR)	12	13	11
13. Elizabeth Manley (CAN)	**23**	**11**	**7**
14. Sanda Dubravčić (YUG)	10	14	19

15. Manuela Ruben (FRG)		18	19	13
16. Sandra Cariboni (SUI)		15	20	16
17. Karen Wood (GRB)		22	18	14
18. Sonja Stanek (AUT)		7	15	25
19. Catarina Lindgren (SWE)		25	17	15
20. Myriam Oberwiler (SUI)		20	21	18
21. Béatrice Farinacci (FRA)		16	26	20
22. Mariko Yoshida (JPN)		21	23	22
23. Diana Rankin (GRB)		19	16	28
24. Parthena Sarafidis (AUT)		24	27	21
25. Hanne Gamborg (DEN)		26	24	23
26. Karin Telser (ITA)		17	25	29
27. Vicki Maree Holland (AUS)		30	22	24
28. Liisa Seitsonen (FIN)		29	28	26
29. Li Scha Wang (NED)		28	31	27
30. Katrien Pauwels (BEL)		27	29	32
31. Rosario Esteban (ESP)		32	30	30
32. Zhenghua Bao (CHN)		34	32	31
33. Hye-kyung Lim (KOR)	33	33	33	
WD. Denyse Adam (NZL)		31	-	-

World Pairs Skating Championships:

	SP	FS
1. Sabine Baeß/Tassilo Thierbach (GDR)	1	1
2. Marina Pestova/Stanislav Leonovich (SOV)	2	2
3. Kitty Carruthers/Peter Carruthers (USA)	4	3
4. Barbara Underhill/Paul Martini (CAN)	**5**	**4**
5. Irina Vorobieva/Igor Lisovski (SOV)	3	5
6. Veronika Pershina/Marat Akbarov (SOV)	6	6
7. Birgit Lorenz/Knut Schubert (GDR)	7	7
8. Lea Ann Miller/Bill Fauver (USA)	9	8
9. Lorri Baier/Lloyd Eisler (CAN)	**8**	**9**
10. Maria DiDomenico/Burt Lancon (USA)	10	10
11. Bettina Hage/Stefan Zins (FRG)	12	11
12. Nathalie Tortel/Xavier Videau (FRA)	11	12
13. Bo Luan/Bin Yao (CHN)	13	13

World Ice Dancing Championships:

	C/OSP	FD
1. Jayne Torvill/Christopher Dean (GRB)	1	1
2. Natalia Bestemianova/Andrei Bukin (SOV)	2	2
3. Irina Moiseeva/Andrei Minenkov (SOV)	4	3
4. Judy Blumberg/Michael Seibert (USA)	3	4
5. Carol Fox/Richard Dalley (USA)	5	5
6. Olga Volozhinskaya/Aleksandr Svinin (SOV)	6	6
7. Karen Barber/Nicky Slater (GRB)	7	8
8. Elisa Spitz/Scott Gregory (USA)	9	7
9. Jana Beránková/Jan Barták (CZE)	8	9
10. Tracy Wilson/Rob McCall (CAN)	**10**	**10**
11. Nathalie Hervé/Pierre Béchu (FRA)	11	11
12. Birgit Goller/Peter Klisch (FRG)	13	12
13. Wendy Sessions/Stephen Williams (GRB)	12	13
14. Petra Born/Rainer Schönborn (FRG)	14	14
15. Noriko Sato/Tadayuki Takahashi (JPN)	16	15
16. Marianne van Bommel/Wayne Deweyert (NED)	15	16
17. Martine Olivier/Philippe Boissier (FRA)	18	17
18. Graziella Ferpozzi/Marco Ferpozzi (SUI)	19	18
19. Saila Saarinen/Kim Jacobson (FIN)	20	19
20. Ulla Örnmarker/Thomas Svedberg (SWE)	21	20
WD. Isabella Micheli/Roberto Pelizzola (ITA)	17	-

For the first time in 18 years, the Soviet Union did not win a gold medal at the World Figure Skating Championships.

Sabine Baeß and Tassilo Thierbach made history as the first and only East German team to win a gold medal in the pairs event at the World Figure Skating Championships.

Saila Saarinen and Kim Jacobson and Ulla Örnmarker and Thomas Svedberg made history as the first ice dance teams from Finland and Sweden to participate in the World Championships.

Elaine Zayak landed a record six triple jumps in her free skate to make a remarkable comeback and win the ladies title. However, her repetition of the triple toe-loop and triple Salchow led the ISU to release a communication which limited the repetition of triple jumps. The rule change also required greater variety in spins and footwork. In skating circles, ISU Communication No. 596 was dubbed "The Zayak Rule".

A trial judging system was tested in Copenhagen. Singles disciplines had two judging panels. One panel judged men's figures and short and the ladies free skate; the other ladies figures and short and men's long. Pairs and dance also had two panels — one for the short program or compulsory dances and OSP, and another for the finals. The trial aimed to reduce bloc judging, but judges complained of an uneven distribution of assignments. The ISU concluded that the trial did not significantly impact competition results.

Sources: Skating magazine, April and May 1982; Canadian Skater magazine, May/June 1982; 100th Anniversary 1892-1992 - International Skating Union: Results 1968-1991 Figure Skating Championships, Elemér Terták, Benjamin T. Wright, Beat Häsler, 1992, courtesy World Figure Skating Museum & Hall of Fame

1983 WORLD FIGURE SKATING CHAMPIONSHIPS
Helsinki, Finland, March 7-13, 1983

World Men's Figure Skating Championships:

	CF	SP	FS
1. Scott Hamilton (USA)	2	1	1
2. Norbert Schramm (FRG)	4	3	3
3. Brian Orser (CAN)	**8**	**2**	**2**
4. Alexandr Fadeev (SOV)	6	4	4
5. Jean-Christophe Simond (FRA)	1	5	7
6. Jozef Sabovčík (CZE)	3	9	5
7. Brian Boitano (USA)	9	7	6
8. Heiko Fischer (FRG)	5	8	9
9. Vladimir Kotin (SOV)	7	6	10
10. Rudi Cerne (FRG)	10	11	8
11. Laurent Depouilly (FRA)	12	13	11
12. Falko Kirsten (GDR)	14	10	12

13. Gary Beacom (CAN)		**11**	**17**	**14**
14. Mark Cockerell (USA)		19	12	13
15. Lars Åkesson (SWE)		13	14	17
16. Miljan Begović (YUG)		15	15	16
17. Masaru Ogawa (JPN)		17	16	15
18. Shinji Someya (JPN)		16	18	19
19. Thomas Hlavik (AUT)		18	21	18
20. Mark Pepperday (GRB)		21	19	20
21. Cameron Medhurst (AUS)		20	20	21
22. Fernando Soria (ESP)	22	22	22	

World Ladies Figure Skating Championships:

	CF	SP	FS1	FS2
1. Rosalynn Sumners (USA)	1	4	1	-
2. Claudia Leistner (FRG)	5	2	3	-
3. Elena Vodorezova (SOV)	3	3	4	-
4. Katarina Witt (GDR)	8	1	2	-
5. Anna Kondrashova (SOV)	9	5	5	-
6. Kristiina Wegelius (FIN) 2	9	9	-	
7. Kay Thomson (CAN)	**6**	**11**	**6**	**-**
8. Manuela Ruben (FRG)	7	10	8	-
9. Tiffany Chin (USA)	14	6	7	-
10. Sandra Cariboni (SUI)	4	16	12	-
11. Janina Wirth (GDR)	15	7	10	-
12. Charlene Wong (CAN)	**13**	**8**	**11**	**-**
13. Sanda Dubravčić (YUG)	11	13	13	-
14. Sonja Stanek (AUT)	10	17	14	-
15. Katrien Pauwels (BEL) 12	20	15	-	
16. Karin Telser (ITA)	21	12	-	3
17. Catarina Lindgren (SWE)	18	15	-	5
18. Juri Ozawa (JPN)	24	18	-	1
19. Susan Jackson (GRB)	25	14	-	2
20. Hanne Gamborg (DEN)	19	19	-	6
21. Elise Ahonen (FIN)	22	22	-	4
22. Li Scha Wang (NED)	20	23	-	7
23. Alison Southwood (GRB)	16	27	-	8
24. Béatrice Farinacci (FRA)	17	24	-	9
25. Susanne Gschwend (AUT)	23	26	-	10

26. Vicki Maree Holland (AUS)	26	21	-	11
27. Rosario Esteban (ESP)	28	25	-	12
WD. Hye-kyung Lim (KOR)		27	28	-	-
WD. Elaine Zayak (USA)	-	-	-	-

World Pairs Skating Championships:

	SP	FS
1. Elena Valova/Oleg Vasiliev (SOV)	2	1
2. Sabine Baeß/Tassilo Thierbach (GDR)	1	2
3. Barbara Underhill/Paul Martini (CAN)	**3**	**3**
4. Kitty Carruthers/Peter Carruthers (USA)	5	4
5. Veronika Pershina/Marat Akbarov (SOV)	6	5
6. Marina Pestova/Stanislav Leonovich (SOV)	4	7
7. Lea Ann Miller/Bill Fauver (USA)	8	6
8. Birgit Lorenz/Knut Schubert (GDR)	7	7
9. Cynthia Coull/Mark Rowsom (CAN)	**9**	**9**
10. Katherina Matousek/Lloyd Eisler (CAN)	**10**	**10**
11. Jill Watson/Burt Lancon (USA)	11	11
12. Babette Preußler/Torsten Ohlow (GDR)	12	12
13. Susan Garland/Ian Jenkins (GRB)	14	13
14. Toshimi Ito/Takashi Mura (JPN)	13	14
15. Jana Havlová/René Novotný (CZE)	15	15
16. Claudia Massari/Leonardo Azzola (FRG)	16	16
17. Maija Pekkala/Pekka Pekkala (FIN)	17	17

World Ice Dancing Championships:

	CD	OSP	FD
1. J. Torvill/C. Dean (GRB)	1	1	1
2. N. Bestemianova/A. Bukin (SOV)	3	3	2
3. Judy Blumberg/Michael Seibert (USA)	2	2	3
4. O. Volozhinskaya/A. Svinin (SOV)	5	4	4
5. Karen Barber/Nicky Slater (GRB)	4	8	5
6. Tracy Wilson/Rob McCall (CAN)	**7**	**5**	**6**
7. Elisa Spitz/Scott Gregory (USA)	6	6	7
8. Elena Batanova/Alexei Soloviev (SOV)	8	7	8
9. Petra Born/Rainer Schönborn (FRG)	10	9	9
10. Kelly Johnson/John Thomas (CAN)	**13**	**11**	**10**
11. I. Micheli/R. Pelizzola (ITA)	12	10	11

12. W. Sessions/S. Williams (GRB)	11	12	12
13. Judit Péterfy/Csaba Bálint (HUN)	14	14	13
14. N. Sato/T. Takahashi (JPN)	15	13	14
15. M. van Bommel/W. Deweyert (NED)	16	15	15
16. Kathrin Beck/Christoff Beck (AUT)	17	16	16
17. C. Schmidlin/D. Schmidlin (SUI)	18	17	17
18. H. Boyanova/Y. Ivanov (BUL)	19	18	18
WD. Nathalie Hervé/ Pierre Béchu (FRA)	9	-	-

Jayne Torvill and Christopher Dean broke all previous records when they received seven perfect 6.0s for their OSP and 6.0s from every judge for their free dance. Torvill and Dean also received an astonishing seventeen 5.9s across the three compulsory dances - nine for the Argentine Tango, six for the Ravensburger Waltz, and two for the Quickstep. The latter achievement was particularly noteworthy, given that judges were typically very stingy with their marks in the compulsory dances.

Ice dancers Hristina Boyanova and Yavor Ivanov made history as the first skaters to represent Bulgaria at the World Figure Skating Championships.

A new 'B' group was created for skaters who ranked outside the top 16 based on the combined scores of the compulsory figures and short program in the ladies event.

During a tour of the Helsinki Jäähalli for a visiting TV crew, Finnish skating official Jane Erkko was asked about the name of the seating area where skaters receive their scores. She referred to it as the 'Kiss and Cry' and the term became part of the skating lexicon.

Sources: Skating magazine, April and May 1983; 100th Anniversary 1892-1992 - International Skating Union: Results 1968-1991 Figure Skating Championships, Elemér Terták, Benjamin T. Wright, Beat Häsler, 1992, courtesy World Figure Skating Museum & Hall of Fame; Cracked Ice: Figure Skating's Inner World, Sonia Bianchetti Garbato, 2004

1984 WORLD FIGURE SKATING CHAMPIONSHIPS
Ottawa, Canada, March 20-25, 1984

World Men's Figure Skating Championships:

	CF	SP	FS1	FS2
1. Scott Hamilton (USA)	1	1	2	-
2. Brian Orser (CAN)	**7**	**2**	**1**	**-**
3. Alexandr Fadeev (SOV)	5	3	3	-
4. Jozef Sabovčík (CZE)	4	4	4	-
5. Rudi Cerne (FRG)	2	5	5	-
6. Brian Boitano (USA)	6	6	7	-
7. Heiko Fischer (FRG)	3	8	9	-
8. Vladimir Kotin (SOV)	9	7	6	-
9. Gordon Forbes (CAN)	**10**	**9**	**8**	**-**
10. Gary Beacom (CAN)	**11**	**10**	**10**	**-**
11. Grzegorz Filipowski (POL)	12	12	12	-
12. Fernand Fédronic (FRA)	8	11	15	-
13. Mark Cockerell (USA)	13	13	13	-
14. Masaru Ogawa (JPN)	16	16	11	-
15. Didier Monge (FRA)	14	14	14	-
16. Petr Barna (CZE)	17	15	-	1
17. Thomas Hlavik (AUT)	15	20	-	2
18. Alessandro Riccitelli (ITA)	19	19	-	3
19. Miljan Begović (YUG)	18	17	-	5
20. Paul Robinson (GRB)	22	21	-	4
21. András Száraz (HUN)	20	22	-	6
22. Perry Meek (AUS)	23	18	-	7
23. Lars Dresler (DEN)	21	24	-	8
24. Fernando Soria (ESP)	24	23	-	9
25. Jae-hyung Cho (KOR)	25	25	-	10
WD. Norbert Schramm (FRG)	-	-	-	-

World Ladies Figure Skating Championships:

	CF	SP	FS
1. Katarina Witt (GDR)	1	1	1
2. Anna Kondrashova (SOV)	4	2	3
3. Elaine Zayak (USA)	9	5	2
4. Kira Ivanova (SOV)	2	3	7

5. Kay Thomson (CAN)	7	6	5
6. Manuela Ruben (FRG)	3	7	8
7. Midori Ito (JPN)	16	4	4
8. Elizabeth Manley (CAN)	**13**	**9**	**6**
9. Sanda Dubravčić (YUG)	6	11	10
10. Sandra Cariboni (SUI)	5	14	15
11. Myriam Oberwiler (SUI)	17	10	11
12. Susan Jackson (GRB)	15	8	13
13. Karin Telser (ITA)	10	15	14
14. Constanze Gensel (GDR)	20	13	9
15. Katrien Pauwels (BEL)	12	16	16
16. Parthena Sarafidis (AUT)	8	17	19
17. Agnès Gosselin (FRA)	19	20	12
18. Cornelia Tesch (FRG)	11	12	20
19. Elise Ahonen (FIN)	18	18	17
20. Susanna Peltola (FIN)	14	19	21
21. Tamara Téglássy (HUN)	21	22	18
22. Diana Zovko-Nicolic (AUS)	23	21	22
23. Hyi-sung Kim (KOR)	22	23	23
WD. Rosalynn Sumners (USA)	-	-	-
WD. Tiffany Chin (USA)	-	-	-

World Pairs Skating Championships:

	SP	FS
1. Barbara Underhill/Paul Martini (CAN)	**2**	**1**
2. Elena Valova/Oleg Vasiliev (SOV)	1	2
3. Sabine Baeß/Tassilo Thierbach (GDR)	4	3
4. Larisa Selezneva/Oleg Makarov (SOV)	3	4
5. Katherina Matousek/Lloyd Eisler (CAN)	**5**	**5**
6. Birgit Lorenz/Knut Schubert (GDR)	8	6
7. Cynthia Coull/Mark Rowsom (CAN)	**7**	**7**
8. Veronika Pershina/Marat Akbarov (SOV)	6	8
9. Babette Preußler/Tobias Schröter (GDR)	11	9
10. Lea Ann Miller/Bill Fauver (USA)	9	10
WD. Claudia Massari/Leonardo Azzola (FRG)	10	-
WD. Jill Watson/Burt Lancon (USA)	12	-
WD. Kitty Carruthers/Peter Carruthers (USA)	-	-

World Ice Dancing Championships:

	CD	OSP	FD
1. J. Torvill/C. Dean (GRB)	1	1	1
2. N. Bestemianova/A. Bukin (SOV)	2	3	2
3. Judy Blumberg/Michael Seibert (USA)	3	2	3
4. M. Klimova/S. Ponomarenko (SOV)	4	4	4
5. Karen Barber/Nicky Slater (GRB)	5	5	5
6. Tracy Wilson/Rob McCall (CAN)	**6**	**8**	**6**
7. Elena Batanova/Alexei Soloviev (SOV)	7	7	7(t)
8. Carol Fox/Richard Dalley (USA)	8	6	7(t)
9. Petra Born/Rainer Schönborn (FRG)	9	9	9
10. Elisa Spitz/Scott Gregory (USA)	10	11	10
11. Kelly Johnson/John Thomas (CAN)	**12**	**10**	**11**
12. W. Sessions/S. Williams (GRB)	11	12	12
13. I. Micheli/R. Pelizzola (ITA)	13	13	13
14. M. van Bommel/W. Deweyert (NED)	14	14	14
15. A. Becherer/F. Becherer (FRG)	15	15	15
16. Kathrin Beck/Christoff Beck (AUT)	16	16	16
17. N. Sato/T. Takahashi (JPN)	17	17	17
18. Klára Engi/Attila Tóth (HUN)	18	18	18
19. Salome Brunner/Markus Merz (SUI)	20	19	19
20. M. Olivier/P. Boissier (FRA)	19	20	20
21. Liane Telling/Michael Fisher (AUS)	21	21	21

Barbara Underhill and Paul Martini were the first Canadians to win gold medals in the pairs event at the World Championships in 22 years.

In the men's event, Norbert Schramm, who finished eleventh and fourteenth in the first two compulsory figures, withdrew mid-way through the first phase of the competition in protest. Schamm had been fourth the year prior. The quality of his figures hadn't declined, but he had fallen out of favour with the West German Federation.

The free dance was delayed by six hours due to a power failure at the Ottawa Civic Centre. Jayne Torvill and Christopher Dean broke their own record from 1983, earning 29 perfect 6.0s - ten more than they earned at the 1984 Winter Olympics in Sarajevo. A perfect 6.0 had never before been awarded in the compulsory dances and Torvill and Dean received seven. Liane Telling and Michael Fisher made history as the first Australian ice dance team to compete at the World Championships.

Sources: Skating magazine, April and May 1984; 100th Anniversary 1892-1992 - International Skating Union: Results 1968-1991 Figure Skating Championships, Elemér Terták, Benjamin T. Wright, Beat Häsler, 1992, courtesy World Figure Skating Museum & Hall of Fame

1985 WORLD FIGURE SKATING CHAMPIONSHIPS
Tokyo, Japan, March 3-10, 1985

World Men's Figure Skating Championships:

	CF	SP	SF	FS
1. Alexandr Fadeev (SOV)	1	1	-	1
2. Brian Orser (CAN)	**4**	**2**	**-**	**2**
3. Brian Boitano (USA)	5	4	-	3
4. Jozef Sabovčík (CZE)	2	3	-	6
5. Vladimir Kotin (SOV)	6	5	-	4
6. Heiko Fischer (FRG)	8	8	-	5
7. Grzegorz Filipowski (POL)	7	6	-	7
8. Mark Cockerell (USA)	16	7	-	8
9. Viktor Petrenko (SOV)	12	13	-	9
10. Neil Paterson (CAN)	**15**	**12**	**-**	**11**
11. Richard Zander (FRG)	11	11	-	14
12. Falko Kirsten (GDR)	19	10	1	10
13. Petr Barna (CZE)	18	9	-	12
14. Masaru Ogawa (JPN)	14	14	-	13
15. Fernand Fédronic (FRA)	3	18	-	18
16. Lars Åkesson (SWE)	9	15	-	17
17. Gordon Forbes (CAN)	**13**	**16**	**-**	**16**
18. Cameron Medhurst (AUS)	17	17	2	15
19. Oliver Höner (SUI)	10	22	-	19
20. Alessandro Riccitelli (ITA)	20	21	3	20
21. Stephen Pickavance (GRB)	23	20	4	-
22. Oula Jääskeläinen (FIN)	21	19	7	-

23. Zhaoxiao Xu (CHN)	24	23	5	-
24. Lars Dresler (DEN)	22	24	6	-
25. Jae-hyung Cho (KOR)	25	25	8	-
26. Fernando Soria (ESP)	26	26	9	-
27. Cheuk-fai Lai (HKG)	27	27	10	-

World Ladies Figure Skating Championships:

	CF	SP	SF	FS
1. Katarina Witt (GDR)	3	1	-	1
2. Kira Ivanova (SOV)	1	3	-	2
3. Tiffany Chin (USA)	2	2	-	3
4. Anna Kondrashova (SOV)	4	4	-	5
5. Debi Thomas (USA)	7	5	-	4
6. Claudia Leistner (FRG)	5	11	-	6
7. Natalia Lebedeva (SOV)	8	7	-	8
8. Agnès Gosselin (FRA)	9	13	-	10
9. Elizabeth Manley (CAN)	**10**	**10**	**-**	**12**
10. Cynthia Coull (CAN)	**18**	**8**	**-**	**9**
11. Constanze Gensel (FRG)	21	9	1	7
12. Patricia Neske (FRG)	11	17	-	11
13. Susan Jackson (GRB)	14	12	-	13
14. Simone Koch (GDR)	17	6	-	15
15. Elise Ahonen (FIN)	13	18	-	16
16. Claudia Villiger (SUI)	12	15	-	18
17. Sandra Cariboni (SUI)	6	19	-	20
18. Masako Kato (JPN)	14	14	-	19
19. Lotta Falkenbäck (SWE)	19	22	2	14
20. Tamara Téglássy (HUN)	16	20	3	17
21. Hye-kyung Lim (KOR)	23	16	4	-
22. Amanda James (AUS)	20	24	6	-
23. Yibing Jiang (CHN)	24	21	5	-
24. Petya Gavazova (BUL)	25	23	7	-
25. Marta Olozagarre (ESP)	22	25	8	-
26. Shuk-ching Ngai (HKG)	26	26	9	-
WD. Midori Ito (JPN)	-	-	-	-
WD. Katrien Pauwels (BEL)	-	-	-	-

World Pairs Skating Championships:

	SP	FS
1. Elena Valova/Oleg Vasiliev (SOV)	2	1
2. Larisa Selezneva/Oleg Makarov (SOV)	1	2
3. Katherina Matousek/Lloyd Eisler (CAN)	**3**	**3**
4. Jill Watson/Peter Oppegard (USA)	6	4
5. Melinda Kunhegyi/Lyndon Johnston (CAN)	**7**	**5**
6. Veronika Pershina/Marat Akbarov (SOV)	5	6
7. Cynthia Coull/Mark Rowsom (CAN)	**4**	**7**
8. Manuela Landgraf/Ingo Steuer (GDR)	8	8
9. Natalie Seybold/Wayne Seybold (USA)	9	9
10. Claudia Massari/Daniele Caprano (FRG)	10	10
11. Danielle Carr/Stephen Carr (AUS)	12	11
12. Fan Jun/Sun Jihong (CHN)	11	12
13. Shuk-ling Ngai/Kwok-yung Mak (HKG)	13	13

World Ice Dancing Championships:

	CD	OSP	FD
1. N. Bestemianova/A. Bukin (SOV)	1	1	1
2. M. Klimova/S. Ponomarenko (SOV)	2	2	2
3. Judy Blumberg/Michael Seibert (USA)	3	3	3
4. Tracy Wilson/Rob McCall (CAN)	**4**	**4**	**4**
5. Petra Born/Rainer Schönborn (FRG)	5	5	5
6. Karen Barber/Nicky Slater (GRB)	6	6	6
7. N. Annenko/G. Sretenski (SOV)	7	7	7
8. I. Micheli/R. Pelizzola (ITA)	8	9	8
9. Kathrin Beck/Christoff Beck (AUT)	9	8	9
10. K. Garossino/R. Garossino (CAN)	**10**	**10**	**10**
11. Renée Roca/Donald Adair (USA)	11	11	11
12. S. Semanick/S. Gregory (USA)	12	12	12
13. N. Sato/T. Takahashi (JPN)	13	13	13
14. Klára Engi/Attila Tóth (HUN)	14	14	14
15. Sharon Jones/Paul Askham (GRB)	16	16	15
16. A. Becherer/F. Becherer (FRG)	15	15	16
17. M. Olivier/P. Boissier (FRA)	17	17	17
18. Luyang Liu/Xiaolei Zhao (CHN)	19	19	18
19. L. Telling/M. Fisher (AUS)	18	18	19

Tiffany Chin made history as the first Asian American skater to win a medal in the ladies event at the World Figure Skating Championships.

Cheuk-fai Lai, Shuk-ching Ngai and Kwok-yung Mak made history as the first skaters to represent Hong Kong at the World Championships. China's Luyang Liu and Xiaolei Zhao became the first Chinese team to compete in the ice dance event. Petya Gavazova made history as the first Bulgarian skater to compete in the ladies event.

After the singles short programs, the 17 skaters with the highest combined ranking qualified for the final. The remaining skaters competed in a semi-final, with the top 3 skaters earning the right to qualify for the free skating final.

Sources: USA Today, March 6 and 8, 1985; The Salt Lake Tribune, March 7, 1985; Skating magazine, April and May 1985; 100th Anniversary 1892-1992 - International Skating Union: Results 1968-1991 Figure Skating Championships, Elemér Terták, Benjamin T. Wright, Beat Häsler, 1992, courtesy World Figure Skating Museum & Hall of Fame

1986 WORLD FIGURE SKATING CHAMPIONSHIPS
Geneva, Switzerland, March 18-23, 1985

World Men's Figure Skating Championships:

	CF	SP	SF	FS
1. Brian Boitano (USA)	4	5	-	1
2. Brian Orser (CAN)	**5**	**1**	**-**	**2**
3. Alexandr Fadeev (SOV)	1	2	-	5
4. Vladimir Kotin (SOV)	9	3	-	3
5. Viktor Petrenko (SOV)	7	6	-	4
6. Jozef Sabovčík (CZE)	2	4	-	9
7. Heiko Fischer (FRG)	3	7	-	10
8. Daniel Doran (USA)	10	9	-	6
9. Scott Williams (USA)	11	8	-	7
10. Masaru Ogawa (JPN)	16	11	-	8
11. Richard Zander (FRG)	6	12	-	14

12. Falko Kirsten (GDR)	14	13	-	11
13. Grzegorz Filipowski (POL)	12	10	-	15
14. Oliver Höner (SUI)	13	16	-	13
15. Laurent Depouilly (FRA)	8	17	-	18
16. Petr Barna (CZE)	19	18	1	12
17. Lars Åkesson (SWE)	15	14	-	20
18. Neil Paterson (CAN)	**17**	**15**	**-**	**19**
19. Lars Dresler (DEN)	21	19	2	17
20. Jaimee Eggleton (CAN)	**24**	**20**	**3**	**16**
21. Alessandro Riccitelli (ITA)	20	21	5	-
22. Cameron Medhurst (AUS)	18	22	6	-
23. Thomas Hlavik (AUT)	23	23	4	-
24. Oula Jääskeläinen (FIN)	25	26	7	-
25. Miljan Begović (YUG)	22	28	8	-
26. András Száraz (HUN)	27	25	9	-
27. Boyko Aleksiev (BUL)	26	27	10	-
28. Fernando Soria (ESP)	28	24	11	-
WD. Wojciech Gwinner (POL)	-	-	-	-
WD. Sung-jin Byun (KOR)	-	-	-	-

World Ladies Figure Skating Championships:

	CF	SP	SF	FS
1. Debi Thomas (USA)	2	1	-	2
2. Katarina Witt (GDR)	3	4	-	1
3. Tiffany Chin (USA)	4	2	-	4
4. Kira Ivanova (SOV)	1	6	-	8
5. Elizabeth Manley (CAN)	**11**	**7**	**-**	**3**
6. Claudia Leistner (FRG)	9	5	-	6
7. Anna Kondrashova (SOV)	6	2	-	9
8. Caryn Kadavy (USA)	7	9	-	7
9. Tracey Wainman (CAN)	**5**	**11**	**-**	**11**
10. Natalia Lebedeva (SOV)	8	10	-	10
11. Midori Ito (JPN)	19	8	-	5
12. Simone Koch (GDR)	16	13	-	12
13. Agnès Gosselin (FRA)	13	18	-	13
14. Katrien Pauwels (BEL)	10	15	-	18
15. Susanne Becher (FRG)	12	20	-	15
16. Claudia Villiger (SUI)	14	12	-	17

17. Constanze Gensel (GDR)	23	19	2	14
18. Tamara Téglássy (HUN)	22	17	1	16
19. Elise Ahonen (FIN)	17	21	4	19
20. Beatrice Gelmini (ITA)	21	14	5	-
21. Željka Čižmešija (YUG)	15	22	6	-
22. Lotta Falkenbäck (SWE)	20	23	3	-
23. Pauline Lee (TPE)	24	24	8	-
24. Hye-kyung Lim (KOR)	26	25	7	-
25. Sandra Escoda (ESP)	25	27	9	-
26. Petya Gavazova (BUL)	27	26	10	-
WD. Susan Jackson (GRB)	18	16	-	-

World Pairs Skating Championships:

	SP	FS
1. Ekaterina Gordeeva/Sergei Grinkov (SOV)	1	1
2. Elena Valova/Oleg Vasiliev (SOV)	2	2
3. Cynthia Coull/Mark Rowsom (CAN)	**4**	**3**
4. Larisa Selezneva/Oleg Makarov (SOV)	3	4
5. Denise Benning/Lyndon Johnston (CAN)	**6**	**6**
6. Jill Watson/Peter Oppegard (USA)	9	5
7. Gillian Wachsman/Todd Waggoner (USA)	5	7
8. Natalie Seybold/Wayne Seybold (USA)	8	8
9. Katrin Kanitz/Tobias Schröter (GDR)	7	9
10. Lenka Knapová/René Novotný (CZE)	10	10
11. Manuela Landgraf/Ingo Steuer (GDR)	11	11
12. Cheryl Peake/Andrew Naylor (GRB)	12	12
13. Kerstin Kimminus/Stefan Pfrengle (FRG)	14	13
14. Danielle Carr/Stephen Carr (AUS)	13	14
15. Sylvie Vaquero/Didier Manaud (FRA)	15	15
WD. Marianne Ocvirek/Holger Maletz (FRG)	-	-

World Ice Dancing Championships:

	CD	OSP	SF	FD
1. Bestemianova/Bukin (SOV)	1	2	-	1
2. Klimova/Ponomarenko (SOV)	2	1	-	2
3. Wilson/McCall (CAN)	**4**	**4**	**-**	**3**
4. Annenko/Sretenski (SOV)	3	3	-	4
5. Semanick/Gregory (USA)	5	5	-	5

6. Roca/Adair (USA)	6	6	-	6
7. Beck/Beck (AUT)	7	7	-	7
8. Becherer/Becherer (FRG)	8	8	-	8
9. Garossino/Garossino (CAN)	**9**	**9**	**-**	**9**
10. Micheli/Pelizzola (ITA)	10	10	-	10
11. Engi/Tóth (HUN)	11	11	-	11
12. Duchesnay/Duchesnay (FRA)	12	12	-	12
13. Jones/Askham (GRB)	13	14	-	13
14. Tanaka/Suzuki (JPN)	14	13	-	14
15. Calegari/Camerlengo (ITA)	15	16	-	15
16. Coates/Abretti (GRB)	16	15	-	16
17. Weppelmann/Schamber. (FRG)	17	17	-	17
18. Schmidlin/Schmidlin (SUI)	18	18	1	18
19. MacDonald/Clarke (AUS)	19	19	2	19
20. Boyanova/Ivanov (BUL)	20	20	3	20
21. Peltola/Jacobson (FIN)	21	21	4	-
22. Park/Han (KOR)	22	22	5	-

Debi Thomas made history as the first skater of colour to win a gold medal in the ladies event at the World Figure Skating Championships.

Kyeung-sook Park and Seung-jong Han made history as the first South Korean ice dance team to compete at the World Championships. Pauline Lee made make history as the first skater to represent Taiwan (Chinese Taipei) at the Worlds. The ISU took special measures to avoid causing issues with China, announcing Lee as a representative of the Republic of Taipei and not Taiwan. A special flag and athem were created for Taipei especially for the event.

Sources: Journal du Jura, March 20, 1986; Le nouvelliste, March 21 and 22, 1986; Skating magazine, March and April 1986; 100th Anniversary 1892-1992 - International Skating Union: Results 1968-1991 Figure Skating Championships, Elemér Terták, Benjamin T. Wright, Beat Häsler, 1992, courtesy World Figure Skating Museum & Hall of Fame; Skate Magazine Yearbook, 1986

1987 WORLD FIGURE SKATING CHAMPIONSHIPS
Cincinnati, Ohio, March 9-14, 1987

World Men's Figure Skating Championships:

	CF	SP	FS
1. Brian Orser (CAN)	**3**	**1**	**1**
2. Brian Boitano (USA)	2	2	2
3. Alexandr Fadeev (SOV)	1	3	3
4. Vladimir Kotin (SOV)	4	5	6
5. Grzegorz Filipowski (POL)	7	6	5
6. Viktor Petrenko (SOV)	5	4	7
7. Christopher Bowman (USA)	11	9	4
8. Petr Barna (CZE)	10	7	9
9. Richard Zander (FRG)	6	11	12
10. Scott Williams (USA)	9	8	13
11. Makoto Kano (JPN)	17	10	8
12. Masaru Ogawa (JPN)	12	14	10
13. Falko Kirsten (GDR)	13	16	11
14. Oliver Höner (SUI)	8	17	16
15. Kurt Browning (CAN)	**14**	**19**	**14**
16. Lars Dresler (DEN)	20	13	15
17. Paul Robinson (GRB)	18	12	18
18. Philippe Roncoli (FRA)	15	20	17
19. Alessandro Riccitelli (ITA)	16	15	21
20. Michael Slipchuk (CAN)	**19**	**21**	**20**
21. Peter Johansson (SWE)	25	18	19
22. Cameron Medhurst (AUS)	23	23	22
23. Oula Jääskeläinen (FIN)	22	24	23
24. Oliver Dechert (FRG)	21	25	24
25. Boyko Aleksiev (BUL)	26	22	-
26. Tomislav Čižmešija (YUG)	24	26	-
27. Chi-man Wong (HKG)	27	27	-
WD. Ralph Burghart (AUT)	-	-	-
WD. András Száraz (HUN)	-	-	-

World Ladies Figure Skating Championships:

	CF	SP	FS
1. Katarina Witt (GDR)	5	1	1
2. Debi Thomas (USA)	2	7	2
3. Caryn Kadavy (USA)	4	5	3
4. Elizabeth Manley (CAN)	**6**	**2**	**6**
5. Kira Ivanova (SOV)	1	6	9
6. Claudia Leistner (FRG)	3	8	8
7. Jill Trenary (USA)	11	4	5
8. Midori Ito (JPN)	14	3	4
9. Anna Kondrashova (SOV)	7	9	7
10. Joanne Conway (GRB)	10	12	10
11. Patricia Schmidt (CAN)	**8**	**10**	**12**
12. Susanne Becher (FRG)	9	18	11
13. Claudia Villiger (SUI)	12	14	13
14. Agnès Gosselin (FRA)	13	16	14
15. Iveta Voralová (CZE)	18	13	15
16. Željka Čižmešija (YUG)	16	19	17
17. Beatrice Gelmini (ITA)	22	15	16
18. Tracy-Lee Brook (AUS)	20	17	18
19. Elina Hänninen (FIN)	19	21	20
20. Yvonne Pokorny (AUT)	17	22	21
21. Hélène Persson (SWE)	23	20	19
22. Hyun-jung Chi (KOR)	21	23	22
23. Sandra Escoda (ESP)	25	24	23
24. Pauline Lee (TPE)	24	26	-
26. Petya Gavazova (BUL)	26	25	-
27. Edith Poon (HKG)	27	27	-
WD. Tamara Téglássy (HUN)	15	11	-
WD. Tiia-Riikka Pietikäinen (FIN)	-	-	-

World Pairs Skating Championships:

	SP	FS
1. Ekaterina Gordeeva/Sergei Grinkov (SOV)	1	1
2. Elena Valova/Oleg Vasiliev (SOV)	2	2
3. Jill Watson/Peter Oppegard (USA)	3	3
4. Larisa Selezneva/Oleg Makarov (SOV)	7	4
5. Denise Benning/Lyndon Johnston (CAN)	**6**	**5**

6. Cynthia Coull/Mark Rowsom (CAN)	4	6
7. Gillian Wachsman/Todd Waggoner (USA)	5	8
8. Christine Hough/Doug Ladret (CAN)	8	7
9. Cheryl Peake/Andrew Naylor (GRB)	9	9
10. Lenka Knapová/René Novotný (CZE)	10	10
11. Sonja Adalbert/Daniele Caprano (FRG)	12	11
12. Danielle Carr/Stephen Carr (AUS)	11	12
13. Shuk-ching Ngai/Cheuk-fai Lai (HKG)	13	13
WD. Katrin Kanitz/Tobias Schröter (GDR)	-	-

World Ice Dancing Championships:

	CD	OSP	FD
1. N. Bestemianova/A. Bukin (SOV)	1	2	1
2. M. Klimova/S. Ponomarenko (SOV)	2	1	2
3. Tracy Wilson/Rob McCall (CAN)	**3**	**3**	**3**
4. N. Annenko/G. Sretenski (SOV)	4	4	4
5. Suzanne Semanick/Scott Gregory (USA)	5	5	5
6. Kathrin Beck/Christoff Beck (AUT)	6	6	6
7. A. Becherer/F. Becherer (FRG)	7	7	7
8. Klára Engi/Attila Tóth (HUN)	8	8	8
9. I. Duchesnay/P. Duchesnay (FRA)	10	9	9
10. K. Garossino/R. Garossino (CAN)	**9**	**10**	**11**
11. L. Trovati/R. Pelizzola (ITA)	11	11	10
12. Susie Wynne/Joseph Druar (USA)	12	13	12
13. Sharon Jones/Paul Askham (GRB)	13	12	13
14. M. Malingambi/A. Gilardi (ITA)	14	14	14
15. H. Górna/A. Dostatni (POL)	16	16	15
16. Tomoko Tanaka/Hiroyuki Suzuki (JPN)	15	15	16
17. J-A. Borlase/S. Chalmers (CAN)	**17**	**17**	**17**
18. A. Weppelmann/H. Schamberger (FRG)	18	18	18
19. M. MacDonald/R. Clarke (AUS)	20	19	19
20. Susanna Rahkamo/Petri Kokko (FIN)	19	21	20
21. H. Boyanova/Y. Ivanov (BUL)	21	20	21
22. K-S. Park/S-J. Han (KOR)	22	22	22
WD. Viera Řeháková/Ivan Havránek (CZE)	-	-	-
WD. L-Y. Cheung/C-K. Chan (HKG)	-	-	-

The ISU discontinued the use of semi-finals and in singles, the results of the compulsory figures and short program were combined, with the short program used as an elimination point for advancement to the free skate.

Sources: Cincinnati Enquirer, March 7, 1987; Skating magazine, April and May 1987; 100th Anniversary 1892-1992 - International Skating Union: Results 1968-1991 Figure Skating Championships, Elemér Terták, Benjamin T. Wright, Beat Häsler, 1992, courtesy World Figure Skating Museum & Hall of Fame

1988 WORLD FIGURE SKATING CHAMPIONSHIPS
Budapest, Hungary, March 21-27, 1988

World Men's Figure Skating Championships:

	CF	SP	FS
1. Brian Boitano (USA)	3	1	2
2. Brian Orser (CAN)	**5**	**2**	**1**
3. Viktor Petrenko (SOV)	6	3	5
4. Grzegorz Filipowski (POL)	2	4	7
5. Christopher Bowman (USA)	7	9	4
6. Kurt Browning (CAN)	**12**	**7**	**3**
7. Heiko Fischer (FRG)	4	6	9
8. Petr Barna (CZE)	11	5	8
9. Paul Wylie (USA)	13	8	6
10. Vladimir Petrenko (SOV)	8	11	10
11. Cameron Medhurst (AUS)	14	10	11
12. Oliver Höner (SUI)	9	13	15
13. Neil Paterson (CAN)	**18**	**12**	**12**
14. Lars Dresler (DEN)	17	15	13
15. Paul Robinson (GRB)	19	14	14
16. Ralph Burghart (AUT)	10	25	20
17. Ronny Winkler (GDR)	23	17	16
18. Peter Johansson (SWE)	25	16	17
19. Daniel Weiss (FRG)	16	18	23
20. András Száraz (HUN)	22	22	18
21. Alessandro Riccitelli (ITA)	21	19	21
22. Oula Jääskeläinen (FIN)	27	21	19
23. Frédéric Lipka (FRA)	20	26	22

24. Tomislav Cizmesija (YUG)	24	28	-
25. David Liu (TPE)	28	24	-
26. Sung-il Jung (KOR)	26	27	-
27. Joaquín Guerrero (MEX)	30	23	-
28. Alexandre Geers (BEL)	29	29	-
WD. Makoto Kano (JPN)	15	20	-
WD. Alexandr Fadeev (SOV)	1	-	-
WD. Vladimir Kotin (SOV)	-	-	-

World Ladies Figure Skating Championships:

	CF	SP	FS
1. Katarina Witt (GDR)	1	2	1
2. Elizabeth Manley (CAN)	**2**	**4**	**2**
3. Debi Thomas (USA)	3	1	4
4. Claudia Leistner (FRG)	5	5	6
5. Jill Trenary (USA)	4	11	5
6. Midori Ito (JPN)	14	3	3
7. Caryn Kadavy (USA)	6	8	7
8. Simone Koch (GDR)	10	6	8
9. Natalia Lebedeva (SOV)	8	7	11
10. Joanne Conway (GRB)	7	10	12
11. Tamara Téglássy (HUN)	15	9	9
12. Marina Kielmann (FRG)	16	14	10
13. Yvonne Gómez (ESP)	11	16	13
14. Natalia Gorbenko (ESP)	9	17	15
15. Beatrice Gelmini (ITA)	12	15	16
16. Lotta Falkenbäck (SWE)	19	25	14
17. Charlene Wong (CAN)	**17**	**12**	**21**
18. Yvonne Pokorny (AUT)	22	13	20
19. Claude Péri (FRA)	24	18	17
20. Stefanie Schmid (SUI)	21	21	18
21. Junko Yaginuma (JPN)	18	26	19
22. Željka Čižmešija (YUG)	13	24	23
23. Mirela Gawłowska (POL)	20	23	22
24. Gina Fulton (GRB)	23	20	23
25. Tracy-Lee Brook (AUS)	26	19	-
26. Anisette Torp-Lind (DEN)	28	22	-
27. Jana Petrušková (CZE)	25	28	-

28. Elina Hänninen (FIN)	27	30	-
29. Hyun-Jung Chi (KOR)	30	27	-
30. Diana Marcos (MEX)	29	31	-
31. Asia Aleksieva (BUL)	31	29	-
WD. Kira Ivanova (SOV)	-	-	-
WD. Anna Kondrashova (SOV)	-	-	-

World Pairs Skating Championships:

	SP	FS
1. Elena Valova/Oleg Vasiliev (SOV)	2	1
2. Ekaterina Gordeeva/Sergei Grinkov (SOV)	1	2
3. Larisa Selezneva/Oleg Makarov (SOV)	3	3
4. Gillian Wachsman/Todd Waggoner (USA)	5	4
5. Denise Benning/Lyndon Johnston (CAN)	**6**	**5**
6. Jill Watson/Peter Oppegard (USA)	4	7
7. Isabelle Brasseur/Lloyd Eisler (CAN)	**7**	**6**
8. Mandy Wötzel/Axel Rauschenbach (GDR)	8	8
9. Christine Hough/Doug Ladret (CAN)	**9**	**9**
10. Natalie Seybold/Wayne Seybold (USA)	10	10
11. Lenka Knapová/René Novotný (CZE)	11	11
12. Cheryl Peake/Andrew Naylor (GRB)	12	12
13. Anuschka Gläser/Stefan Pfrengle (FRG)	13	13
14. Lisa Cushley/Neil Cushley (GRB)	14	14
15. Danielle Carr/Stephen Carr (AUS)	15	15
16. Akiko Nogami/Yoichi Yamazaki (JPN)	16	16

World Ice Dancing Championships:

	CD	OSP	FD
1. N. Bestemianova/A. Bukin (SOV)	1	1	1
2. M. Klimova/S. Ponomarenko (SOV)	2	2	2
3. Tracy Wilson/Rob McCall (CAN)	**3**	**3**	**3**
4. N. Annenko/G. Sretenski (SOV)	4	4	4
5. Kathrin Beck/Christoff Beck (AUT)	5	5	6
6. I. Duchesnay/P. Duchesnay (FRA)	7	6	5
7. Klára Engi/Attila Tóth (HUN)	6	8	7
8. A. Becherer/F. Becherer (FRG)	8	7	8
9. Susie Wynne/Joseph Druar (USA)	9	9	9
10. L. Trovati/R. Pelizzola (ITA)	10	10	10

11. K. Garossino/R. Garossino (CAN)	11	11	11
12. Sharon Jones/Paul Askham (GRB)	12	12	12
13. April Sargent/Russ Witherby (USA)	13	13	13
14. Viera Řeháková/Ivan Havránek (CZE)	14	14	14
15. M. Cole/M. Farrington (CAN)	15	15	15
16. D. Yvon/F. Palluel (FRA)	16	16	16
17. H. Górna/A. Dostatni (POL)	17	17	17
18. A. Weppelmann/H. Schamberger (FRG)	18	19	18
19. Tomoko Tanaka/Hiroyuki Suzuki (JPN)	19	18	19
20. Susanna Rahkamo/Petri Kokko (FIN)	20	20	20
21. K. Kerekes/C. Szentpéteri (HUN)	21	21	21
22. M. MacDonald/R. Clarke (AUS)	22	22	22
23. D. Schlegel/P. Brecht (SUI)	23	23	23
24. B. Pleninger/M. Steiner (AUT)	24	24	24
25. Yucca Liu/Jim Sun (TPE)	25	25	-
WD. S. Semanick/S. Gregory (USA) -	-	-	

Kurt Browning made history as the first skater to land a quadruple jump at the World Figure Skating Championships.

Joaquín Guerrero and Diana Marcos made history as the first skaters to represent Mexico at the World Figure Skating Championships. David Liu and Yucca Liu and Jim Sun were the first skaters to represent Chinese Taipei in the men's and ice dance events.

Sources: The Montreal Gazette, March 21, 1988; Skating magazine, April and May 1988; 100th Anniversary 1892-1992 - International Skating Union: Results 1968-1991 Figure Skating Championships, Elemér Terták, Benjamin T. Wright, Beat Häsler, 1992, courtesy World Figure Skating Museum & Hall of Fame

1989 WORLD FIGURE SKATING CHAMPIONSHIPS
Paris, France, March 14-19, 1989

World Men's Figure Skating Championships:

	CF	OP	FS
1. Kurt Browning (CAN)	5	1	1
2. Christopher Bowman (USA)	4	2	3
3. Grzegorz Filipowski (POL)	3	5	2
4. Alexandr Fadeev (SOV)	1	3	4
5. Petr Barna (CZE)	7	4	5
6. Viktor Petrenko (SOV)	2	6	6
7. Daniel Doran (USA)	6	11	7
8. Oliver Höner (SUI)	10	10	8
9. Michael Slipchuk (CAN)	**13**	**7**	**10**
10. Cameron Medhurst (AUS)	11	9	11
11. Makoto Kano (JPN)	18	8	9
12. Daniel Weiss (FRG)	9	16	12
13. Axel Médéric (FRA)	12	12	14
14. Dmitri Gromov (SOV)	14	15	13
15. András Száraz (HUN)	15	13	18
16. Mirko Eichhorn (GDR)	20	17	15
17. Ralph Burghart (AUT)	8	19	20
18. Alessandro Riccitelli (ITA)	17	20	16
19. Peter Johansson (SWE)	19	14	19
20. Henrik Walentin (DEN)	23	18	17
21. Christian Newberry (GRB)	16	25	-
22. Sung-il Jung (KOR)	22	21	-
23. Iwo Svec (FRG)	21	23	-
24. Oula Jääskeläinen (FIN)	25	22	-
25. David Liu (TPE)	26	24	-
26. Boyko Aleksiev (BUL)	24	26	-
27. Alexandre Geers (BEL)	27	27	-
WD. Ricardo Olavarrieta (MEX)	28	-	-

World Ladies Figure Skating Championships:

	CF	OP	FS
1. Midori Ito (JPN)	6	1	1
2. Claudia Leistner (FRG)	1	3	2

3. Jill Trenary (USA)	2	2	3
4. Patricia Neske (FRG)	5	6	6
5. Natalia Lebedeva (SOV)	3	4	8
6. Kristi Yamaguchi (USA)	12	5	4
7. Evelyn Großmann (GDR)	14	10	5
8. Natalia Gorbenko (SOV)	4	8	11
9. Beatrice Gelmini (ITA)	11	7	10
10. Surya Bonaly (FRA)	16	9	7
11. Karen Preston (CAN)	**17**	**11**	**9**
12. Simone Lang (GDR)	10	13	12
13. Yvonne Pokorny (AUT)	9	14	15
14. Tamara Téglássy (HUN)	13	16	14
15. Junko Yaginuma (JPN)	15	12	16
16. Charlene Wong (CAN)	**8**	**15**	**17**
17. Željka Čižmešija (YUG)	7	19	20
18. Yvonne Gómez (ESP)	24	20	13
19. Hélène Persson (SWE)	21	18	18
20. Petra Vonmoos (SUI)	22	17	19
21. Tracy-Lee Brook (AUS)	23	21	-
22. Lily Lyoonjung Lee (KOR)	20	25	-
23. Louisa Danskin (GRB)	19	27	-
24. Anisette Torp-Lind (DEN)	27	22	-
25. Jacqueline Soames (GRB)	26	23	-
26. Mari Niskanen (FIN)	25	24	-
27. Tsvetelina Yankova (BUL)	30	26	-
28. Diana Marcos (MEX)	28	28	-
29. Charuda Upatham (THA)	29	29	-
WD. Sandy Suy (BEL)	18	-	-

World Pairs Skating Championships:

	OP	FS
1. Ekaterina Gordeeva/Sergei Grinkov (SOV)	1	1
2. Cindy Landry/Lyndon Johnston (CAN)	**2**	**2**
3. Elena Bechke/Denis Petrov (SOV)	4	3
4. Peggy Schwarz/Alexander König (GDR)	3	5
5. Kristi Yamaguchi/Rudy Galindo (USA)	6	4
6. Elena Kvitchenko/Rashid Kadyrkaev (SOV)	5	7
7. Isabelle Brasseur/Lloyd Eisler (CAN)	**8**	**6**

8. Natalie Seybold/Wayne Seybold (USA)		6	8
9. Anuschka Gläser/Stefan Pfrengle (FRG)		9	9
10. Danielle Carr/Stephen Carr (AUS)		10	10
11. Cheryl Peake/Andrew Naylor (GRB)		11	11

World Ice Dancing Championships:

	CD	OSP	FD
1. M. Klimova/S. Ponomarenko (SOV)	1	1	1
2. Maya Usova/Alexandr Zhulin (SOV)	2	2	2
3. I. Duchesnay/P. Duchesnay (FRA)	3	5	3
4. Klára Engi/Attila Tóth (HUN)	4	3	4
5. Susie Wynne/Joseph Druar (USA)	5	4	5
6. L. Fedorinova/E. Platov (SOV)	6	6	6
7. S. Calegari/P. Camerlengo (ITA)	7	7	7
8. K. Garossino/R. Garossino (CAN)	**8**	**8**	**8**
9. Sharon Jones/Paul Askham (GRB)	9	9	9
10. A. Juklová/M. Šimeček (CZE)	11	10	10
11. M. McDonald/M. Mitchell (CAN)	**13**	**11**	**11**
12. D. Yvon/F. Palluel (FRA)	12	12	12
13. Susanna Rahkamo/Petri Kokko (FIN)	15	13	13
14. A. Weppelmann/H. Schamberger (FRG)	14	14	14
15. Anna Croci/Luca Mantovani (ITA)	17	15	15
16. M. Grajcar/A. Dostatni (POL)	16	16	16
17. K. Kerekes/C. Szentpéteri (HUN)	18	17	17
18. D. Gerencser/A. Stanislavov (SUI)	19	18	18
19. Kaoru Takino/Kenji Takino (JPN)	20	19	19
20. P. Zietemann/F. Ladd-Oshiro (FRG)	21	20	20
21. M. MacDonald/D. Smart (AUS)	22	21	-
22. Ursula Holik/Herbert Holik (AUT)	23	22	-
23. K-S. Park/S-J. Han (KOR)	24	23	-
24. P. Gavazova/N. Tonev (BUL)	25	24	-
WD. April Sargent/Russ Witherby (USA)	10	-	-

Midori Ito made history as the first Japanese skater to win a gold medal at the World Figure Skating Championships. She also made history as the first Japanese woman to land a triple Axel and earn a perfect mark of 6.0 at the World Championships.

Charuda Upatham made history as the first skater to represent Thailand at the World Championships.

Security measures at the Palais omnisports de Paris-Bercy were increased, including the use of bomb-sniffing dogs, following a series of troubling incidents seemingly aimed at North American visitors. A Canadian TV crew was attacked at knifepoint. American judge Joan Gruber fainted during the men's compulsory figures and had to be replaced. Gruber was under great strain. Her hotel room was ransacked twice in a 48-hour period. American skater April Sargent's dress was damaged in the dressing room. There were also rumours of bomb threats at the airport. Coach Phillip Mills was at the airport when security detonated two unattended suitcases. The incidents seemed to stop after the American Embassy intervened, but American skaters were instructed not to wear clothing with USA crests or insignia while in Paris.

Sources: The Toronto Star, March 15, 1989; The Baltimore Sun, March 15, 1989; Skating magazine, April and May, 1989; 100th Anniversary 1892-1992 - International Skating Union: Results 1968-1991 Figure Skating Championships, Elemér Terták, Benjamin T. Wright, Beat Häsler, 1992, courtesy World Figure Skating Museum & Hall of Fame

Michelle Kwan, World Champion 1996, 1998, 2000-2001 and 2003. UPI Photo / Tom Theobald / Alamy Stock Photo.

THE AGE OF GLOBALIZATION

1990 WORLD FIGURE SKATING CHAMPIONSHIPS
Halifax and Dartmouth, Nova Scotia, March 6-11, 1990

World Men's Figure Skating Championships:

	CF	OP	FS
1. Kurt Browning (CAN)	**2**	**2**	**1**
2. Viktor Petrenko (SOV)	3	1	2
3. Christopher Bowman (USA)	6	4	3
4. Grzegorz Filipowski (POL)	4	6	4
5. Todd Eldredge (USA)	7	3	7
6. Petr Barna (CZE)	5	9	5
7. Richard Zander (FRG)	1	7	10
8. Viacheslav Zagorodniuk (SOV)	10	5	9
9. Elvis Stojko (CAN)	**16**	**8**	**6**
10. Paul Wylie (USA)	8	14	8
11. Michael Slipchuk (CAN)	**14**	**10**	**11**
12. Cameron Medhurst (AUS)	12	11	12
13. Oliver Höner (SUI)	9	13	17
14. Philippe Candeloro (FRA)	19	12	15
15. Sung-il Jung (KOR)	18	15	14
16. Alessandro Riccitelli (ITA)	13	17	16
17. András Száraz (HUN)	15	16	18
18. Steven Cousins (GRB)	15	18	13
19. Ralph Burghart (AUT)	11	19	19
20. Oula Jaaskelainen (FIN)	17	21	20
21. Mirko Eichhorn (GDR)	22	20	-
22. Peter Johansson (SWE)	20	22	-
23. Lars Dresler (DEN)	21	24	-
24. Tatsuya Fujii (JPN)	24	26	-
25. Jan Erik Digernes (NOR)	30	23	-
26. Cornel Gheorghe (ROM)	28	25	-
27. Alcuin Schulten (NED)	23	29	-

28. David Liu (TPE)	27	28	-
29. Stephen Carr (AUS)	29	27	-
30. Alexandre Geers (BEL)	26	31	-
31. Alexander Mladenov (BUL)	31	30	-
WD. Pavel Vančo (CZE)	-	-	-

World Ladies Figure Skating Championships:

	CF	OP	FS
1. Jill Trenary (USA)	1	5	2
2. Midori Ito (JPN)	10	1	1
3. Holly Cook (USA)	4	3	4
4. Kristi Yamaguchi (USA)	9	2	3
5. Natalia Lebedeva (SOV)	2	4	6
6. Lisa Sargeant (CAN)	**7**	**6**	**5**
7. Patricia Neske (FRG)	3	8	7
8. Evelyn Großmann (GDR)	12	9	8
9. Surya Bonaly (FRA)	15	7	10
10. Marina Kielmann (FRG)	8	15	9
11. Tamara Téglássy (HUN)	11	11	13
12. Junko Yaginuma (JPN)	19	12	11
13. Beatrice Gelmini (ITA)	6	10	18
14. Yuka Sato (JPN)	16	16	12
15. Tanja Krienke (GDR)	13	20	14
16. Sabine Contini (ITA)	21	13	15
17. Lily Lyoonjung Lee (KOR)	18	14	16
18. Željka Čižmešija (YUG)	5	18	20
19. Hélène Persson (SWE)	14	23	17
20. Anisette Torp-Lind (DEN)	17	21	19
21. Laëtitia Hubert (FRA)	25	17	-
22. Emma Murdoch (GRB)	23	19	-
23. Mirjam Wehrli (SUI)	22	22	-
24. Marcela Kochollová (CZE)	20	24	-
25. Natalie Crothers (AUS)	24	27	-
26. Mari Niskanen (FIN)	26	26	-
27. Milena Marinovich (BUL)	29	25	-
28. Sandrine Goes (BEL)	27	28	-
29. Diana Marcos (MEX)	28	29	-
WD. Yvonne Pokorny (AUT)	-	-	-

WD. Natalia Skrabnevskaya (SOV)   -   -   -

World Pairs Skating Championships:

	OP	FS
1. Ekaterina Gordeeva/Sergei Grinkov (SOV)	1	1
2. **Isabelle Brasseur/Lloyd Eisler (CAN)**	**4**	**2**
3. Natalia Mishkutenok/Artur Dmitriev (SOV)	2	3
4. Larisa Selezneva/Oleg Makarov (SOV)	3	4
5. Kristi Yamaguchi/Rudy Galindo (USA)	5	5
6. **Christine Hough/Doug Ladret (CAN)**	**7**	**6**
7. Mandy Wötzel/Axel Rauschenbach (GDR)	6	7
8. Radka Kovaříková/René Novotný (CZE)	8	8
9. **Cindy Landry/Lyndon Johnston (CAN)**	**10**	**9**
10. Peggy Schwarz/Alexander König (FRG)	9	10
11. Natasha Kuchiki/Todd Sand (USA)	11	11
12. Anuschka Gläser/Stefan Pfrengle (FRG)	12	12
13. Sharon Carz/Doug Williams (USA)	13	13
14. Henriette Worner/Andreas Sigurdsson (FRG)	14	14
15. Catherine Barker/Michael Aldred (GRB)	16	15
16. Danielle Carr/Stephen Carr (AUS)	15	16
WD. Katarzyna Głowacka/Krzysztof Korcarz (POL)	-	-
WD. Svetlana Dragaeva/Karel Kovář (ISU)	-	-

World Ice Dancing Championships:

	CD	OD	FS
1. M. Klimova/S. Ponomarenko (SOV)	1	1	2
2. I. Duchesnay/P. Duchesnay (FRA)	3	2	1
3. Maya Usova/Alexandr Zhulin (SOV)	2	3	3
4. Susie Wynne/Joseph Druar (USA)	5	4	4
5. Oksana Grishuk/Evgeni Platov (SOV)	6	5	5
6. Susanna Rahkamo/Petri Kokko (FIN)	7	7	6
7. **Jo-Anne Borlase/Martin Smith (CAN)**	**8**	**8**	**7**
8. April Sargent/Russ Witherby (USA)	9	9	8
9. **M. McDonald/M. Mitchell (CAN)**	**10**	**10**	**9**
10. S. Calegari/P. Camerlengo (ITA)	11	11	10
11. I. Střondalová/M. Brzý (CZE)	13	12	11
12. I. Sarech/X. Debernis (FRA)	12	14	12
13. M. Grajcar/A. Dostatni (POL)	14	13	13

14. Anna Croci/Luca Mantovani (ITA)	15	15	14
15. M. Mandiková/O. Pekár (CZE)	16	16	15
16. R. Woodward/C. Szentpéteri (HUN)	17	17	16
17. Lynn Burton/Andrew Place (GRB)	20	19	17
18. C. Gauthier/A. Dalongeville (FRA)	18	18	19
19. Kaoru Takino/Kenji Takino (JPN)	19	20	18
20. Ann Hall/Jason Blomfield (GRB)	22	21	-
21. P. Zietemann/F. Ladd-Oshiro (FRG)	21	22	-
22. K. Kerekes/G. Kolescanszky (HUN)	23	23	-
23. D. Gerencser/B. Columberg (SUI)	24	24(t)	-
24. M. MacDonald/D. Smart (AUS)	25	24(t)	-
25. P. Gavazova/N. Tonev (BUL)	26	26	-
26. K-S. Park/S-J. Han (KOR)	27	27	-
WD. Klára Engi/Attila Tóth (HUN)	4	6	-
WD. M. Müksch/B. Hatzl (AUT)	-	-	-

Compulsory figures were skated for the final time at the World Figure Skating Championships at the Dartmouth Sportsplex, across the harbour from the Halifax Metro Centre where free skating events were held. David Liu skated the final figure in the men's event. Željka Čižmešija of Yugoslavia skated the final figure ever performed at the World Championships - a paragraph loop.

Sources: Skating magazine, May and June 1990; Protocol, 1990 World Figure Skating Championships; Media Information, 1990 World Figure Skating Championships; 100th Anniversary 1892-1992 - International Skating Union: Results 1968-1991 Figure Skating Championships, Elemér Terták, Benjamin T. Wright, Beat Häsler, 1992, courtesy World Figure Skating Museum & Hall of Fame

1991 WORLD FIGURE SKATING CHAMPIONSHIPS
Munich, Germany, March 12-17, 1991

World Men's Figure Skating Championships:

	OP	FS
1. Kurt Browning (CAN)	2	1
2. Viktor Petrenko (SOV)	1	2
3. Todd Eldredge (USA)	5	3

4. Petr Barna (CZE)	3	4
5. Christopher Bowman (USA)	4	5
6. Elvis Stojko (CAN)	**7**	**6**
7. Michael Slipchuk (CAN)	**8**	**8**
8. Alexei Urmanov (SOV)	6	9
9. Éric Millot (FRA)	9	10
10. Masakazu Kagiyama (JPN)	10	11
11. Paul Wylie (USA)	20	7
12. Oula Jääskeläinen (FIN)	13	13
13. Oliver Höner (SUI)	12	14
14. Sung-il Jung (KOR)	17	12
15. Mirko Eichhorn (GER)	11	15
16. Steven Cousins (GRB)	18	16
17. Cameron Medhurst (AUS)	16	18
18. Daniel Weiss (GER)	19	17
19. Gilberto Viadana (ITA)	15	19
20. Ronny Winkler (GER)	14	20
21. Ralph Burghart (AUT)	21	-
22. Viacheslav Zagorodniuk (SOV)	22	-
23. Cornel Gheorghe (ROM)	23	-
24. Jan Erik Digernes (NOR)	24	-
25. Henrik Walentin (DEN)	25	-
26. Péter Kovács (HUN)	26	-
27. David Liu (TPE)	27	-
28. Tomislav Čižmešija (YUG)	28	-
29. Maarten van Mechelen (LUX)	29	-
30. Jorge La Farga (ESP)	30	-
31. Nikolai Tonev (BUL)	31	-
32. Alexandre Geers (BEL)	32	-
33. Ricardo Olavarrieta (MEX)	33	-
WD. Christopher Blong (NZL)	-	-

World Ladies Figure Skating Championships:

	OP	FS
1. Kristi Yamaguchi (USA)	1	1
2. Tonya Harding (USA)	2	2
3. Nancy Kerrigan (USA)	5	3
4. Midori Ito (JPN)	3	4

5. Surya Bonaly (FRA)	4	6
6. Josée Chouinard (CAN)	**8**	**5**
7. Joanne Conway (GRB)	7	7
8. Marina Kielmann (GER)	6	8
9. Patricia Neske (GER)	9	9
10. Yulia Vorobieva (SOV)	12	11
11. Junko Yaginuma (JPN)	10	12
12. Lu Chen (CHN)	16	10
13. Simone Lang (GER)	11	13
14. Mari Asanuma (JPN)	13	14
15. Lenka Kulovaná (CZE)	15	15
16. Anisette Torp-Lind (DEN)	14	16
17. Zuzanna Szwed (POL)	19	17
18. Lisa Sargeant (CAN)	**18**	**18**
19. Natalia Gorbenko (SOV)	17	19
20. Lily Lyoonjung Lee (KOR)	20	20
21. Marion Krijgsman (NED)	21	-
22. Cathrin Degler (GER)	22	-
23. Tamara Téglássy (HUN)	23	-
24. Beatrice Gelmini (ITA)	24	-
25. Hélène Persson (SWE)	25	-
26. Laetitia Hubert (FRA)	26	-
27. Sabrina Tschudi (SUI)	27	-
28. Željka Čižmešija (YUG)	28	-
29. Mila Kajas (FIN)	29	-
30. Tamara Heggen (AUS)	30	-
31. Marta Andrade Vidal (ESP)	31	-
32. Milena Marinovich (BUL)	32	-
33. Anita Thorenfeldt (NOR)	33	-
34. Isabelle Balhan (BEL)	34	-
35. Christine Czerni (AUT)	35	-
36. Rosanna Blong (NZL)	36	-
37. Diana Marcos (MEX)	37	-

World Pairs Skating Championships:

	OP	FS
1. Natalia Mishkutenok/Artur Dmitriev (SOV)	2	1
2. Isabelle Brasseur/Lloyd Eisler (CAN)	**1**	**2**

3. Natasha Kuchiki/Todd Sand (USA)	4	3
4. Elena Bechke/Denis Petrov (SOV)	3	5
5. Evgenia Shishkova/Vadim Naumov (SOV)	7	4
6. Radka Kovaříková/René Novotný (CZE)	5	6
7. Peggy Schwarz/Alexander König (GER)	6	7
8. Stacey Ball/Jean-Michel Bombardier (CAN)	**8**	**8**
9. Calla Urbanski/Rocky Marval (USA)	9	10
10. Jenni Meno/Scott Wendland (USA)	12	9
11. Christine Hough/Doug Ladret (CAN)	**10**	**11**
12. Anuschka Gläser/Stefan Pfrengle (GER)	11	12
13. Cheryl Peake/Andrew Naylor (GRB)	13	13
14. Anna Gorecki/Arkadius Gorecki (GER)	18	14
15. Rena Inoue/Tomoaki Koyama (JPN)	16	15
16. Danielle Carr/Stephen Carr (AUS)	14	16
17. Anna Tabacchi/Massimo Salvade (ITA)	19	17
18. Saskia Bourgeois/Guy Bourgeois (SUI)	17	18
19. Katarzyna Głowacka/Krzysztof Korcarz (POL)	15	19

World Ice Dancing Championships:

	CD1	CD2	OD	FD
1. Duchesnay/Duchesnay (FRA)	3	3	1	1
2. Klimova/Ponomarenko (SOV)	2	2	3	2
3. Usova/Zhulin (SOV)	1	1	2	3
4. Grishuk/Platov (SOV)	5	4	4	4
5. Engi/Tóth (HUN)	4	5	5	5
6. Calegari/Camerlengo (ITA)	6	6	6	6
7. Rahkamo/Kokko (FIN)	8	8	7	7
8. Yvon/Palluel (FRA)	7	7	8	8
9. Sargent/Witherby (USA)	9	9	9	10
10. Petr/Janoschak (CAN)	**10**	**10**	**10**	**11**
11. Punsalan/Swallow (USA)	12	17	12	9
12. Mrázová/Šimeček (CZE)	11	13	11	12
13. Grajcar/Dostatni (POL)	13	12	13	13
14. Sarech/Debernis (FRA)	15	11	14	15
15. Croci/Mantovani (ITA)	14	14	16	14
16. McDonald/Smith (CAN)	**16**	**16**	**15**	**16**
17. Goolsbee/Schamberger (GER)	17	15	17	17
18. Hall/Blomfield (GRB)	19	19	19	18

19. Stähler/Authorsen (GER)	18	18	18	19
20. Gerencser/Columberg (SUI)	21	22	20	20
21. Takino/Takino (JPN)	20	20	21	-
22. Maritczak/Maritczak (AUT)	23	23	22	-
23. MacDonald/Smart (AUS)	22	21	23	-
24. Uski/Sasi (FIN)	24	24	24(t)	-
25. Hadjiiska/Nikolov (BUL)	25	25	24(t)	-
26. Park/You (KOR)	26	26	26	-

For the first time since the fall of The Berlin Wall, skaters from East and West Germany competed on one unified team and for the last time, the Soviet Union sent a team to the World Figure Skating Championships.

American women swept the podium for the first time at the World Figure Skating Championships and Kristi Yamaguchi made history as the first Asian American skater to win a gold medal in the ladies event. Canadian-born siblings Isabelle and Paul Duchesnay won France's first gold medal in ice dance at the World Championships.

Elvis Stojko made history as the first skater to land a quad jump in combination at the World Championships and Tonya Harding made history as the first North American woman to land a triple Axel at the World Championships.

Sources: Skating magazine, May and June 1991; 100th Anniversary 1892-1992 - International Skating Union: Results 1968-1991 Figure Skating Championships, Elemér Terták, Benjamin T. Wright, Beat Häsler, 1992, courtesy World Figure Skating Museum & Hall of Fame

1992 WORLD FIGURE SKATING CHAMPIONSHIPS
Oakland, United States, March 24-29, 1992

World Men's Figure Skating Championships:

	OP	FS
1. Viktor Petrenko (CIS)	1	1
2. Kurt Browning (CAN)	3	2
3. Elvis Stojko (CAN)	4	3

4. Christopher Bowman (USA)	5	5
5. Mark Mitchell (USA)	8	4
6. Petr Barna (CZE)	2	7
7. Todd Eldredge (USA)	6	6
8. Alexei Urmanov (CIS)	7	9
9. Philippe Candeloro (FRA)	15	8
10. Viacheslav Zagorodniuk (CIS)	12	10
11. Cornel Gheorghe (ROM)	10	11
12. Grzegorz Filipowski (POL)	11	12
13. Michael Slipchuk (CAN)	**9**	**16**
14. Konstantin Kostin (LAT)	16	14
15. Mirko Eichhorn (GER)	14	15
16. Steven Cousins (GRB)	21	13
17. Ralph Burghart (AUT)	17	18
18. Cameron Medhurst (AUS)	20	17
19. Masakazu Kagiyama (JPN)	13	21
20. Gilberto Viadana (ITA)	19	30
21. Michael Tyllesen (DEN)	18	22
22. Zhongyi Jiao (CHN)	23	20
23. Mitsuhiro Murata (JPN)	19	24
24. Jan Erik Digernes (NOR)	24	23
25. Oula Jääskeläinen (FIN)	25	-
26. Tomislav Čizmešija (CRO)	26	-
27. Péter Kovács (HUN)	27	-
28. Alex Chang (TPE)	28	-
29. Patrick Meier (SUI)	29	-
30. Ivan Dinev (BUL)	30	-
31. Christopher Blong (NZL)	31	-
32. Axel Médéric (FRA)	32	-
33. Se-yol Kim (KOR)	33	-
34. Jorge La Farga (ESP)	34	-
35. Dino Quattrocecere (SAF)	35	-

World Ladies Figure Skating Championships:

	OP	FS
1. Kristi Yamaguchi (USA)	1	1
2. Nancy Kerrigan (USA)	3	2
3. Lu Chen (CHN)	2	4

4. Laëtitia Hubert (FRA)	5	3
5. Josée Chouinard (CAN)	**6**	**5**
6. Tonya Harding-Gillooly (USA)	4	6
7. Alice Sue Claeys (BEL)	8	8
8. Yuka Sato (JPN)	11	7
9. Karen Preston (CAN)	**7**	**9**
10. Patricia Neske (GER)	9	10
11. Surya Bonaly (FRA)	10	12
12. Marina Kielmann (GER)	13	11
13. Tatiana Rachkova (CIS)	17	13
14. Joanne Conway (GRB)	12	16
15. Charlene von Saher (GRB)	15	15
16. Nathalie Krieg (SUI)	19	14
17. Krisztina Czakó (HUN)	16	17
18. Lily Lyoonjung Lee (KOR)	14	19
19. Junko Yaginuma (JPN)	18	18
20. Anisette Torp-Lind (DEN)	21	20
21. Irena Zemanová (CZE)	22	21
22. Hélène Persson (SWE)	23	22
23. Tamara Heggen (AUS)	20	24
24. Alma Lepina (LAT)	24	23
25. Mojca Kopač (SLO)	25	-
26. Yulia Vorobieva (CIS)	26	-
27. Viktoria Dimitrova (BUL)	27	-
28. Zuzanna Szwed (POL)	28	-
29. Marion Krijgsman (NED)	29	-
30. Olga Vassiljeva (EST)	30	-
31. Laia Papell (ESP)	31	-
32. Željka Čižmešija (CRO)	32	-
33. Margaret Schlater (ITA)	33	-
34. Mila Kajas (FIN)	34	-
35. Rosanna Blong (NZL)	35	-
36. Anita Thorenfeldt (NOR)	36	-
37. Edita Katkauskaite (LIT)	37	-
38. Janie Ja-lin Weng (TPE)	38	-
39. Juanita-Anne Yorke (SAF)	39	-
40. Lidija Hodzar (YUG)	40	-
WD. Midori Ito (JPN)	-	-

World Pairs Skating Championships:

		OP	FS
1.	Natalia Mishkutenok/Artur Dmitriev (CIS)	1	1
2.	Radka Kovaříková/René Novotný (CZE)	3	2
3.	**Isabelle Brasseur/Lloyd Eisler (CAN)**	**2**	**3**
4.	Elena Bechke/Denis Petrov (CIS)	6	4
5.	Evgenia Shishkova/Vadim Naumov (CIS)	4	5
6.	Peggy Schwarz/Alexander König (GER)	8	6
7.	Calla Urbanski/Rocky Marval (USA)	7	7
8.	Natasha Kuchiki/Todd Sand (USA)	5	8
9.	**Christine Hough/Doug Ladret (CAN)**	**12**	**9**
10.	**Sherry Ball/Kris Wirtz (CAN)**	**10**	**10**
11.	Jenni Meno/Scott Wendland (USA)	9	11
12.	Leslie Monod/Cédric Monod (SUI)	13	12
13.	Anuschka Gläser/Stefan Pfrengle (GER)	11	13
14.	Danielle Carr/Stephen Carr (AUS)	14	14
15.	Anna Tabacchi/Massimo Salvade (ITA)	19	15
16.	Katarzyna Głowacka/Krzysztof Korcarz (POL)	17	16
17.	Kathryn Pritchard/Jason Briggs (GRB)	15	18
18.	Elaine Asanakis/Mark Naylor (GRE)	18	17
19.	Line Haddad/Sylvain Privé (FRA)	16	19
20.	Jung-yoon Choi/Yong-min Lee (KOR)	20	20

European Ice Dancing Championships:

		CD1	CD2	OD	FD
1.	Klimova/Ponomarenko (CIS)	1	1	1	1
2.	Usova/Zhulin (CIS)	2	2	2	2
3.	Grishuk/Platov (CIS)	3	3	3	3
4.	Calegari/Camerlengo (ITA)	4	4	4	4
5.	Rahkamo/Kokko (FIN)	5	5	5	5
6.	Moniotte/Lavanchy (FRA)	6	6	6	6
7.	Yvon/Palluel (FRA)	7	7	7	7
8.	Mrázová/Šimeček (CZE)	8	10	8	8
9.	Sargent/Witherby (USA)	9	8	9	
10.	Stergiadu/Razgulaevs (LAT)	10	9	10	10
11.	Goolsbee/Schamberger (GER)	12	12	11	11
12.	**Petr/Janoschak (CAN)**	**11**	**11**	**12**	**12**
13.	Croci/Mantovani (ITA)	13	13	13	13

14. Woodward/Szentpétery (HUN)	14	14	14	14
15. Mayer/Breen (USA)	15	15	15	15
16. Mann/Noria (CAN)	**16**	**16**	**16**	**16**
17. Drobiazko/Vanagas (LIT)	17	17	17	17
18. Le Tensorer/Kienzle (SUI)	19	22	18	18
19. Bruce/Place (GRB)	18	18	19	19
20. Domańska/Głowacki (POL)	22	19	20	20
21. Denkova/Nikolov (BUL)	21	21	21	21
22. Takino/Takino (JPN)	20	20	22	22
23. Vedres/Szentirmai (HUN)	23	23	23	23
24. MacDonald/Smart (AUS)	24	24	24	24
25. Jung/Jung (KOR)	25	25	25	-
26. Kirk/King (SAF)	26	26	26	-

The International Skating Union celebrated its 100th anniversary at the first World Figure Skating Championships held on the West Coast of the United States.

For the only time, skaters from several former Soviet Socialist Republics entered the World Championships as representatives of the Commonwealth of Independent States. Skaters from this team swept the podium in the ice dance event.

Lu Chen made history as the first skater from China to win a medal at the World Figure Skating Championships.

For the first time since the 1960s, skaters from South Africa competed at the World Championships. Siblings Tomislav and Željka Čižmešija made history as the first skaters to represent Croatia at the World Championships. Konstantin Kostin, Alma Lepina and Aliki Stergiadu and Juris Razgulaevs made history as the first skaters to represent Latvia. Edita Katkauskaite and Margarita Drobiazko and Povilas Vanagas were Lithuania's first representatives. Mojca Kopač was the first skater to represent Slovenia.

Sources: USA Today, March 28, 1992; Skating magazine, May 1992

1993 WORLD FIGURE SKATING CHAMPIONSHIPS
Prague, Czech Republic, March 9-14, 1993

World Men's Figure Skating Championships:

	QRA	QRB	SP	FS
1. Kurt Browning (CAN)	1	-	1	1
2. Elvis Stojko (CAN)	-	1	5	2
3. Alexei Urmanov (RUS)	-	2	3	3
4. Mark Mitchell (USA)	3	-	2	5
5. Philippe Candeloro (FRA)	2	-	8	4
6. Scott Davis (USA)	4	-	7	6
7. Éric Millot (FRA)	-	3	4	8
8. Masakazu Kagiyama (JPN)	9	-	9	7
9. Cornel Gheorghe (ROM)	-	5	14	9
10. Marcus Christensen (CAN)	8	-	12	11
11. Oleg Tataurov (RUS)	-	9	6	14
12. Dmitri Dmitrenko (UKR)	5	-	18	10
13. Konstantin Kostin (LAT)	6	-	15	12
14. Igor Pashkevich (RUS)	7	-	16	13
15. Ronny Winkler (GER)	-	6	10	16
16. Oula Jääskeläinen (FIN)	-	8	11	17
17. Michael Tyllesen (DEN)	-	7	17	15
18. Steven Cousins (GRB)	-	4	13	18
19. Michael Shmerkin (ISR)	12	-	21	19
20. Sung-il Jung (KOR)	-	12	20	20
21. Yueming Liu (CHN)	10	-	24	22
22. Jaroslav Suchý (CZE)	-	11	23	23
23. Jan Erik Digernes (NOR)	11	-	22	24
24. Alexander Murashko (BLS)	-	10	-	-
25. Rastislav Vnučko (SVK)	13	-	-	-
25. Stephen Carr (AUS)	-	13	-	-
27. Roman Martõnenko (EST)	14	-	-	-
27. Dino Quattrocecere (SAF)	-	14	-	-
29. Robert Grzegorczyk (POL)	15	-	-	-
29. Fabrizio Garattoni (ITA)	-	15	-	-
31. Szabolcs Vidrai (HUN)	16	-	-	-
31. David Liu (TPE)	-	16	-	-
33. Nicolas Binz (SUI)	17	-	-	-

33. Daniel Peinado (ESP)	17	-	-	
35. Jan Čejvan (SLO)	18	-	-	-
35. Florian Tuma (AUT)	-	18	-	-
37. Marcus Deen (NED)	19	-	-	-
37. Besarion Tsintsadze (GEO)	-	19	-	-
39. Sergei Umirov (KAZ)	20	-	-	-
39. Tomislav Čižmešija (CRO)	-	20	-	-
41. Christopher Blong (NZL)	21	-	-	-
41. Emanuele Ancorini (SWE)	-	21	-	-
43. Harris Haita (GRE)	22	-	-	-
43. Ivan Dinev (BUL)	-	22	-	-

World Ladies Figure Skating Championships:

	QRA	QRB	SP	FS
1. Oksana Baiul (UKR)	-	2	2	1
2. Surya Bonaly (FRA)	1	-	3	2
3. Lu Chen (CHN)	-	1	5	3
4. Yuka Sato (JPN)	5	-	6	4
5. Nancy Kerrigan (USA)	2	-	1	9
6. Marina Kielmann (GER)	-	3	10	5
7. Tanja Szewczenko (GER)	-	5	8	6
8. Karen Preston (CAN)	**-**	**4**	**7**	**7**
9. Josée Chouinard (CAN)	**4**	**-**	**4**	**10**
10. Lenka Kulovaná (CZE)	-	9	11	8
11. Marie-Pierre Leray (FRA)	-	7	9	12
12. Charlene von Saher (GRB)	6	-	17	11
13. Lisa Ervin (USA)	9	-	14	13
14. Zuzanna Szwed (POL)	-	10	13	14
15. Krisztina Czakó (HUN)	8	-	12	16
16. Bo Zhang (CHN)	-	6	18	15
17. Viktoria Dimitrova (BUL)	7	-	15	17
18. Mila Kajas (FIN)	3	-	16	18
19. Nathalie Krieg (SUI)	-	11	20	19
20. Anisette Torp-Lind (DEN)	-	12	19	20
21. Cristina Mauri (ITA)	12	-	22	21
22. Marta Andrade Vidal (ESP)	11	-	23	22
23. Xin Liu (CHN)	10	-	24	23
24. Olga Vassiljeva (EST)	13	-	-	-

24. Junko Yaginuma (JPN)	-	13	-	-
26. Tamara Heggen (AUS)	14	-	-	-
26. Lily Lyoonjung Lee (KOR)	-	14	-	-
28. Joanna Ng (TPE)	15	-	-	-
28. Maria Butyrskaya (RUS)	-	15	-	-
30. Mojca Kopač (SLO)	16	-	-	-
30. Tonia Kwiatkowski (USA)	-	16	-	-
32. Ann-Marie Söderholm (SWE)	17	-	-	-
32. Melita Juratek (CRO)	-	17	-	-
34. Andrea Kus (AUT)	18	-	-	-
34. M. van der Velden (NED)	-	18	-	-
36. Tatiana Malinina (UZB)	19	-	-	-
36. Alma Lepina (LAT)	-	19	-	-
38. Marianne Aarnes (NOR)	20	-	-	-
38. Lauryna Slavinskaite (LIT)	-	20	-	-
40. Sandra Brajdic (ISU)	21	-	-	-
40. Inna Ovsiannikova (BLS)	-	21	-	-
42. Mayda Navarro (MEX)	22	-	-	-
42. Rosanna Blong (NZL)	-	22	-	-
44. Jalina Kakadyi (KAZ)	23	-	-	-
44. Kim Harris (SAF)	-	23	-	-
WD. Alice Sue Claeys (BEL)	-	8	21	-

World Pairs Skating Championships:

	SP	FS
1. Isabelle Brasseur/Lloyd Eisler (CAN)	**1**	**1**
2. Mandy Wötzel/Ingo Steuer (GER)	3	2
3. Evgenia Shishkova/Vadim Naumov (RUS)	2	3
4. Radka Kovaříková/René Novotný (CZE)	6	4
5. Jenni Meno/Todd Sand (USA)	4	6
6. Marina Eltsova/Andrei Bushkov (RUS)	5	7
7. M. Menzies/J-M. Bombardier (CAN)	**8**	**6**
8. Calla Urbanski/Rocky Marval (USA)	7	8
9. Leslie Monod/Cédric Monod (SUI)	9	10
10. Jodeyne Higgins/Sean Rice (CAN)	**13**	**9**
11. Danielle Carr/Stephen Carr (AUS)	12	11
12. Peggy Schwarz/Alexander König (GER)	10	12
13. Svetlana Pristav/Viacheslav Tkachenko (UKR)	11	14

14. Elena Berezhnaya/Oleg Shliakhov (LAT)	15	13
15. Oksana Kazakova/Dmitri Sukhanov (RUS)	14	15
16. Jacqueline Soames/John Jenkins (GRB)	18	16
17. Beata Zielińska/Mariusz Siudek (POL)	19	17
18. Elena Grigoreva/Sergei Sheiko (BLS)	17	18
19. Sarah Abitbol/Stéphane Bernadis (FRA)	16	19
20. Claire Auret/Christoff van Rensburg (SAF)	21	20
WD. Elaine Asanakis/Mark Naylor (GRE)	20	-

World Ice Dancing Championships:

	CD1	CD2	OD	FD
1. Usova/Zhulin (RUS)	1	1	1	1
2. Grishuk/Platov (RUS)	2	2	2	2
3. Krylova/Fedorov (RUS)	4	3	3	3
4. Rahkamo/Kokko (FIN)	3	4	4	4
5. Moniotte/Lavanchy (FRA)	6	6	5	5
6. Calegari/Camerlengo (ITA)	5	5	6	7
7. Romanova/Yaroshenko (UKR)	7	7	7	6
8. Mrázová/Šimeček (CZE)	8	8	8	8
9. Navka/Gezalian (BLS)	10	10	10	9
10. Stergiadu/Razgulajevs (UZB)	9	9	9	11
11. Roca/Sur (USA)	11	11	11	10
12. Goolsbee/Schamberger (GER)	12	12	12	12
13. Drobiazko/Vanagas (LIT)	14	14	13	14
14. Bourne/Kraatz (CAN)	**15**	**15**	**16**	**13**
15. Wynne/Witherby (USA)	13	13	14	15
16. Le Bed/Piton (FRA)	15	16	16	18
17. Humphreys/Lanning (GRB)	19	18	18	16
18. Woodward/Szentpétery (HUN)	18	19	19	17
19. Stekolnikova/Kazarly. (KAZ)	17	17	17	19
20. Chroboková/Brzý (CZE)	20	20	20	20
21. Domańska/Głowacki (POL)	22	21	21	21
22. Fusar-Poli/Reani (ITA)	21	22	22	22
23. Führing/Wilczek (AUT)	24	24	23	23
24. Gerencser/Stanislavov (SUI)	23	23	24	24
25. Shirahata/Tanaka (JPN)	25	25	25	-
26. Denkova/Nikolov (BUL)	26	26	26	-
27. Trocenko/Samovich (LAT)	28	27	27	-

28. Ruby/Kaplan (ISR)	27	28	28	-
29. v.d. Riet/van Eeden (SAF)	29	29	29	-

Qualifying rounds were held for the first time at the World Figure Skating Championships.

Oksana Baiul made history as the first skater to win a gold medal for Ukraine at the World Figure Skating Championships. It was the first year that a team from Ukraine was sent to the event.

Jaroslav Suchý, Lenka Kulovaná, Radka Kovaříková and René Novotný and Radmila Chroboková and Milan Brzý were the first skaters to represent the Czech Republic at the World Championships, skating on home ice. Rastislav Vnučko was the first skater to represent Slovakia at the World Championships.

Alexander Murashko, Inna Ovsiannikova, Elena Grigoreva and Sergei Sheiko and Tatiana Navka and Samvel Gezalian made history as the first skaters to represent Belarus at the World Championships. Besarion Tsintsadze was the first skater to represent Georgia. Michael Shmerkin and Tamara Ruby and Konstantin Kaplin were the first skaters to represent Israel. Sergei Umirov, Jalina Kakadyi and Elizaveta Stekolnikova and Dmitri Kazarlyga were the first skaters to represent Kazakhstan. Tatiana Malinina and Aliki Stergiadu and Juris Razgulajevs were the first skaters to represent Uzbekistan.

Oksana Grishuk and Evgeni Platov, Angelika Krylova and Vladimir Fedorov and Maya Usova and Alexander Zhulin, the trio of Russian teams that swept the podium in the ice dance event, were also the first ice dancers to represent Russia at the World Championships.

Sources: Eissport magazine, March 1993; Skating magazine, May 1993

1994 WORLD FIGURE SKATING CHAMPIONSHIPS
Chiba, Japan, March 20-27, 1994

World Men's Figure Skating Championships:

	QRA	QRB	SP	FS
1. Elvis Stojko (CAN)	1	-	1	1
2. Philippe Candeloro (FRA)	2	-	2	2
3. Viacheslav Zagorodniuk (UKR)	-	2	3	3
4. Alexei Urmanov (RUS)	-	1	4	4
5. Éric Millot (FRA)	3	-	5	6
6. Masakazu Kagiyama (JPN)	-	6	9	5
7. Scott Davis (USA)	-	3	8	7
8. Sébastien Britten (CAN)	-	4	12	8
9. Igor Pashkevich (RUS)	7	-	10	9
10. Steven Cousins (GRB)	-	8	7	11
11. Andrejs Vlascenko (LAT)	5	-	11	10
12. Oleg Tataurov (RUS)	-	5	13	12
13. Aren Nielsen (USA)	9	-	6	16
14. Michael Shmerkin (ISR)	-	7	14	13
15. Marcus Christensen (CAN)	6	-	16	14
16. Zsolt Kerekes (HUN)	-	10	17	15
17. Michael Tyllesen (DEN)	4	-	15	18
18. Ronny Winkler (GER)	-	11	18	17
19. Besarion Tsintsadze (GEO)	10	-	22	19
20. Sung-il Jung (KOR)	8	-	20	21
21. David Liu (TPE)	-	9	23	20
22. Stephen Carr (AUS)	-	12	21	23
23. Markus Leminen (FIN)	12	-	19	24
24. Fumihiro Oikawa (JPN)	11	-	24	22
25. Igor Lyutikov (AZE)	13	-	-	-
25. Hristo Turlakov (BUL)	-	13	-	-
27. Alexander Murashko (BLS)	14	-	-	-
27. M.C. Negrea (ROM)	-	14	-	-
29. Dino Quattrocecere (SAF)	15	-	-	-
29. F.C. Retamar (ESP)	-	15	-	-
31. Fabrizio Garattoni (ITA)	16	-	-	-
31. Zbigniew Komorowski (POL)	-	16	-	-
33. Min Zhang (CHN)	17	-	-	-

33. Margus Hernits (EST)	-	17	-	-
35. Rastislav Vnučko (SVK)	18	-	-	-
35. Yuri Litvinov (KAZ)	-	18	-	-
37. Emrah Polatoğlu (TUR)	19	-	-	-
37. Ricardo Olavarrieta (MEX)	-	19	-	-
39. Tomislav Čižmešija (CRO)	20	-	-	-
39. Vaidotas Juraitis (LIT)	-	20	-	-
41. Alexandros Kypreos (GRE)	21	-	-	-
WD. Kurt Browning (CAN)	-	-	-	-
WD. Brian Boitano (USA)	-	-	-	-
WD. Viktor Petrenko (UKR)	-	-	-	-

World Ladies Figure Skating Championships:

	QRA	QRB	SP	FS
1. Yuka Sato (JPN)	1	-	1	1
2. Surya Bonaly (FRA)	2	-	2	2
3. Tanja Szewczenko (GER)	3	-	4	3
4. Marina Kielmann (GER)	-	3	5	4
5. Josée Chouinard (CAN)	-	1	3	5
6. Elena Liashenko (LIT)	6	-	6	6
7. Marie-Pierre Leray (FRA)	-	10	12	7
8. Michelle Kwan (USA)	5	-	11	8
9. Susan Humphreys (CAN)	7	-	**10**	9
10. Olga Markova (RUS)	4	-	7	11
11. Mila Kajas (FIN)	-	4	8	13
12. Krisztina Czakó (HUN)	-	5	18	10
13. Rena Inoue (JPN)	-	6	15	12
14. Nathalie Krieg (SUI)	-	9	13	15
15. Anna Rechnio (POL)	-	7	9	17
16. Lenka Kulovaná (CZE)	10	-	17	14
17. Lyudmila Ivanova (UKR)	8	-	14	16
18. Charlene Von Saher (GRB)	11	-	16	18
19. Alice Sue Claeys (BEL)	-	11	22	19
20. Viktoria Dimitrova (BUL)	9	-	21	20
21. Tatiana Malinina (UZB)	-	8	19	21
22. Ying Liu (CHN)	-	12	20	23
23. Inna Zayets (UKR)	12	-	23	22
24. Silvia Fontana (ITA)	13	-	-	-

24. Nicole Bobek (USA)	-	13	-	-
26. Marta Andrade Vidal (ESP)	14	-	-	-
26. Laëtitia Hubert (FRA)	-	14	-	-
28. Kateřina Beránková (CZE)	15	-	-	-
28. Yulia Vorobieva (AZE)	-	15	-	-
30. Lily Lyoonjung Lee (KOR)	16	-	-	-
30. Olga Vassiljeva (EST)	-	16	-	-
32. Alma Lepina (LAT)	17	-	-	-
32. Tamara Panjkret (CRO)	-	17	-	-
34. Guona Zhao (CHN)	18	-	-	-
34. Ingrida Zenkeviciute (LIT)	-	18	-	-
36. Valentina Gazeleridou (KAZ)	19	-	-	-
36. Claire Auret (SAF)	-	19(t)	-	-
36. Lefki Terzaki (GRE)	-	19(t)	-	-
39. Miriam Manzano (AUS)	20	-	-	-
40. Sandra Brajdic (ISU)	21	-	-	-
40. Zaneta Štefániková (SVK)	-	21	-	-
WD. Lu Chen (CHN)	-	2	-	-
WD. Katarina Witt (GER)	-	-	-	-
WD. Oksana Baiul (UKR)	-	-	-	-
WD. Nancy Kerrigan (USA)	-	-	-	-
WD. Tonya Harding (USA)	-	-	-	-

World Pairs Skating Championships:

	SP	FS
1. Evgenia Shishkova/Vadim Naumov (RUS)	1	1
2. Isabelle Brasseur/Lloyd Eisler (CAN)	**2**	**2**
3. Marina Eltsova/Andrei Bushkov (RUS)	3	3
4. Mandy Wötzel/Ingo Steuer (GER)	5	4
5. Radka Kovaříková/René Novotný (CZE)	4	5
6. Jenni Meno/Todd Sand (USA)	6	8
7. Elena Berezhnaya/Oleg Shliakhov (LAT)	11	6
8. Maria Petrova/Anton Sikharulidze (RUS)	10	7
9. Peggy Schwarz/Alexander König (GER)	7	9
10. Danielle Carr/Stephen Carr (AUS)	8	11
11. Kristy Sargeant/Kris Wirtz (CAN)	**9**	**12**
12. Kyoko Ina/Jason Dungjen (USA)	14	10
13. N. Krestianinova/A. Torchinski (AZE)	12	13

14. Anuschka Gläser/Axel Rauschenbach (GER)	15	14
15. Yukiko Kawasaki/Alexei Tikhonov (JPN)	13	15
16. Jamie Salé/Jason Turner (CAN)	**18**	**16**
17. Karen Courtland/Todd Reynolds (USA)	16	17
18. Marina Khalturina/Andrei Kriukov (KAZ)	17	19
19. Line Haddad/Sylvain Privé (FRA)	20	18
20. Elena Beloussovskaya/Igor Maliar (UKR)	19	20
21. Xue Shen/Hongbo Zhao (CHN)	23	21
22. Marta Głuchowska/Mariusz Siudek (POL)	22	22
23. Marta Andrella/Dmitri Kaploun (ITA)	21	24
24. Elena Grigoreva/Sergei Sheiko (BLS)	24	23
25. Dana Mednick/Jason Briggs (GRB)	25	-
26. Claire Auret/Christoff Van Rensburg (SAF)	26	-
27. Nigora Karabaeva/Evgeni Sviridov (UZB)	27	-
28. Hoi-san Poon/Wai-tung Cheung (HKG)	28	-
WD. Ekaterina Gordeeva/Sergei Grinkov (RUS)	-	-
WD. Natalia Mishkutenok/Artur Dmitriev (RUS)	-	-

World Ice Dancing Championships:

	CD1	CD2	OD	FD
1. Grishuk/Platov (RUS)	1	1	1	1
2. Moniotte/Lavanchy (FRA)	2	2	2	2
3. Rahkamo/Kokko (FIN)	3	3	3	3
4. Romanova/Yaroshenko (UKR)	4	5	4	4
5. Navka/Gezalian (BLS)	6	6	5	6
6. Bourne/Kraatz (CAN)	**9**	**7**	**6**	**6**
7. Goolsbee/Schamberger (GER)	7	9	7	7
8. Mrázová/Šimeček (CZE)	8	8	8	8
9. Drobiazko/Vanagas (LIT)	10	11	9	9
10. Anissina/Peizerat (FRA)	11	10	10	10
11. Stergiadu/Razgulaevs (UZB)	12	12	11	11
12. Punsalan/Swallow (USA)	13	13	12	12
13. Lobacheva/Averbukh (RUS)	14	14	13	13
14. Stekolnikova/Kazarly. (KAZ)	15	15	14	14
15. Gerencser/Stanislavov (SUI)	18	17	15	15
16. Humphreys/Lanning (GRB)	16	16	16	16
17. Fusar-Poli/Reani (ITA)	17	18	17	17
18. Grushina/Goncharov (UKR)	20	19	18	18

19. Chroboková/Brzý (CZE)	19	20	19	19
20. Führing/Wilczek (AUT)	21	21	20	20
21. Pershankova/Morozov (AZE)	23	22	22	21
22. Bonardi/Reani (ITA)	24	23	21	22
23. Nowak/Kolasiński (POL)	22	25	23	23
24. Tsuzuki/Nakamura (JPN)	27	24	27	24
25. Poráčová/Poráč (SVK)	28	26	25	-
26. Denkova/Nikolov (BUL)	25	27	26	-
27. Chait/Sevastianov (ISR)	29	29	28	-
28. Grebenkina/Samovich (LAT)	30	30	29	-
29. Mosenkova/Kurakin (EST)	31	33	30	-
30. Lai/Lai (TPE)	32	31	31	-
31. Park/Ryu (KOR)	35	32	32	-
32. Nurdbaeva/Settarov (UZB)	34	36	33	-
33. Seydel/Smart (AUS)	33	34	34	-
34. Kirk/King (SAF)	36	35	35	-
WD. Vedres/Szentirmai (HUN)	26	28	24	-
WD. Krylova/Fedorov (RUS)	5	4	-	-
WD. Torvill/Dean (GRB)	-	-	-	-
WD. Usova/Zhulin (RUS)	-	-	-	-

In the aftermath of the attack on Nancy Kerrigan and the 1994 Winter Olympic Games in Lillehammer, both Kerrigan and Tonya Harding did not compete at the World Figure Skating Championships.

France's Surya Bonaly caused a major controversy when she refused to stand on the medal podium after winning the silver medal in the ladies event. After ISU President Olaf Poulsen coaxed her onto the podium, she took off her medal in protest and was booed by the Japanese audience. After the incident, she told reporters, "They say I am too much of this way, so I change. Then they say I am too much of that way and I change again. I don't know what I have to do. It's not right. It's crazy. It's nothing against Yuka [Sato]. I like her. I saw her program. It was nice and clean." At the time, Bonaly was widely criticized for showing poor sportsmanship. In the years since, the incident became part an important conversation about race, gender and expectations in figure skating.

Susanna Rahkamo and Petri Kokko won Finland's first medal in ice dancing at the World Championships.

Igor Lyutikov, Yulia Vorobieva, Natalia Krestianinova and Alexei Torchinski and Olga Pershankova and Nikolai Morozov made history as the first skaters to represent Azerbaijan at the World Championships. Emrah Polatoglu made history as the first skater to represent Turkey.

The event was attended by Crown Prince and Princess (now Emperor and Empress) of Japan Naruhito and Masako.

Sources: The Journal, March 3, 1994; The Leader-Post, March 8, 1994; USA Today, March 9, 1994; The Sacramento Bee, March 20, 1994; The Columbian, March 20, 1994; The Ottawa Citizen, March 27, 1994; Eissport magazine, April 1994

1995 WORLD FIGURE SKATING CHAMPIONSHIPS
Birmingham, England, March 7-12, 1995

World Men's Figure Skating Championships:

	QRA	QRB	SP	FS
1. Elvis Stojko (CAN)	-	-	2	1
2. Todd Eldredge (USA)	1	-	1	2
3. Philippe Candeloro (FRA)	-	-	5	3
4. Alexei Urmanov (RUS)	-	-	4	5
5. Éric Millot (FRA)	-	-	8	4
6. Viacheslav Zagorodniuk (UKR)	-	-	7	6
7. Scott Davis (USA)	-	-	3	8
8. Steven Cousins (GRB)	-	-	6	9
9. Ilia Kulik (RUS)	2	-	11	7
10. Zsolt Kerekes (HUN)	5	-	9	11
11. Michael Shmerkin (ISR)	-	1	14	10
12. Dmitri Dmitrenko (UKR)	3	-	10	12
13. Vasili Eremenko (UKR)	4	-	12	14
14. Cornel Gheorghe (ROM)	9	-	17	13
15. Markus Leminen (FIN)	6	-	15	15
16. Thierry Cerez (FRA)	-	4	13	16

17. Sébastien Britten (CAN)	-	-	18	17
18. Ronny Winkler (GER)	-	3	19	19
19. Clive Shorten (GRB)	7	-	22	18
20. Alexander Murashko (BLS)	8	-	16	21
21. Fabrizio Garattoni (ITA)	-	5	20	20
22. Zhongyi Jiao (CHN)	-	2	23	22
23. Naoki Shigematsu (JPN)	10	-	21	23
24. Florian Tuma (AUT)	-	6	24	24
25. Michael Tyllesen (DEN)	11	-	25	-
26. Robert Grzegorczyk (POL)	-	8	26	-
27. Jan Erik Digernes (NOR)	-	11	27	-
28. Shin Amano (JPN)	-	10	28	-
29. David Liu (TPE)	-	7	29	-
30. Margus Hernits (EST)	-	9	30	-
31. Marcus Christensen (CAN)	12	-	-	-
31. Ivan Dinev (BUL)	-	12	-	-
33. Besarion Tsintsadze (GEO)	13	-	-	-
33. Radek Horák (CZE)	-	13	-	-
35. Yuri Litvinov (KAZ)	14	-	-	-
35. Róbert Kažimír (SVK)	-	14	-	-
37. Stephen Carr (AUS)	15	-	-	-
37. Emrah Polatoğlu (TUR)	-	15	-	-
39. Sung-il Jung (KOR)	16	-	-	-
39. Patrick Meier (SUI)	-	16	-	-
41. Ricardo Olavarrieta (MEX)	17	-	-	-
41. Jan Čejvan (SLO)	-	17	-	-
WD. Daniel Peinado (ESP)	-	-	-	-

World Ladies Figure Skating Championships:

	QRA	QRB	SP	FS
1. Lu Chen (CHN)	-	2	3	1
2. Surya Bonaly (FRA)	-	-	4	2
3. Nicole Bobek (USA)	-	1	1	4
4. Michelle Kwan (USA)	-	-	5	3
5. Olga Markova (RUS)	-	-	2	5
6. Laëtitia Hubert (FRA)	-	3	7	7
7. Irina Slutskaya (RUS)	1	-	12	6
8. Marie-Pierre Leray (FRA)	-	-	8	9

9. Elena Liashenko (UKR)	-	-	6	10
10. Hanae Yokoya (JPN)	2	-	16	8
11. Yulia Lavrenchuk (UKR)	8	-	10	12
12. Junko Yaginuma (JPN)	4	-	14	11
13. Marina Kielmann (GER)	-	-	9	14
14. Anna Rechnio (POL)	3	-	17	13
15. Kateřina Beránková (CZE)	12	-	13	15
16. Kumiko Koiwai (JPN)	5	-	15	17
17. Simone Lang (GER)	9	-	18	16
18. Lucinda Ruh (SUI)	-	4	23	18
19. Jennifer Robinson (CAN)	**-**	**9**	**22**	**19**
20. Maria Nikitochkina (BLS)	10	-	21	21
21. T.S. Bombardieri (ITA)	7	-	24	20
22. Tatiana Malinina (UZB)	-	5	20	22
23. Krisztina Czakó (HUN)	6	-	19	23
24. Jenna Arrowsmith (GRB)	-	13	29	24
25. Marta Andrade Vidal (ESP)	-	7	25	-
26. Ivana Jakupčević (CRO)	-	10	26	-
27. Mila Kajas (FIN)	-	6	27	-
28. Mojca Kopač (SLO)	-	8	28	-
29. M. van der Velden (NED)	-	11	30	-
30. Julia Lautowa (AUT)	11	-	31	-
31. Alma Lepina (LAT)	-	12	-	-
32. Miriam Manzano (AUS)	13	-	-	-
33. Netty Kim (CAN)	**14**	**-**	**-**	**-**
33. Zuzana Paurová (SVK)	-	14	-	-
35. J. Golovatenko (EST)	15	-	-	-
35. Helena Grundberg (SWE)	-	15	-	-
37. Boon-sun Park (KOR)	16	-	-	-
37. Janie Ja-lin Weng (TPE)-	16	-	-	-
38. Tsvetelina Abrasheva (BUL)	17	-	-	-
38. Lauryna Slavinskaite (LIT)	-	17	-	-
40. Claire Auret (SAF)	18	-	-	-
40. Carole Ren (HKG)	-	18	-	-
WD. Tanja Szewczenko (GER)	-	-	11	-

World Pairs Skating Championships:

	SP	FS
1. Radka Kovaříková/René Novotný (CZE)	1	1
2. Evgenia Shishkova/Vadim Naumov (ROM)	3	2
3. Jenni Meno/Todd Sand (USA)	5	3
4. Marina Eltsova/Andrei Bushkov (RUS)	4	4
5. Mandy Wötzel/Ingo Steuer (GER)	2	5
6. Maria Petrova/Anton Sikharulidze (RUS)	6	6
7. Elena Berezhnaya/Oleg Shliakhov (LAT)	7	7
8. Kyoko Ina/Jason Dungjen (USA)	10	8
9. Sarah Abitbol/Stéphane Bernadis (FRA)	8	9
10. M. Menzies/J-M. Bombardier (CAN)	**11**	**10**
11. Danielle Carr/Stephen Carr (AUS)	9	13
12. Elena Beloussovskaya/Sergei Potalov (UKR)	12	12
13. Marina Khalturina/Andrei Kriukov (KAZ)	15	11
14. Jodeyne Higgins/Sean Rice (CAN)	**14**	**14**
15. Allison Gaylor/David Pelletier (CAN)	**16**	**15**
16. Dorota Zagórska/Mariusz Siudek (POL)	13	17
17. Lesley Rogers/Michael Aldred (GRB)	17	16
18. Silvia Dimitrov/Rico Rex (GER)	19	18
19. Marta Andrella/Dmitri Kaploun (ITA)	18	19
20. Ulrike Gerstl/Björn Lobenwein (AUT)	20	20
21. Polina Djo/Evgeni Sviridov (UZB)	21	21
WD. Veronika Joukalová/Otto Dlabola (CZE)	-	-
WD. Jekaterina Silnitskaya/Mirko Müller (GER)	-	-

World Ice Dancing Championships:

	CD1	CD2	OD	FD
1. Grishuk/Platov (RUS)	1	1	1	1
2. Rahkamo/Kokko (FIN)	2	2	2	2
3. Moniotte/Lavanchy (FRA)	3	3	3	3
4. Bourne/Kraatz (CAN)	**5**	**4**	**4**	**4**
5. Krylova/Ovsiannikov (RUS)	4	5	5	5
6. Anissina/Peizerat (FRA)	6	6	6	6
7. Navka/Gezalian (BLS)	7	7	7	7
8. Romanova/Yaroshenko (UKR)	8	8	8	8
9. Mrázová/Šimeček (CZE)	9	9	9	9
10. Roca/Sur (USA)	11	11	11	10

11. Goolsbee/Schamberger (GER)	10	10	10	11
12. Drobiazko/Vanagas (LIT)	12	12	12	12
13. Stekolnikova/Kazarly. (KAZ)	13	14	13	14
14. Nowak/Kolasiński (POL)	15	16	14	13
15. Lobacheva/Averbukh (RUS)	14	13	15	15
16. Gerencser/Stanislavov (SUI)	17	15	16	16
17. Boyce/Brunet (CAN)	**19**	**18**	**17**	**18**
18. MacLean/Schaub (AUT)	21	21	18	17
19. Winkler/Lohse (GER)	20	19	19	19
20. Piton/Piton (FRA)	16	17	21	20
21. Fitzgerald/Vincent (GRB)	18	20	20	21
22. Grushina/Goncharov (UKR)	22	22	22	22
23. Koinuma/Arakekian (ARM)	23	23	23	24
24. Denkova/Nikolov (BUL)	24	27	24	23
25. Fermi/Baldi (ITA)	27	25	25	-
26. Kawai/Tanaka (JPN)	25	24	26	-
27. Vondrková/Král (CZE)	26	26	27	-
28. Bárány/Szombathelyi (HUN)	29	28	28	-
29. Mosenkova/Kurakin (EST)	30	29	29	-
30. Kuusniemi/Walker (FIN)	28	30	30	-
31. Seydel/Smart (AUS)	31	31	-	-
32. Kirk/King	32	32	-	-
WD. Lai/Lai (TPE)	-	-	-	-

Lu Chen and Radka Kovaříková and René Novotný made history as the first skaters from China and the Czech Republic to win a gold medal at the World Figure Skating Championships. Kaho Koinuma and Tigran Arakekian made history as the first skaters to represent Armenia at the World Championships.

The qualifying rounds were adapted. "Seeded" skaters weren't required to participate, based on a classification sheet published by the ISU. The classification sheet was based on the results of several competitions, including the previous year's World Championships.

British skater Jenna Arrowsmith failed to place high enough in her group to qualify, but earned the right to compete in the short program and free skate because of the ISU's rule that the host country automatically qualified one skater.

Sources: Eissport magazine, March 1995; The Plain Dealer, March 6 and 7, 1995; Skating magazine, May 1995

1996 WORLD FIGURE SKATING CHAMPIONSHIPS
Edmonton, Canada, March 14-24, 1996

World Men's Figure Skating Championships:

	QRA	QRB	SP	FS
1. Todd Eldredge (USA)	-	-	2	1
2. Ilia Kulik (RUS)	-	-	1	2
3. Rudy Galindo (USA)	1	-	4	4
4. Elvis Stojko (CAN)	**-**	**-**	**7**	**3**
5. Alexei Urmanov (RUS)	-	-	3	5
6. Viacheslav Zagorodniuk (UKR)	-	-	8	6
7. Éric Millot (FRA)	-	-	6	9
8. Andrejs Vlascenko (GER)	-	4	11	8
9. Philippe Candeloro (FRA)	-	-	16	17
10. Dan Hollander (USA)	2	-	13	10
11. Michael Shmerkin (ISR)	7	-	12	11
12. Thierry Cerez (FRA)	-	5	15	12
13. Takeshi Honda (JPN)	-	1	14	13
14. Cornel Gheorghe (ROM)	5	-	10	15
15. Steven Cousins (GRB)	-	-	5	18
16. Dmitri Dmitrenko (UKR)	4	-	9	19
17. Sébastien Britten (CAN)	**-**	**2**	**20**	**14**
18. Szabolcs Vidrai (HUN)	-	7	18	16
19. Michael Tyllesen (DEN)	-	3	17	17
20. Neil Wilson (GRB)	6	-	22	20
21. Patrick Schmit (LUX)	-	10	23	21
22. Fabrizio Garattoni (ITA)	-	6	21	22
23. Robert Grzegorczyk (POL)	9	-	19	23
24. Alexander Murashko (BLS)	10	-	24	24
25. Patrick Meier (SUI)	11	-	25	-
26. Zhengxin Guo (CHN)	3	-	26	-
27. Marcus Christensen (CAN)	**-**	**8**	**27**	**-**
28. Margus Hernits (EST)	-	9	28	-

29. Yuri Litvinov (KAZ)	8	-	29	-
30. Markus Leminen (FIN)	12	-	-	-
30. Radek Horák (CZE)	-	12	-	-
32. Ivan Dinev (BUL)	13	-	-	-
32. Róbert Kažimír (SVK)	-	13	-	-
34. Kyu-hyun Lee (KOR)	14	-	-	-
34. Jan Čejvan (SLO)	-	14	-	-
36. Zoltán Kőszegi (HUN)	15	-	-	-
36. Ricardo Olavarrieta (MEX)	-	15	-	-
38. Stephen Carr (AUS)	16	-	-	-
38. Robert Ward (SAF)	-	16	-	-
40. Jordi Pedro Roya (ESP)	17	-	-	-
40. Aramayis Grigorian (ARM)	-	17	-	-
WD. Florian Tuma (AUT)	-	11	-	-
WD. David Liu (TPE)	-	-	-	-
WD. Igor Lyutikov (AZE)	-	-	-	-
WD. Vahktang Murvanidze (GEO)	-	-	-	-

World Ladies Figure Skating Championships:

	QRA	QRB	SP	FS
1. Michelle Kwan (USA)	-	-	1	1
2. Lu Chen (CHN)	-	-	2	2
3. Irina Slutskaya (RUS)	-	-	3	3
4. Maria Butyrskaya (RUS)	-	1	4	4
5. Surya Bonaly (FRA)	-	-	7	5
6. Tanja Szewczenko (GER)	-	3	5	6
7. Midori Ito (JPN)	1	-	6	7
8. Tonia Kwiatkowski (USA)	-	4	9	8
9. Yulia Vorobieva (AZE)	-	2	8	9
10. Hanae Yokoya (JPN)	-	-	11	10
11. Krisztina Czakó (HUN)	3	-	12	12
12. Elena Liashenko (UKR)	-	-	10	14
13. Tatiana Malinina (UZB)	5	-	13	15
14. Vanessa Gusmeroli (FRA)	-	9	18	13
15. Tara Lipinski (USA)	2	-	23	11
16. Lenka Kulovaná (CZE)	-	6	17	16
17. Yulia Lavrenchuk (UKR)	-	11	16	17
18. Mojca Kopač (SLO)	-	7	15	18

19. Lucinda Ruh (SUI)	-	8	20	19
20. Meijia Lu (CHN)	4	-	14	22
21. Jennifer Robinson (CAN)	-	**5**	**24**	**20**
22. Stephanie Main (GRB)	12	-	22	21
23. Maria Nikitochkina (BLS)	-	12	19	23
24. Silvia Fontana (ITA)	7	-	21	24
25. Zuzanna Szwed (POL)	-	10	25	-
26. Marta Andrade Vidal (ESP)	10	-	26	-
27. Helena Grundberg (SWE)	8	-	27	-
28. Sofia Penkova (BUL)	11	-	28	-
29. Ivana Jakupčević (CRO)	9	-	29	-
30. Denise Jaschek (AUT)	6	-	30	-
31. Alma Lepina (LAT)	13	-	-	-
31. Miriam Manzano (AUS)	-	13	-	-
33. Hyung-kyung Choi (KOR)	14	-	-	-
33. Véronique Fleury (FRA)	-	14	-	-
35. Marta Chisu (ROM)	15	-	-	-
35. Shirene Human (SAF)	-	15	-	-
37. Janie Ja-lin Weng (TPE)	-	16	-	-
WD. Mila Kajas (FIN)	-	-	-	-
WD. Elen Hambartsoumian (ARM)	-	-	-	-
WD. Jelena Golovatenko (EST)	-	-	-	-

World Pairs Skating Championships:

	SP	FS
1. Marina Eltsova/Andrei Bushkov (RUS)	2	1
2. Mandy Wötzel/Ingo Steuer (GER)	1	2
3. Jenni Meno/Todd Sand (USA)	5	3
4. Evgenia Shishkova/Vadim Naumov (RUS)	3	4
5. Oksana Kazakova/Artur Dmitriev (RUS)	4	5
6. Kyoko Ina/Jason Dungjen (USA)	8	6
7. Kristy Sargeant/Kris Wirtz (CAN)	**6**	**7**
8. M. Menzies/J-M. Bombardier (CAN)	**10**	**8**
9. Elena Beloussovskaya/Sergei Potalov (UKR)	9	9
10. Shelby Lyons/Brian Wells (USA)	11	10
11. Sarah Abitbol/Stéphane Bernadis (FRA)	7	12
12. Danielle McGrath/Stephen Carr (AUS)	12	11
13. Dorota Zagórska/Mariusz Siudek (POL)	15	14

14. Silvia Dimitrov/Rico Rex (GER)		13	15
15. Xue Shen/Hongbo Zhao (CHN)		18	13
16. Lesley Rogers/Michael Aldred (GRB)		16	16
17. Marina Khalturina/Andrei Kriukov (KAZ)		17	17
18. Line Haddad/Sylvain Privé (FRA)		14	19
19. Elaine Asanakis/Joel McKeever (GRE)		20	18
20. Veronika Joukalová/Otto Dlabola (CZE)		19	20
21. Anna Kaverzina/Gennadi Emeljenenko (BLS)		21	21
22. Jekaterina Nekrassova/Valdis Mintals (EST)		23	22
23. Olga Bogouslavska/Juri Salmonov (LAT)		22	23

World Ice Dancing Championships:

	CD1	CD2	OD	FD
1. Grishuk/Platov (RUS)	1	1	1	1
2. Krylova/Ovsiannikov (RUS)	2	2	2	2
3. Bourne/Kraatz (CAN)	**3**	**3**	**3**	**3**
4. Anissina/Peizerat (FRA)	4	4	4	4
5. Romanova/Yaroshenko (UKR)	5	5	5	5
6. Lobacheva/Averbukh (RUS)	6	6	6	6
7. Punsalan/Swallow (USA)	8	7	7	7
8. Drobiazko/Vanagas (LIT)	9	8	8	8
9. Mrázová/Šimeček (CZE)	7	9	9	9
10. Fusar-Poli/Margaglio (ITA)	12	10	10	10
11. Nowak/Kolasiński (POL)	10	12	11	11
12. Stekolnikova/Kazarly. (KAZ)	11	11	12	12
13. Winkler/Lohse (GER)	13	13	13	13
14. Roca/Sur (USA)	14	14	14	14
15. Lefebvre/Brunet (CAN)	**16**	**17**	**15**	**15**
16. Tsuzuki/Razgulajevs (JPN)	17	18	17	16
17. Humphreys/Askew (GRB)	15	15	16	18
18. MacLean/Schaub (AUT)	18	16	18	17
19. Grushina/Goncharov (UKR)	20	20	20	19
20. Piton/Piton (FRA)	19	19	19	20
21. Jacquemard/Gayet (FRA)	21	21	21	21
22. Vondrková/Král (CZE)	22	23	22	23
23. Chait/Sakhnovski (ISR)	24	25	24	22
24. Berkes/Szentirmai (HUN)	23	24	23	24
25. Diener/Pospelov (SUI)	25	22	25	-

26. Hanley/Serkov (EST)	29	27	26	-
27. Lai/Lai (TPE)	27	29	27	-
28. Koinuma/Arakelian (ARM)	26	26	29	-
29. Loyer/Bell (AUS)	28	28	28	-
30. Kuusnuemi/Walker (FIN)	30	30	30	-
31. Uotila/Mattila (FIN)	31	31	-	-
32. Mosenkova/Kurakin (EST)	32	32	-	-
33. Kim/Kim (KOR)	33	33	-	-

For the first time in history, two rainbow Pride flags were displayed at the World Figure Skating Championships, in support of U.S. Champion Rudy Galindo, who was openly gay.

For the first time in a decade, American skaters won gold medals in both the men's and ladies events at the World Championships.

The event also marked the first time that the World Figure Skating Championships had an official website. The website featured news, a photo gallery, competitor list, polls, educational information, results.

There was a minor controversy when ISU President Ottavio Cinquanta banned Kurt Browning from performing with singer Michael Burgess in the Opening Ceremony, because he was a professional. Browning and Kristi Yamaguchi were ultimately invited to perform after the Parade of Champions ended.

Sources: Edmonton Journal, March 7 and 25, 1996; The Ottawa Citizen, March 17, 1996; Bay Area Reporter, March 28, 1996; Skating magazine, April 1996; Eissport magazine, April 1996; Website, 1996 World Figure Skating Championships

1997 WORLD FIGURE SKATING CHAMPIONSHIPS
Lausanne, Switzerland, March 16-23, 1997

World Men's Figure Skating Championships:

	QRA	QRB	SP	FS
1. Elvis Stojko (CAN)	2	-	4	1

2. Todd Eldredge (USA)	1	-	2	2
3. Alexei Yagudin (RUS)	6	-	5	3
4. Viacheslav Zagorodniuk (UKR)	3	-	6	4
5. Ilia Kulik (RUS)	-	2	3	6
6. Andrejs Vlascenko (GER)	4	-	10	5
7. Michael Weiss (USA)	-	4	9	8
8. Igor Pashkevich (AZE)	5	-	12	7
9. Jeffrey Langdon (CAN)	**-**	**5**	**11**	**9**
10. Takeshi Honda (JPN)	-	7	7	12
11. Steven Cousins (GRB)	-	9	17	11
12. Éric Millot (FRA)	-	3	13	13
13. Laurent Tobel (FRA)	-	6	20	10
14. Cornel Gheorghe (ROM)	9	-	18	14
15. Michael Shmerkin (ISR)	11	-	8	20
16. Szabolcs Vidrai (HUN)	8	-	15	17
17. Konstantin Kostin (LAT)	-	8	14	18
18. Michael Tyllesen (DEN)	-	12	19	16
19. Zhengxin Guo (CHN)	12	-	22	15
20. Roman Skorniakov (UZB)	-	13	16	19
21. Michael Hopfes (GER)	-	10	21	21
22. Anthony Liu (AUS)	7	-	24	22
23. Ivan Dinev (BUL)	13	-	23	24
24. Patrick Meier (SUI)	16	-	26	23
25. Markus Leminen (FIN)	14	-	25	-
26. Gilberto Viadana (ITA)	-	14	27	-
27. Kyu-hyun Lee (KOR)	-	11	28	-
28. Robert Grzegorczyk (POL)	-	15	29	-
29. Patrick Schmit (LUX)	10	-	30	-
30. Vakhtang Murvanidze (GEO)	15	-	31	-
31. Jordi Pedro Roya (ESP) -	16	-	-	-
32. Alexander Murashko (BLS)	17	-	-	-
32. Margus Hernits (EST)	-	17	-	-
34. Karel Nekola (CZE)	18	-	-	-
34. Dan Hollander (USA)	-	18	-	-
36. Ferdi Skoberla (SAF)	19	-	-	-
36. Róbert Kažimír (SLO)	-	19	-	-
38. Yuri Litvinov (KAZ)	20	-	-	-
38. David Liu (TPE)	-	20	-	-

40. Ricardo Olaverrieta (MEX)	21	-	-	-
40. Florian Tuma (AUT)	-	21	-	-
42. Yan-ho Brian Chan (HKG)	22	-	-	-
42. M. van den Broeck (BEL)	-	22	-	-
WD. Alexei Urmanov (RUS)	-	1	-	-
WD. Armen Asoyan (ARM)	-	-	-	-
WD. Aleksander Terentjev (EST)	-	-	-	-

World Ladies Figure Skating Championships:

	QRA	QRB	SP	FS
1. Tara Lipinski (USA)	-	1	1	2
2. Michelle Kwan (USA)	1	-	4	1
3. Vanessa Gusmeroli (FRA)	2	-	2	4
4. Irina Slutskaya (RUS)	3	-	6	3
5. Maria Butyrskaya (RUS)	-	3	3	5
6. Laëtitia Hubert (FRA)	9	-	7	7
7. Krisztina Czakó (HUN)	4	-	5	8
8. Julia Lautowa (AUT)	-	5	11	6
9. Yulia Lavrenchuk (UKR)	-	4	9	10
10. Eva-Maria Fitze (GER)	8	-	16	9
11. Joanne Carter (AUS)	10	-	10	12
12. Olga Markova (RUS)	-	7	15	11
13. Nicole Bobek (USA)	-	2	8	15
14. Zuzanna Szwed (POL)	5	-	12	14
15. Lucinda Ruh (SUI)	-	6	18	13
16. Lenka Kulovaná (CZE)	7	-	14	18
17. Tatiana Malinina (UZB)	-	12	17	19
18. Fumie Suguri (JPN)	-	10	24	16
19. Alisa Drei (FIN)	-	8	22	17
20. Mojca Kopač (SLO)	13	-	13	22
21. Yulia Vorobieva (AZE)	6	-	20	20
22. Helena Grundberg (SWE)	-	13	23	21
23. Hanae Yokoya (JPN)	-	9	19	23
24. Lu Chen (CHN)	-	11	25	-
26. T.S. Bombardieri (ITA)	15	-	26	-
27. Zuzana Paurová (SVK)	14	-	27	-
28. Marta Andrade Vidal (ESP)	11	-	28	-
29. Ivana Jakupčević (CRO)	-	15	29	-

30. Sofia Penkova (BUL)	-	14	30	-
31. Valeria Trifancova (LAT)	16	-	-	-
31. Yankun Du (CHN)	-	16	-	-
33. Valentina Gazeleridou (GRE)	17	-	-	-
33. Shirene Human (SAF)	-	17	-	-
35. Noemi Bedo (ROM)	18	-	-	-
35. Zoe Jones (GRB)	-	18	-	-
37. Patricia Ferriot (BEL)	19	-	-	-
37. Min-ju Jung (KOR)	-	19	-	-
39. Janie Ja-lin Weng (TPE)	20	-	-	-
39. Kaja Hanevold (NOR)	-	20	-	-
41. Liina-Grete Lilender (EST)	21	-	-	-
41. Rita Dolly Auyeung (HKG)	-	21	-	-
WD. Susan Humphreys (CAN)	**12**	**-**	**21**	**-**
WD. Veronika Dytrt (GER)	-	-	-	-

World Pairs Skating Championships:

	SP	FS
1. Mandy Wötzel/Ingo Steuer (GER)	1	1
2. Marina Eltsova/Andrei Bushkov (RUS)	2	2
3. Oksana Kazakova/Artur Dmitriev (RUS)	6	3
4. Kyoko Ina/Jason Dungjen (USA)	5	4
5. Jenni Meno/Todd Sand (USA)	4	5
6. Kristy Sargeant/Kris Wirtz (CAN)	**8**	**6**
7. Sarah Abitbol/Stéphane Bernadis (FRA)	7	7
8. Dorota Zagórska/Mariusz Siudek (POL)	11	8
9. Elena Berezhnaya/Anton Sikharulidze (RUS)	3	12
10. Peggy Schwarz/Mirko Müller (GER)	9	10
11. Xue Shen/Hongbo Zhao (CHN)	14	9
12. Marina Khalturina/Andrei Kriukov (KAZ)	10	11
13. Silvia Dimitrov/Rico Rex (GER)	12	13
14. M-C. Savard-Gagnon/L. Bradet (CAN)	**15**	**14**
15. Stephanie Stiegler/John Zimmerman (USA)	13	15
16. Danielle McGrath/Stephen Carr (AUS)	16	16
17. Elaine Asanakis/Joel McKeever (GRE)	18	17
18. E. Beloussovskaya/S. Morozov (UKR)	17	18
19. Svetlana Plachonina/Dmitri Kaploun (BLS)	19	19
20. Elena Sirokhvatova/Oleg Shliakhov (LAT)	20	20

21. Inga Rodionova/Alexander Anichenko (AZE)   22   21
22. J. Nekrassova/V. Mintals (EST)   24   22
23. M. Krasiltseva/A. Chestnikh (ARM)   23   23
24. Elena Ershova/Evgeni Sviridov (UZB)   25   -
WD. Lesley Rogers/Michael Aldred (GRB)   21   -
WD. Evgenia Filonenko/Igor Marchenko (UKR)   -   -
WD. Oľga Beständigová/Jozef Beständig (SVK)   -   -

European Ice Dancing Championships:

	CD1	CD2	OD	FD
1. Grishuk/Platov (RUS)	1	1	1	1
2. Krylova/Ovsiannikov (RUS)	2(t)	2	2	2
3. Bourne/Kraatz (CAN)	**2(t)**	**3**	**3**	**3**
4. Moniotte/Lavanchy (FRA)	4	5	4	4
5. Anissina/Peizerat (FRA)	5	4	5	5
6. Punsalan/Swallow (USA)	6	6	6	6
7. Lobacheva/Averbukh (RUS)	7	7	7	7
8. Romanova/Yaroshenko (UKR)	8	8	8	8
9. Fusar-Poli/Margaglio (ITA)	9	10	10	9
10. Drobiazko/Vanagas (LIT)	10	9	9	10
11. Nowak/Kolasiński (POL)	12	12	11	11
12. Winkler/Lohse (GER)	13	14	13	12
13. Mrázová/Šimeček (CZE)	11	11	12	14
14. Navka/Morozov (BLS)	14	13	14	13
15. Stekolnikova/Kazarly. (KAZ)	15	15	15	15
16. Humphreys/Askew (GRB)	16	16	16	16
17. Chalom/Gates (USA)	18	17	18	17
18. Chait/Sakhnovski (ISR)	17	18	17	18
19. Denkova/Staviski (BUL)	20	19	19	19
20. Lefebvre/Brunet (CAN)	**19**	**20**	**20**	**20**
21. Führing/Ellinger (AUT)	22	23	22	21
22. Kawai/Tanaka (JPN)	21	21	21	23
23. Vondrková/Král (CZE)	23	24	23	22
24. Dahlen/Razgulajevs (LAT)	24	22	24	24
25. Loyer/Bell (AUS)	25	25	25	-
26. Kalesnik/Terentjev (EST)	26	27	26	-
27. Szijgyarto/Tóth (HUN)	27	26	27	-
28. Slobodova/Beljk (UZB)	28	29	28	-

29. Chakmakjian/Lapaige (BEL)	29	28	29	-
WD. Koinuma/Arakekian (ARM)	-	-	-	-
WD. Bárány/Rosnik (HUN)	-	-	-	-

14-year-old Tara Lipinski made history as the youngest skater to win a gold medal in the ladies event at the World Figure Skating Championships. Not everyone was thrilled about the participation of such young competitors. 22-year-old French skater Laëtitia Hubert told reporters, "With such young skaters, it seems to me like we're returning to the days of baby gymnasts. Meanwhile, skaters my age are very capable of landing triple jumps, but with experience and femininity added to that."

While attending the World Championships with his students Nicole Bobek and Cornel Gheorghe, legendary coach Carlo Fassi suffered a heart attack and passed away at the Canton Hospital University Vaud. A memorial service for Fassi was held at Lausanne's Olympic Museum.

China's Zhengxin Guo made history as the first skater to land two quadruple jumps in one program and Canada's Elvis Stojko made history as the first skater to land a quadruple/triple combination at the World Championships.

Sources: USA Today, March 21, 1997; The Ann Arbor News, March 22, 1997; Eissport magazine, April 1997; Skating magazine, May 1997; Entries, 1997 World Figure Skating Championships

Laëtitia Hubert of France, a nine-time competitor at the World Championships who narrowly missed out on winning a medal twice. PA Images / Alamy Stock Photo.

1998 WORLD FIGURE SKATING CHAMPIONSHIPS
Minneapolis, United States, March 29-April 5, 1998

World Men's Figure Skating Championships:

	QRA	QRB	SP	FS
1. Alexei Yagudin (RUS)	-	2	1	2
2. Todd Eldredge (USA)	1	-	4	1
3. Evgeni Plushenko (RUS)	-	1	2	4
4. Viacheslav Zagorodniuk (UKR)	3	-	5	3
5. Andrejs Vlascenko (GER)	-	7	6	5
6. Michael Weiss (USA)	2	-	3	7
7. Steven Cousins (GRB)	7	-	7	6
8. Jeffrey Langdon (CAN)	**5**	**-**	**8**	**8**
9. Evgeni Pliuta (UKR)	-	5	9	10
10. Szabolcs Vidrai (HUN)	-	4	12	9
11. Takeshi Honda (JPN)	-	3	11	11
12. Zhengxin Guo (CHN)	-	9	14	12
13. Michael Tyllesen (DEN)	13	-	18	14
14. Roman Skorniakov (UZB)	6	-	21	13
15. Michael Shmerkin (ISR)	11	-	10	19
16. Laurent Tobel (FRA)	-	11	19	16
17. Anthony Liu (AUS)	-	12	22	15
18. Margus Hernits (EST)	12	-	17	18
19. Markus Leminen (FIN)	-	13	13	20
20. Patrick Meier (SUI)	-	6	23	17
21. Ivan Dinev (BUL)	4	-	15	21
22. Robert Grzegorczyk (POL)	10	-	16	23
23. Sven Meyer (GER)	-	10	24	22
24. Gilberto Viadana (ITA)	-	8	20	24
25. Patrick Schmit (LUX)	14	-	25	-
26. Yamato Tamura (JPN)	9	-	26	-
27. Sergejs Telenkov (LAT)	-	15	27	-
28. Vakhtang Murvanidze (GEO)	15	-	28	-
29. Emanuel Sandhu (CAN)	**8**	**-**	**29**	**-**
30. Kyu-hyun Lee (KOR)	-	14	30	-
31. Gheorghe Chiper (ROM)	16	-	-	-
31. David Liu (TPE)	-	16	-	-
33. Juraj Sviatko (SVK)	17	-	-	-

33. Daniel Peinado (ESP)	-	17	-	-
35. Panagiotis Markouizos (GRE)	18	-	-	-
35. Ricardo Olavarrieta (MEX)	-	18	-	-
WD. Ilia Kulik (RUS)	-	-	-	-
WD. Elvis Stojko (CAN)	**-**	**-**	**-**	**-**
WD. Philippe Candeloro (FRA)	-	-	-	-
WD. Igor Pashkevich (AZE)	-	-	-	-
WD. Armen Asoyan (ARM)	-	-	-	-
WD. Sergei Rylov (AZE)	-	-	-	-
WD. Derek Hay-wai Leung (HKG)	-	-	-	-

World Ladies Figure Skating Championships:

	QRA	QRB	SP	FS
1. Michelle Kwan (USA)	1	-	1	1
2. Irina Slutskaya (RUS)	2	-	4	2
3. Maria Butyrskaya (RUS)	-	1	5	3
4. Laëtitia Hubert (FRA)	8	-	3	4
5. Anna Rechnio (POL)	-	2	2	5
6. Tonia Kwiatkowski (USA)	4	-	8	6
7. Elena Liashenko (UKR)	-	3	6	7
8. Elena Sokolova (RUS)	3	-	13	8
9. Tanja Szewczenko (GER)	-	6	10	10
10. Diána Póth (HUN)	-	8	15	9
11. Yulia Vorobieva (AZE)	5	-	11	11
12. Yulia Lavrenchuk (UKR)	-	4	12	13
13. Joanne Carter (AUS)	6	-	16	12
14. Tatiana Malinina (UZB)	-	5	7	18
15. Lenka Kulovaná (CZE)	10	-	17	14
16. Vanessa Gusmeroli (FRA)	-	7	9	19
17. Marie-Pierre Leray (FRA)	14	-	18	16
18. Silvia Fontana (ITA)	-	9	21	15
19. Júlia Sebestyén (HUN)	9	-	20	17
20. Angela Derochie (CAN)	**11**	**-**	**19**	**20**
21. Zuzana Paurová (SVK)	-	11	14	23
22. Shizuka Arakawa (JPN)	7	-	22	21
23. Lucinda Ruh (SUI)	-	10	24	22
24. Mojca Kopač (SLO)	-	12	23	24
25. Alisa Drei (FIN)	12	-	25	-

26. Anna Wenzel (AUT)	-	14	26	-
27. Anna Lundström (SWE)	13	-	27	-
28. Marta Andrade Vidal (ESP)	-	13	28	-
29. Hyung-kyung Choi (KOR)	15	-	29	-
30. Yankun Du (CHN)	-	15	30	-
31. Ivana Jakupčević (CRO)	16	-	-	-
31. Olga Vassiljeva (EST)	-	16	-	-
33. Shirene Human (SAF)	17	-	-	-
33. Valeria Trifancova (LAT)	-	17	-	-
35. Lauryna Slavinskaite (LIT)	18	-	-	-
35. Helena Pajović (YUG) -	18	-	-	
37. A. Chatziathanassiou (GRE)	19	-	-	-
37. Roxana Luca (ROM)	-	19	-	-
39. Rocia Salas Visuet (MEX)	-	20	-	-
WD. Tara Lipinski (USA)	-	-	-	-
WD. Lu Chen (CHN)	-	-	-	-
WD. Surya Bonaly (FRA)	-	-	-	-
WD. Nicole Bobek (USA)	-	-	-	-
WD. Kaja Hanevold (NOR)	-	-	-	

-

World Pairs Skating Championships:

	SP	FS
1. Elena Berezhnaya/Anton Sikharulidze (RUS)	2	1
2. Jenni Meno/Todd Sand (USA)	1	2
3. Peggy Schwarz/Mirko Müller (GER)	3	3
4. Shen Xue/Zhao Hongbo (CHN)	6	4
5. Dorota Zagórska/Mariusz Siudek (POL)	4	6
6. Marina Eltsova/Andrei Bushkov (RUS)	7	5
7. Kristy Sargeant/Kris Wirtz (CAN)	**5**	**7**
8. Sarah Abitbol/Stéphane Bernadis (FRA)	8	8
9. M-C. Savard-Gagnon/L. Bradet (CAN)	**12**	**9**
10. Shelby Lyons/Brian Wells (USA)	10	10
11. Marina Khalturina/Andrei Kriukov (KAZ)	9	11
12. Evgenia Filonenko/Igor Marchenko (UKR)	11	12
13. Marsha Poluliaschenko/Andrew Seabrook (GRB)	15	13
14. Kateřina Beránková/Otto Dlabola (CZE)	13	14
15. Danielle McGrath/Stephen Carr (AUS)	14	15

16. Elaine Asanakis/Alcuin Schulten (GRE) 16 16
17. Inga Rodionova/Aleksandr Anichenko (AZE) 18 17
18. Oľga Beständigová/Jozef Beständig (SVK) 17 18
19. Jelena Sirokhvatova/Jurijs Salmanovs (LAT) 20 19
20. Jekaterina Nekrassova/Valdis Mintals (EST) 19 20
WD. Mandy Wötzel/Ingo Steuer (GER) - -
WD. Oksana Kazakova/Artur Dmitriev (RUS) - -
WD. Kyoko Ina/Jason Dungjen (USA) - -
WD. Natalia Ponomareva/Evgeni Sviridov (UZB) - -

World Ice Dancing Championships:

	CD1	CD2	OD	FD
1. Krylova/Ovsiannikov (RUS)	1	1	1	1
2. Anissina/Peizerat (FRA)	3	2	2	2
3. Bourne/Kraatz (CAN)	**2**	**3**	**3**	**3**
4. Lobacheva/Averbukh (RUS)	4	4	4	4
5. Fusar-Poli/Margaglio (ITA)	6	6	5	5
6. Punsalan/Swallow (USA)	5	5	6	6
7. Romanova/Yaroshenko (UKR)	9	8	7	7
8. Drobiazko/Vanagas (LIT)	7	7	8	8
9. Winkler/Lohse (GER)	8	9	9	9
10. Navka/Morozov (BLS)	11	12	10	10
11. Nowak/Kolasiński (POL)	10	10	11	11
12. Mrázová/Šimeček (CZE)	12	11	12	12
13. Grushina/Goncharov (UKR)	13	13	13	13
14. Chait/Sakhnovski (ISR)	16	15	15	14
15. Semenovich/Fedorov (RUS)	15	14	14	15
16. Gerencser/Camerlengo (ITA)	14	16	16	16
17. Denkova/Staviski (BUL)	17	17	17	17
18. Delobel/Schoenfelder (FRA)	19	19	18	18
19. Lefebvre/Brunet (CAN)	**18**	**18**	**19**	**19**
20. Merzová/Morbacher (SVK)	21	20	21	20
21. Führing/Ellinger (AUT)	23	23	22	21
22. Stekolnikova/Kazarly. (KAZ)	20	21	20	24
23. Clements/Shortland (GRB)	24	25	23	22
24. Deniaud/Jaffredo (FRA)	23	22	24	23
25. Joseph/Butler (USA)	26	24	25	-
26. Hugentob./Hugentob. (SUI)	28	28	26	-

27. Smetanenko/Gezalian (ARM)	27	26	27	-
28. Kawai/Tanaka (JPN)	25	27	28	-
29. Bárány/Rosnik (HUN)	29	29	29	-
30. Fourer/Heinecke (AUS)	30	30	30	-
WD. Grishuk/Platov (RUS)	-	-	-	-

After a high-profile scandal at the 1998 Winter Olympics, which involved Ukrainian judge Yuri Balkov, ice dancing was under great scrutiny and IOC President Dick Pound was openly discussing removing the sport from the Olympic lineup. The judging in Minneapolis was criticized for being predictable and ISU President Ottavio Cinquanta remarked during the World Championships, "We must acknowledge and we cannot deny that the results of ice dance [are] too stable."

Sources: The Toronto Star, March 26, 1998; USA Today, March 27, 1998; The Ottawa Citizen, March 30, 1998; Skating magazine, June 1998; Protocol, 1998 World Figure Skating Championships

1999 WORLD FIGURE SKATING CHAMPIONSHIPS
Helsinki, Finland, March 20-28, 1999

World Men's Figure Skating Championships:

	QRA	QRB	SP	FS
1. Alexei Yagudin (RUS)	1	-	2	1
2. Evgeni Plushenko (RUS)	-	1	1	2
3. Michael Weiss (USA)	-	2	4	3
4. Elvis Stojko (CAN)	**-**	**3**	**3**	**5**
5. Alexei Urmanov (RUS)	2	-	5	6
6. Takeshi Honda (JPN)	3	-	8	4
7. Guo Zhengxin (CHN)	-	7	6	8
8. Laurent Tobel (FRA)	6	-	10	7
9. Andrejs Vlascenko (GER)	4	-	7	10
10. Anthony Liu (AUS)	-	4	16	9
11. Dmitri Dmitrenko (UKR)	-	6	12	11
12. Timothy Goebel (USA)	5	-	13	12
13. Stefan Lindemann (GER)	7	-	9	14
14. Ivan Dinev (BUL)	-	8	11	13

15. Evgeni Pliuta (UKR)	9	8	14	15
16. Trifun Živanović (USA)	-	5	15	16
17. Vakhtang Murvanidze (GEO)	-	9	17	18
18. Emanuel Sandhu (CAN)	**11**	**-**	**20**	**17**
19. Margus Hernits (EST)	12	-	18	19
20. Szabolcs Vidrai (HUN)	-	10	19	21
21. Roman Skorniakov (UZB)	-	11	21	20
22. Patrick Meier (SUI)	8	-	22	22
23. Robert Grzegorczyk (POL)	10	-	23	24
24. Markus Leminen (FIN)	-	12	25	23
25. Sergei Rylov (AZE)	15	-	24	-
26. Kyu-hyun Lee (KOR)	14	-	26	-
27. Róbert Kažimír (SVK)	-	13	27	-
28. Cornel Gheorghe (ROM)	-	14	28	-
29. Michael Tyllesen (DEN)	13	-	30	-
30. Aleksandr Chestnikh (ARM)	-	15	29	-
31. Vitali Danilchenko (UKR)	16	-	-	-
31. Clive Shorten (GRB)	-	16	-	-
33. Neil Wilson (GRB)	17	-	-	-
33. Yuri Litvinov (KAZ)	-	17	-	-
35. Lukáš Rakowski (CZE)	18	-	-	-
35. Konstantin Beliaev (BLS)	-	18	-	-
37. Jan Čejvan (SLO)	19	-	-	-
37. Yon García (ESP)	-	19	-	-
39. Sergejs Telenkov (LAT)	20	-	-	-
39. David Del Pozo (MEX)	-	20	-	-
41. Angelo Dolfini (ITA)	21	-	-	-
41. Panagiotis Markouizos (GRE)	-	21	-	-

World Ladies Figure Skating Championships:

	QRA	QRB	SP	FS
1. Maria Butyrskaya (RUS)	-	1	1	1
2. Michelle Kwan (USA)	1	-	4	2
3. Julia Soldatova (RUS)	-	3	2	4
4. Tatiana Malinina (UZB)	-	2	5	3
5. Vanessa Gusmeroli (FRA)	2	-	3	5
6. Anna Rechnio (POL)	5	-	6	7
7. Sarah Hughes (USA)	4	-	10	6

8. Elena Liashenko (UKR)	-	4	7	8
9. Yulia Lavrenchuk (UKR)	8	-	9	10
10. Viktoria Volchkova (RUS)	3	-	11	14
11. Diána Póth (HUN)	6	-	8	15
12. Angela Nikodinov (USA)	-	9	17	9
13. Lucinda Ruh (SUI)	9	-	12	12
14. Alisa Drei (FIN)	-	12	13	13
15. Julia Lautowa (AUT)	-	10	22	11
16. Silvia Fontana (ITA)	-	5	18	16
17. Yulia Vorobieva (AZE)	-	7	15	18
18. Jennifer Robinson (CAN)	**-**	**8**	**14**	**20**
19. Júlia Sebestyén (HUN)	14	-	16	17
20. Fumie Suguri (JPN)	-	6	20	21
21. Eva-Maria Fitze (GER)	7	-	19	22
22. Sabina Wojtala (POL)	-	11	23	19
23. Valeria Trifancova (LAT)	11	-	21	24
24. Caroline Gülke (GER)	-	13	24	23
25. Idora Hegel (CRO)	12	-	25	-
26. Marta Andrade Vidal (ESP)	10	-	27	-
27. Veronika Dytrtová (CZE)	-	14	26	-
28. Zuzana Paurová (SVK)	-	15	28	-
29. Olga Vassiljeva (EST)	13	-	30	-
30. Meijia Lu (CHN)	15	-	29	-
31. Min-ju Jung (KOR)	16	-	-	-
31. Ingrida Snieskiene (LIT)	-	16	-	-
33. Anna Dimova (BUL)	17	-	-	-
33. Marion Krijgsman (NED)	-	17(t)	-	-
33. Klara Bramfeldt (SWE)	-	17(t)	-	-
36. Kaja Hanevold (NOR)	18	-	-	-
37. Rocio Salas Visuet (MEX)	19	-	-	-
37. Shirene Human (SAF)	-	19	-	-
39. A. Chatziathanassiou (GRE)	20	-	-	-
39. Dow-jane Chi (TPE)	-	20	-	-
41. Helena Pajović (SCG)	-	21	-	-
WD. Laëtitia Hubert (FRA)	-	-	-	-

World Pairs Skating Championships:

	SP	FS
1. Elena Berezhnaya/Anton Sikharulidze (RUS)	1	1
2. Xue Shen/Hongbo Zhao (CHN)	2	2
3. Dorota Zagórska/Mariusz Siudek (POL)	3	3
4. Maria Petrova/Alexei Tikhonov (RUS)	5	4
5. Sarah Abitbol/Stéphane Bernadis (FRA)	6	5
6. Kristy Sargeant/Kris Wirtz (CAN)	**4**	**6**
7. Tatiana Totmianina/Maxim Marinin (RUS)	7	7
8. Peggy Schwarz/Mirko Müller (GER)	9	8
9. Kyoko Ina/John Zimmerman (USA)	8	9
10. Danielle Hartsell/Steven Hartsell (USA)	13	10
11. Yulia Obertas/Dmitri Palamarchuk (UKR)	11	11
12. Kateřina Beránková/Otto Dlabola (CZE)	12	12
13. V. Saurette/J-S. Fecteau (CAN)	**10**	**13**
14. Qing Pang/Jian Tong (CHN)	15	14
15. Inga Rodionova/Aleksandr Anichenko (AZE)	16	15
16. Mariana Kautz/Norman Jeschke (GER)	19	16
17. Oľga Beständigová/Jozef Beständig (CZE)	18	17
18. Ekaterina Danko/Gennadi Emeljenenko (BLS)	17	18
19. Maria Krasiltseva/Artem Znachkov (ARM)	20	19
20. Natalia Ponomareva/Evgeni Sviridov (UZB)	21	-
WD. Laura Handy/Paul Binnebose (USA)	14	-

World Ice Dancing Championships:

	CD1	CD2	OD	FD
1. Krylova/Ovsiannikov (RUS)	1	1	2	1
2. Anissina/Peizerat (FRA)	3	2	1	2
3. Bourne/Kraatz (CAN)	**2**	**3**	**3**	**3**
4. Lobacheva/Averbukh (RUS)	4	4	4	4
5. Fusar-Poli/Margaglio (ITA)	6	5	5	5
6. Drobiazko/Vanagas (LIT)	5	6	6	6
7. Winkler/Lohse (GER)	7	7	7	7
8. Grushina/Goncharov (UKR)	8	8	8	8
9. Nowak/Kolasiński (POL)	9	9	9	9
10. Lang/Tchernyshev (USA)	10	10	10	10
11. Denkova/Staviski (BUL)	11	11	11	11
12. Navka/Kostomarov (RUS)	12	12	12	12

13. Chait/Sakhnovski (ISR)	13	13	13	13
14. Delobel/Schoenfelder (FRA)	14	14	15	14
15. Lefebvre/Brunet (CAN)	**15**	**15**	**14**	**15**
16. Clements/Shortland (GRB)	16	18	16	16
17. Chalom/Gates (USA)	17	16	17	17
18. Hugentob./Hugentob. (SUI)	18	17	18	18
19. Rauer/Rauer (GER)	21	19	19	19
20. Tsuzuki/Farkhoutdinov (JPN)	22	21	20	20
21. Fermi/Rinaldi (ITA)	19	20	22	21
22. Zhang/Cao (CHN)	20	24	21	22
23. Hrázská/Procházka (CZE)	25	22	23	23
24. Führing/Ellinger (AUT)	24	23	24	24
25. Gustafsson/Gronlund (FIN)	31	31	31	25
26. Kurkudym/Kocherzh. (UKR)	26	25	25	-
27. Stekolnik./Fitzgerald (KAZ)	23	27	26	-
28. Bárány/Rosnik (HUN)	28	26	28	-
29. Kalesnik/Terentjev (EST)	29	29	27	-
30. Dahlen/Lukanin (AZE)	27	28	29	-
31. Yang/Lee (KOR)	30	30	30	-
32. R-Smith/N-Bond (AUS)	32	32	-	-

For the first time, Russians claimed gold medals in all four disciplines at the World Figure Skating Championships.

Maria Butyrskaya made history as the first Russian skater to win a gold medal in the ladies event at the World Figure Skating Championships. At 26, she was also the oldest skater to win gold in the ladies event.

In the pairs event, Xue Shen and Hongbo Zhao and Dorota Zagórska and Mariusz Siudek made history as the first pairs from China and Poland to win medals at the World Championships. Ice dancers Ana Galitch and Andrei Griazev made history as the first skaters to represent Bosnia and Herzegovina at the World Championships.

Timothy Goebel made history as the first skater to land a quad Salchow at the World Championships, in the qualifying rounds.

This was the first time that the qualifying rounds for both men's and ladies events contributed to the overall score, with qualifying making up 20%, the short program 30%, and free skating 50%.

Canadian television network CTV released footage of Ukrainian judge Alfred Korytek and Russian judge Sviatoslav Babenko making gestures at one another during the pairs free skate. After Russian pair Elena Berezhnaya and Anton Sikharulidze won, ISU official Sally Anne-Stapleford reviewed the footage and admitted, "There appears to have been some kind of collusion. There appears to have been some kind of communication... It doesn't look particularly good." Korytek and Babenko were both swiftly suspended by the ISU.

Sources: USA Today, March 23, 1999; The Flint Journal, March 26, 1999; Calgary Herald, March 28, 1999; Saint John Telegraph-Journal, March 29, 1999; Protocol, 1999 World Figure Skating Championships

2000 WORLD FIGURE SKATING CHAMPIONSHIPS
Nice, France, March 23-April 3, 2000

World Men's Figure Skating Championships:

	QRA	QRB	SP	FS
1. Alexei Yagudin (RUS)	1	-	1	1
2. Elvis Stojko (CAN)	-	**1**	**5**	**2**
3. Michael Weiss (USA)	2	-	3	3
4. Evgeni Plushenko (RUS)	-	2	2	4
5. Chengjiang Li (CHN)	3	-	8	6
6. Alexandr Abt (RUS)	-	3	4	12
7. Stanick Jeannette (FRA)	-	5	10	8
8. Zhengxin Guo (CHN)	-	4	9	9
9. Vincent Restencourt (FRA)	7	-	11	7
10. Takeshi Honda (JPN)	5	-	17	5
11. Timothy Goebel (USA)	-	8	7	10
12. Anthony Liu (AUS)	-	7	6	14
13. Vitali Danilchenko (UKR)	-	6	12	11
14. Stefan Lindemann (GER)	4	-	13	13

15. Dmitri Dmitrenko (UKR)	8	-	15	15
16. Andrejs Vlascenko (GER)	6	-	16	16
17. Roman Skorniakov (UZB)	-	10	18	17
18. Ivan Dinev (BUL)	-	9	14	20
19. Ben Ferreira (CAN)	**-**	**11**	**20**	**18**
20. Michael Tyllesen (DEN)	10	-	19	19
21. Markus Leminen (FIN)	12	-	22	22
22. Patrick Meier (SUI)	9	-	21	24
23. Sergei Rylov (AZE)	-	13	24	21
24. Konstantin Kostin (LAT)	-	12	23	23
25. Vakhtang Murvanidze (GEO)	13	-	25	-
26. Szabolcs Vidrai (HUN)	11	-	27	-
27. Yamato Tamura (JPN)	-	14	26	-
28. Cornel Gheorghe (ROM)	14	-	28	-
29. Matthew Davies (GRB)	-	15	29	-
30. Yuri Litvinov (KAZ)	15	-	30	-
31. Kevin van der Perren (BEL)	16	-	-	-
31. Robert Grzegorczyk (POL)	-	16	-	-
33. Róbert Kažimír (SVK)	17	-	-	-
33. Kyu-hyun Lee (KOR)	-	17	-	-
35. Patrick Schmit (LUX)	18	-	-	-
35. Michael Shmerkin (ISR)	-	18	-	-
37. Angelo Dolfini (ITA)	19	-	-	-
37. Bradley Santer (AUS)	-	19	-	-
39. Ricky Cockerill (NZL)	20	-	-	-
39. Jan Čejvan (SLO)	-	20	-	-
41. Clemens Jonas (AUT)	21	-	-	-
41. Lukáš Rakowski (CZE)	-	21	-	-
43. Jordi Pedro Roya (ESP)	22	-	-	-
43. Margus Hernits (EST)	-	22	-	-
45. Panagiotis Markouizos (GRE)	23	-	-	-
45. Filip Stiller (SWE)	-	23	-	-
47. Ricardo Olavarrieta (MEX)	-	24	-	-
WD. Gheorghe Chiper (ROM)	-	-	-	-
WD. Gregor Urbas (SLO)	-	-	-	-

World Ladies Figure Skating Championships:

	QRA	QRB	SP	FS
1. Michelle Kwan (USA)	-	2	3	1
2. Irina Slutskaya (RUS)	-	1	2	2
3. Maria Butyrskaya (RUS)	1	-	1	3
4. Vanessa Gusmeroli (FRA)	-	7	4	4
5. Sarah Hughes (USA)	-	3	5	5
6. Viktoria Volchkova (RUS)	-	4	8	7
7. Júlia Sebestyén (HUN)	3	-	7	9
8. Jennifer Robinson (CAN)	**-**	**6**	**11**	**6**
9. Angela Nikodinov (USA)	-	5	6	11
10. Elena Liashenko (UKR)	4	-	10	10
11. Mikkeline Kierkgaard (DEN)	2	-	15	8
12. Yoshie Onda (JPN)	-	8	12	12
13. Sabina Wojtala (POL)	-	9	9	15
14. Diána Póth (HUN)	11	-	13	13
15. Alisa Drei (FIN)	7	-	14	16
16. Anna Rechnio (POL)	9(t)	-	17	14
17. Zoya Douchine (GER)	6	-	20	18
18. Tatiana Malinina (UZB)	5	-	19	19
19. Silvia Fontana (ITA)	-	10	21	17
20. Anna Lundström (SWE)	8	-	18	20
21. Galina Maniachenko (UKR)	9(t)	-	16	21
22. Siyin Sun (CHN)	-	13	22	22
23. Ivana Jakupčević (CRO)	-	12	25	23
24. Shirene Human (SAF)	13	-	23	24
25. Kaja Hanevold (NOR)	15	-	24	-
26. Roxana Luca (ROM)	12	-	26	-
27. Yulia Lebedeva (ARM)	-	14	27	-
28. A. Gimazetdinova (UZB)	-	11	29	-
29. Valeria Trifancova (LAT)	14	-	28	-
30. Marion Krijgsman (NED)	-	15	30	-
31. Yulia Vorobieva (AZE)	16	-	-	-
31. Mojca Kopač (SLO)	-	16	-	-
33. Ellen Mareels (BEL)	17	-	-	-
33. Olga Vassiljeva (EST)	-	17	-	-
35. Lucia Starovičová (SVK)	18	-	-	-
35. Anna Wenzel (AUT)	-	18	-	-

37. Sarah-Yvonne Prytula (AUS)	19	-	-	-
37. Tamsin Sear (GRB)	-	19	-	-
39. Diane Chen (TPE)	20	-	-	-
39. Nicole Skoda (SUI)	-	20	-	-
41. Liza Menagia (GRE)	21	-	-	-
41. Marta Andrade Vidal (ESP)	-	21	-	-
43. Rocio Salas Visuet (MEX)	22	-	-	-
43. Young-eun Choi (KOR)	-	22	-	-
45. Helena Pajović (YUG) -	23	-	-	
WD. Laëtitia Hubert (FRA)	-	-	-	-
WD. Julia Lautowa (AUT)	-	-	-	-
WD. Eva Chudá (CZE)	-	-	-	-
WD. Angeliki Menaya (GRE)	-	-	-	-
WD. Dominyka Valiukeviciute	-	-	-	-

World Pairs Skating Championships:

	SP	FS
1. Maria Petrova/Alexei Tikhonov (RUS)	2	1
2. Xue Shen/Hongbo Zhao (CHN)	1	2
3. Sarah Abitbol/Stéphane Bernadis (FRA)	4	3
4. Jamie Salé/David Pelletier (CAN)	**3**	**4**
5. Dorota Zagórska/Mariusz Siudek (POL)	7	5
6. Tatiana Totmianina/Maxim Marinin (BLS)	8	6
7. Kyoko Ina/John Zimmerman (USA)	6	7
8. Peggy Schwarz/Mirko Müller (GER)	5	9
9. Tiffany Scott/Phillip Dulebohn (USA)	9	8
10. Kristy Sargeant/Kris Wirtz (CAN)	**11**	**10**
11. Mariana Kautz/Norman Jeschke (GER)	12	12
12. Marina Khalturina/Valeri Artyuchov (KAZ)	16	11
13. Kateřina Beránková/Otto Dlabola (CZE)	13	13
14. Inga Rodionova/Andrei Kriukov (AZE)	14	14
15. Qing Pang/Jian Tong (CHN)	15	15
16. Evgenia Filonenko/Alexander Chestnikh (GEO)	18	16
17. Viktoria Shklover/Valdis Mintals (EST)	17	17
18. Oľga Beständigová/Jozef Beständig (SVK)	19	18
19. Ekaterina Danko/Gennadi Emelienenko (BLS)	20	19
20. Catherine Huc/Vivien Rolland (FRA)	21	-
21. Tatjana Zaharjeva/Jurijs Salmanovs (LAT)	22	-

WD. Yulia Obertas/Dmitri Palamarchuk (UKR) 10 -
WD. Maria Krasiltseva/Artem Znachkov (ARM) - -
WD. Olga Semkina/Alexey Minin (BUL) - -
DQ. Elena Berezhnaya/Anton Sikharulidze (RUS) - -
DQ. Natalia Ponomareva/Evgeni Sviridov (UZB) - -

World Ice Dancing Championships:

	CD1	CD2	OD	FD
1. Anissina/Peizerat (FRA) 1	1	2	1	
2. Fusar-Poli/Margaglio (ITA)	2	2	1	2
3. Drobiazko/Vanagas (LIT)	4	4	4	3
4. Lobacheva/Averbukh (RUS)	3	3	3	4
5. Chait/Sakhnovski (ISR)	6	6	5	5
6. Winkler/Lohse (GER)	5	5	6	6
7. Grushina/Goncharov (UKR)	7	7	7	7
8. Lang/Tchernyshev (USA)	8	9	9	8
9. Nowak/Kolasiński (POL)	9	8	10	9
10. Dubreuil/Lauzon (CAN)	**10**	**11**	**11**	**10**
11. Delobel/Schoenfelder (FRA)	12	12	12	11
12. Silverstein/Pekarek (USA)	14	14	13	12
13. Semenovich/Kostomarov (RUS)	13	13	14	13
14. Hugentob./Hugentob. (SUI)	15	16	15	14
15. Wing/Lowe (CAN)	**17**	**15**	**16**	**15**
16. Romaniuta/Barantsev (RUS)	18	17	18	16
17. Kauc/Bernadowski (POL)	19	19	19	18
18. Tsuzuki/Farkhoutdinov (JPN)	21	20	20	17
19. Rauer/Rauer (GER)	20	21	21	19
20. Gebora/Visontai (HUN)	25	24	22	20
21. Keeble/Zalewski (GRB)	24	23	23	21
22. Zhang/Cao (CHN)	23	22	24	22
23. Führing/Ellinger (AUT)	22	25	26	-
24. Kovalová/Szurman (CZE)	26	26	25	-
25. de Carbonnel/Malkov (BLS)	28	28	27	-
26. Ďurkovská/Mesároš (SVK)	27	27	28	-
27. Mosenkova/Sychov (EST)	30	30	29	-
28. Hyden/Azrojan (ARM)	29	29	30	-
29. Galitch/Griazev (BIH)	31	31	-	-
30. Duval-Rigby/Rigby (AUS)	32	32	-	-

WD. Denkova/Staviski (BUL)	11	10	8	-
WD. Faiella/Milo (ITA)	16	18	17	-
WD. Bourne/Kraatz (CAN)	-	-	-	-
WD. Krylova/Ovsiannikov (RUS)	-	-	-	-
WD. Potdykova/Petukhov (RUS)	-	-	-	-
WD. Kobaladze/Voiko (UKR)	-	-	-	-

The World Figure Skating Championships were originally awarded to Brisbane, Australia and the event would have been the first senior ISU Championship in the Southern Hemisphere. In 1999, the World Championships were relocated to Nice, France. In a press release, the ISU claimed, "The reason for the new decision of the ISU Council is that there were irreconcilable problems, which prevented an agreement with television resources in Australia to act as 'host broadcaster' under agreeable technical and financial conditions that would assure adequate service and coverage to the ISU and its world-wide television broadcast licensees." The Australian federation disputed this statement, noting that nothing had changed with regard to their arrangements for television coverage since the time their bid to host the event was approved, sued for expenses and filed a complaint against the ISU with the Court of Arbitration for Sport.

Margarita Drobiazko and Povilas Vanagas made history as the first Lithuanians to win medals at the World Figure Skating Championships.

Several skaters suffered serious injuries. Ukraine's Dmitri Palamarchuk suffered a concussion after a fall during an overhead lift and Bulgaria's Albena Denkova required surgery to her left leg after being slashed by American skater Peter Tchernyshev's blade during practice. French skater Stéphane Bernadis was attacked by an unknown intruder in his hotel room yielding a razor. He suffered a 25-centimeter gash on his left forearm that required stitches and was given an injection of painkillers before competing. Weeks prior to the competition, a threatening note was left on Bernadis' car that said, "You will die soon."

Elena Berezhnaya and Anton Sikharulidze were not permitted to compete, after Berezhnaya's positive doping test at the European Championships. At the time, she was dealing with bronchitis and had been prescribed medication containing the prohibited substance by a physician in New Jersey. Uzbekistan's Natalia Ponomareva and Evgeniy Sviridov were also not permitted to compete, after Sviridov tested positive for a banned substance at the Four Continents Championships.

Sources: CBS Sportsline, September 1, 1999; ISU Press Release, November 27, 1999; ESPN, February 14, March 26 and 28, 2000; Kingston Whig-Standard, March 28 and April 6, 2000; The Hamilton Spectator, March 31, 2000; The Age, March 31, 2000; The Sydney Morning Herald, April 3, 2000; Skating magazine, May 2000; Entries, 2000 World Figure Skating Championships; Protocol, 2000 World Figure Skating Championships

2001 WORLD FIGURE SKATING CHAMPIONSHIPS
Vancouver, Canada, March 17-25, 2001

World Men's Figure Skating Championships:

	QRA	QRB	SP	FS
1. Evgeni Plushenko (RUS)	1	-	1	1
2. Alexei Yagudin (RUS)	5	-	2	2
3. Todd Eldredge (USA)	2	-	3	3
4. Timothy Goebel (USA)	3	-	4	4
5. Takeshi Honda (JPN)	-	1	10	6
6. Yunfei Li (CHN)	6	-	5	7
7. Chengjiang Li (CHN)	-	8	6	8
8. Alexandr Abt (RUS)	4	-	7	9
9. Emanuel Sandhu (CAN)	**-**	**4**	**16**	**5**
10. Elvis Stojko (CAN)	**-**	**2**	**11**	**11**
11. Stanick Jeannette (FRA)	-	3	9	12
12. Ivan Dinev (BUL)	7	-	12	10
13. Sergei Rylov (AZE)	-	7	15	13
14. Anthony Liu (AUS)	-	10	8	16
15. Min Zhang (CHN)	-	6	17	15
16. Patrick Meier (SUI)	8	-	13	18
17. Yamato Tamura (JPN)	-	5	24	14

18. Stefan Lindemann (GER)	-	9	14	20
19. Vincent Restencourt (FRA)	13	-	18	17
20. Roman Skorniakov (UZB)	-	13	19	19
21. Gheorghe Chiper (ROM)	11	-	22	21
22. Vitali Danilchenko (UKR)	9	-	20	23
23. Dmitri Dmitrenko (UKR)	10	-	21	24
24. Markus Leminen (FIN)	-	14	23	22
25. Vakhtang Murvanidze (GEO)	-	11	26	-
26. Neil Wilson (GRB)	14	-	25	-
27. Angelo Dolfini (ITA)	12	-	28	-
28. Róbert Kažimír (SVK)	-	15	27	-
29. Sergei Davydov (BLS)	-	12	29	-
30. Gregor Urbas (SLO)	15	-	30	-
31. Alexei Kozlov (EST)	16	-	-	-
31. Kristoffer Berntsson (SWE)	-	16	-	-
33. Kevin van der Perren (BEL)	17	-	-	-
33. Michael Shmerkin (ISR)	-	17	-	-
35. Konstantin Kostin (LAT)	18	-	-	-
35. Zoltán Tóth (HUN)	-	18	-	-
37. Yuri Litvinov (KAZ)	19	-	-	-
37. Gareth Echardt (SAF)	-	19	-	-
39. Yon García (ESP)	20	-	-	-
39. Mauricio Medellin (MEX)	-	20	-	-
41. Ricky Cockerill (NZL)	21	-	-	-
41. Miloš Milanović (YUG)	-	21	-	-
43. Panagiotis Markouizos (ISU)	22	-	-	-
WD. Kyu-hyun Lee (KOR)	-	-	-	-

World Ladies Figure Skating Championships:

	QRA	QRB	SP	FS
1. Michelle Kwan (USA)	1	-	2	1
2. Irina Slutskaya (RUS)	-	1	1	2
3. Sarah Hughes (USA)	2	-	4	4
4. Maria Butyrskaya (RUS)	4	-	5	3
5. Angela Nikodinov (USA)	3	-	3	5
6. Viktoria Volchkova (RUS)	-	2	6	6
7. Fumie Suguri (JPN)	5	-	7	7
8. Elena Liashenko (UKR)	-	5	9	8

9. Vanessa Gusmeroli (FRA)	-	3	8	10
10. Silvia Fontana (ITA)	-	4	10	9
11. Elina Kettunen (FIN)	7	-	12	11
12. Sarah Meier (SUI)	-	10	11	12
13. Tatiana Malinina (UZB)	6	-	14	13
14. Mikkeline Kierkgaard (DEN)	8	-	17	14
15. Jennifer Robinson (CAN)	-	7	**16**	**15**
16. Susanne Stadlmüller (GER)	11	-	13	16
17. Laëtitia Hubert (FRA)	-	6	19	17
18. Júlia Sebestyén (HUN)	9	-	18	18
19. Tamara Dorofejev (HUN)	-	8	21	19
20. Julia Soldatova (BLS)	10	-	15	22
21. Annie Bellemare (CAN)	-	13	**20**	**20**
22. Karen Venhuizen (NED)	-	14	23	21
23. Bit-na Park (KOR)	-	9	24	23
24. Zuzana Babiaková (SVK)	-	11	22	24
25. Idora Hegel (CRO)	-	12	25	-
26. Hristina Vassileva (BUL)	12	-	27	-
27. Roxana Luca (ROM)	14	-	26	-
28. Siyin Sun (CHN)	-	15	28	-
29. Carina Chen (TPE)	13	-	30	-
30. Marta Andrade Vidal (ESP)	15	-	29	-
31. Galina Maniachenko (UKR)	16	-	-	-
31. Zoe Jones (GRB)	-	16	-	-
33. Lenka Šeniglová (CZE)	17	-	-	-
33. Natalie Hoste (BEL)	-	17	-	-
35. Anna Wenzel (AUT)	18	-	-	-
35. Sabina Wojtala (POL)	-	18	-	-
37. Georgina Papavasilou (ISU)	19	-	-	-
37. Stephanie Zhang (AUS)	-	19	-	-
39. Shirene Human (SAF)	20	-	-	-
39. Marina Khalturina (KAZ)	-	20	-	-
41. Dirke O'Brien Baker (NZL)	21	-	-	-
41. Olga Vassiljeva (EST)	-	21	-	-
43. Rocio Salas Visuet (MEX)	22	-	-	-
43. Yulia Vorobieva (AZE)	-	22	-	-
45. Christine Lee (HKG)	23	-	-	-
45. Darya Zuravicky (ISR)	-	23	-	-

47. Ksenia Jastsenjski (YUG) - 24 - -

World Pairs Skating Championships:

	SP	FS
1. Jamie Salé/David Pelletier (CAN)	**3**	**1**
2. Elena Berezhnaya/Anton Sikharulidze (RUS)	1	2
3. Xue Shen/ Hongbo Zhao (CHN)	2	3
4. Maria Petrova/Alexei Tikhonov (RUS)	4	5
5. Tatiana Totmianina/Maxim Marinin (RUS)	8	4
6. Dorota Zagórska/Mariusz Siudek (POL)	5	6
7. Kyoko Ina/John Zimmerman (USA)	6	7
8. Kristy Wirtz/Kris Wirtz (CAN)	**14**	**8**
9. Aliona Savchenko/Stanislav Morozov (UKR)	12	9
10. Qing Pang/Jian Tong (CHN)	10	10
11. Tiffany Scott/Philip Dulebohn (USA)	9	12
12. Kateřina Beránková/Otto Dlabola (CZE)	13	11
13. Inga Rodionova/Andrei Kriukov (AZE)	11	15
14. Sabrina Lefrançois/Jérôme Blanchard (FRA)	17	13
15. Yuko Kawaguchi/Alexander Markuntsov (JPN)	15	14
16. Mariana Kautz/Norman Jeschke (GER)	16	16
17. Natalia Ponomareva/Evgeni Sviridov (UZB)	18	17
18. Viktoria Shklover/Valdis Mintals (EST)	19	18
19. Maria Krasiltseva/Artem Znachkov (ARM)	20	19
20. Jelena Sirokhvatova/Jurijs Salmanovs (LAT)	21	-
21. Oľga Beständigová/Jozef Beständig (SVK)	22	-
22. Michela Cobisi/Ruben De Pra (ITA)	23	-
23. Ivana Durin/Andrei Maximov (YUG)	24	-
WD. Sarah Abitbol/Stéphane Bernadis (FRA)	7	-

World Ice Dancing Championships:

	CDA	CDB	OD	FD
1. Fusar-Poli/Margaglio (ITA)	-	1	1	1
2. Anissina/Peizerat (FRA)	1	-	2	2
3. Lobacheva/Averbukh (RUS)	-	2(t)	3	3
4. Bourne/Kraatz (CAN)	**-**	**2(t)**	**4**	**4**
5. Drobiazko/Vanagas (LIT)	2	-	5	5
6. Chait/Sakhnovski (ISR)	3	-	6	6
7. Winkler/Lohse (GER)	-	4	7	7

8. Grushina/Goncharov (UKR)	4	-	8	8
9. Lang/Tchernyshev (USA)	-	5	9	9
10. Denkova/Staviski (BUL)	5	-	10	10
11. Dubreuil/Lauzon (CAN)	**-**	**6**	**11**	**11**
12. Navka/Kostomarov (RUS)	6(t)	-	12	12
13. Delobel/Schoenfelder (FRA)	8	-	13	13
14. Nowak/Kolasiński (POL)	6(t)	-	14	14
15. Hugentob./Hugentob. (SUI)	-	7	15	15
16. Humphreys/Baranov (GRB)	9	-	16	16
17. Belbin/Agosto (USA)	-	8(t)	17	17
18. Sauri/Stifunin (FRA)	-	8(t)	18	18
19. Fraser/Lukanin (AZE)	-	10	20	19
20. Błażowska/Kozubek (POL)	10(t)	-	19	20
21. Agogliati/Milo (ITA)	10(t)	-	21	21
22. Gebora/Visontai (HUN)	13	-	23	22
23. Kovalová/Szurman (CZE)	-	11	24	23
24. Tsuzuki/Farkhoutdinov (JPN)	12	-	22	24
25. Gudina/Beleteski (ISR)	-	12	25	-
26. Anselmi/Pedrazzini (ITA)	-	13(t)	26	-
27. Rauer/Rauer (GER)	-	13(t)	27	-
28. Zhang/Cao (CHN)	-	13(t)	28	-
29. Mosenkova/Sychov (EST)	14(t)	-	29	-
30. de Carbonnel/Malkov (BLS)	14(t)	-	30	-
31. Yang/Lee (KOR)	-	16	-	-
32. Duval-Rigby/Rigby (AUS)	16(t)	-	-	-
33. Szolnoki/Illes (CRO)	16(t)	-	-	-
34. Ďurkovská/Mesároš (SVK)	-	17	-	-
35. Galitch/Shishkov (BIH)	-	18	-	-

Barbara Fusar-Poli and Maurizio Margaglio made history as the first Italians to win gold medals at the World Figure Skating Championships.

For the first time at the World Championships, there were so many entries in the ice dance event that the compulsory dances were broken into two qualifying groups. The top fifteen teams from each group advanced to the original dance.

The Canadian organizers presented a unique SkateFest in conjunction with the Championships. There were figure skating history exhibits and autograph sessions with skating greats like Barbara Ann Scott, Barbara Wagner and Bob Paul and Tracy Wilson. Colin James gave a free concert at Centre Stage, which was followed by a fireworks display. A highlight of SkateFest was the Theatre of Champions at the Plaza Theatre - a series of biographical skating documentary screenings hosted by Debbi Wilkes, which doubled as Q&A and meet and greet sessions with the subjects of the documentaries. Brian Orser, Barbara Underhill and Paul Martini and Jayne Torvill and Christopher Dean were among the featured skaters. SkateFest set a new gold standard for the off-ice experience at the World Championships.

Sources: The Province, February 9 and 15 and March 15 and 16, 2001; Skating magazine, May 2001; Protocol, 2001 World Figure Skating Championships

2002 WORLD FIGURE SKATING CHAMPIONSHIPS
Nagano, Japan, March 16-24, 2002

World Men's Figure Skating Championships:

	QRA	QRB	SP	FS
1. Alexei Yagudin (RUS)	1	-	1	1
2. Timothy Goebel (USA)	-	1	4	2
3. Takeshi Honda (JPN)	3	-	3	3
4. Alexandr Abt (RUS)	2	-	2	4
5. Chengjiang Li (CHN)	-	3	6	5
6. Michael Weiss (USA)	-	2	5	6
7. Anthony Liu (AUS)	-	7	11	7
8. Jeffrey Buttle (CAN)	**-**	**4**	**7**	**12**
9. Min Zhang (CHN)	4	-	15	8
10. Andrejs Vlascenko (GER)	-	11	9	9
11. Frédéric Dambier (FRA)	5	-	12	10
12. Matthew Savoie (USA)	6	-	14	11
13. Brian Joubert (FRA)	-	5	8	15
14. Kevin van der Perren (BEL)	7	-	10	14
15. Ben Ferreira (CAN)	**10**	**-**	**17**	**13**

16. Song Gao (CHN)	-	9	16	16
17. Ivan Dinev (BUL)	-	10	13	18
18. Stéphane Lambiel (SUI)	-	6	18	17
19. Roman Skorniakov (UZB)	-	8	21	19
20. Vakhtang Murvanidze (GEO)	9	-	19	20
21. Markus Leminen (FIN)	-	13	20	22
22. Dmitri Dmitrenko (UKR)	12	-	23	21
23. Sergei Rylov (AZE)	8	-	24	23
24. Sergei Davydov (BLS)	-	12	22	24
25. Juraj Sviatko (SVK)	11	-	25	-
26. Tomáš Verner (CZE)	15	-	26	-
27. Yosuke Takeuchi (JPN)	14	-	27	-
28. Gregor Urbas (SLO)	-	14	28	-
29. Kristoffer Berntsson (SWE)	13	-	29	-
30. Sergei Kotov (ISR)	-	15	30	-
31. Zoltán Tóth (HUN)	16	-	-	-
31. Yon García (ESP)	-	16	-	-
33. Clemens Jonas (AUT)	17	-	-	-
33. Aidas Reklys (LIT)	-	17	-	-
35. James Black (GRB)	18	-	-	-
35. Miloš Milanović (YUG)	-	18	-	-
37. Dino Quattrocecere (SAF)	19	-	-	-
37. Panagiotis Markouizos (GRE)	-	19	-	-
WD. Margus Hernits (EST)	-	-	-	-
WD. Evgeni Plushenko (RUS)	-	-	-	-
WD. Todd Eldredge (USA)	-	-	-	-

World Ladies Figure Skating Championships:

	QRA	QRB	SP	FS
1. Irina Slutskaya (RUS)	-	1	1	1
2. Michelle Kwan (USA)	1	-	3	2
3. Fumie Suguri (JPN)	2	-	2	3
4. Sasha Cohen (USA)	-	2	5	4
5. Yoshie Onda (JPN)	-	3	4	5
6. Elena Liashenko (UKR)	-	4	6	6
7. Viktoria Volchkova (RUS)	-	9	8	7
8. Júlia Sebestyén (HUN)	3	-	7	11
9. Jennifer Robinson (CAN)	**5**	**-**	**14**	**8**

#	Skater				
10.	Silvia Fontana (ITA)	7	-	10	10
11.	Susanna Pöykiö (FIN)	-	6	13	9
12.	Laëtitia Hubert (FRA)	-	8	12	12
13.	Zuzana Babiaková (SVK)	11	-	9	13
14.	Idora Hegel (CRO)	-	10	16	15
15.	Tatiana Malinina (UZB)	-	5	11	21
16.	Miriam Manzano (AUS)	-	13	18	16
17.	Galina Maniachenko (UKR)	10	-	24	14
18.	Julia Soldatova (BLS)	-	7	22	17
19.	Marta Andrade Vidal (ESP)	12	-	17	18
20.	Dan Fang (CHN)	-	12	19	19
21.	Vanessa Giunchi (ITA)	14	-	20	20
22.	Julia Lautowa (AUT)	9	-	21	22
23.	Åsa Persson (SWE)	-	11	23	23
24.	Lucie Krausová (CZE)	8	-	26	-
25.	Gintarė Vostrecovaitė (LIT)	13	-	25	-
26.	Natalie Hoste (BEL)	-	15	27	-
27.	Sabina Wojtala (POL)	15	-	28	-
28.	Georgina Papavasiliou (GRE)	-	14	29	-
29.	Anne-Sophie Calvez (FRA)	16	-	-	-
29.	Yea-ji Shin (KOR)	-	16	-	-
31.	Roxana Luca (ROM)	17	-	-	-
31.	Darya Zuravicky (ISR)	-	17	-	-
33.	Shirene Human (SAF)	-	18	-	-
33.	Hristina Vassileva (BUL)	18	-	-	-
35.	Christine Lee (HKG)	19	-	-	-
35.	Gladys Orozco (MEX)	-	19	-	-
37.	Diana Y. Chen (TPE)	20	-	-	-
37.	Ksenija Jastsenski (YUG)	-	20	-	-
WD.	Jennifer Kirk (USA)	4	-	15	-
WD.	Maria Butyrskaya (RUS)	6	-	-	-
WD.	Sarah Hughes (USA)	-	-	-	-

World Pairs Skating Championships:

	SP	FS
1. Xue Shen/Hongbo Zhao (CHN)	1	1
2. Tatiana Totmianina/Maxim Marinin (RUS)	2	2
3. Kyoko Ina/John Zimmerman (USA)	3	3

4. Maria Petrova/Alexei Tikhonov (RUS)	4	4
5. Qing Pang/Jian Tong (CHN)	5	5
6. Dorota Zagórska/Mariusz Siudek (POL)	6	6
7. Tiffany Scott/Philip Dulebohn (USA)	7	7
8. Jacinthe Larivière/Lenny Faustino (CAN)	**8**	**8**
9. Dan Zhang/Hao Zhang (CHN)	10	9
10. Anabelle Langlois/Patrice Archetto (CAN)	**11**	**10**
11. Kateřina Beránková/Otto Dlabola (CZE)	9	12
12. Valérie Marcoux/Bruno Marcotte (CAN)	**12**	**11**
13. Yuko Kawaguchi/Alexander Markuntsov (JPN)	13	13
14. Mariana Kautz/Norman Jeschke (GER)	14	14
15. Viktoria Borzenkova/Andrei Chuvilyaev (RUS)	16	15
16. Tatiana Chuvaeva/Dmitri Palamarchuk (UKR)	15	16
17. Viktoria Shklover/Valdis Mintals (EST)	17	17
18. Maria Krasiltseva/Artem Znachkov (ARM)	19	18
19. Jelena Sirokhvatova/Jurijs Salmanovs (LAT)	18	19
20. Marina Aganina/Artem Knyazev (UZB)	20	20
WD. Jamie Salé/David Pelletier (CAN)	**-**	**-**
WD. Elena Berezhnaya/Anton Sikharulidze (RUS)	-	-

World Ice Dancing Championships:

	CD1	CD2	OD	FD
1. Lobacheva/Averbukh (RUS)	1	1	1	1
2. Bourne/Kraatz (CAN)	**2**	**2**	**2**	**2**
3. Chait/Sakhnovski (ISR)	4	4	4	3
4. Drobiazko/Vanagas (LIT)	3	3	3	4
5. Denkova/Staviski (BUL)	5	5	5	5
6. Grushina/Goncharov (UKR)	6	6	6	6
7. Winkler/Lohse (GER)	7	7	7	7
8. Navka/Kostomarov (RUS)	8	8	8	8
9. Lang/Tchernyshev (USA)	9	9	9	9
10. Dubreuil/Lauzon (CAN)	**11**	**10**	**10**	**10**
11. Nowak/Kolasiński (POL)	10	12	11	11
12. Delobel/Schoenfelder (FRA)	15	11	12	12
13. Belbin/Agosto (USA)	13	13	14	13
14. Humphreys/Baranov (GRB)	12	14	13	14
15. Fraser/Lukanin (AZE)	16	15	15	15
16. Faiella/Scali (ITA)	14	16	16	16

17. Ouabdelsselam/Delmas (FRA)	17	17	17	17
18. Morávková/Procházka (CZE)	19	18	18	18
19. Rauer/Rauer (GER)	18	19	19	20
20. Zhang/Cao (CHN)	20	20	20	19
21. Gebora/Visontai (HUN)	21	22	21	21
22. Anselmi/Pedrazzini (ITA)	23	21	22	22
23. Yang/Lee (KOR)	23	23	24	23
24. Arikawa/Miyamoto (JPN)	26	24	23	24
25. Beknazarova/Kocherzh. (UKR)	22	25	25	-
26. Huot/Valkama (FIN)	25	26	26	-
27. Mosenkova/Sychov (EST)	27	27	27	-
28. Buck/Nelson-Bond (AUS)	28	28	28	-
WD. Anissina/Peizerat (FRA)	-	-	-	-
WD. Fusar-Poli/Margaglio (ITA)	-	-	-	-

Xue Shen and Hongbo Zhao made history as the first Chinese team to win a gold medal in the pairs event at the World Figure Skating Championships.

Galit Chait and Sergei Sakhnovski made history as the first skaters from Israel to win a medal at the Championships. Chait and Sakhnovski won the bronze medal over Lithuania's Margarita Drobiazko and Povilas Vanagas in a four-three split of the judging panel, and afterwards the The Lithuanian Skating Federation filed a petition protesting the results. The petition was signed by more than 30 skaters, including American ice dancers Naomi Lang and Peter Tchernyshev and Muriel Boucher-Zazoui, the coach of Marina Anissina and Gwendal Peizerat. The ISU swiftly rejected the protest, which referee Courtney Jones called "unfounded". Drobiazko and Vanagas filed a similar complaint a month prior at the 2002 Winter Olympic Games in Salt Lake City, which was also rejected. Vanagas stated, "The main reason overall [for the protest] for us is to try to [take care] of the people living in the ISU system and taking part in the competition. Knowing our situation, how sad it was for many years, we just tried to somehow help the skaters who will be going on."

Sources: Saint John Times-Transcript, February 20, 2002; Star Tribune,

March 6, 2002; The Hamilton Spectator, March 25, 2002; Skating magazine, May 2002; Protocol, 2002 World Figure Skating Championships

2003 WORLD FIGURE SKATING CHAMPIONSHIPS
Washington, United States, March 24-30, 2003

World Men's Figure Skating Championships:

	QRA	QRB	SP	FS
1. Evgeni Plushenko (RUS)	1	-	1	1
2. Timothy Goebel (USA)	2	-	2	2
3. Takeshi Honda (JPN)	-	2	3	3
4. Chengjiang Li (CHN)	4	-	4	4
5. Michael Weiss (USA)	-	1	5	5
6. Brian Joubert (FRA)	-	9	6	6
7. Sergei Davydov (BLS)	-	6	7	7
8. Emanuel Sandhu (CAN)	**5**	**-**	**10**	**8**
9. Ilia Klimkin (RUS)	-	4	13	11
10. Stéphane Lambiel (SUI)	3	-	16	10
11. Min Zhang (CHN)	-	5	18	9
12. Stanislav Timchenko (RUS)	-	8	11	13
13. Ryan Jahnke (USA)	-	3	9	18
14. Ivan Dinev (BUL)	-	7	14	14
15. Jeffrey Buttle (CAN)	**6**	**-**	**8**	**19**
16. Stanick Jeannette (FRA)	-	12	12	16
17. Andrejs Vlascenko (GER)	11	-	21	12
18. Gheorghe Chiper (ROM)	8	-	17	17
19. Kevin van der Perren (BEL)	7	-	22	15
20. Roman Skorniakov (UZB)	-	10	15	20
21. Vakhtang Murvanidze (GEO)	9	-	19	22
22. Tomáš Verner (CZE)	-	11	20	21
23. Silvio Smalun (GER)	10	-	25	23
24. Gregor Urbas (SLO)	-	13	23	24
25. Karel Zelenka (ITA)	-	14	24	-
26. Sergei Kotov (ISR)	13	-	27	-
27. Zoltán Tóth (HUN)	-	15	26	-
28. Ari-Pekka Nurmenkari (FIN)	12	-	28	-
29. Juraj Sviatko (SVK)	14	-	29	-
30. Konstantin Tupikov (UKR)	15	-	30	-

31. Maciej Kuś (POL)	16	-	-	-
31. Kristoffer Berntsson (SWE)	-	16	-	-
33. Yon García (ESP)	17	-	-	-
33. Dong-whun Lee (KOR)	-	17	-	-
35. Aidas Reklys (LIT)	18	-	-	-
35. Clemens Jonas (AUT)	-	18	-	-
37. Bradley Santer (AUS)	19	-	-	-
37. Manuel Segura Munoz (MEX)	-	19	-	-
39. Aramayis Grigoryan (ARM)	20	-	-	-
39. Sean Carlow (AUS)	-	20	-	-
WD. Alexandr Abt (RUS)	-	-	-	-
WD. Panagiotis Markouizos (GRE)	-	-	-	-

World Ladies Figure Skating Championships:

	QRA	QRB	SP	FS
1. Michelle Kwan (USA)	1	-	1	1
2. Elena Sokolova (RUS)	2	-	2	2
3. Fumie Suguri (JPN)	-	1	3	4
4. Sasha Cohen (USA)	3	-	5(t)	3
5. Viktoria Volchkova (RUS)	-	3	5(t)	5
6. Sarah Hughes (USA)	6	-	8	6
7. Elena Liashenko (UKR)	5	-	7	8
8. Shizuka Arakawa (JPN)	4	-	11	7
9. Jennifer Robinson (CAN)	-	2	**9**	**9**
10. Carolina Kostner (ITA)	-	9	4	11
11. Yoshie Onda (JPN)	-	4	12	15
12. Alisa Drei (FIN)	8	-	18	10
13. Ludmila Nelidina (RUS)	-	5	15	13
14. Júlia Sebestyén (HUN)	10	-	10	14
15. Julia Lautowa (AUT)	12	-	17	12
16. Galina Maniachenko (UKR)	-	7	14	16
17. Joannie Rochette (CAN)	**9**	-	**16**	**19**
18. Dan Fang (CHN)	7	-	13	22
19. Sarah Meier (SUI)	13	-	20	18
20. Mojca Kopač (SLO)	-	13	22	17
21. Jenna McCorkell (GRB)	11	-	19	20
22. Anne-Sophie Calvez (FRA)	-	6	21	21
23. A. Gimazetdinova (UZB)	-	8	23	24

24. Idora Hegel (CRO)	-	10	27	23
25. Sara Falotico (BEL)	15	-	24	-
26. Miriam Manzano (AUS)	14	-	25	-
27. Olga Vassiljeva (EST)	-	15	26	-
28. Vanessa Giunchi (ITA)	-	12	28	-
29. Johanna Götesson (SWE)	-	11	29	-
30. Tuğba Karademir (TUR)	-	14	30	-
31. Tamara Dorofejev (HUN)	16	-	-	-
31. Daria Timoshenko (AZW)	-	16	-	-
33. Zuzana Babiaková (SVK)	17	-	-	-
33. Gintarė Vostrecovaitė (LIT)	-	17	-	-
35. Lucie Krausová (CZE)	18	-	-	-
35. Georgina Papavasiliou (GRE)	-	18	-	-
37. Roxana Luca (ROM)	19	-	-	-
37. Diane Chen (TPE)	-	19	-	-
39. Ana Cecilia Cantú (MEX)	20	-	-	-
39. Hristina Vassileva (BUL)	-	20	-	-
41. Shirene Human (SAF)	21	-	-	-
41. Hae-lyeum Cho (KOR)	-	21	-	-
WD. Irina Slutskaya (RUS)	-	-	-	-
WD. Sabin Wojtala (POL)	-	-	-	-
WD. Aleksandra Petushko (LAT)	-	-	-	-

World Pairs Skating Championships:

	SP	FS
1. Shen Xue/Zhao Hongbo (CHN)	2	1
2. Tatiana Totmianina/Maxim Marinin (RUS)	1	2
3. Maria Petrova/Alexei Tikhonov (RUS)	3	3
4. Qing Pang/Jian Tong (CHN)	8	4
5. Anabelle Langlois/Patrice Archetto (CAN)	**6**	**5**
6. Dan Zhang/Hao Zhang (CHN)	7	6
7. Dorota Zagórska/Mariusz Siudek (POL)	5	7
8. Yulia Obertas/Alexei Sokolov (RUS)	4	8
9. Tiffany Scott/Philip Dulebohn (USA)	13	9
10. Rena Inoue/John Baldwin Jr. (USA)	11	10
11. Kateřina Beránková/Otto Dlabola (CZE)	10	12
12. Sarah Abitbol/Stéphane Bernadis (FRA)	9	13
13. Jacinthe Larivière/Lenny Faustino (CAN)	**15**	**11**

14. Yuko Kavaguti/Alexander Markuntsov (JPN)	12	14
15. Eva-Maria Fitze/Rico Rex (GER)	16	15
16. Katie Orscher/Garrett Lucash (USA)	14	16
17. Tatiana Volosozhar/Petro Kharchenko (UKR)	17	17
18. Maria Guerassimenko/Vladimir Futáš (SVK)	18	18
19. Diana Rennik/Aleksei Saks (EST)	19	19
20. Marina Aganina/Artem Knyazev (UZB)	20	20
21. Olga Boguslavska/Andrei Brovenko (LAT)	21	-

World Ice Dancing Championships:

	CDA	CDB	OD	FD
1. Bourne/Kraatz (CAN)	-	1	2	1
2. Lobacheva/Averbukh (RUS)	1	-	1	2
3. Denkova/Staviski (BUL)	-	2	3	3
4. Navka/Kostomarov (RUS)	-	3	4	4
5. Grushina/Goncharov (UKR)	2	-	5	5
6. Chait/Sakhnovski (ISR)	3	-	6	6
7. Belbin/Agosto (USA)	-	4	7	7
8. Lang/Tchernyshev (USA)	4	-	8	8
9. Delobel/Schoenfelder (FRA)	5	-	9	9
10. Dubreuil/Lauzon (CAN)	-	5	10	10
11. Faiella/Scali (ITA)	-	6	11	11
12. Wing/Lowe (CAN)	7	-	12	12
13. Fraser/Lukanin (AZE)	6	-	13	13
14. Gudina/Beletski (ISR)	-	8	14	14
15. Domnina/Shabalin (RUS)	-	7	15	15
16. Morávková/Procházka (CZE)	8	-	16	16
17. Zhang/Cao (CHN)	-	9	18	17
18. Hoffmann/Elek (HUN)	9	-	17	18
19. O'Connor/O'Dougherty (GRB)	-	11	19	19
20. Watanabe/Kido (JPN)	10	-	20	20
21. Huot/Valkama (FIN)	11	-	23	21
22. Golovina/Voiko (UKR)	-	10	21	23
23. Petetin/Jost (FRA)	-	12	22	22
24. Grebenkina/Azrojan (ARM)	12	-	24	24
25. Buck/Nelson-Bond (AUS)	-	13	25	-
26. Timofejeva/Striganov (EST)	-	14	26	-
27. Dulej/Janicki (POL)	13	-	27	-

28. Zatzman/Radisauskas (LIT)	-	15	28	-
29. Siniaver/Tukvadze (GEO)	14	-	29	-
WD. Winkler/Lohse (GER)	-	-	-	-
WD. Steinel/Tsvetkov (GER)	-	-	-	-

For the first time, only one compulsory dance was skated at the World Championships, accounting for 20% of the total score. Teams were broken into two groups, due to the large number of entries.

Shae-Lynn Bourne and Victor Kraatz made history as the first Canadian ice dance team to win a gold medal at the World Figure Skating Championships. Albena Denkova and Maxim Staviski made history as the first Bulgarian skaters to win medals at the World Championships. China's Xue Shen and Hongbo Zhao earned four perfect 6.0's - the most perfect marks any pair had received at the World Championships in over a decade.

The World Skating Federation, a new initiative launched during the World Championships, hoped to replace the ISU as the sport's governing body. The ISU was growing increasingly unpopular after years of judging scandals under the leadership of President Ottavio Cinquanta and the World Skating Federation aimed to gain the approval of the International Olympic Committee. A founding member of the WSF, veteran Hungarian judge Judit Fürst-Tombor, was one of the first to feel the ISU's wrath, when she was dismissed from the ladies judging panel at the World Championships for her involvement. At a high profile press conference, WSF organizers screened a video that showed ISU President Ottavio Cinquanta evading and bumbling through questions about judging scandals. The WSF movement gained the support of many former World Champions, including Dick Button, Scott Hamilton, Kurt Browning, Todd Eldredge, Kristi Yamaguchi, Katarina Witt and Jamie Salé and David Pelletier. Though the WSF was ultimately unsuccessful in its bid to takeover international governance of figure skating, the support it received spoke volumes about how unhappy many in the skating community were the status quo at the time.

Sources: USA Today, March 26, 2003; Star-Phoenix, March 26, 2003; Tri-City Herald, March 26, 2003; The Toronto Star, March 27, 2003; Skating magazine, May 2003; Entries, 2003 World Figure Skating Championships; Protocol, 2003 World Figure Skating Championships; Sixes Across The Board, Skate Guard Blog, August 21, 2022

Tessa Virtue and Scott Moir, World Champions 2010, 2012 and 2017. Daiju Kitamura / AFLO SPORT / Aflo Co. Ltd. / Alamy Stock Photo.

THE DIGITAL REVOLUTION

2004 WORLD FIGURE SKATING CHAMPIONSHIPS
Dortmund, Germany, March 22-28, 2004

World Men's Figure Skating Championships:

	QRA	QRB	SP	FS
1. Evgeni Plushenko (RUS)	1	-	1	1
2. Brian Joubert (FRA)	-	2	2	2
3. Stefan Lindemann (GER)	3	-	3	3
4. Stéphane Lambiel (SUI)	-	3	6	4
5. Johnny Weir (USA)	-	7	4	5
6. Michael Weiss (USA)	5	-	5	6
7. Min Zhang (CHN)	4	-	7	7
8. Emanuel Sandhu (CAN)	-	1	**13**	**8**
9. Frédéric Dambier (FRA)	-	4	10	9
10. Chengjiang Li (CHN)	-	5	12	10
11. Daisuke Takahashi (JPN)	7	-	11	11
12. Andrei Griazev (RUS)	-	6	8	16
13. Ben Ferreira (CAN)	-	9	**14**	**14**
14. Kevin van der Perren (BEL)	-	8	19	12
15. Ivan Dinev (BUL)	-	11	18	13
16. Matthew Savoie (USA)	-	10	17	15
17. Gheorghe Chiper (ROM)	6	-	15	18
18. Sergei Davydov (BLS)	9	-	16	17
19. Tomáš Verner (CZE)	-	13	20	19
20. Gregor Urbas (SLO)	8	-	21	21
21. Kristoffer Berntsson (SWE)	11	-	24	20
22. Yamato Tamura (JPN)	-	12	22	23
23. Neil Wilson (GRB)	-	14	23	22
24. Zoltán Tóth (HUN)	12	-	26	-
25. Ari-Pekka Nurmenkari (FIN)	14	-	25	-
26. Vitali Danilchenko (UKR)	10	-	29	-
27. Vakhtang Murvanidze (GEO)	13	-	28	-

28. Trifun Živanović (SCG)	15	-	27	-
29. Juraj Sviatko (SVK)	-	15	30	-
30. Dong-whun Lee (KOR)	16	-	-	-
30. Patrick Meier (SUI)	-	16	-	-
32. Clemens Jonas (AUT)	17	-	-	-
32. Sergei Kotov (ISR)	-	17	-	-
34. Aidas Reklys (LIT)	18	-	-	-
34. Bradley Santer (AUS)	-	18	-	-
36. Pavel Kersha (BLS)	19	-	-	-
36. Yon García (ESP)	-	19	-	-
37. Andrei Dobrokhodov (AZE)	-	20	-	-
38. Miguel Ángel Moyron (MEX)	-	21	-	-
WD. Ilia Klimkin (RUS)	2	-	9	-
WD. Gareth Echardt (SAF)	-	-	-	-

World Ladies Figure Skating Championships:

	QRA	QRB	SP	FS
1. Shizuka Arakawa (JPN)	1	-	2	1
2. Sasha Cohen (USA)	-	1	1	3
3. Michelle Kwan (USA)	3	-	4	2
4. Miki Ando (JPN)	2	-	3	4
5. Carolina Kostner (ITA)	6	-	5	6
6. Júlia Sebestyén (HUN)	-	3	6	7
7. Fumie Suguri (JPN)	8	-	7	5
8. Joannie Rochette (CAN)	**-**	**5**	**9**	**8**
9. Irina Slutskaya (RUS)	5	-	8	11
10. Elena Sokolova (RUS)	-	2	14	9
11. Elena Liashenko (UKR)	-	4	10	12
12. Susanna Pöykiö (FIN)	4	-	15	10
13. Sarah Meier (SUI)	-	9	12	13
14. Jennifer Robinson (CAN)	**-**	**6**	**13**	**15**
15. Viktoria Volchkova (RUS)	7	-	11	19
16. Idora Hegel (CRO)	-	8	19	14
17. Anne-Sophie Calvez (FRA)	9	-	17	16
18. Jennifer Kirk (USA)	-	7	16	18
19. Dan Fang (CHN)	11	-	22	17
20. Miriam Manzano (AUS)	12	-	18	20
21. Annette Dytrt (GER)	-	10	20	22

22. Zuzana Babiaková (SVK)	10	-	24	21
23. Valentina Marchei (ITA)	-	11	21	23
24. Jenna McCorkell (GRB)	-	13	23	24
25. Julia Lautowa (AUT)	15	-	25	-
26. Michele Cantú (MEX)	-	15	26	-
27. Mojca Kopač (SLO)	14	-	27	-
28. Sara Falotico (BEL)	13	-	28	-
29. Daria Timoshenko (AZE)	-	12	29	-
30. Ji-eun Choi (KOR)	-	14	30	-
31. Hristina Vassileva (BUL)	16	-	-	-
31. Diane Chen (TPE)	-	16(t)	-	-
31. Gintarė Vostrecovaitė (LIT)	-	16(t)	-	-
34. Karen Venhuizen (NED)	17	-	-	-
35. Tuğba Karademir (TUR)	18	-	-	-
35. Jenna-Anne Buys (SAF)	-	18	-	-
37. Lucie Krausová (CZE)	19	-	-	-
37. Ksenija Jastsenjski (SCG)	-	19	-	-
39. Anna Bernauer (LUX)	20	-	-	-
39. Olga Vassiljeva (EST)	-	20	-	-
41. Keren Shua Haim (ISR)	21	-	-	-
41. Nina Bates (BIH)	-	21	-	-

World Pairs Skating Championships:

	SP	FS
1. Tatiana Totmianina/Maxim Marinin (RUS)	1	2
2. Xue Shen/Hongbo Zhao (CHN)	4	1
3. Qing Pang/Jian Tong (CHN)	3	3
4. Maria Petrova/Alexei Tikhonov (RUS)	2	4
5. Dan Zhang/Hao Zhang (CHN)	6	5
6. Dorota Zagórska/Mariusz Siudek (POL)	5	6
7. Yulia Obertas/Sergei Slavnov (RUS)	7	7
8. Anabelle Langlois/Patrice Archetto (CAN)	**8**	**8**
9. Valérie Marcoux/Craig Buntin (CAN)	**10**	**9**
10. Rena Inoue/John Baldwin Jr. (USA)	9	10
11. Sabrina Lefrançois/Jérôme Blanchard (FRA)	12	11
12. Eva-Maria Fitze/Rico Rex (GER)	11	12
13. Kathryn Orscher/Garrett Lucash (USA)	14	13
14. Tatiana Volosozhar/Petr Kharchenko (UKR)	13	14

15. Milica Brozović/Vladimir Futás (SVK) 15 15
16. Julia Shapiro/Vadim Akolzin (ISR) 16 16
17. Olga Boguslavska/Andrei Brovenko (LAT) 18 17
18. Diana Rennik/Aleksei Saks (EST) 17 18
19. Marina Aganina/Artem Knyazev (UZB) 19 19

World Ice Dancing Championships

	CDA	CDB	OD	FD
1. Navka/Kostomarov (RUS)	1	-	1	1
2. Denkova/Staviski (BUL) -	1	2	2	
3. Winkler/Lohse (GER)	2	-	4	3
4. Grushina/Goncharov (UKR)	-	2	3	4
5. Belbin/Agosto (USA)	-	4	5	5
6. Delobel/Schoenfelder (FRA)	3	-	6	6
7. Chait/Sakhnovski (ISR)	4	-	8	7
8. Dubreuil/Lauzon (CAN)	-	3	7	**8**
9. Faiella/Scali (ITA)	5	-	9	9
10. Domnina/Shabalin (RUS)	6	-	10	10
11. Wing/Lowe (CAN)	-	5	**12**	**11**
12. Gregory/Petukhov (USA)	7	-	11	12
13. Kulikova/Novikov (RUS)	9	-	13	13
14. Kerr/Kerr (GRB)	-	8	14	14
15. Gudina/Beletski (ISR)	-	6	15	15
16. Fraser/Lukanin (AZE)	8	-	16	17
17. Watanabe/Kido (JPN)	10	-	18	16
18. Hoffmann/Elek (HUN)	-	7	17	18
19. Grebenkina/Azrojan (ARM)	-	10	20	19
20. Péchalat/Bourzat (FRA)	-	9	19	20
21. Golovina/Voiko (UKR)	11	-	22	21
22. Yang/Gao (CHN)	-	12	21	23
23. Piché/Denis (CAN)	**12**	-	**24**	**22**
24. Kauc/Zych (POL)	-	11	23	24
25. Janošťáková/Procházka (CZE)	14	-	25	-
26. Buck/Nelson-Bond (AUS)	13	-	26	-
27. Herzog/Matsjuk (AUT)	-	13	27	-
28. Huot/Valkama (FIN)	-	14	28	-
29. Zatzman/Radisauskas (LIT)	15	-	29	-

For the final time, the 6.0 judging system was used at the World Figure Skating Championships. Forty-two perfect marks were awarded.

Stefan Lindemann and Kati Winkler and René Lohse won Germany's first medals in the men's and ice dancing events at the World Championships since the fall of The Berlin Wall. Trifun Živanović and Ksenija Jastsenjski made history as the first skaters to represent Serbia and Montenegro at the World Championships.

Michelle Kwan received a controversial one-tenth deduction in the short program, because her program went two seconds over the time limit. A disturbing incident occurred during the ladies free skate, when a tutu-wearing streaker took off his shirt and got on the ice right before Kwan started her program. On his chest was the website address of GoldenPalace.com, an online casino. The man, who had snuck a pair of skates through security, was removed from the ice by five security guards and identified as thirty-year-old Ron Bensimhon of Montreal, Quebec. Following the incident, Kwan told reporters, "I was skating around and I thought he was a big flower girl. Then I thought he might have a gun. Who knows what he was thinking? He was crazy, but thank God he wasn't that crazy." Kwan noted that there were no metal detectors at the Dortmund Westfalenhalle. Bensimhon was briefly detained and then released. He was later sent to jail after similarly disrupting a synchronized diving event at the 2004 Summer Olympics in Athens, Greece.

Sources: The Tribune, March 28, 2004; Press and Sun-Bulletin, March 29, 2004; Skating magazine, May 2004; Telegraph-Journal, August 19, 2004; Protocol, 2004 World Figure Skating Championships; Sixes Across The Board, Skate Guard Blog, August 21, 2022

2005 WORLD FIGURE SKATING CHAMPIONSHIPS
Moscow, Russia, March 14-20, 2005

World Men's Figure Skating Championships:

	QRA	QRB	SP	FS
1. Stéphane Lambiel (SUI)	-	1	1	1

2. **Jeffrey Buttle (CAN)**	-	4	3	2
3. Evan Lysacek (USA)	-	3	4	4
4. Johnny Weir (USA)	4	-	9	6
5. Chengjiang Li (CHN)	3	-	6	7
6. Brian Joubert (FRA)	-	2	2	13
7. **Emanuel Sandhu (CAN)**	7	-	11	3
8. Kevin van der Perren (BEL)	-	8	12	5
9. Frédéric Dambier (FRA)	-	11	10	8
10. Timothy Goebel (USA)	-	9	14	9
11. Andrei Griazev (RUS)	8	-	8	16
12. Stefan Lindemann (GER)	2	-	23	10
13. Ivan Dinev (BUL)	6	-	18	11
14. Kristoffer Berntsson (SWE)	-	12	13	14
15. Daisuke Takahashi (JPN)	-	6	7	18
16. Min Zhang (CHN)	-	7	22	12
17. Sergei Dobrin (RUS)	5	-	15	15
18. Gheorghe Chiper (ROM)	-	10	17	17
19. Roman Serov (ISR)	-	13	16	20
20. Karel Zelenka (ITA)	10	-	19	19
21. Jamal Othman (SUI)	11	-	21	21
22. Sergei Davydov (BLS)	9	-	26	22
23. Viktor Pfeifer (AUT)	-	14	20	23
24. Vakhtang Murvanidze (GEO)	12	-	24	-
25. Samuel Contesti (FRA)	-	5	29	-
26. Zoltán Tóth (HUN)	15	-	25	-
27. Ari-Pekka Nurmenkari (FIN)	13	-	27	-
28. John Hamer (GRB)	14	-	28	-
29. Trifun Živanović (SCG)	-	15	30	-
30. Bradley Santer (AUS)	16	-	-	-
30. Tomáš Verner (CZE)	-	16	-	-
32. Andrei Dobrokhodov (AZE)	17	-	-	-
32. Silvio Smalun (GER)	-	17	-	-
34. Konstantin Tupikov (UKR)	18	-	-	-
34. Maciej Kuś (POL)	-	18	-	-
36. Gregor Urbas (SLO)	19	-	-	-
36. Yon García (ESP)	-	19	-	-
38. Aidas Reklys (LIT)	20	-	-	-
38. Alper Uçar (TUR)	-	20	-	-

40. Ricky Cockerill (NZL)	21	-	-	-
40. Humberto Contreras (MEX)	-	21	-	-
42. Gareth Echardt (SAF)	22	-	-	-
42. Edward Ka-yin Chow (HKG)	-	22	-	-
WD. Evgeni Plushenko (RUS)	1	-	-	-
WD. Takeshi Honda (JPN)	-	-	-	-

World Ladies Figure Skating Championships:

	QRA	QRB	SP	FS
1. Irina Slutskaya (RUS)	1	-	1	1
2. Sasha Cohen (USA)	-	1	2	2
3. Carolina Kostner (ITA)	3	-	4	4
4. Michelle Kwan (USA)	5	-	3	3
5. Fumie Suguri (JPN)	2	-	10	5
6. Miki Ando (JPN)	-	2	7	7
7. Elena Sokolova (RUS)	-	3	6	8
8. Susanna Pöykiö (FIN)	-	4	8	6
9. Shizuka Arakawa (POL)	4	-	5	9
10. Elena Liashenko (UKR)	6	-	11	12
11. Joannie Rochette (CAN)	-	5	9	**15**
12. Júlia Sebestyén (HUN)	-	6	12	16
13. Idora Hegel (CRO)	-	8	13	13
14. Sarah Meier (SUI)	7	-	20	10
15. Annette Dytrt (GER)	-	7	14	14
16. Joanne Carter (AUS)	-	9	15	11
17. Jennifer Kirk (USA)	9	-	18	17
18. Viktória Pavuk (HUN)	-	12	17	18
19. Lina Johansson (SWE)	-	11	19	20
20. Cynthia Phaneuf (CAN)	**8**	-	**22**	**21**
21. Yan Liu (CHN)	-	10	25	19
22. Jenna McCorkell (GRB)	10	-	16	22
23. Candice Didier (FRA)	12	-	21	23
24. Karen Venhuizen (NED)	11	-	24	24
25. Andrea Kreuzer (AUT)	14	-	23	-
26. Sara Falotico (BEL)	-	13	27	-
27. Tuğba Karademir (TUR)	-	15	26	-
28. Roxana Luca (ROM)	13	-	28	-
29. Fleur Maxwell (LUX)	15	-	29	-

30. Ji-eun Choi (KOR)	-	14	30	-
31. Tamar Katz (ISR)	16	-	-	-
31. Sonia Radeva (BUL)	-	16	-	-
33. Laura Fernandez (ESP)	17	-	-	-
33. Elena Glebova (EST)	-	17	-	-
35. Evgenia Melnik (BLS)	18	-	-	-
35. Michele Cantú (MEX)	-	18	-	-
37. Daria Timoshenko (AZE)	19	-	-	-
38. Gintarė Vostrecovaitė (LIT)	20	-	-	-
39. Shirene Human (SAF)	21	-	-	-
WD. Nina Bates (BIH)	-	-	-	-
WD. Diane Chen (TPE)	-	-	-	-

World Pairs Skating Championships:

	SP	FS
1. Tatiana Totmianina/Maxim Marinin (RUS)	1	1
2. Maria Petrova/Alexei Tikhonov (RUS)	2	2
3. Dan Zhang/Hao Zhang (CHN)	4	3
4. Qing Pang/Jian Tong (CHN)	5	4
5. Yulia Obertas/Sergei Slavnov (RUS)	6	5
6. Aliona Savchenko/Robin Szolkowy (GER)	8	6
7. Dorota Zagórska/Mariusz Siudek (POL)	7	7
8. U. Wakamatsu/J-S. Fecteau (CAN)	**9**	**8**
9. Valérie Marcoux/Craig Buntin (CAN)	**10**	**9**
10. Tatiana Volosozhar/Stanislav Morozov (UKR)	11	11
11. Rena Inoue/John Baldwin Jr. (USA)	12	10
12. Kathryn Orscher/Garrett Lucash (USA)	14	12
13. Marylin Pla/Yannick Bonheur (FRA)	13	13
14. Marina Aganina/Artem Knyazev (UZB)	15	15
15. Oľga Beständigová/Jozef Beständig (SVK)	18	14
16. Diana Rennik/Aleksei Saks (EST)	16	16
17. Rumiana Spassova/Stanimir Todorov (BUL)	20	17
18. Julia Shapiro/Vadim Akolzin (ISR)	17	18
19. Olga Boguslavska/Andrei Brovenko (LAT)	19	19
WD. Xue Shen/Hongbo Zhao (CHN)	3	-

World Ice Dancing Championships:

	CD	SP	FS

1. Tatiana Navka/Roman Kostomarov (RUS)	1	1	1
2. Tanith Belbin/Benjamin Agosto (USA)	2	2	2
3. E. Grushina/R. Goncharov (UKR)	3	3	4
4. I. Delobel/O. Schoenfelder (FRA)	6	6	3
5. Albena Denkova/Maxim Staviski (BUL)	4	4	5
6. Galit Chait/Sergei Sakhnovski (ISR)	7	5	6
7. M-F. Dubreuil/P. Lauzon (CAN)	**5**	**8**	**7**
8. Oksana Domnina/Maxim Shabalin (RUS)	8	7	8
9. Federica Faiella/Massimo Scali (ITA)	9	9	9
10. Megan Wing/Aaron Lowe (CAN)	**10**	**10**	**10**
11. M. Gregory/D. Petukhov (USA)	11	12	11
12. Sinead Kerr/John Kerr (GRB)	12	11	13
13. Kristin Fraser/Igor Lukanin (AZE)	14	13	12
14. S. Kulikova/V. Novikov (RUS)	13	14	14
15. Nóra Hoffmann/Attila Elek (HUN)	15	17	16
16. Nozomi Watanabe/Akiyuki Kido (JPN)	17	15	18
17. A. Grebenkina/V. Azrojan (ARM)	18	16	17
18. N. Gudina/A. Beletski (ISR)	19	18	15
19. N. Péchalat/F. Bourzat (FRA)	16	23	19
20. Christina Beier/William Beier (GER)	21	20	20
21. Julia Golovina/Oleg Voiko (UKR)	23	21	21
22. Alexandra Kauc/Michał Zych (POL)	22	22	22
23. Fang Yang/Chongbo Gao (CHN)	20	19	23
24. Alessia Aureli/Andrea Vaturi (ITA)	26	24	24
25. Laura Munana/Luke Munana (MEX)	25	25	-
26. J. Haunstetter/A. Hönlein (GER)	27	27	-
27. O. Akimova/A. Shakalov (UZB)	24	29	-
28. N. Buck/T. Nelson-Bond (AUS)	28	28	-
29. D. Keller/F. Keller (SUI)	29	26	-
30. A. Galcheniuk/O. Krupen (BLS)	30	30	-

Elena Grushina and Ruslan Goncharov made history as the first Ukrainians to win a medal in ice dancing at the World Figure Skating Championships.

The new IJS Code of Points judging system, which debuted in September of 2003, was first used at the World Figure Skating Championships. For the first time at the event, skaters were rewarded Technical Element Scores (TES) and a Program Component Component Scores (PCS). Many in the skating world had mixed feelings on the new system. World Champion Paul Martini said, "Skaters love it. They know what the rules are. That's so encouraging to the athlete to know where they stand. There's some subjective aspects on the second mar, but the kid gets a straight answer. The positives significantly outweigh any negatives." Four-time World Champion Katarina Witt didn't share Martini's enthusiasm. She told reporters, "You can throw this new system in the garbage."

Yulia Obertas and Sergei Slavnov made history as the first pair to receive positive GOE on a throw triple flip jump at the World Championships.

Sources: The Daily Herald-Tribune, March 4, 2005; The Toronto Star, March 13, 2005; The Boston Globe, March 14, 2005; Skating magazine, May 2005; Protocol, 2005 World Figure Skating Championships

2006 WORLD FIGURE SKATING CHAMPIONSHIPS
Calgary, Canada, March 19-26, 2006

World Men's Figure Skating Championships:

	QRA	QRB	SP	FS
1. Stéphane Lambiel (SUI)	1	-	4	1
2. Brian Joubert (FRA)	-	3	1	2
3. Evan Lysacek (USA)	2	-	8	3
4. Nobunari Oda (JPN)	-	1	3	5
5. Emanuel Sandhu (CAN)	**6**	**-**	**2**	**4**
6. Jeffrey Buttle (CAN)	**-**	**2**	**7**	**7**
7. Johnny Weir (USA)	-	4	5	8
8. Alban Préaubert (FRA)	-	5	17	6
9. Chengjiang Li (CHN)	5	-	6	15
10. Ilia Klimkin (RUS)	3	-	10	10
11. Matthew Savoie (USA)	-	8	9	9
12. Sergei Davydov (BLS)	-	6	12	11
13. Tomáš Verner (CZE)	-	7	11	14
14. Gheorghe Chiper (ROM)	-	9	15	12

15. Min Zhang (CHN)	4	-	19	13
16. Anton Kovalevski (UKR)	9	-	14	19
17. Andrei Griazev (RUS)	-	10	21	16
18. Roman Serov (ISR)	8	-	16	20
19. Ivan Dinev (BUL)	11	-	18	18
20. Silvio Smalun (GER)	7	-	13	21
21. Shawn Sawyer (CAN)	**10**	**-**	**25**	**17**
22. Gregor Urbas (SLO)	-	11	20	23
23. Kristoffer Berntsson (SWE)	-	12	23	22
24. Trifun Živanović (SCG)	-	14	22	24
25. Karel Zelenka (ITA)	-	13	24	-
26. Viktor Pfeifer (AUT)	12	-	26	-
27. Igor Macypura (SVK)	13	-	28	-
28. Jamal Othman (SUI)	14	-	27	-
29. Ari-Pekka Nurmenkari (FRA)	15	-	29	-
30. John Hamer (GRB)	-	15	30	-
31. Aidas Reklys (LIT)	16	-	-	-
31. Sean Carlow (AUS)	-	16	-	-
33. Bertalan Zákány (HUN)	17	-	-	-
33. Alper Uçar (TUR)	-	17	-	-
35. Tristan Thode (NZL)	18	-	-	-
35. Michael Novales (PHI)	-	18	-	-
37. Zeus Issariotis (GRE)	19	-	-	-
37. Luis Hernandez Olea (MEX)	-	19	-	-
39. Justin Pietersen (SAF)	20	-	-	-
39. Edward Ka-yin Chow (HKG)	-	20	-	-

World Ladies Figure Skating Championships:

	QRA	QRB	SP	FS
1. Kimmie Meissner (USA)	2	-	5	1
2. Fumie Suguri (JPN)	1	-	2	2
3. Sasha Cohen (USA)	3	-	1	4
4. Elena Sokolova (RUS)	-	6	3	3
5. Yukari Nakano (JPN)	-	2	6	6
6. Sarah Meier (SUI)	5	-	4	5
7. Joannie Rochette (CAN)	**-**	**1**	**7**	**8**
8. Emily Hughes (USA)	-	3	10	7
9. Susanna Pöykiö (FIN)	7	-	9	9

10. Kiira Korpi (FIN)	-	5	11	10
11. Yoshie Onda (JPN)	6	-	12	12
12. Carolina Kostner (ITA)	-	4	16	11
13. Mira Leung (CAN)	**4**	**-**	**14**	**13**
14. Elene Gedevanishvili (GEO)	-	9	8	17
15. Idora Hegel (CRO)	-	7	17	14
16. Yan Liu (CHN)	-	8	19	15
17. Amanda Nylander (SWE)	10	-	18	19
18. Tuğba Karademir (TUR)	14	-	22	16
19. Arina Martynova (RUS)	13	-	15	21
20. Galina Efremenko (UKR)	-	14	21	18
21. A. Gimazetdinova (UZB)	-	11	13	22
22. Júlia Sebestyén (HUN)	11	-	24	20
23. Valentina Marchei (ITA)	12	-	20	23
24. Annette Dytrt (GER)	-	10	23	24
25. Viktória Pavuk (HUN)	8	-	28	-
26. Katarina Gerboldt (RUS)	-	13	27	-
27. Michele Cantú (MEX)	15	-	25	-
28. N. Bobillier-Chaumont (FRA)	9	-	29	-
29. Andrea Kreuzer (AUT)	-	15	26	-
30. Teodora Poštič (SLO)	-	12	30	-
31. Miriam Manzano (AUS)	16	-	-	-
31. Tammy Sutan (THA)	-	16	-	-
33. Roxana Luca (ROM)	17	-	-	-
33. Sonia Radeva (BUL)	-	17	-	-
35. J. Belenyesiová (SVK)	18	-	-	-
35. Diane Chen (TPE)	-	18	-	-
37. Alisa Kireeva (UKR)	19	-	-	-
37. Ksenia Jastsenjski (SCG)	-	19	-	-
39. Jenna-Anne Buys (SAF)	20	-	-	-
39. Ji-eun Choi (KOR)	-	20	-	-
41. Elena Muhhina (EST)	21	-	-	-
41. Olga Zadvornova (LAT)	-	21	-	-
43. Laura Fernandez (ESP)	-	22	-	-
WD. Kristina Mikhailova (BLS)	-	-	-	-
WD. Viktoria Volchkova (RUS)	-	-	-	-

World Pairs Skating Championships:

	SP	FS
1. Qing Pang/Jian Tong (CHN)	2	1
2. Dan Zhang/Hao Zhang (CHN)	1	4
3. Maria Petrova/Alexei Tikhonov (RUS)	3	2
4. Rena Inoue/John Baldwin Jr. (USA)	6	3
5. Valérie Marcoux/Craig Buntin (CAN)	**4**	**5**
6. Aliona Savchenko/Robin Szolkowy (GER)	5	7
7. Jessica Dubé/Bryce Davison (CAN)	**7**	**6**
8. Julia Obertas/Sergei Slavnov (RUS)	8	8
9. Dorota Zagórska/Mariusz Siudek (POL)	9	9
10. Tatiana Volosozhar/Stanislav Morozov (UKR)	11	10
11. Marcy Hinzmann/Aaron Parchem (USA)	10	13
12. Maria Mukhortova/Maxim Trankov (RUS)	12	12
13. Marylin Pla/Yannick Bonheur (FRA)	14	11
14. Dominika Piątkowska/Dmitri Khromin (POL)	13	14
15. Rumiana Spassova/Stanimir Todorov (BUL)	16	15
16. Marina Aganina/Artem Knyazev (UZB)	15	16
17. Stacey Kemp/David King (GRB)	18	18
18. Mari Vartmann/Florian Just (GER)	19	17
19. Julia Beloglazova/Andrei Bekh (UKR)	17	19
20. Emma Brien/Stuart Beckingham (AUS)	20	20

World Ice Dancing Championships:

	CD	OD	FD
1. Albena Denkova/Maxim Staviski (BUL)	1	1	3
2. M-F. Dubreuil/P. Lauzon (CAN)	**2**	**3**	**1**
3. Tanith Belbin/Benjamin Agosto (USA)	3	4	4
4. M. Drobiazko/P. Vanagas (LIT)	5	5	2
5. I. Delobel/O. Schoenfelder (FRA)	4	2	5
6. Galit Chait/Sergei Sakhnovski (ISR)	6	7	6
7. O. Domnina/M. Shabalin (RUS)	7	6	7
8. F. Faiella/M. Scali (ITA)	9	10	8
9. M. Gregory/D. Petukhov (USA)	10	9	10
10. Megan Wing/Aaron Lowe (CAN)	**8**	**8**	**11**
11. Sinead Kerr/John Kerr (GRB)	12	11	9
12. J. Khokhlova/S. Novitski (RUS) 11	16	12	
13. C. Beier/W. Beier (GER)	13	14	13

14. Kristin Fraser/Igor Lukanin (AZE)	14	13	15
15. N. Péchalat/F. Bourzat (FRA)	15	12	17
16. M. Matthews/M. Zavozin (USA)	16	18	14
17. Nozomi Watanabe/Akiyuki Kido (JPN)	17	15	16
18. Nóra Hoffmann/Attila Elek (HUN)	18	17	18
19. Alexandra Kauc/Michał Zych (POL)	19	20	19
20. A. Zaretski/R. Zaretski (ISR) 24	22	20	
21. A. Zadorozhniuk/S. Verbillo (UKR)	21	21	21
22. Xiaoyang Yu/Chen Wang (CHN)	23	23	22
23. E. Romanovskaya/A. Grachev (RUS)	20	19	24
24. A. Beknazarova/V. Zuev (UKR)	22	24	23
25. O. Akimova/A. Shakalov (UZB)	27	25	-
26. Laura Munana/Luke Munana (MEX)	26	27	-
27. Kamila Hájková/David Vincour (CZE)	28	26	-
28. N. Buck/T. Nelson-Bond (AUS)	29	28	-
29. A. Allapach/P. Kongkasem (THA)	30	29	-
WD. A. Grebenkina/V. Azrojan (ARM)	-	-	-

Albena Denkova and Maxim Staviski made history as the first Bulgarian skaters to win gold medals at the World Figure Skating Championships.

Michael Novales made history as the first skater to represent The Philippines at the World Championships.

For the last time, the system of using two qualifying rounds to eliminate entries in the men's and ladies figure skating was used at the World Championships.

Sources: CNN News, March 2, 2006; Protocol, 2006 World Figure Skating Championships

2007 WORLD FIGURE SKATING CHAMPIONSHIPS
Tokyo, Japan, March 20-25, 2007

World Men's Figure Skating Championships:

	SP	FS
1. Brian Joubert (FRA)	1	3

2. Daisuke Takahashi (JPN)	3	1
3. Stéphane Lambiel (SUI)	6	2
4. Tomáš Verner (CZE)	9	4
5. Evan Lysacek (USA)	5	5
6. Jeffrey Buttle (CAN)	**2**	**8**
7. Nobunari Oda (JPN)	14	6
8. Johnny Weir (USA)	4	10
9. Kristoffer Berntsson (SWE)	15	7
10. Sergei Davydov (BLS)	8	12
11. Alban Préaubert (FRA)	10	11
12. Stefan Lindemann (GER)	16	9
13. Christopher Mabee (CAN)	**7**	**14**
14. Yannick Ponsero (FRA)	12	15
15. Ryan Bradley (USA)	19	13
16. Emanuel Sandhu (CAN)	**11**	**16**
17. Karel Zelenka (ITA)	17	17
18. Jamal Othman (SUI)	18	20
19. Sergei Voronov (RUS)	22	19
20. Andrei Lutai (RUS)	24	18
21. Igor Macypura (SVK)	21	22
22. Gregor Urbas (SLO)	23	21
23. Jialiang Wu (CHN)	13	24
24. Anton Kovalevski (UKR)	20	23
25. Ari-Pekka Nurmenkari (FIN)	25	-
26. Ming Xu (CHN)	26	-
27. Alper Uçar (TUR)	27	-
28. Sean Carlow (AUS)	28	-
29. Christian Rauchbauer (AUT)	29	-
30. Trifun Zivanovic (SRB)	30	-
31. Naiden Borichev (BUL)	31	-
32. Sergei Kotov (ISR)	32	-
33. Przemysław Domański (POL)	33	-
34. Dong-whun Lee (KOR)	34	-
35. Javier Fernández (ESP)	35	-
36. Luis Hernandez Olea (MEX)	36	-
37. Justin Pietersen (SAF)	37	-
38. Boris Martinec (CRO)	38	-
39. Zeus Issariotis (GRE)	39	-

40. Edward Ka-yin Chow (HKG)	40	-
41. Zoltán Kelemen (ROM)	41	-
42. Joel Watson (NZL)	42	-

World Ladies Figure Skating Championships:

	SP	FS
1. Miki Ando (JPN)	2	2
2. Mao Asada (JPN)	5	1
3. Yu-na Kim (KOR)	1	4
4. Kimmie Meissner (USA)	4	3
5. Yukari Nakano (JPN)	7	6
6. Carolina Kostner (ITA)	3	9
7. Sarah Meier (SUI)	9	8
8. Susanna Pöykiö (FIN)	10	7
9. Emily Hughes (USA)	6	13
10. Joannie Rochette (CAN)	**16**	**5**
11. Valentina Marchei (ITA)	14	10
12. Júlia Sebestyén (HUN)	8	15
13. Elena Sokolova (RUS)	11	14
14. Kiira Korpi (FIN)	17	11
15. Alissa Czisny (USA)	18	12
16. Arina Martynova (RUS)	12	16
17. Elene Gedevanishvili (GEO)	13	17
18. Elena Glebova (EST)	22	18
19. Anastasia Gimazetdinova (UZB)	15	20
20. Joanne Carter (AUS)	19	21
21. Idora Hegel (CRO)	24	19
22. Yan Liu (CHN)	21	23
23. Tamar Katz (ISR)	23	22
24. Mira Leung (CAN)	**20**	**24**
25. Kathrin Freudelsperger (AUT)	25	-
26. Lina Johansson (SWE)	26	-
27. Tuğba Karademir (TUR)	27	-
28. Irina Movchan (UKR)	28	-
29. Kristin Wieczorek (GER)	29	-
30. Roxana Luca (ROM)	30	-
31. Anna Jurkiewicz (POL)	31	-
32. Hristina Vassileva (BUL)	32	-

33. Radka Bártová (SVK)	33	-
34. Isabelle Pieman (BEL)	34	-
35. Ivana Hudziecová (CZE)	35	-
36. Teodora Poštič (SLO)	36	-
37. Mérovée Ephrem (MON)	37	-
38. Maria-Elena Papasotiriou (GRE)	38	-
39. Julia Teplih (LAT)	39	-
40. Charissa Tansomboon (THA)	40	-
41. Jocelyn Ho (TPE)	41	-
42. Ana Cecilia Cantú (MEX)	42	-
43. Ksenia Jastsenjski (SRB)	43	-
44. Ami Parekh (IND)	44	-
45. Kristine Y. Lee (HKG)	45	-
WD. Kristina Shlobina (AZE)	-	-
WD. Anne-Sophie Calvez (FRA)	-	-
WD. Jenna McCorkell (GRB)	-	-

World Pairs Skating Championships:

	SP	FS
1. Xue Shen/Hongbo Zhao (CHN)	1	1
2. Qing Pang/Jian Tong (CHN)	3	2
3. Aliona Savchenko/Robin Szolkowy (GER)	2	3
4. Tatiana Volosozhar/Stanislav Morozov (UKR)	8	5
5. Dan Zhang/Hao Zhang (CHN)	10	4
6. Valérie Marcoux/Craig Buntin (CAN)	**5**	**6**
7. Jessica Dubé/Bryce Davison (CAN)	**7**	**7**
8. Rena Inoue/John Baldwin Jr. (USA)	6	8
9. Yuko Kawaguchi/Alexander Smirnov (RUS)	4	10
10. Anabelle Langlois/Cody Hay (CAN)	**13**	**9**
11. Maria Mukhortova/Maxim Trankov (RUS)	12	11
12. Brooke Castile/Benjamin Okolski (USA)	14	13
13. Dominika Piątkowska/Dmitri Khromin (POL)	15	12
14. Marylin Pla/Yannick Bonheur (FRA)	16	16
15. Angelika Pylkina/Niklas Hogner (SWE)	17	15
16. Laura Magitteri/Ondřej Hotárek (ITA)	18	14
17. Stacey Kemp/David King (GRB)	19	17
18. Mari Vartmann/Florian Just (GER)	20	18
19. Marina Aganina/Artem Knyazev (UZB)	21	-

20. Diana Rennik/Aleksei Saks (EST)	22	-
WD. Dorota Siudek/Mariusz Siudek (POL)	9	-
WD. Maria Petrova/Alexei Tikhonov (RUS)	11	-
WD. Julia Belogazova/Andrei Bekh (UKR)	-	-

World Ice Dancing Championships:

	CD	OD	FD
1. Albena Denkova/Maxim Staviski (BUL)	2	1	1
2. M-F. Dubreuil/P. Lauzon (CAN)	**1**	**3**	**2**
3. Tanith Belbin/Benjamin Agosto (USA)	5	2	4
4. I. Delobel/O. Schoenfelder (FRA)	4	5	3
5. Oksana Domnina/Maxim Shabalin (RUS)	3	4	5
6. Tessa Virtue/Scott Moir (CAN)	**9**	**6**	**6**
7. Meryl Davis/Charlie White (USA)	10	8	7
8. Jana Khokhlova/Sergei Novitski (RUS)	6	7	8
9. Federica Faiella/Massimo Scali (ITA)	7	9	11
10. M. Gregory/D. Petukhov (USA)	11	10	9
11. Sinead Kerr/John Kerr (GRB)	8	11	12
12. N. Péchalat/F. Bourzat (FRA)	14	13	10
13. Anna Cappellini/Luca Lanotte (ITA)	12	16	13
14. A. Zaretski/R. Zaretski (ISR)	13	12	14
15. Nozomi Watanabe/Akiyuki Kido (JPN)	15	17	15
16. Kristin Fraser/Igor Lukanin (AZE)	16	14	16
17. A. Zadorozhniuk/S. Verbillo (UKR)	17	15	17
18. N. Zhiganshina/A. Gazsi (GER)	20	18	19
19. Grethe Grünberg/Kristjan Rand (EST)	23	19	18
20. Kaitlyn Weaver/Andrew Poje (CAN)	**18**	**23**	**20**
21. Xintong Huang/Xun Zheng (CHN)	19	22	21
22. A. Grebenkina/V. Azrojan (ARM)	21	21	23
23. K. Copely/D. Stagniūnas (LIT)	24	20	22
24. O. Akimova/A. Shakalov (UZB)	22	24	24
25. Barbora Silná/Dmitri Matsyuk (AUT)	25	25	-
26. Zsuzsanna Nagy/György Elek (HUN)	26	28	-
27. N.A. House/A. Reklys (LIT)	28	26	-
28. Goulakos/Neumann-Aubichon (GRE)	29	27	-
29. Laura Munana/Luke Munana (MEX)	27	29	-
WD. Kamila Hájková/David Vincour (CZE)	-	-	-
WD. Joanna Budner/Jan Mościcki (POL)	-	-	-

Romance was in the air in Tokyo. After delivering a winning performance in the pairs free skate, Hongbo Zhao proposed to his partner Xue Shen on the ice. Spoiler alert: she said yes!

Ami Parekh and Mérovée Ephrem made history as the first skaters to represent India and Monaco at the World Figure Skating Championships.

Sources: The Globe and Mail, April 12, 2007; Skating magazine, May 2007; Entries, 2007 World Figure Skating Championships; Protocol, 2007 World Figure Skating Championships

2008 WORLD FIGURE SKATING CHAMPIONSHIPS
Göteborg, Sweden, March 16-23, 2008

World Men's Figure Skating Championships:

	SP	FS
1. Jeffrey Buttle (CAN)	**1**	**1**
2. Brian Joubert (FRA)	6	2
3. Johnny Weir (USA)	2	5
4. Daisuke Takahashi (JPN)	3	6
5. Stéphane Lambiel (SUI)	5	7
6. Kevin van der Perren (BEL)	9	3
7. Sergei Voronov (RUS)	15	4
8. Takahiko Kozuka (JPN)	8	8
9. Patrick Chan (CAN)	**7**	**11**
10. Stephen Carriere (USA)	11	9
11. Jeremy Abbott (USA)	14	10
12. Sergei Davydov (BLS)	12	12
13. Adrian Schultheiss (SWE)	13	13
14. Kristoffer Berntsson (SWE)	10	15
15. Tomáš Verner (CZE)	4	20
16. Karel Zelenka (ITA)	17	16
17. Gregor Urbas (SLO)	18	14
18. Yannick Ponsero (FRA)	16	18
19. Yasuharu Nanri (JPN)	20	17
20. Anton Kovalevski (UKR)	21	19
21. Igor Macypura (SVK)	19	21

22. Jamal Othman (SUI)	22	22
23. Chengjiang Li (CHN)	23	23
24. Abzal Rakimgaliev (KAZ)	24	24
25. Alexandr Kazakov (BLS)	25	-
26. Michael Chrolenko (NOR)	26	-
27. Pavel Kaška (CZE)	27	-
28. Boris Martinec (CRO)	28	-
29. Elliot Hilton (GRB)	29	-
30. Javier Fernández (ESP)	30	-
31. Mikko Minkkinen (FIN)	31	-
32. Peter Liebers (GER)	32	-
33. Zoltán Kelemen (ROM)	33	-
34. Maxim Shipov (ISR)	34	-
35. Sean Carlow (AUS)	35	-
36. Luis Hernández Olea (MEX)	36	-
37. Manuel Koll (AUT)	37	-
38. Justin Pietersen (SAF)	38	-
39. Naiden Borichev (BUL)	39	-
40. Konstantin Tupikov (POL)	40	-
41. Tristan Thode (NZL)	41	-
42. Kutay Eryoldaş (TUR)	42	-
43. Danil Privalov (AZE)	43	-
44. Tigran Vardanjan (HUN)	44	-
45. Saulius Ambrulevičius (LIT)	45	-
WD. Alban Préaubert (FRA)	-	-
WD. Evan Lysacek (USA)	-	-
WD. Jialang Wu (CHN)	-	-

World Ladies Figure Skating Championships:

	SP	FS
1. Mao Asada (JPN)	2	2
2. Carolina Kostner (ITA)	1	3
3. Yu-na Kim (KOR)	5	1
4. Yukari Nakano (JPN)	3	4
5. Joannie Rochette (CAN)	**6**	**5**
6. Sarah Meier (SUI)	7	6
7. Kimmie Meissner (USA)	9	12
8. Laura Lepistö (FIN)	21	7

9. Kiira Korpi (FIN)	4	17
10. Beatrisa Liang (USA)	10	13
11. Júlia Sebestyén (HUN)	19	8
12. Annette Dytrt (GER)	12	11
13. Valentina Marchei (ITA)	17	9
14. Mira Leung (CAN)	**14**	**14**
15. Elena Glebova (EST)	20	10
16. Ashley Wagner (USA)	11	15
17. Ksenia Doronina (RUS)	15	16
18. Viktoria Helgesson (SWE)	16	20
19. Na-young Kim (KOR)	18	19
20. Elene Gedevanishvili (GEO)	23	18
21. Anastasia Gimazetdinova (UZB)	13	21
22. Tamar Katz (ISR)	24	22
23. Melinda Sherilyn Wang (TPE)	22	23
24. Jenna McCorkell (GRB)	25	-
25. Ivana Reitmayerová (SVK)	26	-
26. Tuğba Karademir (TUR)	27	-
27. Mérovée Ephrem (MON)	28	-
28. Victoria Muniz (PRI)	29	-
29. Sonia Lafuente (ESP)	30	-
30. Yan Liu (CHN)	31	-
31. Nella Simaová (CZE)	32	-
32. Sonia Radeva (BUL)	33	-
33. Anna Jurkiewicz (POL)	34	-
34. Irina Movchan (UKR)	35	-
35. Julia Sheremet (BLS)	36	-
36. Tina Wang (AUS)	37	-
37. Candice Didier (FRA)	38	-
38. Roxana Luca (ROM)	39	-
39. Viviane Käser (SUI)	40	-
40. Mirna Librić (CRO)	41	-
41. Ksenia Jastsenjski (SRB)	42	-
42. Barbara Klerk (BEL)	43	-
43. Loretta Hamui (MEX)	44	-
44. Gracielle Jeanne Tan (PHI)	45	-
45. Denise Koegl (AUT)	46	-
46. Charissa Tansomboon (THA)	47	-

47. Stasia Rage (LAT)	48	-
48. Tamami Ono (HKG)	49	-
49. Maria-Elena Papasotiriou (GRE)	50	-
50. Lejeanne Marais (SAF)	51	-
51. Morgan Figgins (NZL)	52	-
52. Beatričė Rožinskaitė (LIT)	53	-
WD. Miki Ando (JPN)	8	-
WD. Teodora Poštič (SLO)	-	-

World Pairs Skating Championships:

	SP	FS
1. Aliona Savchenko/Robin Szolkowy (GER)	2	1
2. Dan Zhang/Hao Zhang (CHN)	1	3
3. Jessica Dubé/Bryce Davison (CAN)	**4**	**2**
4. Yuko Kawaguchi/Alexander Smirnov (RUS)	3	4
5. Qing Pang/Jian Tong (CHN)	5	5
6. Meagan Duhamel/Craig Buntin (CAN)	**7**	**6**
7. Maria Mukhortova/Maxim Trankov (RUS)	6	9
8. Anabelle Langlois/Cody Hay (CAN)	**9**	**7**
9. Tatiana Volosozhar/Stanislav Morozov (UKR)	8	10
10. Rena Inoue/John Baldwin Jr. (USA)	10	8
11. Brooke Castile/Benjamin Okolski (USA)	12	11
12. Huibo Dong/Yiming Wu (CHN)	11	12
13. Laura Magitteri/Ondřej Hotárek (ITA)	14	13
14. Adeline Canac/Maximin Coia (FRA)	16	14
15. Stacey Kemp/David King (GRB)	13	15
16. Dominika Piątkowska/Dmitri Khromin (POL)	17	16
17. Hayley Anne Sacks/Vadim Akolzin (ISR)	15	17
18. Marina Aganina/Dmitri Zobnin (UZB)	18	19
19. Ariel Fay Gagnon/Chad Tsagris (GRE)	19	18
20. Amy Ireland/Michael Bahoric (CRO)	20	20
WD. Ekaterina Kostenko/Roman Talan (UKR)	-	-
WD. Mélodie Chataigner/Medhi Bouzzine (FRA)	-	-

World Ice Dancing Championships:

	CD	OD	FD
1. I. Delobel/O. Schoenfelder (FRA)	1	1	2
2. Tessa Virtue/Scott Moir (CAN)	**2**	**3**	**1**

3. Jana Khokhlova/Sergei Novitski (RUS)	3	2	5
4. Tanith Belbin/Benjamin Agosto (USA)	5	4	3
5. Federica Faiella/Massimo Scali (ITA)	4	5	4
6. Meryl Davis/Charlie White (USA)	7	7	6
7. N. Péchalat/F. Bourzat (FRA)	6	6	7
8. Sinead Kerr/John Kerr (GRB)	8	8	8
9. A. Zaretski/R. Zaretski (ISR)	9	9	10
10. Anna Cappellini/Luca Lanotte (ITA)	11	10	9
11. Kristin Fraser/Igor Lukanin (AZE)	10	11	11
12. K. Navarro/B. Bommentre (USA)	12	13	14
13. E. Bobrova/D. Soloviev (RUS)	16	12	13
14. K. Copely/D. Stagniūnas (LIT)	13	14	12
15. Ekaterina Rubleva/Ivan Shefer (RUS)	15	15	15
16. Cathy Reed/Chris Reed (JPN)	18	18	16
17. Kaitlyn Weaver/Andrew Poje (CAN)	**20**	**17**	**17**
18. A. Zadorozhniuk/S. Verbillo (UKR)	14	16	21
19. A. Hann-McCurdy/M. Coreno (CAN)	**17**	**19**	**18**
20. N. Zhiganshina/A. Gazsi (GER)	19	21	19
21. Barbora Silná/Dmitri Matsyuk (AUT)	21	20	20
22. Xiaoyang Yu/Chen Wang (CHN)	23	23	23
23. Kamila Hájková/David Vincour (CZE)	22	25	22
24. Leonie Krail/Oscar Peter (SUI)	25	22	24
25. Krisztina Barta/Ádám Tóth (HUN)	27	24	-
26. Joanna Budner/Jan Mościcki (POL)	24	28	-
27. D. O'Brien/G. Merriman (AUS)	28	27	-
28. Ksenia Shmirina/Egor Maistrov (BLS)	29	26	-
29. Seon-hye Yu/Ramil Sarkulov (UZB)	26	30	-
30. Ina Demireva/Juri Kurakin (BUL)	30	29	-
31. K. Kiudmaa/A. Trohlev (EST)	31	-	-
WD. O. Domnina/M. Shabalin (RUS)	-	-	-
WD. Christina Beier/William Beier (GER)	-	-	-

Isabelle Delobel and Olivier Schoenfelder's winning performance to music from the Academy Award–winning film "The Piano" featured a first at the World Figure Skating Championships - the incorporation of French Sign Language in the choreography. Delobel and Schoenfelder worked with Patricia Mazoyer, a multi-disciplinary artist who is hard of hearing, to develop the innovative piece.

Meagan Duhamel and Craig Buntin made history as the first pair to receive positive GOE on a throw triple Lutz jump at the World Championships.

American ice dancer Brent Bommentre's luggage was missing in action when he arrived in Göteborg. He skated the compulsory dance in a brand new pair of skates and a costume bought at a department store. His costumes and skates showed up in time for the original dance, but he elected to continue competing in his new skates.

Victoria Muniz made history as the first skater to represent Puerto Rico at the World Figure Skating Championships.

Sources: RFI, March 22, 2008; Skating magazine, May 2008; Media Kit, Patricia Mazoyer, La Main Tatouée; Entries, 2008 World Figure Skating Championships; Protocol, 2008 World Figure Skating Championships

2009 WORLD FIGURE SKATING CHAMPIONSHIPS
Los Angeles, United States, March 23-29, 2009

World Men's Figure Skating Championships:

	SP	FS
1. Evan Lysacek (USA)	2	1
2. Patrick Chan (CAN)	**3**	**2**
3. Brian Joubert (FRA)	1	3
4. Tomáš Verner (CZE)	4	4
5. Samuel Contesti (ITA)	6	5
6. Takahiko Kozuka (JPN)	5	7
7. Nobunari Oda (JPN)	7	8
8. Denis Ten (KAZ)	17	6
9. Brandon Mroz (USA)	8	13
10. Andrei Lutai (RUS)	15	9
11. Jeremy Abbott (USA)	10	10
12. Vaughn Chipeur (CAN)	**12**	**12**
13. Sergei Voronov (RUS)	9	14

14. Kevin van der Perren (BEL)		14	15
15. Takahito Mura (JPN)		13	16
16. Yannick Ponsero (FRA)		11	17
17. Jeremy Ten (CAN)		**21**	**11**
18. Adrian Schultheiss (SWE)		18	18
19. Javier Fernández (ESP)		20	19
20. Kristoffer Berntsson (SWE)		16	20
21. Gregor Urbas (SLO)		22	21
22. Anton Kovalevski (UKR)		19	23
23. Przemysław Domański (POL)		24	22
24. Igor Macypura (SVK)		23	24
25. Peter Liebers (GER)		25	-
26. Jamal Othman (SUI)		26	-
27. Ari-Pekka Nurmenkari (FIN)		27	-
28. Jialiang Wu (CHN)		28	-
29. Viktor Pfeifer (AUT)		29	-
30. Elliot Hilton (GRB)		30	-
31. Tigran Vardanjan (HUN)		31	-
32. Zoltán Kelemen (ROM)		32	-
33. Damjan Ostojič (BIH)		33	-
34. Luis Hernández Olea (MEX)		34	-
35. Alper Uçar (TUR)		35	-
36. Maxim Shipov (ISR)		36	-
37. Kevin Alves (BRA)		37	-
38. Charles Shou-san Pao (TPE)		38	-
39. Min-seok Kim (KOR)		39	-
40. Beka Shankulashvili (GEO)		40	-
41. Boris Martinec (CRO)		41	-
42. Mikael Redin (SUI)		42	-
43. Alexandr Kazakov (BLS)		43	-
44. Justin Pietersen (SAF)		44	-
45. Georgi Kenchadze (BUL)		45	-
46. Mark Webster (AUS)		46	-
47. Andrew Huertas (PRI)		47	-
48. Gegham Vardanyan (ARM)		48	-
49. Saulius Ambrulevičius (LIT)		49	-
50. Michael Dimalanta (PHI)		50	-
WD. Joffrey Bourdon (MNE)		51	-

World Men's Figure Skating Championships:

		SP	FS
1.	Yu-na Kim (KOR)	1	1
2.	**Joannie Rochette (CAN)**	**2**	**3**
3.	Miki Ando (JPN)	4	2
4.	Mao Asada (JPN)	3	4
5.	Rachael Flatt (USA)	7	5
6.	Laura Lepistö (FIN)	6	7
7.	Alena Leonova (RUS)	11	6
8.	Fumie Suguri (JPN)	9	9
9.	Sarah Meier (SUI)	10	10
10.	Elene Gedevanishvili (GEO)	8	11
11.	Alissa Czisny (USA)	14	8
12.	Carolina Kostner (ITA)	5	15
13.	Susanna Pöykiö (FIN)	12	12
14.	Ivana Reitmayerová (SVK)	16	13
15.	**Cynthia Phaneuf (CAN)**	**15**	**14**
16.	Elena Glebova (EST)	13	17
17.	Na-young Kim (KOR)	17	21
18.	Annette Dytrt (GER)	18	19
19.	Anna Jurkiewicz (POL)	20	16
20.	Jenna McCorkell (GRB)	21	18
21.	Tuğba Karademir (TUR)	22	20
22.	Candice Didier (FRA)	19	22
23.	Kerstin Frank (AUT)	23	23
24.	Ana Cecilia Cantu (MEX)	24	24
25.	Tamar Katz (ISR)	25	-
26.	Sonia Lafuente (ESP)	26	-
27.	Viktoria Helgesson (SWE)	27	-
28.	Chaochih Liu (TPE)	28	-
29.	Gracielle Jeanne Tan (PHI)	29	-
30.	Nella Simaová (CZE)	30	-
31.	Anastasia Gimazetdinova (UZB)	31	-
32.	Emma Hagieva (AZE)	32	-
33.	Cheltzie Lee (AUS)	33	-
34.	Irina Movchan (UKR)	34	-
35.	Teodora Poštič (SLO)	35	-

36. Roxana Luca (ROM)   36   -
37. Tamami Ono (HKG)   37   -
38. Zanna Pugaca (LAT)   38   -
39. Bianka Pádár (HUN)   39   -
40. Isabelle Pieman (BEL)   40   -
41. Sonia Radeva (BUL)   41   -
42. Yan Liu (CHN)   42   -
43. Victoria Muniz (PRI)   43   -
44. Lejeanne Marais (SAF)   44   -
45. Charissa Tansomboon (THA)   45   -
46. Mirna Librić (CRO)   46   -
47. Maria Papasotiriou (GRE)   47   -
48. Beatrice Rozinskaite (LIT)   48   -
49. Ksenia Jastsenjski (SRB)   49   -
50. Mérovée Ephrem (MON)   50   -
51. Stacy Perfetti (BRA)   51   -
52. Clara Peters (IRL)   52   -
53. Yoniko Eva Washington (IND)   53   -
WD. Sonja Mugoša (MNE)   -   -
WD. Noémie Silberer (SUI)   -   -

World Pairs Skating Championships:

	SP	FS
1. Aliona Savchenko/Robin Szolkowy (GER)	1	1
2. Dan Zhang/Hao Zhang (CHN)	3	2
3. Yuko Kavaguti/Alexander Smirnov (RUS)	2	3
4. Qing Pang/Jian Tong (CHN)	5	4
5. Maria Mukhortova/Maxim Trankov (RUS)	4	7
6. Tatiana Volosozhar/Stanislav Morozov (UKR)	6	5
7. Jessica Dubé/Bryce Davison (CAN)	**7**	**6**
8. Meagan Duhamel/Craig Buntin (CAN)	**8**	**8**
9. Caydee Denney/Jeremy Barrett (USA)	10	9
10. Mylène Brodeur/John Mattatall (CAN)	**11**	**10**
11. Keauna McLaughlin/Rockne Brubaker (USA)	9	12
12. Vanessa James/Yannick Bonheur (FRA)	17	11
13. Stacey Kemp/David King (GRB)	13	13
14. Anaïs Morand/Antoine Dorsaz (SUI)	12	14
15. Maylin Hausch/Daniel Wende (GER)	15	15

16. Yue Zhang/Lei Wang (CHN)	14	16
17. Maria Sergejeva/Ilja Glebov (EST)	16	17
18. Nicole Della Monica/Yannick Kocon (ITA)	18	18
19. Joanna Sulej/Mateusz Chruściński (POL)	19	19
20. Jessica Crenshaw/Chad Tsagris (GRE)	20	20
21. Ekaterina Sokolova/Fedor Sokolov (ISR)	21	-
22. A. Sunyoto-Yang/D. Sulindro-Yang (TPE)	22	-
23. Nina Ivanova/Filip Zalevski (BUL)	23	-
24. Ksenia Ozerova/Alexander Enbert (RUS)	24	-
25. Marina Aganina/Dmitri Zobnin (UZB)	25	-
WD. Lubov Ilyushechkina/Nodari Maisuradze (RUS)	-	-

World Ice Dancing Championships:

	CD	OD	FD
1. Oksana Domnina/Maxim Shabalin (RUS)	1	2	1
2. Tanith Belbin/Benjamin Agosto (USA)	2	1	2
3. Tessa Virtue/Scott Moir (CAN)	**3**	**6**	**4**
4. Meryl Davis/Charlie White (USA)	4	3	3
5. N. Péchalat/F. Bourzat (FRA)	6	4	5
6. Jana Khokhlova/Sergei Novitski (RUS)	5	5	6
7. Sinead Kerr/John Kerr (GRB)	8	7	7
8. Federica Faiella/Massimo Scali (ITA)	7	10	8
9. Pernelle Carron/Matthieu Jost (FRA)	9	8	10
10. Anna Cappellini/Luca Lanotte (ITA)	11	9	11
11. Emily Samuelson/Evan Bates (USA)	13	11	9
12. Vanessa Crone/Paul Poirier (CAN)	**10**	**12**	**12**
13. A. Zaretski/R. Zaretski (ISR)	12	13	14
14. K. Copely/D. Stagniūnas (LIT)	16	14	13
15. A. Zadorozhniuk/S. Verbillo (UKR)	15	19	15
16. Cathy Reed/Chris Reed (JPN)	18	15	16
17. C. Hermann/D. Hermann (GER)	20	16	18
18. Kristin Fraser/Igor Lukanin (AZE)	14	18	20
19. Zoé Blanc/Pierre-Loup Bouquet (FRA)	19	17	19
20. Caitlin Mallory/Kristjan Rand (EST)	23	21	17
21. L. Myslivečková/M. Novák (CZE)	17	20	21
22. Xintong Huang/Xun Zheng (CHN)	22	23	22
23. P. Towler-Green/P. Poole (USA)	21	22	23
24. Joanna Budner/Jan Mościcki (POL)	24	25	24

25. D. O'Brien/G. Merriman (AUS)	27	24	-
26. N. Georgiadis/G. Hockley (GRE)	26	26	-
27. Leonie Krail/Oscar Peter (SUI)	25	27	-
28. Emese László/Máté Fejes (HUN)	29	28	-
29. Ina Demireva/Juri Kurakin (BUL)	28	30	-
30. K. Shmirina/Y. Maistrov (BLS)	30	28	-
WD. I. Delobel/O. Schoenfelder (FRA)	-	-	-
WD. N. Hoffmann/M. Zavozin (HUN)	-	-	-

Yu-na Kim made history as the first Korean skater to win a gold medal at the World Figure Skating Championships.

Clara Peters made history as the first skater to represent Ireland at the World Championships. Kevin Alves and Stacey Perfetti were the first skaters from Brazil to participate.

Sources: ESPN, March 28, 2009; Skating magazine, May 2009; Entries, 2009 World Figure Skating Championships; Protocol, 2009 World Figure Skating Championships

2010 WORLD FIGURE SKATING CHAMPIONSHIPS
Torino, Italy, March 22-28, 2010

World Men's Figure Skating Championships:

	SP	FS
1. Daisuke Takahashi (JPN)	1	1
2. Patrick Chan (CAN)	**2**	**2**
3. Brian Joubert (FRA)	3	4
4. Michal Březina (CZE)	5	3
5. Jeremy Abbott (USA)	6	6
6. Adam Rippon (USA)	7	5
7. Samuel Contesti (ITA)	8	11
8. Kevin van der Perren (BEL)	10	9
9. Adrian Schultheiss (SWE)	12	7
10. Takahiko Kozuka (JPN)	4	12
11. Kevin Reynolds (CAN)	**14**	**8**
12. Javier Fernández (ESP)	13	10
13. Denis Ten (KAZ)	9	15

14. Sergei Voronov (RUS)	11	14
15. Florent Amodio (FRA)	15	13
16. Anton Kovalevski (UKR)	16	19
17. Jinlin Guan (CHN)	19	16
18. Ryan Bradley (USA)	21	17
19. Alexandr Kazakov (BLS)	24	18
20. Viktor Pfeifer (AUT)	17	21
21. Abzal Rakimgaliev (KAZ)	22	20
22. Jamal Othman (SUI)	20	22
23. Min-seok Kim (KOR)	18	24
24. Ari-Pekka Nurmenkari (FIN)	23	23
25. Peter Liebers (GER)	25	-
26. Pavel Kaška (CZE)	26	-
27. Kevin Alves (BRA)	27	-
28. Nobunari Oda (JPN)	28	-
29. Boris Martinec (CRO)	29	-
30. Matthew Parr (GRB)	30	-
31. Peter Reitmayer (SVK)	31	-
32. Zoltán Kelemen (ROM)	32	-
33. Damjan Ostojič (BIH)	33	-
34. Andrew Huertas (PRI)	34	-
35. Maciej Cieplucha (POL)	35	-
36. Viktor Romanenkov (EST)	36	-
37. Stephen Li-chung Kuo (TPE)	37	-
38. Saulius Ambrulevičius (LIT)	38	-
39. Mark Webster (AUS)	39	-
40. Georgi Kenchadze (BUL)	40	-
41. Tigran Vardanjan (HUN)	41	-
42. Sarkis Hayrapetyan (ARM)	42	-
43. Maxim Shipov (ISR)	43	-
44. Humberto Contreras (MEX)	44	-
45. Ali Demirboğa (TUR)	45	-
46. Girts Jekabsons (LAT)	46	-
WD. Joffrey Bourdon (MNE)	-	-
WD. Artem Borodulin (RUS)	-	-
WD . Paolo Bacchini (ITA)	-	-

World Ladies Figure Skating Championships:

	SP	FS
1. Mao Asada (JPN)	2	2
2. Yu-na Kim (KOR)	7	1
3. Laura Lepistö (FIN)	3	6
4. Miki Ando (JPN)	11	3
5. Cynthia Phaneuf (CAN)	**8**	**4**
6. Carolina Kostner (ITA)	4	5
7. Mirai Nagasu (USA)	1	11
8. Ksenia Makarova (RUS)	5	8
9. Rachael Flatt (USA)	6	9
10. Viktoria Helgesson (SWE)	9	10
11. Akiko Suzuki (JPN)	20	7
12. Sarah Hecken (GER)	13	13
13. Alena Leonova (RUS)	14	14
14. Jenna McCorkell (GRB)	15	12
15. Júlia Sebestyén (HUN)	10	15
16. Yan Liu (CHN)	18	16
17. Cheltzie Lee (AUS)	17	17
18. Elene Gedevanishvili (GEO)	12	21
19. Kiira Korpi (FIN)	16	20
20. Sonia Lafuente (ESP)	21	18
21. Elena Glebova (EST)	22	19
22. Min-jeong Kwak (KOR)	23	22
23. Anastasia Gimazetdinova (UZB)	19	23
24. Manouk Gijsman (NED)	24	24
25. Ivana Reitmayerová (SVK)	25	-
26. Sarah Meier (SUI)	26	-
27. Tamar Katz (ISR)	27	-
28. Tuğba Karademir (TUR)	28	-
29. Myriane Samson (CAN)	**29**	**-**
30. Kerstin Frank (AUT)	30	-
31. Victoria Muniz (PRI)	31	-
32. Bettina Heim (SUI)	32	-
33. Fleur Maxwell (LUX)	33	-
34. Teodora Poštič (SLO)	34	-
35. Karina Sinding Johnson (DEN)	35	-
36. Zanna Pugaca (LAT)	36	-

37. Mirna Libric (CRO)	37	-
38. Lauren Ko (PHI)	38	-
39. Martina Boček (CZE)	39	-
40. Irina Movchan (UKR)	40	-
41. Sonia Radeva (BUL)	41	-
42. Ana Cecilia Cantú (MEX)	42	-
43. Crystal Kiang (TPE)	43	-
44. Georgia Glastris (GRE)	44	-
45. Gwendoline Didier (FRA)	45	-
46. Marina Seeh (SRB)	46	-
47. Clara Peters (IRL)	47	-
48. Tamami Ono (HKG)	48	-
49. Abigail Pietersen (SAF)	49	-
50. Charissa Tansomboon (THA)	50	-
51. Sabina Paquier (ROM)	51	-
52. Yoniko Eva Washington (IND)	52	-
53. Beatričė Rožinskaitė (LIT)	53	-
WD. Isabelle Pieman (BEL)	-	-
WD. Sonja Mugoša (MNE)	-	-

World Pairs Skating Championships:

	SP	FS
1. Qing Pang/Jian Tong (CHN)	1	1
2. Aliona Savchenko/Robin Szolkowy (GER)	3	2
3. Yuko Kavaguti/Alexander Smirnov (RUS)	2	3
4. Maria Mukhortova/Maxim Trankov (RUS)	4	4
5. Dan Zhang/Hao Zhang (CHN)	5	5
6. Jessica Dubé/Bryce Davison (CAN)	**8**	**6**
7. Caydee Denney/Jeremy Barrett (USA)	6	8
8. Vera Bazarova/Yuri Larionov (RUS)	7	7
9. Amanda Evora/Mark Ladwig (USA)	9	9
10. Anabelle Langlois/Cody Hay (CAN)	**12**	**10**
11. Stefania Berton/Ondřej Hotárek (ITA)	11	11
12. Vanessa James/Yannick Bonheur (FRA)	10	13
13. Anaïs Morand/Antoine Dorsaz (SUI)	13	14
14. Maylin Hausch/Daniel Wende (GER)	14	12
15. Joanna Sulej/Mateusz Chruściński (POL)	15	15
16. Stacey Kemp/David King (GRB)	16	16

17. Huibo Dong/Yiming Wu (CHN) — 17 -
18. Maria Sergejeva/Ilja Glebov (EST) — 18 -
19. Lubov Bakirova/Mikalai Kamianchuk (BLS) — 19 -
20. A. Sunyoto-Yang/D. Sulindro-Yang (TPE) — 20 -
21. Jessica Crenshaw/Chad Tsagris (GRE) — 21 -
22. Ekaterina Kostenko/Roman Talan (UKR) — 22 -
23. Nina Ivanova/Filip Zalevski (BUL) — 23 -
24. Gabriela Čermanová/Martin Hanulák (SVK) — 24 -
25. D. Montalbano/E. Krasnopolski (ISR) — 25 -

World Ice Dancing Championships:

	CD	OD	FD
1. Tessa Virtue/Scott Moir (CAN)	**1**	**1**	**2**
2. Meryl Davis/Charlie White (USA)	2	2	1
3. Federica Faiella/Massimo Scali (ITA)	3	3	4
4. N. Péchalat/F. Bourzat (FRA)	4	4	3
5. Sinead Kerr/John Kerr (GRB)	6	5	5
6. A. Zaretski/R. Zaretski (ISR)	8	6	6
7. Vanessa Crone/Paul Poirier (CAN)	**9**	**7**	**7**
8. E. Bobrova/D. Soloviev (RUS)	11	8	8
9. Emily Samuelson/Evan Bates (USA)	10	10	10
10. Nóra Hoffmann/Maxim Zavozin (HUN)	13	11	9
11. Anna Cappellini/Luca Lanotte (ITA)	7	12	14
12. Pernelle Carron/Lloyd Jones (FRA)	15	13	12
13. Ekaterina Rubleva/Ivan Shefer (RUS)	16	16	11
14. K. Navarro/B. Bommentre (USA)	14	15	15
15. Cathy Reed/Chris Reed (JPN)	23	14	13
16. L. Myslivečková/M. Novák (CZE)	18	17	17
17. Caitlin Mallory/Kristjan Rand (EST)	20	21	16
18. Xiaoyang Yu/Chen Wang (CHN)	17	19	19
19. Kira Geil/Dmitri Matsyuk (AUT)	19	18	18
20. Allison Reed/Otar Japaridze (GEO)	22	22	-
21. C. Hermann/Daniel Hermann (GER)	21	23	-
22. C. Chitwood/M. Hanretty (GRB)	24	20	-
23. Katelyn Good/Nikolaj Sørensen (DEN)	25	24	-
24. D. O'Brien/G. Merriman (AUS)	26	25	-
25. Jenette Maitz/Alper Uçar (TUR)	27	26	-
WD. J. Khokhlova/S. Novitski (RUS)	5	9	-

WD. A. Zadorozhniuk/S. Verbillo (UKR)   12   -   -

For the final time, the compulsory and original dances were included in the ice dance event at the World Figure Skating Championships. Snippets of compulsory dance patterns were subsequently incorporated into the short dance, which replaced the original dance. Italians Federica Faiella and Massimo Scali were the last skaters to perform a full compulsory dance at the World Championships - the Golden Waltz. The last skaters to perform an original dance at the World Championships were Israeli siblings Alexandra and Roman Zaretski.

Daisuke Takahashi made history as the first skater from Japan to win a gold medal in the men's event at the World Championships. It was the first year skaters from Japan won both the men's and ladies events.

Laura Lepistö made history as the first skater from Finland to win a medal in the ladies event at the World Championships.

Sources: Skating magazine, May 2010; Entries, 2010 World Figure Skating Championships; Protocol, 2010 World Figure Skating Championships

2011 WORLD FIGURE SKATING CHAMPIONSHIPS
Moscow, Russia, April 25-May 1, 2011

World Men's Figure Skating Championships:

	PR	SP	FS
1. Patrick Chan (CAN)	-	1	1
2. Takahiko Kozuka (JPN)	1	6	2
3. Artur Gachinski (RUS)	-	4	3
4. Michal Březina (CZE)	3	7	5
5. Daisuke Takahashi (JPN)	-	3	6
6. Nobunari Oda (JPN)	-	2	9
7. Florent Amodio (FRA)	-	5	7
8. Brian Joubert (FRA)	-	9	4
9. Richard Dornbush (USA)	-	11	8
10. Javier Fernández (ESP)	-	14	10

11. Ross Miner (USA)	-	13	11
12. Tomáš Verner (CZE)	-	8	13
13. Ryan Bradley (USA)	-	12	12
14. Denis Ten (KAZ)	-	10	14
15. Peter Liebers (GER)	4	16	15
16. Anton Kovalevski (UKR)	-	17	16
17. Kevin van der Perren (BEL)	-	15	18
18. Samuel Contesti (ITA)	-	18	17
19. Jorik Hendrickx (BEL)	10	22	19
20. Kevin Reynolds (CAN)	**-**	**19**	**21**
21. Paolo Bacchini (ITA)	6	23	20
22. Nan Song (CHN)	-	20	23
23. Kim Lucine (MON)	8	24	22
24. Joey Russell (CAN)	**7**	**21**	**24**
25. Adrian Schultheiss (SWE)	-	25	-
26. Viktor Pfeifer (AUT)	5	26	-
27. Min-seok Kim (KOR)	12	27	-
28. Alexander Majorov (SWE)	2	28	-
29. Maxim Shipov (ISR)	9	29	-
30. Misha Ge (UZB)	11	30	-
31. Mark Webster (AUS)	13	-	-
32. Justus Strid (DEN)	14	-	-
33. David Richardson (GRB)	15	-	-
34. Tigran Vardanjan (HUN)	16	-	-
35. Mikael Redin (SUI)	17	-	-
36. Kutay Eryoldaş (TUR)	18	-	-
37. Stephen Li-chung Kuo (TPE)	19	-	-
38. Bela Papp (FIN)	20	-	-
39. Harry Hau Yin Lee (HKG)	21	-	-
40. Vitali Luchanok (BLS)	22	-	-
41. Sarkis Hayrapetyan (ARM)	23	-	-
42. Georgi Kenchadze (BUL)	24	-	-
WD. Shawn Sawyer (CAN)	**-**	**-**	**-**
WD. Damjan Ostojič (BIH)	-	-	-
WD. Jordan Ju (TPE)	-	-	-
WD. Viktor Romanenkov (EST)	-	-	-

World Ladies Figure Skating Championships:

	PR	SP	FS
1. Miki Ando (JPN)	-	2	1
2. Yu-na Kim (KOR)	-	1	2
3. Carolina Kostner (ITA)	-	6	3
4. Alena Leonova (RUS)	-	5	4
5. Alissa Czisny (USA)	-	4	5
6. Mao Asada (JPN)	-	7	6
7. Ksenia Makarova (RUS)	3	9	
8. Kanako Murakami (JPN)	-	10	7
9. Kiira Korpi (FIN)	-	9	8
10. Elene Gedevanishvili (GEO)	-	15	10
11. Sarah Hecken (GER)	-	12	11
12. Rachael Flatt (USA)	-	8	14
13. Cynthia Phaneuf (CAN)	**-**	**13**	**12**
14. Maé-Bérénice Méité (FRA)	1	11	15
15. Joshi Helgesson (SWE)	2	16	13
16. Amélie Lacoste (CAN)	**5**	**14**	**18**
17. Viktoria Helgesson (SWE)	-	24	16
18. Bingwa Geng (CHN)	-	19	17
19. Ira Vannut (BEL)	4	17	20
20. Juulia Turkkila (FIN)	6	22	19
21. Cheltzie Lee (AUS)	-	18	21
22. Elena Glebova (EST)	9	20	22
23. Irina Movchan (UKR)	10	23	23
24. Jenna McCorkell (GRB)	-	21	24
25. Sonia Lafuente Martínez (ESP)	3	25	-
26. Karina Sinding Johnson (DEN)	7	26	-
27. Bettina Heim (SUI)	12	27	-
28. Daša Grm (SLO)	8	28	-
29. Belinda Schönberger (AUT)	11	29	-
30. Viktória Pavuk (HUN)	-	30	-
31. Roberta Rodeghiero (ITA)	13	-	-
32. Sabina Măriuţă (ROM)	14	-	-
33. Min-jeong Kwak (KOR)	15	-	-
34. Birce Atabey (TUR)	16	-	-
35. Mericien Venzon (PHI)	17	-	-
36. Lejeanne Marais (SAF)	18	-	-

37. Hristina Vassileva (BUL)	19	-	-
38. Melinda Wang (TPE)	20	-	-
39. Clara Peters (IRL)	21	-	-
40. Taryn Jurgensen (THA)	22	-	-
41. Mary Ro Reyes (MEX)	23	-	-
42. Georgia Glastris (GRE)	24	-	-
43. Marina Seeh (SRB)	25	-	-
44. Tiffany Packard Yu (HKG)	26	-	-
WD. Laura Lepistö (FIN)	-	-	-
WD. Myriane Samson (CAN)	**-**	**-**	**-**
WD. Qiuying Zhu (CHN)	-	-	-
WD. Elene Gedevanishvili (GEO)	-	-	-
WD. Valentina Marchei (ITA)	-	-	-
WD. Fleur Maxwell (LUX)	-	-	-
WD. Patricia Gleščič (SLO)	-	-	-

World Pairs Skating Championships:

	SP	FS
1. Aliona Savchenko/Robin Szolkowy (GER)	2	1
2. Tatiana Volosozhar/Maxim Trankov (RUS)	3	2
3. Qing Pang/Jian Tong (CHN)	1	3
4. Yuko Kavaguti/Alexander Smirnov (RUS)	5	4
5. Vera Bazarova/Yuri Larionov (RUS)	4	5
6. Caitlin Yankowskas/John Coughlin (USA)	8	6
7. Meagan Duhamel/Eric Radford (CAN)	**7**	**7**
8. K. Moore-Towers/D. Moscovitch (CAN)	**10**	**8**
9. Narumi Takahashi/Mervin Tran (JPN)	6	10
10. Stefania Berton/Ondřej Hotárek (ITA)	9	11
11. Amanda Evora/Mark Ladwig (USA)	11	9
12. Maylin Hausch/Daniel Wende (GER)	12	12
13. Yue Zhang/Lei Wang (CHN)	13	13
14. Huibo Dong/Yiming Wu (CHN)	14	14
15. Klára Kadlecová/Petr Bidař (CZE)	15	15
16. Natalia Zabiiako/Sergei Kulbach (EST)	16	16
17. Stacey Kemp/David King (GRB)	17	-
18. Adeline Canac/Yannick Bonheur (FRA)	18	-
19. Lubov Bakirova/Mikalai Kamianchuk (BLS)	19	-
20. D. Montalbano/E. Krasnopolski (ISR)	20	-

21. Stina Martini/Severin Kiefer (AUT) 21 -
22. Alexandra Malakhova/Leri Kenchadze (BUL) 22 -
WD. Narumi Takahashi/Mervin Tran (JPN) - -

World Ice Dancing Championships:

	PR	SD	FD
1. Meryl Davis/Charlie White (USA)	-	2	1
2. Tessa Virtue/Scott Moir (CAN)	**-**	**1**	**2**
3. Maia Shibutani/Alex Shibutani (USA)	-	4	3
4. N. Péchalat/F. Bourzat (FRA)	-	3	6
5. Kaitlyn Weaver/Andrew Poje (CAN)	**1**	**7**	**4**
6. E. Bobrova/D. Soloviev (RUS)	-	5	5
7. E. Ilinykh/N. Katsalapov (RUS)	-	6	10
8. Anna Cappellini/Luca Lanotte (ITA)	-	8	9
9. Madison Chock/Greg Zuerlein (USA)	-	9	7
10. Vanessa Crone/Paul Poirier (CAN)	**-**	**10**	**8**
11. N. Zhiganshina/A. Gazsi (GER)	2	12	11
12. Pernelle Carron/Lloyd Jones (FRA)	-	11	12
13. Cathy Reed/Chris Reed (JPN)	-	13	13
14. I. Tobias/D. Stagniūnas (LIT)	3	14	14
15. S. Heekin-Canedy/A. Shakalov (UKR)	5	15	15
16. P. Coomes/N. Buckland (GRB)	-	17	16
17. Xintong Huang/Xun Zheng (CHN)	4	16	17
18. Allison Reed/Otar Japaridze (GEO)	6	19	18
19. C. Guignard/M. Fabbri (ITA)	-	18	19
20. Louise Walden/Owen Edwards (GRB)	9	20	20
21. Dóra Turóczi/Balázs Major (HUN)	-	21	-
22. L. Myslivečková/M. Novák (CZE)	8	22	-
23. S. Hurtado/A. Díaz Bronchud (ESP)	7	23	-
24. Brooke Frieling/Lionel Rumi (ISR)	-	24	-
25. Ramona Elsener/Florian Roost (SUI)	10	25	-
26. Kira Geil/Tobias Eisenbauer (AUT)	11	-	-
27. D. O'Brien/G. Merriman (AUS)	12	-	-
28. Zsuzsanna Nagy/Máté Fejes (HUN)	13	-	-
29. Katelyn Good/Nikolaj Sørensen (DEN)	14	-	-
30. C. Bruhns/B. Westenberger (MEX)	15	-	-
31. K. Tremasova/D. Lichev (BUL)	16	-	-
32. L. Valadzenkava/V. Vakunov (BLS)	17	-	-

WD. Sinead Kerr/John Kerr (GRB) - - -
WD. Nóra Hoffmann/Attila Elek (HUN) - - -
WD. Alisa Agafonova/Alper Uçar (TUR) - - -

The World Figure Skating Championships were originally assigned to Nagano, Japan, then moved to Tokyo. The aftermath of the devastating Tōhoku earthquake and tsunami and concerns about nuclear plant safety led to several countries issuing advisories to citizens travelling to Japan. Ultimately, the ISU opted to cancel the event and there were discussions rescheduling the event for the fall of 2011. Instead, the World Championships were rescheduled to be held in the late spring in Moscow, Russia, on very short notice. Japanese skaters wore patches on their practice outfits reading "Rebirth Japan" and "We are always with you". Russian President Vladimir Putin honoured Japan in the Opening Ceremony, stating, "In Russia, we know from experience what a disaster at a nuclear power plant is like. We are confident that the Japanese people... will courageously traverse this uphill road."

Following a five-year hiatus, a qualifying "preliminary" round was reintroduced to address the large volume of number of entries. Skaters were granted a bye to the short program or original dance, on the basis of their country's standings in the previous year's World Championships and their own ISU standings. For the first time in history, skaters were also required to obtain a minimum Technical Elements Score (TES) at an international event in order to be eligible to compete at the World Championships. As minimum Technical Elements Scores increased over the years, this requirement had a significant and enduring effect on all disciplines, severely restricting opportunities for development and growth for skaters representing small and developing skating federations around the world.

North Americans swept the podium in the ice dance event at the World Figure Skating Championships. Meryl Davis and Charlie White made history as the first American ice dancers to win a World title and Maia and Alex Shibutani made history as the first Asian American skaters to win a medal at the World Championships. The short dance replaced the compulsory and original dances.

Sources: ISU *Communication No. 1513, July 14, 2008;* ISU *Communication No. 1621, June 28, 2010;* La Gazzetta dello Sport, *March 17, 2011;* The New York Times, *April 27, 2011; Speech by Vladimir Putin, April 27, 2011, Government of the Russian Federation;* Skating *magazine, June 2011; Entries, 2011 World Figure Skating Championships; Protocol, 2011 World Figure Skating Championships*

2012 WORLD FIGURE SKATING CHAMPIONSHIPS
Nice, France, March 26-April 1, 2012

World Men's Figure Skating Championships:

	PR	SP	FS
1. Patrick Chan (CAN)	-	**1**	**1**
2. Daisuke Takahashi (JPN)	-	3	3
3. Yuzuru Hanyu (JPN)	-	7	2
4. Brian Joubert (FRA)	-	4	5
5. Florent Amodio (FRA)	-	6	4
6. Michal Březina (CZE)	-	2	7
7. Denis Ten (KAZ)	-	8	6
8. Jeremy Abbott (USA)	-	9	8
9. Javier Fernández (ESP)	-	5	14
10. Samuel Contesti (ITA)	-	11	9
11. Takahiko Kozuka (JPN)	-	13	11
12. Kevin Reynolds (CAN)	-	**12**	**13**
13. Adam Rippon (USA)	-	10	16
14. Nan Song (CHN)	1	15	12
15. Kevin van der Perren (BEL)	-	18	10
16. Tomáš Verner (CZE)	-	14	17
17. Sergei Voronov (RUS)	2	17	15
18. Artur Gachinski (RUS)	-	16	18
19. Misha Ge (UZB)	4	19	23
20. Peter Liebers (GER)	-	23	19
21. Christopher Caluza (PHI)	8	20	20
22. Viktor Pfeifer (AUT)	6	21	21
23. Kim Lucine (MON)	5	22	22
24. Javier Raya (ESP)	9	24	24

25. Maciej Cieplucha (POL)	3	25	-
26. Alexander Majorov (SWE)	7	26	-
27. Min-seok Kim (KOR)	11	27	-
28. Dmitri Ignatenko (UKR)	-	28	-
29. Alexei Bychenko (ISR)	12	29	-
30. Justus Strid (DEN)	10	30	-
31. Ari-Pekka Nurmenkari (FIN)	13	-	-
32. Zoltán Kelemen (ROM)	14	-	-
33. Brendan Kerry (AUS)	15	-	-
34. Laurent Alvarez (SUI)	16	-	-
35. Damjan Ostojič (BIH)	17	-	-
36. Slavik Hayrapetyan (ARM)	18	-	-
37. Luke Chilcott (GRB)	19	-	-
38. Jordan Ju (TPE)	20	-	-
39. Márton Markó (HUN)	21	-	-
40. Ali Demirboğa (TUR)	22	-	-
41. Vitali Luchanok (BLS)	23	-	-
42. Saulius Ambrulevičius (LIT)	24	-	-
43. Taras Rajec (SVK)	25	-	-
44. Manol Atanassov (BUL)	26	-	-
45. Harry Hau Yin Lee (HKG)	27	-	-
WD. Kevin Alves (BRA)	-	-	-

World Ladies Figure Skating Championships:

	PR	SP	FS
1. Carolina Kostner (ITA)	-	3	1
2. Alena Leonova (RUS)	-	1	4
3. Akiko Suzuki (JPN)	-	5	2
4. Ashley Wagner (USA)	-	8	3
5. Kanako Murakami (JPN)	-	2	5
6. Mao Asada (JPN)	-	4	6
7. Kexin Zhang (CHN)	-	9	7
8. Valentina Marchei (ITA)	4	11	9
9. Ksenia Makarova (RUS)	-	6	14
10. Elene Gedevanishvili (GEO)	-	7	15
11. Viktoria Helgesson (SWE)	-	10	11
12. Yrétha Silété (FRA)	-	15	8
13. Elena Glebova (EST)	2	14	10

14. Jenna McCorkell (GRB)	1	12	12
15. Sonia Lafuente (ESP)	3	18	13
16. Amélie Lacoste (CAN)	**-**	**13**	**17**
17. Natalia Popova (UKR)	8	20	16
18. Juulia Turkkila (FIN)	-	17	18
19. Polina Korobeynikova (RUS)	7	19	19
20. Sarah Hecken (GER)	-	21	20
21. Kerstin Frank (AUT)	5	22	21
22. Alissa Czisny (USA)	-	16	22
23. Romy Bühler (SUI)	6	24	23
24. Alisa Mikonsaari (FIN)	-	23	24
25. Victoria Muniz (PRI)	9	25	-
26. Isabelle Pieman (BEL)	-	26	-
27. Alina Fjodorova (LAT)	10	27	-
28. Min-jeong Kwak (KOR)	-	28	-
29. Clara Peters (IRL)	11	29	-
30. Lejeanne Marais (SAF)	12	30	-
31. Melinda Wang (TPE)	13	-	-
32. Reyna Hamui (MEX)	14	-	-
33. Sıla Saygı (TUR)	15	-	-
34. Inga Janulevičiūtė (LIT)	16	-	-
35. Karina Sinding Johnson (DEN)	17	-	-
36. Mimi Tanasorn Chindasook (THA)	18	-	-
37. Fleur Maxwell (LUX)	19	-	-
38. Chae-yeon Suhr (KOR)	20	-	-
39. Daša Grm (SLO)	21	-	-
40. Chantelle Kerry (AUS)	22	-	-
41. Eliška Březinová (CZE)	23	-	-
42. Anine Rabe (NOR)	24	-	-
43. Sabina Măriuţă (ROM)	25	-	-
44. Alexandra Kunová (SVK)	26	-	-
45. Georgia Glastris (GRE)	27	-	-
46. Ami Parekh (IND)	28	-	-
47. Zhaira Costiniano (PHI)	29	-	-
48. Daniela Stoeva (BUL)	30	-	-
49. Marina Seeh (SRB)	31	-	-
50. Mirna Librić (CRO)	32	-	-
51. Viktória Pavuk (HUN)	33	-	-

WD. Kiira Korpi (FIN)	-	-	-
WD. Gerli Liinamäe (EST)	-	-	-
WD. Anne Line Gjersem (NOR)	-	-	-

World Pairs Skating Championships:

	PR	SP	FS
1. A. Savchenko/R. Szolkowy (GER)	-	1	2
2. T. Volosozhar/M. Trankov (RUS)	-	8	1
3. Narumi Takahashi/Mervin Tran (JPN)	-	3	3
4. Qing Pang/Jian Tong (CHN)	-	2	6
5. M. Duhamel/E. Radford (CAN)	**-**	**5**	**5**
6. Vera Bazarova/Yuri Larionov (RUS)	-	4	7
7. Y. Kavaguti/A. Smirnov (RUS)	-	11	4
8. Caydee Denney/John Coughlin (USA)	-	7	8
9. Wenjing Sui/Cong Han (CHN)	1	6	9
10. M.B. Marley/R. Brubaker (USA)	-	10	10
11. S. Berton/O. Hotárek (ITA)	-	9	11
12. Jessica Dubé/Sébastien Wolfe (CAN)	**-**	**12**	**12**
13. Maylin Hausch/Daniel Wende (GER)	-	15	13
14. M. Vartmann/A. van Cleave (GER)	3	16	14
15. N. Della Monica/M. Guarise (ITA)	7	14	15
16. Vanessa James/Morgan Ciprès (FRA)	2	13	16
17. D. Montalbano/E. Krasnopolski (ISR)	5	17	-
18. Anaïs Morand/Timothy Leemann (SUI)	8	18	-
19. Stacey Kemp/David King (GRB)	4	19	-
20. Ji-hyang Ri/Won-hyok Thae (PRK)	6	20	-
21. L. Bakirova/M. Kamianchuk (BLS)	9	-	-
22. Stina Martini/Severin Kiefer (AUT)	10	-	-
23. E. Makarova/L. Kenchadze (BUL)	11	-	-

World Ice Dancing Championships:

	PR	SP	FS
1. Tessa Virtue/Scott Moir (CAN)	**-**	**1**	**1**
2. Meryl Davis/Charlie White (USA)	-	2	2
3. N. Péchalat/F. Bourzat (FRA)	-	3	3
4. Kaitlyn Weaver/Andrew Poje (CAN)	**-**	**4**	**4**
5. E. Ilinykh/N. Katsalapov (RUS)	1	5	5
6. A. Cappellini/L. Lanotte (ITA)	-	6	6

7. E. Bobrova/D. Soloviev (RUS)	-	9	7
8. Maia Shibutani/Alex Shibutani (USA)	-	7	11
9. E. Riazanova/I. Tkachenko (RUS)	-	10	8
10. M. Hubbell/Z. Donohue (USA)	-	8	10
11. N. Zhiganshina/A. Gazsi (GER)	-	11	9
12. Xintong Huang/Xun Zheng (CHN)	2	13	13
13. Kharis Ralph/Asher Hill (CAN)	**-**	**15**	**14**
14. P. Coomes/N. Buckland (GRB)	4	12	17
15. S. Heekin-Canedy/D. Dun (UKR)	-	17	12
16. L. Alessandrini/S. Vaturi (ITA)	7	14	16
17. J. Zlobina/A. Sitnikov (AZE)	5	19	15
18. I. Tobias/D. Stagniūnas (LIT)	-	16	19
19. S. Hurtado/A. Díaz Bronchud (ESP)	6	18	18
20. D. O'Brien/G. Merriman (AUS)	8	20	20
21. Pernelle Carron/Lloyd Jones (FRA)	-	21	-
22. Irina Shtork/Taavi Rand (EST)	3	22	-
23. Zsuzsanna Nagy/Máté Fejes (HUN)	10	23	-
24. Cathy Reed/Chris Reed (JPN)	-	24	-
25. A. Nagornyuk/V. Kovalenko (UZB)	9	25	-
26. G. Kubová/D. Kiselev (CZE)	11	-	-
27. Federica Testa/Lukáš Csölley (SVK)	12	-	-
28. Henna Lindholm/Ossi Kanervo (FIN)	13	-	-
29. A. Zvorigina/M. Bernadowski (POL)	14	-	-
30. Ramona Elsener/Florian Roost (SUI)	15	-	-
31. Alisa Agafonova/Alper Uçar (TUR)	16	-	-
32. K. Pecherkina/A. Jakushin (LAT)	17	-	-
33. C. Bruhns/R. Van Natten (MEX)	18	-	-
34. Ekaterina Bugrov/Vasili Rogov (ISR)	19	-	-
35. C. Mansour/D. Zhunussov (KAZ)	20	-	-
36. Barbora Silná/Juri Kurakin (AUT)	21	-	-
37. A. Chistiakova/D. Lichev (BUL)	22	-	-
38. L. Valadzenkava/V. Vakunov (BLS)	23	-	-

Narumi Takahashi and Mervin Tran made history as the first Japanese pair to win a medal at the World Figure Skating Championships. Two men from Japan stood on the podium in the men's event for the first time.

Sources: *Skating magazine*, May 2012; Entries, 2012 World Figure Skating Championships; Protocol, 2012 World Figure Skating Championships

2013 WORLD FIGURE SKATING CHAMPIONSHIPS
London, Ontario, March 11-17, 2013

World Men's Figure Skating Championships:

	SP	FS
1. Patrick Chan (CAN)	**1**	**2**
2. Denis Ten (KAZ)	2	1
3. Javier Fernández (ESP)	7	4
4. Yuzuru Hanyu (JPN)	9	3
5. Kevin Reynolds (CAN)	**3**	**7**
6. Daisuke Takahashi (JPN)	4	8
7. Max Aaron (USA)	8	6
8. Takahito Mura (JPN)	11	5
9. Brian Joubert (FRA)	5	10
10. Michal Březina (CZE)	6	11
11. Peter Liebers (GER)	13	12
12. Florent Amodio (FRA)	10	15
13. Andrei Rogozine (CAN)	**18**	**9**
14. Ross Miner (USA)	14	13
15. Nan Song (CHN)	12	18
16. Misha Ge (UZB)	15	16
17. Maxim Kovtun (RUS)	19	14
18. Alexander Majorov (SWE)	16	17
19. Jorik Hendrickx (BEL)	23	19
20. Viktor Pfeifer (AUT)	21	20
21. Tomáš Verner (CZE)	17	22
22. Viktor Romanenkov (EST)	20	23
23. Yakov Godorozha (UKR)	24	21
24. Justus Strid (DEN)	22	24
25. Maciej Cieplucha (POL)	25	-
26. Jin-seo Kim (KOR)	26	-
27. Paolo Bacchini (ITA)	27	-
28. Abzal Rakimgaliev (KAZ)	28	-
29. Zoltán Kelemen (ROM)	29	-
30. Ronald Lam (HKG)	30	-

31. Alexei Bychenko (ISR)	31	-
32. Kim Lucine (MON)	32	-
33. Paul Bonifacio Parkinson (ITA)	33	-
34. Christopher Caluza (PHI)	34	-
WD. Pavel Ignatenko (BLS)	-	-
WD. Luiz Manella Pereira (BRA)	-	-
WD. Manol Atanassov (BUL)	-	-
WD. Valtter Virtanen (FIN)	-	-
WD. Romain Ponsart (FRA)	-	-
WD. Harry Mattick (GRB)	-	-
WD. Stéphane Walker (SUI)	-	-

World Ladies Figure Skating Championships:

	SP	FS
1. Yu-na Kim (KOR)	1	1
2. Carolina Kostner (ITA)	2	3
3. Mao Asada (JPN)	6	2
4. Kanako Murakami (JPN)	3	7
5. Ashley Wagner (USA)	5	6
6. Gracie Gold (USA)	9	5
7. Zijun Li (CHN)	12	4
8. Kaetlyn Osmond (CAN)	**4**	**10**
9. Adelina Sotnikova (RUS)	8	9
10. Elizaveta Tuktamysheva (RUS)	14	8
11. Maé-Bérénice Méité (FRA)	11	11
12. Akiko Suzuki (JPN)	7	13
13. Alena Leonova (RUS)	13	14
14. Viktoria Helgesson (SWE)	10	15
15. Natalia Popova (UKR)	17	12
16. Elena Glebova (EST)	15	16
17. Monika Simančíková (SVK)	19	17
18. Valentina Marchei (ITA)	21	18
19. Nathalie Weinzierl (GER)	24	19
20. Jenna McCorkell (GRB)	18	21
21. Brooklee Han (AUS)	20	20
22. Sonia Lafuente (ESP)	16	23
23. Kexin Zhang (CHN)	23	22
24. Kerstin Frank (AUT)	22	24

25. Isadora Williams (BRA)	25	-
26. Anita Madsen (DEN)	26	-
27. Carol Bressanutti (ITA)	27	-
28. Kaat Van Daele (BEL)	28	-
29. Elene Gedevanishvili (GEO)	29	-
30. Tina Stürzinger (SUI)	30	-
31. Juulia Turkkila (FIN)	31	-
32. Anne Line Gjersem (NOR)	32	-
33. Inga Janulevičiūtė (LIT)	33	-
34. Patricia Gleščič (SLO)	34	-
35. Alina Fjodorova (LAT)	35	-
WD. Anna Afonkina (BUL)	-	-
WD. Laura Raszyková (CZE)	-	-
WD. Fleur Maxwell (LUX)	-	-
WD. Reyna Hamui (MEX)	-	-

World Pairs Skating Championships:

	SP	FS
1. Tatiana Volosozhar/Maxim Trankov (RUS)	1	1
2. Aliona Savchenko/Robin Szolkowy (GER)	3	2
3. Meagan Duhamel/Eric Radford (CAN)	**2**	**3**
4. K. Moore-Towers/D. Moscovitch (CAN)	**5**	**5**
5. Qing Pang/Jian Tong (CHN)	6	4
6. Yuko Kavaguti/Alexander Smirnov (RUS)	4	7
7. Vera Bazarova/Yuri Larionov (RUS)	7	6
8. Vanessa James/Morgan Ciprès (FRA)	8	8
9. Alexa Scimeca/Chris Knierim (USA)	12	9
10. Stefania Berton/Ondřej Hotárek (ITA)	9	10
11. Cheng Peng/ Hao Zhang (CHN)	10	11
12. Wenjing Sui/Cong Han (CHN)	11	13
13. Marissa Castelli/Simon Shnapir (USA)	13	12
14. Nicole Della Monica/Matteo Guarise (ITA)	15	14
15. Stacey Kemp/David King (GRB)	14	16
16. Mari Vartmann/Aaron Van Cleave (GER)	16	15
17. Elizaveta Makarova/Leri Kenchadze (BUL)	17	-
18. Magdalena Klatka/Radosław Chruściński (POL)	18	-
WD. Stina Martini/Severin Kiefer (AUT)	-	-
WD. Camille Foucher/Márk Magyar (HUN)	-	-

	SD	FD
WD. Julia Lavrentieva/Yuri Rudik (UKR)	-	-
WD. Caydee Denney/John Coughlin (USA)	-	-

World Ice Dancing Championships:

	SD	FD
1. Meryl Davis/Charlie White (USA)	1	1
2. Tessa Virtue/Scott Moir (CAN)	**2**	**2**
3. Ekaterina Bobrova/Dmitri Soloviev (RUS)	3	4
4. Anna Cappellini/Luca Lanotte (ITA)	5	3
5. Kaitlyn Weaver/Andrew Poje (CAN)	**6**	**5**
6. Nathalie Péchalat/Fabian Bourzat (FRA)	4	7
7. Madison Chock/Evan Bates (USA)	7	6
8. Maia Shibutani/Alex Shibutani (USA)	8	9
9. Elena Ilinykh/Nikita Katsalapov (RUS)	9	10
10. Nelli Zhiganshina/Alexander Gazsi (GER)	11	8
11. Ekaterina Riazanova/Ilia Tkachenko (RUS)	13	11
12. Pernelle Carron/Lloyd Jones (FRA)	12	12
13. Penny Coomes/Nicholas Buckland (GRB)	10	17
14. Siobhan Heekin-Canedy/Dmitri Dun (UKR)	14	16
15. Isabella Tobias/Deividas Stagniūnas (LIT)	18	13
16. Julia Zlobina/Alexei Sitnikov (AZE)	17	14
17. Charlene Guignard/Marco Fabbri (ITA)	16	15
18. Piper Gilles/Paul Poirier (CAN)	**15**	**18**
19. Sara Hurtado/Adrià Díaz Bronchud (ESP)	20	19
20. Cathy Reed/Chris Reed (JPN)	19	20
21. Lucie Myslivečková/Neil Brown (CZE)	21	-
22. Olesia Karmi/Max Lindholm (FIN)	22	-
23. Allison Reed/Vasili Rogov (ISR)	23	-
24. Zsuzsanna Nagy/Máté Fejes (HUN)	24	-
25. Irina Shtork/Taavi Rand (EST)	25	-
26. Federica Testa/Lukáš Csölley (SVK)	26	-
27. Justyna Plutowska/Peter Gerber (POL)	27	-
28. Alisa Agafonova/Alper Uçar (TUR)	28	-
29. Viktoria Kavaliova/Yurii Bieliaiev (UKR)	29	-
WD. Danielle O'Brien/Gregory Merriman (AUS)	-	-
WD. Sarah Coward/Georgo Kenchadze (BUL)	-	-
WD. Xintong Huang/Xun Zheng (CHN)	-	-
WD. Olesia Karmi/Max Lindholm (FIN)	-	-

WD. Ramona Elesener/Florian Roost (SUI)   -   -
WD. Anna Nagornyuk/Viktor Kovalenko (UKR)   -   -

Denis Ten and Javier Fernández made history as the first skaters from Kazakhstan and Spain to win medals at the World Figure Skating Championships.

In their home country, Meagan Duhamel and Eric Radford made history as the first pairs team to land side-by-side triple Lutzes at the World Championships. Duhamel and Radford landed the jump in both the short program and free skate.

The "preliminary" qualifying rounds were eliminated from all disciplines at the World Championships.

Sources: Skating magazine, May 2013; Entries, 2013 World Figure Skating Championships; Results, 2013 World Figure Skating Championships

2014 WORLD FIGURE SKATING CHAMPIONSHIPS
Saitama, Japan, March 24-30, 2014

World Men's Figure Skating Championships:

	SP	FS
1. Yuzuru Hanyu (JPN)	3	1
2. Tatsuki Machida (JPN)	1	2
3. Javier Fernández (ESP)	2	3
4. Maxim Kovtun (RUS)	7	5
5. Jeremy Abbott (USA)	8	4
6. Takahiko Kozuka (JPN)	6	6
7. Han Yan (CHN)	5	11
8. Max Aaron (USA)	9	8
9. Chafik Besseghier (FRA)	10	7
10. Tomáš Verner (CZE)	4	15
11. Kevin Reynolds (CAN)	**15**	**10**
12. Nam Nguyen (CAN)	**16**	**9**
13. Ivan Righini (ITA)	14	12
14. Peter Liebers (GER)	11	14
15. Alexei Bychenko (ISR)	12	13

16. Jin-seo Kim (KOR)	13	16
17. Jorik Hendrickx (BEL)	17	18
18. Elladj Baldé (CAN)	**22**	**17**
19. Christopher Caluza (PHI)	18	19
20. Abzal Rakimgaliev (KAZ)	24	20
21. Zoltán Kelemen (ROM)	20	21
22. Maciej Cieplucha (POL)	21	22
23. Stéphane Walker (SUI)	19	23
24. Yakov Godorozha (UKR)	25	-
25. Viktor Romanenkov (EST)	26	-
26. Misha Ge (UZB)	27	-
27. Ronald Lam (HKG)	28	-
28. Kim Lucine (MON)	29	-
29. Viktor Pfeifer (AUT)	30	-
30. Justus Strid (DEN)	31	-
31. Alexander Majorov (SWE)	32	-
WD. Michal Březina (CZE)	23	-
WD. Patrick Chan (CAN)	-	-
WD. Florent Amodio (FRA)	-	-
WD. Javier Raya (ESP)	-	-

World Ladies Figure Skating Championships:

	SP	FS
1. Mao Asada (JPN)	1	1
2. Yulia Lipnitskaya (RUS)	3	2
3. Carolina Kostner (ITA)	2	6
4. Anna Pogorilaya (RUS)	6	3
5. Gracie Gold (USA)	5	7
6. Akiko Suzuki (JPN)	4	8
7. Ashley Wagner (USA)	7	4
8. Polina Edmunds (USA)	12	5
9. So-youn Park (KOR)	13	9
10. Kanako Murakami (JPN)	10	10
11. Kaetlyn Osmond (CAN)	**8**	**13**
12. Nathalie Weinzierl (GER)	11	15
13. Gabrielle Daleman (CAN)	**14**	**11**
14. Joshi Helgesson (SWE)	15	12
15. Maé-Bérénice Méité (FRA)	9	16

16. Valentina Marchei (ITA)	22	14
17. Zijun Li (CHN)	16	17
18. Eliška Březinová (CZE)	24	18
19. Brooklee Han (AUS)	18	19
20. Anna Ovcharova (SUI)	17	20
21. Natalia Popova (UKR)	21	21
22. Anne Line Gjersem (NOR)	23	22
23. Hae-jin Kim (KOR)	19	23
24. Nicole Rajičová (SVK)	25	-
25. Elena Glebova (EST)	26	-
26. Inga Janulevičiūtė (LIT)	27	-
27. Kaat Van Daele (BEL)	28	-
28. Juulia Turkkila (FIN)	29	-
29. Anita Madsen (DEN)	30	-
30. Kerstin Frank (AUT)	31	-
31. Sonia Lafuente (ESP)	32	-
32. Netta Schreiber (ISR)	33	-
WD. Jenna McCorkell (GRB)	20	-

World Pairs Skating Championships:

	SP	FS
1. Aliona Savchenko/Robin Szolkowy (GER)	1	1
2. Ksenia Stolbova/Fedor Klimov (RUS)	3	2
3. Meagan Duhamel/Eric Radford (CAN)	**2**	**4**
4. K. Moore-Towers/D. Moscovitch (CAN)	**6**	**3**
5. Cheng Peng/Hao Zhang (CHN)	5	5
6. Wenjing Sui/Cong Han (CHN)	4	9
7. Vera Bazarova/Yuri Larionov (RUS)	7	6
8. Julia Antipova/Nodari Maisuradze (RUS)	8	10
9. Stefania Berton/Ondřej Hotárek (ITA)	10	7
10. Vanessa James/Morgan Ciprès (FRA)	9	8
11. Marissa Castelli/Simon Shnapir (USA)	11	11
12. Paige Lawrence/Rudi Swiegers (CAN)	**12**	**12**
13. Maylin Wende/Daniel Wende (GER)	13	13
14. Felicia Zhang/Nathan Bartholomay (USA)	14	14
15. Daria Popova/Bruno Massot (FRA)	15	15
16. Nicole Della Monica/Matteo Guarise (ITA)	16	16
17. Narumi Takahashi/Ryuichi Kihara (JPN)	17	-

18. Amani Fancy/Christopher Boyadji (GRB)	18	-
19. Natalia Zabiiako/Alexandr Zaboev (EST)	19	-
20. Maria Paliakova/Nikita Bochkov (BLS)	20	-
21. Julia Lavrentieva/Yuri Rudyk (UKR)	21	-
22. Miriam Ziegler/Severin Kiefer (AUT)	22	-
23. Elizaveta Makarova/Leri Kenchadze (BUL)	23	-
WD. Caydee Denney/John Coughlin (USA)	-	-

World Ice Dancing Championships:

	SD	FD
1. Anna Cappellini/Luca Lanotte (ITA)	1	4
2. Kaitlyn Weaver/Andrew Poje (CAN)	**2**	**3**
3. Nathalie Péchalat/Fabian Bourzat (FRA)	3	2
4. Elena Ilinykh/Nikita Katsalapov (RUS)	5	1
5. Madison Chock/Evan Bates (USA)	4	5
6. Maia Shibutani/Alex Shibutani (USA)	6	6
7. Victoria Sinitsina/Ruslan Zhiganshin (RUS)	8	8
8. Piper Gilles/Paul Poirier (CAN)	**10**	**7**
9. Penny Coomes/Nicholas Buckland (GRB)	9	9
10. Alexandra Paul/Mitchell Islam (CAN)	**11**	**10**
11. Nelli Zhiganshina/Alexander Gazsi (GER)	7	14
12. Julia Zlobina/Alexei Sitnikov (AZE)	12	11
13. Gabriella Papadakis/Guillaume Cizeron (FRA)	15	13
14. Charlène Guignard/Marco Fabbri (ITA)	17	12
15. Isabella Tobias/Deividas Stagniūnas (LIT)	13	15
16. Sara Hurtado/Adrià Díaz Bronchud (ESP)	16	17
17. Alexandra Aldridge/Daniel Eaton (USA)	18	16
18. Cathy Reed/Chris Reed (JPN)	14	18
19. Irina Shtork/Taavi Rand (EST)	20	19
20. Alisa Agafonova/Alper Uçar (TUR)	19	20
21. Tanja Kolbe/Stefano Caruso (GER)	21	-
22. Justyna Plutowska/Peter Gerber (POL)	22	-
23. Federica Testa/Lukáš Csölley (SVK)	23	-
24. Danielle O'Brien/Gregory Merriman (AUS)	24	-
25. Ramona Elsener/Florian Roost (SUI)	25	-
26. Henna Lindholm/Ossi Kanervo (FIN)	26	-
27. Gabriela Kubová/Matěj Novák (CZE)	27	-
28. Dóra Turóczi/Balázs Major (HUN)	28	-

29. L. Fournier Beaudry/N. Sørensen (DEN)	29	-
30. Allison Reed/Vasili Rogov (ISR)	30	-
31. Angelina Telegina/Otar Japaridze (GEO)	31	-
32. Viktoria Kavaliova/Yuri Bieliaiev (BLS)	32	-
WD. Ekaterina Bobrova/Dmitri Soloviev (RUS)	-	-
WD. Meryl Davis/Charlie White (USA)	-	-
WD. Tessa Virtue/Scott Moir (CAN)	**-**	**-**
WD. Madison Hubbell/Zachary Donohue (USA)	-	-
WD. Nadezhda Frolenkova/Vitali Nikiforov (UKR)	-	-

Sources: Toronto Star, March 3, 2014; Skating magazine, May 2014; Entries, 2014 World Figure Skating Championships; Protocol, 2014 World Figure Skating Championships

2015 WORLD FIGURE SKATING CHAMPIONSHIPS
Shanghai, China, March 23-29, 2015

World Men's Figure Skating Championships:

	SP	FS
1. Javier Fernández (ESP)	2	2
2. Yuzuru Hanyu (JPN)	1	3
3. Denis Ten (KAZ)	3	1
4. Jason Brown (USA)	6	5
5. Nam Nguyen (CAN)	**9**	**4**
6. Misha Ge (UZB)	8	7
7. Maxim Kovtun (RUS)	16	6
8. Adam Rippon (USA)	11	8
9. Florent Amodio (FRA)	7	11
10. Han Yan (CHN)	5	13
11. Joshua Farris (USA)	13	10
12. Takahiko Kozuka (JPN)	19	9
13. Sergei Voronov (RUS)	4	17
14. Ronald Lam (HKG)	14	14
15. Michal Březina (CZE)	10	15
16. Takahito Mura (JPN)	23	12
17. Alexei Bychenko (ISR)	12	16
18. Chafik Besseghier (FRA)	18	19
19. June-hyoung Lee (KOR)	24	18

	SP	FS
20. Brendan Kerry (AUS)	17	21
21. Michael Christian Martinez (PHI)	22	20
22. Jeremy Ten (CAN)	**15**	**22**
23. Alexander Majorov (SWE)	21	23
24. Yaroslav Paniot (UKR)	20	24
25. Ivan Righini (ITA)	25	-
26. Nan Song (CHN)	26	-
27. Petr Coufal (CZE)	27	-
28. Pavel Ignatenko (BLS)	28	-
29. Peter Liebers (GER)	29	-
30. Stéphane Walker (SUI)	30	-

World Ladies Figure Skating Championships:

	SP	FS
1. Elizaveta Tuktamysheva (RUS)	1	1
2. Satoko Miyahara (JPN)	3	4
3. Elena Radionova (RUS)	2	6
4. Gracie Gold (USA)	8	2
5. Ashley Wagner (USA)	11	3
6. Rika Hongo (JPN)	5	5
7. Kanako Murakami (JPN)	4	8
8. Polina Edmunds (USA)	7	7
9. Zijun Li (CHN)	6	11
10. Maé-Bérénice Méité (FRA)	12	10
11. Alaine Chartrand (CAN)	**10**	**12**
12. So-youn Park (KOR)	15	9
13. Anna Pogorilaya (RUS)	9	13
14. Joshi Helgesson (SWE)	13	14
15. Nicole Rajičová (SVK)	14	15
16. Angelīna Kučvaļska (LAT)	23	16
17. Anne Line Gjersem (NOR)	20	17
18. Daša Grm (SLO)	22	18
19. Hae-jin Kim (KOR)	18	19
20. Roberta Rodeghiero (ITA)	17	21
21. Gabrielle Daleman (CAN)	**21**	**20**
22. Elene Gedevanishvili (GEO)	16	22
23. Nicole Schott (GER)	19	23
24. Giada Russo (ITA)	24	24

25. Natalia Popova (UKR)	25	-
26. Ivett Tóth (HUN)	26	-
27. Eliška Březinová (CZE)	27	-
28. Aleksandra Golovkina (LIT)	28	-
29. Anastasia Galustyan (ARM)	29	-
30. Netta Schreiber (ISR)	30	-
31. Kiira Korpi (FIN)	31	-
32. Niki Wories (NED)	32	-
33. Eveline Brunner (SUI)	33	-
34. Alisson Krystle Perticheto (PHI)	34	-
35. Brooklee Han (AUS)	35	-
WD. Kerstin Frank (AUT)	-	-
WD. Anna Ovcharova (SUI)	-	-

World Pairs Skating Championships:

	SP	FS
1. Meagan Duhamel/Eric Radford (CAN)	**1**	**1**
2. Wenjing Sui/Cong Han (CHN)	3	2
3. Qing Pang/Jian Tong (CHN)	2	3
4. Cheng Peng/Hao Zhang (CHN)	5	4
5. Yuko Kavaguti/Alexander Smirnov (RUS)	4	6
6. Evgenia Tarasova/Vladimir Morozov (RUS)	6	5
7. Alexa Scimeca/Chris Knierim (USA)	7	7
8. Julianne Séguin/Charlie Bilodeau (CAN)	**10**	**10**
9. Vanessa James/Morgan Ciprès (FRA)	12	8
10. Kristina Astakhova/Alexei Rogonov (RUS)	13	9
11. Valentina Marchei/Ondřej Hotárek (ITA)	9	11
12. Haven Denney/Brandon Frazier (USA)	8	12
13. L. Ilyushechkina/D. Moscovitch (CAN)	**11**	**13**
14. Nicole Della Monica/Matteo Guarise (ITA)	14	15
15. Mari Vartmann/Aaron Van Cleave (GER)	15	14
16. Amani Fancy/Christopher Boyadji (GRB)	16	16
17. Maria Paliakova/Nikita Bochkov (BLS)	17	-
18. Miriam Ziegler/Severin Kiefer (AUT)	18	-
19. Narumi Takahashi/Ryuichi Kihara (JPN)	19	-

World Ice Dancing Championships:

	SD	FD
1. Gabriella Papadakis/Guillaume Cizeron (FRA)	4	1
2. Madison Chock/Evan Bates (USA)	1	2
3. Kaitlyn Weaver/Andrew Poje (CAN)	**2**	**3**
4. Anna Cappellini/Luca Lanotte (ITA)	3	4
5. Maia Shibutani/Alex Shibutani (USA)	6	5
6. Piper Gilles/Paul Poirier (CAN)	**7**	**6**
7. Elena Ilinykh/Ruslan Zhiganshin (RUS)	5	9
8. Ksenia Monko/Kirill Khaliavin (RUS)	10	8
9. Alexandra Stepanova/Ivan Bukin (RUS)	14	7
10. Madison Hubbell/Zachary Donohue (USA)	11	10
11. L. Fournier Beaudry/N. Sørensen (DEN)	9	11
12. Charlène Guignard/Marco Fabbri (ITA)	12	12
13. Alexandra Paul/Mitchell Islam (CAN)	**8**	**14**
14. Sara Hurtado/Adrià Díaz Bronchud (ESP)	15	13
15. Federica Testa/Lukáš Csölley (SVK)	13	15
16. Alisa Agafonova/Alper Uçar (TUR)	16	16
17. Alexandra Nazarova/Maxim Nikitin (UKR)	17	17
18. Carolina Moscheni/Ádám Lukács (HUN)	19	18
19. Shiyue Wang/Xinyu Liu (CHN)	18	19
20. Allison Reed/Vasili Rogov (ISR)	20	20
21. Barbora Silná/Juri Kurakin (AUT)	21	-
22. Cathy Reed/Chris Reed (JPN)	22	-
23. Irina Shtork/Taavi Rand (EST)	23	-
24. Natalia Kaliszek/Maksym Spodyriev (POL)	24	-
25. Cecilia Törn/Jussiville Partanen (FIN)	25	-
26. Rebeka Kim/Kirill Minov (KOR)	26	-
27. Olivia Smart/Joseph Buckland (GRB)	27	-
28. Viktoria Kavaliova/Yurii Bieliaiev (BLS)	28	-
29. Olga Jakushina/Andrey Nevskiy (LAT)	29	-
WD. Nelli Zhiganshina/Alexander Gazsi (GER)	-	-
WD. Penny Coomes/Nicholas Buckland (GRB)	-	-

For the first time, China played host to the World Figure Skating Championships. An estimated one hundred and twenty thousand fans attended the competition and several events were sold out.

Sources: Skating magazine, May 2015; Entries, 2015 World Figure Skating Championships; Protocol, 2015 World Figure Skating Championships

2016 WORLD FIGURE SKATING CHAMPIONSHIPS
Boston, United States, March 28-April 3, 2016

World Men's Figure Skating Championships:

	SP	FS
1. Javier Fernández (ESP)	2	1
2. Yuzuru Hanyu (JPN)	1	2
3. Boyang Jin (CHN)	5	3
4. Mikhail Kolyada (RUS)	6	5
5. Patrick Chan (CAN)	**3**	**8**
6. Adam Rippon (USA)	7	4
7. Shoma Uno (JPN)	4	6
8. Max Aaron (USA)	8	7
9. Michal Březina (CZE)	11	10
10. Grant Hochstein (USA)	16	9
11. Denis Ten (KAZ)	12	12
12. Ivan Righini (ITA)	9	13
13. Alexei Bychenko (ISR)	19	11
14. Deniss Vasiļjevs (LAT)	10	16
15. Misha Ge (UZB)	15	14
16. Jorik Hendrickx (BEL)	14	15
17. Brendan Kerry (AUS)	17	17
18. Maxim Kovtun (RUS)	13	21
19. Michael Christian Martinez (PHI)	23	18
20. Chafik Besseghier (FRA)	20	20
21. Julian Zhi Jie Yee (MAS)	22	19
22. Phillip Harris (GRB)	21	22
23. Ivan Pavlov (UKR)	24	23
24. June-hyoung Lee (KOR)	18	24
25. Javier Raya (ESP)	25	-
26. Han Yan (CHN)	26	-
27. Nam Nguyen (CAN)	**27**	-
28. Franz Streubel (GER)	28	-
29. Denis Margalik (ARG)	29	-
30. Slavik Hayrapetyan (ARM)	30	-

WD. Nathan Chen (USA) - -
WD. Liam Firus (CAN) - -
WD. Alexander Majorov (SWE) - -

World Ladies Figure Skating Championships:

	SP	FS
1. Evgenia Medvedeva (RUS)	3	1
2. Ashley Wagner (USA)	4	2
3. Anna Pogorilaya (RUS)	2	4
4. Gracie Gold (USA)	1	6
5. Satoko Miyahara (JPN)	6	3
6. Elena Radionova (RUS)	5	5
7. Mao Asada (JPN)	9	7
8. Rika Hongo (JPN)	7	8
9. Gabrielle Daleman (CAN)	**8**	**9**
10. Mirai Nagasu (USA)	10	11
11. Zijun Li (CHN)	11	12
12. Elizabet Tursynbaeva (KAZ)	12	10
13. Nicole Rajičová (SVK)	15	13
14. Da-bin Choi (KOR)	16	15
15. Angelīna Kučvaļska (LAT)	18	14
16. Roberta Rodeghiero (ITA)	13	19
17. Alaine Chartrand (CAN)	**17**	**17**
18. So-youn Park (KOR)	22	18
19. Anna Khnychenkova (UKR)	19	20
20. Viveca Lindfors (FIN)	23	16
21. Amy Lin (TPE)	14	22
22. Niki Wories (NED)	24	21
23. Ziquan Zhao (CHN)	21	23
24. Anastasia Galustyan (ARM)	20	24
25. Maé-Bérénice Méité (FRA)	25	-
26. Anne Line Gjersem (NOR)	26	-
27. Kailani Craine (AUS)	27	-
28. Ivett Tóth (HUN)	28	-
29. Eliška Březinová (CZE)	29	-
30. Joshi Helgesson (SWE)	30	-
31. Laurine Lecavelier (FRA)	31	-
32. Kerstin Frank (AUT)	32	-

33. Aleksandra Golovkina (LIT)	33	-
34. Yasmine Kimiko Yamada (SUI)	34	-
35. Nathalie Weinzierl (GER)	35	-
36. Kristen Spours (GRB)	36	-
37. Sonia Lafuente (ESP)	37	-
38. Daša Grm (SLO)	38	-
WD. Polina Edmunds (USA)	-	-

World Pairs Skating Championships:

	SP	FS
1. Meagan Duhamel/Eric Radford (CAN)	**2**	**1**
2. Wenjing Sui/Cong Han (CHN)	1	2
3. Aliona Savchenko/Bruno Massot (GER)	4	3
4. Ksenia Stolbova/Fedor Klimov (RUS)	5	4
5. Evgenia Tarasova/Vladimir Morozov (RUS)	6	5
6. Tatiana Volosozhar/Maxim Trankov (RUS)	3	7
7. L. Ilyushechkina/D. Moscovitch (CAN)	**8**	**6**
8. K. Moore-Towers/M. Marinaro (CAN)	**10**	**8**
9. Alexa Scimeca/Chris Knierim (USA)	7	12
10. Vanessa James/Morgan Ciprès (FRA)	9	10
11. Nicole Della Monica/Matteo Guarise (ITA)	11	13
12. Cheng Peng/Hao Zhang (CHN)	12	9
13. Tarah Kayne/Danny O'Shea (USA)	14	11
14. Valentina Marchei/Ondřej Hotárek (ITA)	13	15
15. Xuehan Wang/Lei Wang (CHN)	15	14
16. Lola Esbrat/Andrei Novoselov (FRA)	16	16
17. Goda Butkutė/Nikita Ermolaev (LIT)	17	-
18. Ioulia Chtchetinina/Noah Scherer (SUI)	18	-
19. Adel Tankova/Evgeni Krasnopolski (ISR)	19	-
20. Tatiana Danilova/Mikalai Kamianchuk (BLS)	20	-
21. Miriam Ziegler/Severin Kiefer (AUT)	21	-
22. Sumire Suto/Francis Boudreau Audet (JPN)	22	-
WD. Julianne Séguin/Charlie Bilodeau (CAN)	**-**	**-**
WD. Xiaoyu Yu/Yang Jin (CHN)	-	-

World Ice Dancing Championships:

	SD	FD
1. Gabriella Papadakis/Guillaume Cizeron (FRA)	1	1

2. Maia Shibutani/Alex Shibutani (USA)	2	2
3. Madison Chock/Evan Bates (USA)	3	3
4. Anna Cappellini/Luca Lanotte (ITA)	6	4
5. Kaitlyn Weaver/Andrew Poje (CAN)	**4**	**5**
6. Madison Hubbell/Zachary Donohue (USA)	7	6
7. Penny Coomes/Nicholas Buckland (GRB)	8	7
8. Piper Gilles/Paul Poirier (CAN)	**5**	**8**
9. Victoria Sinitsina/Nikita Katsalapov (RUS)	9	10
10. Charlène Guignard/Marco Fabbri (ITA)	10	9
11. Alexandra Stepanova/Ivan Bukin (RUS)	11	11
12. Isabella Tobias/Ilia Tkachenko (ISR)	13	12
13. L. Fournier Beaudry/N. Sørensen (DEN)	15	13
14. Federica Testa/Lukáš Csölley (SVK)	12	15
15. Kana Muramoto/Chris Reed (JPN)	16	14
16. Natalia Kaliszek/Maksim Spodirev (POL)	14	16
17. Kavita Lorenz/Joti Polizoakis (GER)	18	17
18. Cecilia Törn/Jussiville Partanen (FIN)	17	19
19. Alexandra Nazarova/Maxim Nikitin (UKR)	20	18
20. Barbora Silná/Juri Kurakin (AUT)	19	20
21. Alisa Agafonova/Alper Uçar (TUR)	21	-
22. Shiyue Wang/Xinyu Liu (CHN)	22	-
23. É. Paradis/F-X. Ouellette (CAN)	**23**	**-**
24. Cortney Mansour/Michal Češka (CZE)	24	-
25. Rebeka Kim/Kirill Minov (KOR)	25	-
26. Celia Robledo/Luis Fenero (ESP)	26	-
27. T. Garabedian/S. Proulx-Sénécal (ARM)	27	-
28. Viktoria Kavaliova/Yurii Bieliaiev (BLS)	28	-
29. Olga Jakushina/Andrey Nevskiy (LAT)	29	-
30. Anastasia Khromova/Daryn Zhunussov (KAZ)	30	-

Denis Margalik and Julian Zhi Jie Yee made history as the first skaters to represent Argentina and Malaysia at the World Figure Skating Championships.

Meagan Duhamel and Eric Radford made history as the first pair to receive positive GOE on a throw quadruple jump at the World Championships.

Sources: *Skating magazine*, May 2016; Entries, 2016 World Figure Skating Championships; Protocol, 2016 World Figure Skating Championships

2017 WORLD FIGURE SKATING CHAMPIONSHIPS
Helsinki, Finland, March 29-April 2, 2017

World Men's Figure Skating Championships:

		SP	FS
1.	Yuzuru Hanyu (JPN)	5	1
2.	Shoma Uno (JPN)	2	2
3.	Boyang Jin (CHN)	4	3
4.	Javier Fernández (ESP)	1	6
5.	**Patrick Chan (CAN)**	**3**	**5**
6.	Nathan Chen (USA)	6	4
7.	Jason Brown (USA)	8	7
8.	Mikhail Kolyada (RUS)	7	9
9.	**Kevin Reynolds (CAN)**	**12**	**8**
10.	Alexei Bychenko (ISR)	11	12
11.	Maxim Kovtun (RUS)	10	14
12.	Misha Ge (UZB)	16	10
13.	Morisi Kvitelashvili (GEO)	19	11
14.	Deniss Vasiļjevs (LAT)	14	13
15.	Brendan Kerry (AUS)	13	15
16.	Denis Ten (KAZ)	9	20
17.	Chafik Besseghier (FRA)	17	16
18.	Michal Březina (CZE)	15	18
19.	Keiji Tanaka (JPN)	22	17
20.	Paul Fentz (GER)	20	21
21.	Jorik Hendrickx (BEL)	21	22
22.	Julian Zhi Jie Yee (MAS)	23	19
23.	Alexander Majorov (SWE)	18	23
24.	Michael Christian Martinez (PHI)	24	24
25.	Ivan Pavlov (UKR)	25	-
26.	Jin-seo Kim (KOR)	26	-
27.	Javier Raya (ESP)	27	-
28.	Stéphane Walker (SUI)	28	-
29.	Igor Reznichenko (POL)	29	-
30.	Matteo Rizzo (ITA)	30	-

31. Graham Newberry (GRB)	31	-
32. Chih-I Tsao (TPE)	32	-
33. Valtter Virtanen (FIN)	33	-
34. Nicholas Vrdoljak (CRO)	34	-
35. Slavik Hayrapetyan (ARM)	35	-
36. Larry Loupolover (AZE)	36	-
WD. Han Yan (CHN)	-	-
WD. Ivan Righini (ITA)	-	-

World Ladies Figure Skating Championships:

	SP	FS
1. Evgenia Medvedeva (RUS)	1	1
2. Kaetlyn Osmond (CAN)	**2**	**2**
3. Gabrielle Daleman (CAN)	**3**	**3**
4. Karen Chen (USA)	5	6
5. Mai Mihara (JPN)	15	4
6. Carolina Kostner (ITA)	8	5
7. Ashley Wagner (USA)	7	10
8. Maria Sotskova (RUS)	6	11
9. Elizabet Tursynbayeva (KAZ)	10	8
10. Da-bin Choi (KOR)	11	7
11. Wakaba Higuchi (JPN)	9	12
12. Mariah Bell (USA)	13	9
13. Anna Pogorilaya (RUS)	4	15
14. Xiangning Li (CHN)	16	13
15. Loena Hendrickx (BEL)	17	14
16. Rika Hongo (JPN)	12	18
17. Nicole Rajičová (SVK)	18	16
18. Laurine Lecavelier (FRA)	22	17
19. Nicole Schott (GER)	24	19
20. Ivett Tóth (HUN)	14	21
21. Zijun Li (CHN)	20	20
22. Angelīna Kučvaļska (LAT)	21	22
23. Anastasia Galustyan (ARM)	23	23
24. Kailani Craine (AUS)	19	24
25. Jessica Shuran Yu (SGP)	25	-
26. Joshi Helgesson (SWE)	26	-
27. Helery Hälvin (EST)	27	-

28. Amy Lin (TPE)	28	-
29. Emmi Peltonen (FIN)	29	-
30. Isadora Williams (BRA)	30	-
31. Kerstin Frank (AUT)	31	-
32. Natasha McKay (GRB)	32	-
33. Yasmine Kimiko Yamada (SUI)	33	-
34. Anne Line Gjersem (NOR)	34	-
35. Anna Khnychenkova (UKR)	35	-
36. Daša Grm (SLO)	36	-
37. Michaela Lucie Hanzlíková (CZE)	37	-
WD. Satoko Miyahara (JPN)	-	-
WD. Niki Wories (NED)	-	-
WD. Ziquan Zhao (CHN)	-	-

World Pairs Skating Championships:

	SP	FS
1. Wenjing Sui/Cong Han (CHN)	1	1
2. Aliona Savchenko/Bruno Massot (GER)	2	2
3. Evgenia Tarasova/Vladimir Morozov (RUS)	3	4
4. Xiaoyu Yu/Hao Zhang (CHN)	4	5
5. Ksenia Stolbova/Fedor Klimov (RUS)	13	3
6. L. Ilyushechkina/D. Moscovitch (CAN)	**6**	**8**
7. Meagan Duhamel/Eric Radford (CAN)	**7**	**7**
8. Vanessa James/Morgan Ciprès (FRA)	10	6
9. Valentina Marchei/Ondřej Hotárek (ITA)	9	9
10. Alexa Scimeca Knierim/Chris Knierim (USA)	8	11
11. Julianne Séguin/Charlie Bilodeau (CAN)	**12**	**10**
12. Natalia Zabiiako/Alexander Enbert (RUS)	5	13
13. Nicole Della Monica/Matteo Guarise (ITA)	11	12
14. Anna Dušková/Martin Bidař (CZE)	15	14
15. Tae-ok Ryom/Ju-sik Kim (PRK)	14	15
16. E. Alexandrovskaya/H. Windsor (AUS)	16	16
17. Sumire Suto/Francis Boudreau-Audet (JPN)	17	-
18. Miriam Ziegler/Severin Kiefer (AUT)	18	-
19. Minerva Fabienne Hase/Nolan Seegert (GER)	19	-
20. Haven Denney/Brandon Frazier (USA)	20	-
21. L. Petranović/A. Souza-Kordeiru (CRO)	21	-
22. Goda Butkutė/Nikita Ermolaev (LIT)	22	-

23. Tatiana Danilova/Mikalai Kamianchuk (BLS) 23 -
24. Daria Beklemisheva/Márk Magyar (HUN) 24 -
25. Emilia Simonen/Matthew Penasse (FIN) 25 -
26. Zoe Jones/Christopher Boyadji (GRB) 26 -
27. Lola Esbrat/Andrei Novoselov (FRA) 27 -
28. Ioulia Chtchetinina/Noah Scherer (SUI) 28 -
WD. Men-ji Ji/Themistocles Leftheris (KOR) - -

World Ice Dancing Championships:

	SD	FD
1. Tessa Virtue/Scott Moir (CAN)	**1**	**2**
2. Gabriella Papadakis/Guillaume Cizeron (FRA)	2	1
3. Maia Shibutani/Alex Shibutani (USA)	5	4
4. Kaitlyn Weaver/Andrew Poje (CAN)	**6**	**6**
5. Ekaterina Bobrova/Dmitri Soloviev (RUS)	8	3
6. Anna Cappellini/Luca Lanotte (ITA)	7	5
7. Madison Chock/Evan Bates (USA)	4	8
8. Piper Gilles/Paul Poirier (CAN)	**9**	**7**
9. Madison Hubbell/Zachary Donohue (USA)	3	10
10. Alexandra Stepanova/Ivan Bukin (RUS)	10	9
11. Charlène Guignard/Marco Fabbri (ITA)	11	11
12. Isabella Tobias/Ilia Tkachenko (ISR)	12	12
13. L. Fournier Beaudry/N. Sørensen (DEN)	13	14
14. Natalia Kaliszek/Maksym Spodyriev (POL)	15	13
15. Oleksandra Nazarova/Maxim Nikitin (UKR)	14	15
16. Shiyue Wang/Xinyu Liu (CHN)	18	16
17. Alisa Agafonova/Alper Uçar (TUR)	17	17
18. Olivia Smart/Adrià Díaz Bronchud (ESP)	16	19
19. Kavita Lorenz/Joti Polizoakis (GER)	20	18
20. Yura Min/Alexander Gamelin (KOR)	19	20
21. Marie-Jade Lauriault/Romain Le Gac (FRA)	21	-
22. Lilah Fear/Lewis Gibson (GRB)	22	-
23. Kana Muramoto/Chris Reed (JPN)	23	-
24. Cecilia Törn/Jussiville Partanen (FIN)	24	-
25. T. Garabedian/S. Proulx-Sénécal (ARM)	25	-
26. Nicole Kuzmichová/Alexandr Sinicyn (CZE)	26	-
27. Viktoria Kavaliova/Yurii Bieliaiev (BLS)	27	-
28. L. Alessandrini/P. Souquet-Basiège (FRA)	28	-

29. Olga Jakushina/Andrey Nevskiy (LAT)	29	-
30. Taylor Tran/Saulius Ambrulevičius (LIT)	30	-
31. Anastasia Galyeta/Avidan Brown (AZE)	31	-
32. Tatiana Kozmava/Oleksii Shumskyi (GEO)	32	-
WD. Lucie Myslivečková/Lukáš Csölley (SVK)	-	-

The International Skating Union celebrated its 125th anniversary.

For the first time, three men from Asia and two Canadian women stood on the podium in the men's and ladies events at the World Figure Skating Championships.

Jessica Shuran Yu made history as the first skater to represent Singapore at the World Championships.

Yuzuru Hanyu set a record for the highest overall score awarded in the men's event at the World Championships under the IJS System prior to the 2018/2019 season (223.20). Hanyu also made history as the first skater to land a quadruple loop jump at the World Championships.

Boyang Jin made history as the first skater to receive positive GOE on the quadruple Lutz jump at the World Championships. Nathan Chen and Shoma Uno made history as the first skaters to receive positive GOE on the quadruple flip jump at the World Championships. Both skaters performed the jump in the short program.

Evgenia Medvedeva set a record for the highest overall score awarded in the ladies event at the World Championships under the IJS System prior to the 2018/2019 season (154.40).

Sources: Skating magazine, May 2017; CBC Sports, December 29, 2017; Entries, 2017 World Figure Skating Championships; Protocol, 2017 World Figure Skating Championships; ISU Highest Total Scores Statistics

Kaetlyn Osmond, World Champion 2018. Enrico Calderoni / AFLO SPORT / Aflo Co. Ltd. / Alamy Stock Photo.

2018 WORLD FIGURE SKATING CHAMPIONSHIPS
Milan, Italy, March 19-25, 2018

World Men's Figure Skating Championships:

	SP	FS
1. Nathan Chen (USA)	1	1
2. Shoma Uno (JPN)	5	2
3. Mikhail Kolyada (RUS)	2	4
4. Alexei Bychenko (ISR)	7	7
5. Kazuki Tomono (JPN)	11	3
6. Deniss Vasiljevs (LAT)	9	5
7. Dmitri Aliev (RUS)	13	6
8. Keegan Messing (CAN)	**6**	**11**
9. Misha Ge (UZB)	8	9
10. Michal Březina (CZE)	17	8
11. Max Aaron (USA)	15	10
12. Alexander Majorov (SWE)	10	13
13. Keiji Tanaka (JPN)	14	12
14. Vincent Zhou (USA)	3	19
15. Paul Fentz (GER)	12	16
16. Romain Ponsart (FRA)	16	14
17. Matteo Rizzo (ITA)	18	17
18. Brendan Kerry (AUS)	19	15
19. Boyang Jin (CHN)	4	23
20. Daniel Samohin (ISR)	20	18
21. Julian Zhi Jie Yee (MAS)	21	20
22. Donovan Carrillo (MEX)	24	21
23. Slavik Hayrapetyan (ARM)	23	22
24. Phillip Harris (GRB)	22	24
25. Nam Nguyen (CAN)	**25**	-
26. Morisi Kvitelashvili (GEO)	26	-
27. Stéphane Walker (SUI)	27	-
28. Burak Demirboğa (TUR)	28	-
29. Ivan Pavlov (UKR)	29	-
30. Chih-I Tsao (TPE)	30	-
31. Larry Loupolover (AZE)	31	-
32. Abzal Rakimgaliev (KAZ)	32	-
33. Jin-seo Kim (KOR)	33	-

34. Nicholas Vrdoljak (CRO)	34	-
35. Valtter Virtanen (FIN)	35	-
36. Igor Reznichenko (POL)	36	-
37. Javier Raya (ESP)	37	-
WD. Patrick Chan (CAN)	-	-
WD. Javier Fernández (ESP)	-	-
WD. Yuzuru Hanyu (JPN)	-	-
WD. Denis Ten (KAZ)	-	-
WD. Adam Rippon (USA)	-	-

World Ladies Figure Skating Championships:

	SP	FS
1. Kaetlyn Osmond (CAN)	**4**	**1**
2. Wakaba Higuchi (JPN)	8	2
3. Satoko Miyahara (JPN)	3	3
4. Carolina Kostner (ITA)	1	5
5. Alina Zagitova (RUS)	2	7
6. Bradie Tennell (USA)	7	4
7. Gabrielle Daleman (CAN)	**6**	**8**
8. Maria Sotskova (RUS)	5	9
9. Loena Hendrickx (BEL)	10	6
10. Mirai Nagasu (USA)	9	11
11. Elizabet Tursynbayeva (KAZ)	11	10
12. Mariah Bell (USA)	17	12
13. Nicole Schott (GER)	12	14
14. Laurine Lecavelier (FRA)	15	13
15. Ha-nul Kim (KOR)	14	15
16. Viveca Lindfors (FIN)	13	16
17. Kailani Craine (AUS)	20	18
18. Eliška Březinová (CZE)	18	19
19. Stanislava Konstantinova (RUS)	16	20
20. Alexia Paganini (SUI)	19	22
21. Elisabetta Leccardi (ITA)	23	17
22. Daša Grm (SLO)	22	21
23. Ivett Tóth (HUN)	24	23
24. Larkyn Austman (CAN)	**25**	-
25. Xiangning Li (CHN)	26	-
26. Nicole Rajičová (SVK)	27	-

27. Amy Lin (TPE)	28	-
28. Anita Östlund (SWE)	29	-
29. Alisa Stomakhina (AUT)	30	-
30. Elżbieta Kropa (LIT)	31	-
31. Natasha McKay (GRB)	32	-
32. Anne Line Gjersem (NOR)	33	-
33. Gerli Liinamäe (EST)	34	-
34. Isadora Williams (BRA)	35	-
35. Antonina Dubinina (SRB)	36	-
36. Angelīna Kučvaļska (LAT)	37	-
WD. Da-bin Choi (KOR)	21	-
WD. Evgenia Medvedeva (RUS)	-	-
WD. Karen Chen (USA)	-	-
WD. Anna Khnychenkova (UKR)	-	-
WD. Alisson Krystle Perticheto (PHI)	-	-

World Pairs Skating Championships:

	SP	FS
1. Aliona Savchenko/Bruno Massot (GER)	1	1
2. Evgenia Tarasova/Vladimir Morozov (RUS)	2	2
3. Vanessa James/Morgan Ciprès (FRA)	3	3
4. Natalia Zabiiako/Alexander Enbert (RUS)	4	6
5. Nicole Della Monica/Matteo Guarise (ITA)	5	5
6. K. Moore-Towers/M. Marinaro (CAN)	**10**	**4**
7. Xiaoyu Yu/Hao Zhang (CHN)	9	7
8. Kristina Astakhova/Alexei Rogonov (RUS)	7	9
9. Cheng Peng/Yang Jin (CHN)	6	10
10. Valentina Marchei/Ondřej Hotárek (ITA)	8	8
11. Anna Dušková/Martin Bidař (CZE)	13	11
12. Tae-ok Ryom/Ju-sik Kim (PRK)	12	12
13. Annika Hocke/Ruben Blommaert (GER)	16	13
14. Miriam Ziegler/Severin Kiefer (AUT)	14	14
15. Alexa Scimeca Knierim/Chris Knierim (USA)	11	15
16. E. Alexandrovskaya/H. Windsor (AUS)	15	16
17. D. Stellato-Dudek/N. Bartholomay (USA)	17	-
18. Camille Ruest/Andrew Wolfe (CAN)	**18**	**-**
19. Paige Conners/Evgeni Krasnopolski (ISR)	19	-
20. L. Barquero Jiménez/A. Maestu Babarro (ESP)	20	-

21. L. Petranović/A. Souza-Kordeiru (CRO)	21	-
22. Julianne Séguin/Charlie Bilodeau (CAN)	**22**	**-**
23. Ioulia Chtchetinina/Mikhail Akulov (SUI)	23	-
24. Miu Suzaki/Ryuichi Kihara (JPN)	24	-
25. Lola Esbrat/Andrei Novoselov (FRA)	25	-
26. Kyu-eun Kim/Alex Kang-chan Kam (KOR)	26	-
27. Zoe Jones/Christopher Boyadji (GRB)	27	-
28. Elizaveta Kashitsyna/Márk Magyar (HUN)	28	-
WD. Meagan Duhamel/Eric Radford (CAN)	**-**	**-**
WD. Wenjing Sui/Cong Han (CHN)	-	-
WD. Ksenia Stolbova/Fedor Klimov (RUS)	-	-
WD. Tarah Kayne/Danny O'Shea (USA)	-	-
WD. Sofiya Karagodina/Semyon Stepanov (AZE)	-	-

World Ice Dancing Championships:

	SD	FD
1. Gabriella Papadakis/Guillaume Cizeron (FRA)	1	1
2. Madison Hubbell/Zachary Donohue (USA)	2	2
3. Kaitlyn Weaver/Andrew Poje (CAN)	**3**	**4**
4. Anna Cappellini/Luca Lanotte (ITA)	4	3
5. Madison Chock/Evan Bates (USA)	5	5
6. Piper Gilles/Paul Poirier (CAN)	**6**	**6**
7. Alexandra Stepanova/Ivan Bukin (RUS)	7	7
8. Tiffany Zahorski/Jonathan Guerreiro (RUS)	8	8
9. Charlène Guignard/Marco Fabbri (ITA)	9	9
10. Kaitlin Hawayek/Jean-Luc Baker (USA)	15	10
11. Kana Muramoto/Chris Reed (JPN)	10	11
12. Olivia Smart/Adriàn Díaz Bronchud (ESP)	12	12
13. Marie-Jade Lauriault/Romain Le Gac (FRA)	14	13
14. Carolane Soucisse/Shane Firus (CAN)	**11**	**14**
15. Alexandra Nazarova/Maxim Nikitin (UKR)	16	15
16. Kavita Lorenz/Joti Polizoakis (GER)	17	16
17. Natalia Kaliszek/Maksym Spodyriev (POL)	13	19
18. Shiyue Wang/Xinyu Liu (CHN)	19	17
19. Alisa Agafonova/Alper Uçar (TUR)	20	18
20. Allison Reed/Saulius Ambrulevičius (LIT)	18	20
21. Yura Min/Alexander Gamelin (KOR)	21	-
22. Tina Garabedian/Simon Proulx-Sénécal (ARM)	22	-

23. Cecilia Törn/Jussiville Partanen (FIN)	23	-
24. Lilah Fear/Lewis Gibson (GRB)	24	-
25. Lucie Myslivečková/Lukáš Csölley (SVK)	25	-
26. Cortney Mansour/Michal Češka (CZE)	26	-
27. Anna Yanovskaya/Ádám Lukács (HUN)	27	-
28. Viktoria Kavaliova/Yurii Bieliaiev (BLS)	28	-
29. Teodora Markova/Simon Daze (BUL)	29	-
30. Chantelle Kerry/Andrew Dodds (AUS)	30	-
31. Adel Tankova/Ronald Zilberberg (ISR)	31	-
WD. Tessa Virtue/Scott Moir (CAN)	**-**	**-**
WD. Maia Shibutani/Alex Shibutani (USA)	-	-
WD. Penny Coomes/Nicholas Buckland (GRB)	-	-
WD. Ekaterina Bobrova/Dmitri Soloviev (RUS)	-	-

Kaetlyn Osmond won Canada's first gold medal in the ladies event at the World Figure Skating Championships since 1973.

Aliona Savchenko and Bruno Massot set a record for the highest overall score awarded in the pairs event at the World Championships under the IJS System prior to the 2018/2019 season (162.86).

Gabriella Papadakis and Guillaume Cizeron set a record for the highest overall score awarded in the ice dance event at the World Championships under the IJS System prior to the 2018/2019 season (203.16).

Sources: Skating magazine, May 2018; Entries, 2018 World Figure Skating Championships; Protocol, 2018 World Figure Skating Championships; ISU Highest Total Scores Statistics

2019 WORLD FIGURE SKATING CHAMPIONSHIPS
Saitama, Japan, March 18-24, 2019

World Men's Figure Skating Championships:

	SP	FS
1. Nathan Chen (USA)	1	1
2. Yuzuru Hanyu (JPN)	3	2

3. Vincent Zhou (USA)	4	3
4. Shoma Uno (JPN)	6	4
5. Boyang Jin (CHN)	9	5
6. Mikhail Kolyada (RUS)	10	6
7. Matteo Rizzo (ITA)	5	10
8. Michal Březina (CZE)	8	8
9. Jason Brown (USA)	2	14
10. Andrei Lazukin (RUS)	11	9
11. Kévin Aymoz (FRA)	7	12
12. Alexander Samarin (RUS)	20	7
13. Morisi Kvitelashvili (GEO)	12	13
14. Keiji Tanaka (JPN)	19	11
15. Keegan Messing (CAN)	**14**	**15**
16. Nam Nguyen (CAN)	**13**	**16**
17. Vladimir Litvintsev (AZE)	16	19
18. Alexander Majorov (SWE)	17	17
19. Jun-hwan Cha (KOR)	18	18
20. Brendan Kerry (AUS)	21	21
21. Deniss Vasiļjevs (LAT)	23	20
22. Alexei Bychenko (ISR)	22	22
23. Julian Zhi Jie Yee (MAS)	24	23
24. Daniel Samohin (ISR)	15	24
25. Peter James Hallam (GRB)	25	-
26. Luc Maierhofer (AUT)	26	-
27. Aleksandr Selevko (EST)	27	-
28. Paul Fentz (GER)	28	-
29. Ivan Shmuratko (UKR)	29	-
30. Burak Demirboğa (TUR)	30	-
31. Slavik Hayrapetyan (ARM)	31	-
32. Valtter Virtanen (FIN)	32	-
33. Donovan Carrillo (MEX)	33	-
34. Lukas Britschgi (SUI)	34	-
35. Igor Reznichenko (POL)	35	-
WD. Maxim Kovtun (RUS)	-	-

World Ladies Figure Skating Championships:

	SP	FS
1. Alina Zagitova (RUS)	1	1

2. Elizabet Tursynbaeva (KAZ)	3	4
3. Evgenia Medvedeva (RUS)	4	3
4. Rika Kihira (JPN)	7	2
5. Kaori Sakamoto (JPN)	2	5
6. Satoko Miyahara (JPN)	8	6
7. Bradie Tennell (USA)	10	7
8. Sofia Samodurova (RUS)	9	8
9. Mariah Bell (USA)	6	9
10. Eun-soo Lim (KOR)	5	10
11. Gabrielle Daleman (CAN)	**11**	**12**
12. Loena Hendrickx (BEL)	13	11
13. Ekaterina Ryabova (AZE)	17	13
14. Yi Christy Leung (HKG)	14	14
15. Laurine Lecavelier (FRA)	19	15
16. Nicole Schott (GER)	12	17
17. Alexandra Feigin (BUL)	20	16
18. Daša Grm (SLO)	16	18
19. Hongyi Chen (CHN)	15	19
20. Eliška Březinová (CZE)	18	20
21. Natasha McKay (GRB)	21	21
22. Eva Lotta Kiibus (EST)	23	22
23. Alaine Chartrand (CAN)	**22**	**23**
24. Isadora Williams (BRA)	24	24
25. Ivett Tóth (HUN)	25	-
26. Pernille Sørensen (DEN)	26	-
27. Marina Piredda (ITA)	27	-
28. Emmi Peltonen (FIN)	28	-
29. Julia Sauter (ROM)	29	-
30. Anita Östlund (SWE)	30	-
31. Roberta Rodeghiero (ITA)	31	-
32. Nicole Rajičová (SVK)	32	-
33. Alexia Paganini (SUI)	33	-
34. Valentina Matos (ESP)	34	-
35. Aurora Cotop (CAN)	**35**	**-**
36. Kailani Craine (AUS)	36	-
37. Sophia Schaller (AUT)	37	-
38. Elžbieta Kropa (LIT)	38	-
39. Anastasia Galustyan (ARM)	39	-

40. Kyarha van Tiel (NED) — 40 / -
WD. Viveca Findfors (FIN) — - / -
WD. Matilda Algotsson (SWE) — - / -
WD. Stanislava Konstantinova (RUS) — - / -

World Pairs Skating Championships:

	SP	FS
1. Wenjing Sui/Cong Han (CHN)	2	1
2. Evgenia Tarasova/Vladimir Morozov (RUS)	1	2
3. Natalia Zabiiako/Alexander Enbert (RUS)	4	4
4. Cheng Peng/Yang Jin (CHN)	3	5
5. Vanessa James/Morgan Ciprès (FRA)	7	3
6. Aleksandra Boikova/Dmitrii Kozlovskii (RUS)	6	6
7. K. Moore-Towers/M. Marinaro (CAN)	**5**	**8**
8. Nicole Della Monica/Matteo Guarise (ITA)	8	7
9. Ashley Cain/Timothy LeDuc (USA)	9	9
10. Miriam Ziegler/Severin Kiefer (AUT)	11	11
11. Tae-ok Ryom/Ju-sik Kim (PRK)	13	10
12. Evelyn Walsh/Trennt Michaud (CAN)	**12**	**12**
13. Minerva Fabienne Hase/Nolan Seegert (GER)	10	14
14. Annika Hocke/Ruben Blommaert (GER)	16	13
15. L. Barquero Jiménez/A. Maestu Babarro (ESP)	14	15
16. L. Petranović/A. Souza-Kordeiru (CRO)	15	17
17. Zoe Jones/Christopher Boyadji (GRB)	17	16
18. Hanna Abrazhevich/Martin Bidař (CZE)	19	18
19. Rebecca Ghilardi/Filippo Ambrosini (ITA)	18	19
WD. Miu Suzaki/Ryuichi Kihara (JPN)	-	-

World Ice Dancing Championships:

	RD	FD
1. Gabriella Papadakis/Guillaume Cizeron (FRA)	1	1
2. Victoria Sinitsina/Nikita Katsalapov (RUS)	2	2
3. Madison Hubbell/Zachary Donohue (USA)	4	3
4. Alexandra Stepanova/Ivan Bukin (RUS)	3	4
5. Kaitlyn Weaver/Andrew Poje (CAN)	**5**	**5**
6. Madison Chock/Evan Bates (USA)	6	6
7. Piper Gilles/Paul Poirier (CAN)	**8**	**7**
8. Charlène Guignard/Marco Fabbri (ITA)	7	8

9. Kaitlin Hawayek/Jean-Luc Baker (USA)	9	10
10. L. Fournier Beaudry/N. Sørensen (CAN)	**10**	**9**
11. Natalia Kaliszek/Maksym Spodyriev (POL)	11	12
12. Sara Hurtado/Kirill Khaliavin (ESP)	12	13
13. Lilah Fear/Lewis Gibson (GRB)	15	11
14. Marie-Jade Lauriault/Romain Le Gac (FRA)	13	14
15. Shiyue Wang/Xinyu Liu (CHN)	14	15
16. Juulia Turkkila/Matthias Versluis (FIN)	18	16
17. Allison Reed/Saulius Ambrulevičius (LIT)	16	17
18. Shari Koch/Christian Nüchtern (GER)	17	18
19. Anna Yanovskaya/Ádám Lukács (HUN)	20	19
20. Alexandra Nazarova/Maxim Nikitin (UKR)	19	20
21. Misato Komatsubara/Tim Koleto (JPN)	21	-
22. Anna Kublikova/Yuri Hulitski (BLS)	22	-
23. Victoria Manni/Carlo Rothlisberger (SUI)	23	-
24. Jasmine Tessari/Francesco Fioretti (ITA)	24	-
25. Shira Ichilov/Vadim Davidovich (ISR)	25	-
26. Chantelle Kerry/Andrew Dodds (AUS)	26	-
27. Katerina Bunina/German Frolov (EST)	27	-

Alina Zagitova set a record for the highest overall score awarded in the ladies event at the World Championships under the IJS System after the 2018/2019 season (237.50).

The short dance was rebranded as the rhythm dance.

Wenjing Sui and Cong Han set a record for the highest overall score awarded in the pairs event at the World Championships under the IJS System after the 2018/2019 season (234.84).

Elizaveta Tursynbaeva made history as the first woman to receive positive GOE for quadruple jump (Salchow) at the World Figure Skating Championships. Tursynbaeva was also the first skater from Kazakhstan to win a medal in the ladies event.

Sources: Skating magazine, May 2019; Entries, 2019 World Figure Skating Championships; Protocol, 2019 World Figure Skating Championships; ISU Highest Total Scores Statistics

Yuzuru Hanyu, World Champion 2014 and 2017. Jessica Gow / TT News Agency / Alamy Stock Photo.

THE PANDEMIC

2020
*EVENT NOT HELD**

*The 2020 World Figure Skating Championships were scheduled to be held in Montreal, Canada. Despite an alarming rise of cases during the first wave, Skate Canada planned on moving forward with the event, with screening protocols in place. However, as the gravity and extent of the situation became clear, The Quebec Health Ministry held a press conference to discuss "all major events in the province... with input from the Public Health Agency of Canada." The next day, it was announced the 2020 World Figure Skating Championships were cancelled. It was the first year the World Championships were not held since the tragic crash of Sabena Flight 548 resulted in the event's cancellation in 1961. As countries around the world went into lockdown, it became apparent to skaters worldwide that had the World Championships proceeded, they likely would have been a dangerous super-spreader event. A potential disaster had been avoided.

Sources: CBC News, March 9, 2020; Global News, March 10, 2020; Skating magazine, May 2020

2021 WORLD FIGURE SKATING CHAMPIONSHIPS
Stockholm, Sweden, March 22-28, 2021

World Men's Figure Skating Championships:

	SP	FS
1. Nathan Chen (USA)	3	1
2. Yuma Kagiyama (JPN)	2	2
3. Yuzuru Hanyu (JPN)	1	4
4. Shoma Uno (JPN)	6	3
5. Mikhail Kolyada (FSR)	4	5
6. Keegan Messing (CAN)	**5**	**6**
7. Jason Brown (USA)	7	8

8. Evgeni Semenenko (FSR)	10	7
9. Kévin Aymoz (FRA)	9	9
10. Jun-hwan Cha (KOR)	8	13
11. Matteo Rizzo (ITA)	11	11
12. Daniel Grassl (ITA)	15	10
13. Han Yan (CHN)	12	14
14. Morisi Kvitelashvili (GEO)	17	16
15. Lukas Britschgi (SUI)	24	15
16. Aleksandr Selevko (EST)	16	17
17. Konstantin Milyukov (BLS)	14	18
18. Deniss Vasiļjevs (LAT)	13	21
19. Michal Březina (CZE)	23	19
20. Donovan Carrillo (MEX)	23	19
21. Ivan Shmuratko (UKR)	22	20
22. Boyang Jin (CHN)	19	22
23. Nikolaj Majorov (SWE)	20	23
24. Alexei Bychenko (ISR)	18	24
25. Vincent Zhou (USA)	25	-
26. Paul Fentz (GER)	26	-
27. Vladimir Litvintsev (AZE)	27	-
28. Başar Oktar (TUR)	28	-
29. Maurizio Zandron (AUT)	29	-
30. Peter James Hallam (GRB)	30	-
31. Valtter Virtanen (FIN)	31	-
32. Mikhail Shaidorov (KAZ)	32	-
33. Larry Loupolover (BUL)	33	-
WD. Slavik Hayrapetyan (ARM)	-	-
WD. Brendan Kerry (AUS)	-	-

World Ladies Figure Skating Championships:

	SP	FS
1. Anna Shcherbakova (FSR)	1	2
2. Elizaveta Tuktamysheva (FSR)	3	3
3. Alexandra Trusova (FSR)	12	1
4. Karen Chen (USA)	4	6
5. Loena Hendrickx (BEL)	10	4
6. Kaori Sakamoto (JPN)	6	5
7. Rika Kihira (JPN)	2	9

8. Olga Mikutina (AUT)	11	7
9. Bradie Tennell (USA)	7	8
10. Hae-in Lee (KOR)	8	11
11. Ye-lim Kim (KOR)	5	13
12. Ekaterina Ryabova (AZE)	13	10
13. Madeline Schizas (CAN)	**9**	**14**
14. Eva-Lotta Kiibus (EST)	19	12
15. Josefin Taljegård (SWE)	15	16
16. Lindsay van Zundert (NED)	24	15
17. Alexandra Feigin (BUL)	17	18
18. Nicole Schott (GER)	20	17
19. Satoko Miyahara (JPN)	16	19
20. Alina Urushadze (GEO)	18	20
21. Hongyi Chen (CHN)	22	21
22. Eliška Březinová (CZE)	21	22
23. Natasha McKay (GRB)	23	23
24. Jenni Saarinen (FIN)	14	24
25. Alexia Paganini (SUI)	25	-
26. Kailani Craine (AUS)	26	-
27. Emily Bausback (CAN)	**27**	**-**
28. Lara Naki Gutmann (ITA)	28	-
29. Emmy Ma (TPE)	29	-
30. Júlia Láng (HUN)	30	-
31. Nelli Ioffe (ISR)	31	-
32. Ekaterina Kurakova (POL)	32	-
33. Angelīna Kučvaļska (LAT)	33	-
34. Daša Grm (SLO)	34	-
35. Anastasia Arkhipova (UKR)	35	-
36. Emilea Zingas (CYP)	36	-
37. Elžbieta Kropa (LIT)	37	-
WD. Yi Christy Leung (HKG)	-	-
WD. Maé-Bérénice Méité (FRA)	-	-
WD. Anastasia Galustyan (ARM)	-	-
WD. Alisson Krystle Perticheto (PHI)	-	-
WD. Viktoriia Safonova (BLS)	-	-

World Pairs Skating Championships:

	SP	FS
1. Anastasia Mishina/Aleksandr Galliamov (FSR)	3	1
2. Wenjing Sui/Cong Han (CHN)	2	2
3. Aleksandra Boikova/Dmitrii Kozlovskii (FSR)	1	4
4. Evgenia Tarasova/Vladimir Morozov (FSR)	4	3
5. Cheng Peng/Yang Jin (CHN)	5	6
6. K. Moore-Towers/M. Marinaro (CAN)	**10**	**5**
7. Alexa Scimeca Knierim/Brandon Frazier (USA)	7	7
8. Nicole Della Monica/Matteo Guarise (ITA)	11	8
9. Ashley Cain-Gribble/Timothy LeDuc (USA)	6	9
10. Riku Miura/Ryuichi Kihara (JPN)	8	10
11. Miriam Ziegler/Severin Kiefer (AUT)	9	11
12. Evelyn Walsh/Trennt Michaud (CAN)	**12**	**12**
13. Annika Hocke/Robert Kunkel (GER)	13	14
14. Ioulia Chtchetinina/Márk Magyar (HUN)	18	13
15. Elizaveta Zhuk/Martin Bidař (CZE)	16	15
16. Anastasiia Metelkina/Daniil Parkman (GEO)	14	16
17. Rebecca Ghilardi/Filippo Ambrosini (ITA)	15	18
18. B. Lukashevich/A. Stepanov (BLS)	20	17
19. Anna Vernikov/Evgeni Krasnopolski (ISR)	17	20
20. Cléo Hamon/Denys Strekalin (FRA)	19	19
21. L. Petranović/A. Souza-Kordeiru (CRO)	21	-
22. Daria Danilova/Michel Tsiba (NED)	22	-
23. Coline Keriven/Noël-Antoine Pierre (FRA)	23	-
24. Zoe Jones/Christopher Boyadji (GRB)	24	-
WD. Minerva Fabienne Hase/Nolan Seegert (GER)	-	-
WD. Sofiia Holichenko/Artem Darenskyi (UKR)	-	-
WD. Yuchen Wang/Yihang Huang (CHN)	-	-
WD. Jessica Calalang/Brian Johnson (USA)	-	-

World Ice Dancing Championships:

	RD	FD
1. Victoria Sinitsina/Nikita Katsalapov (FSR)	1	1
2. Madison Hubbell/Zachary Donohue (USA)	2	3
3. Piper Gilles/Paul Poirier (CAN)	**4**	**2**
4. Madison Chock/Evan Bates (USA)	3	4
5. Alexandra Stepanova/Ivan Bukin (FSR)	5	5
6. Charlène Guignard/Marco Fabbri (ITA)	6	6
7. Lilah Fear/Lewis Gibson (GRB)	8	7
8. L. Fournier Beaudry/N. Sørensen (CAN)	**7**	**8**
9. Kaitlin Hawayek/Jean-Luc Baker (USA)	11	9
10. Tiffany Zahorski/Jonathan Guerreiro (FSR)	10	10
11. Sara Hurtado/Kirill Khaliavin (ESP)	12	11
12. Natalia Kaliszek/Maksym Spodyriev (POL)	9	14
13. Shiyue Wang/Xinyu Liu (CHN)	13	12
14. Marjorie Lajoie/Zachary Lagha (CAN)	**14**	**13**
15. Allison Reed/Saulius Ambrulevičius (LIT)	15	15
16. Adelina Galyavieva/Louis Thauron (FRA)	16	16
17. Evgeniia Lopareva/Geoffrey Brissaud (FRA)	19	17
18. Katharina Müller/Tim Dieck (GER)	17	19
19. Misato Komatsubara/Tim Koleto (JPN)	18	20
20. Alexandra Nazarova/Maxim Nikitin (UKR)	20	18
21. Juulia Turkkila/Matthias Versluis (FIN)	21	-
22. Natálie Taschlerová/Filip Taschler (CZE)	22	-
23. Anna Yanovskaya/Ádám Lukács (HUN)	23	-
24. Holly Harris/Jason Chan (AUS)	24	-
25. Carolina Moscheni/Francesco Fioretti (ITA)	25	-
26. Shira Ichilov/Laurent Abecassis (ISR)	26	-
27. Yuliia Zhata/Berk Akalın (TUR)	27	-
28. Viktoria Semenjuk/Ilya Yukhimuk (BLS)	28	-
29. Chelsea Verhaegh/Sherim van Geffen (NED)	29	-
30. E. Kuznetsova/O. Kolosovskyi (AZE)	30	-
31. Mina Zdravkova/Christopher M. Davis (BUL)	31	-
WD. Tina Garabedian/Simon Proulx-Sénécal (ARM)	-	-
WD. Olivia Smart/Adriá Díaz Bronchud (ESP)	-	-
WD. Maxine Weatherby/Temirlan Yerzhanov (KAZ)	-	-
WD. Yura Min/Daniel Eaton (KOR)	-	-
WD. Maria Kazakova/Georgy Reviya (GEO)	-	-

The World Figure Skating Championships were held under strict health protocols. Attendees remained in a "bubble" - a group of individuals that were isolated and tested to prevent the spread of the virus. Many expressed valid concerns about the safety of the event. A petition called #NoQuarantineNoWorlds circulated prior to the event, criticizing the ISU and organizers for "woefully inadequate measures", such as a lack of a two-week self-isolation period before the event. Several skaters tested positive upon their arrival in Stockholm and photos circulated on social media of participants not adhering to safety protocols. On social media, World Champion Meagan Duhamel remarked, "The complete lack of any COVID safety regulations just stresses me out. I'd love to know how [the ISU] will enforce COVID safety for Worlds. Will [Russia], a country that doesn't believe or follow protocol be in its own hotel?"

The Court of Arbitration of Sport (CAS) ruled in favour of the World Anti-Doping Agency (WADA), declaring the Russian Anti-Doping Agency (RUSADA) as non-compliant with the World Anti-Doping Code and imposing a two-year sanction. The ISU allowed Russian skaters to compete as "representatives of the Figure Skating Federation of Russia" (FSR) instead of representatives of their country. At medal ceremonies, a selection from Tchaikovsky's "Piano Concerto No. 1 in B-Flat Minor" was played instead of the Russian national anthem. This music was played when Russian skaters swept the podium for the first time in the ladies event at the World Championships.

Alexandra Trusova, the FSR athlete with RUS in her name, made history as the first woman to receive positive GOE on a quadruple Lutz jump at the European Championships.

Emilea Zingas made history as the first skater to represent Cyprus at the World Championships.

Sources: WADA Statement on Court of Arbitration decision to declare FSRsian Anti-Doping Agency as non-compliant, December 1, 2020; Inside The Games, March 17, 2021; NBC Sports, March 29, 2021; Skating magazine, May 2021; *Music & Politics*, Vol. 17, Issue 2, Summer 2023; Entries, 2021 World Figure Skating Championships; Results, 2021 World Figure Skating Championships

2022 WORLD FIGURE SKATING CHAMPIONSHIPS
Montpellier, France, March 21-27, 2022

World Men's Figure Skating Championships:

	SP	FS
1. Shoma Uno (JPN)	1	1
2. Yuma Kagiyama (JPN)	2	2
3. Vincent Zhou (USA)	6	4
4. Morisi Kvitelashvili (GEO)	7	5
5. Camden Pulkinen (USA)	12	3
6. Kazuki Tomono (JPN)	3	8
7. Daniel Grassl (ITA)	5	7
8. Adam Siao Him Fa (FRA)	10	6
9. Ilia Malinin (USA)	4	11
10. Matteo Rizzo (ITA)	8	10
11. Kévin Aymoz (FRA)	15	12
12. Roman Sadovsky (CAN)	**18**	**9**
13. Deniss Vasiljevs (LAT)	11	14
14. Keegan Messing (CAN)	**9**	**17**
15. Mihhail Selevko (EST)	20	13
16. Vladimir Litvintsev (AZE)	14	15
17. Maurizio Zandron (AUT)	16	16
18. Si-hyeong Lim (KOR)	13	18
19. Nikolaj Majorov (SWE)	19	20
20. Graham Newberry (GRB)	19	20
21. Tomàs-Llorenç Guarino Sabaté (ESP)	24	19
22. Nikita Starostin (GER)	23	22
23. Ivan Shmuratko (UKR)	22	23
24. Mark Gorodnitsky (ISR)	25	-
25. Adam Hagara (SVK)	26	-
26. Vladimir Samoilov (POL)	27	-
27. Burak Demirboğa (TUR)	28	-
28. Aleksandr Vlasenko (HUN)	29	-
WD. Jun-hwan Cha (KOR)	17	-

WD. Donovan Carrillo (MEX) - -
WD. Nathan Chen (USA) - -
WD. Yuzuru Hanyu (JPN) - -
WD. Lukas Britschgi (SUI) - -
WD. Kao Miura (JPN) - -
WD. Mikhail Shaidorov (KAZ) - -
WD. Georgii Reshtenko (CZE) - -
WD. Larry Loupolover (BUL) - -
WD. Slavik Hayrapetyan (ARM) - -

World Women's Figure Skating Championships:

	SP	FS
1. Kaori Sakamoto (JPN)	1	1
2. Loena Hendrickx (BEL)	2	2
3. Alysa Liu (USA)	5	3
4. Mariah Bell (USA)	3	4
5. Young You (KOR)	4	6
6. Anastasiia Gubanova (GEO)	14	5
7. Hae-in Lee (KOR)	11	7
8. Karen Chen (USA)	8	8
9. Ekaterina Ryabova (AZE)	9	11
10. Nicole Schott (GER)	6	14
11. Wakaba Higuchi (JPN)	7	12
12. Madeline Schizas (CAN)	**10**	**10**
13. Ekaterina Kurakova (POL)	16	9
14. Olga Mikutina (AUT)	15	13
15. Mana Kawabe (JPN)	12	15
16. Niina Petrõkina (EST)	17	16
17. Lindsay van Zundert (NED)	18	17
18. Julia Sauter (ROM)	19	18
19. Alexia Paganini (SUI)	13	19
20. Lara Naki Gutmann (ITA)	20	20
21. Josefin Taljegård (SWE)	21	21
22. Kailani Craine (AUS)	22	22
23. Natasha McKay (GRB)	24	23
24. Daša Grm (SLO)	23	24
25. Jenni Saarinen (FIN)	25	-
26. Tzu-Han Ting (TPE)	26	-

27. Eliška Březinová (CZE) — 27 — -
28. Alexandra Feigin (BUL) — 28 — -
29. Léa Serna (FRA) — 29 — -
30. Marilena Kitromilis (CYP) — 30 — -
31. Júlia Láng (HUN) — 31 — -
32. Stefanie Pesendorfer (AUT) — 32 — -
33. Anete Lāce (LAT) — 33 — -
WD. Anastasiia Shabotova (UKR) — - — -
WD. Ye-lim Kim (KOR) — - — -

World Pairs Skating Championships:

	SP	FS
1. Alexa Scimeca Knierim/Brandon Frazier (USA)	1	1
2. Riku Miura/Ryuichi Kihara (JPN)	3	3
3. Vanessa James/Eric Radford (CAN)	**5**	**2**
4. Karina Safina/Luka Berulava (GEO)	4	4
5. Minerva Fabienne Hase/Nolan Seegert (GER)	6	5
6. Evelyn Walsh/Trennt Michaud (CAN)	**8**	**6**
7. Miriam Ziegler/Severin Kiefer (AUT)	7	7
8. Camille Kovalev/Pavel Kovalev (FRA)	9	8
9. Daria Danilova/Michel Tsiba (NED)	11	9
10. Zoe Jones/Christopher Boyadji (GRB)	10	10
11. Dorota Broda/Pedro Betegón Martín (ESP)	12	11
12. Hailey Kops/Evgeni Krasnopolski (ISR)	14	12
WD. Ashley Cain-Gribble/Timothy LeDuc (USA)	2	-
WD. Sofiia Holichenko/Artem Darenskyi (UKR)	13	-
WD. K. Moore-Towers/M. Marinaro (CAN)	**-**	**-**
WD. Sara Conti/Niccolò Macii (ITA)	-	-
WD. A. Golubeva/H. Giotopoulos Moore (AUS)	-	-
WD. Rebecca Ghilardi/Filippo Ambrosini (ITA)	-	-
WD. Jelizaveta Žuková/Martin Bidař (CZE)	-	-
WD. Anastasiia Metelkina/Daniil Parkman (GEO)	-	-

World Ice Dancing Championships:

	RD	FD
1. Gabriella Papadakis/Guillaume Cizeron (FRA)	1	1
2. Madison Hubbell/Zachary Donohue (USA)	2	2
3. Madison Chock/Evan Bates (USA)	3	3
4. Charlène Guignard/Marco Fabbri (ITA)	4	4
5. Piper Gilles/Paul Poirier (CAN)	**5**	**5**
6. Lilah Fear/Lewis Gibson (GRB)	7	6
7. Olivia Smart/Adriá Díaz Bronchud (ESP)	6	7
8. Kaitlin Hawayek/Jean-Luc Baker (USA)	9	8
9. L. Fournier Beaudry/N. Sørensen (DEN)	8	9
10. Allison Reed/Saulius Ambrulevičius (LIT)	10	11
11. Marjorie Lajoie/Zachary Lagha (CAN)	**13**	**10**
12. Juulia Turkkila/Matthias Versluis (FIN)	12	12
13. Natálie Taschlerová/Filip Taschler (CZE)	11	14
14. Tina Garabedian/Simon Proulx-Sénécal (ARM)	14	13
15. Maria Kazakova/Georgy Reviya (GEO)	17	15
16. Kana Muramoto/Daisuke Takahashi (JPN)	15	16
17. Sasha Fear/George Waddell (GRB)	18	18
18. Holly Harris/Jason Chan (AUS)	19	17
19. S. Mazingue/M.J. Gaidajenko (EST)	20	19
20. Shira Ichilov/Volodymyr Byelikov (ISR)	16	-
21. Mariia Ignateva/Danijil Szemko (HUN)	22	-
22. Jasmine Tessari/Stéphane Walker (SUI)	23	-
23. C. Lafond-Fournier/R. Kang-in Kam (NZL)	24	-
24. Mária Sofia Pucherová/Nikita Lysak (SVK)	25	-
25. Carolina Moscheni/Francesco Fioretti (ITA)	26	-
26. E. Mitrofanova/V. Kasinskij (BIH)	27	-
27. A. Polibina/P. Golovishnikov (POL)	28	-
28. E. Kuznetsova/O. Kolosovskyi (AZE)	29	-
29. Aurelija Ipolito/Luke Russell (LAT)	30	-
30. Gaukhar Nauryzova/Boyisangur Datiev (KAZ)	31	-
WD. Alexandra Nazarova/Maxim Nikitin (UKR)	-	-
WD. J. Janse van Rensburg/B. Steffan (GER)	-	-
WD. Natalia Kaliszek/Maksym Spodyriev (POL)	-	-
WD. M. Nosovitskaya/M. Nosovitskiy (ISR)	-	-

Eight skaters were forced to withdraw after testing positive for the virus.

The International Skating Union (ISU) ceased the use of the term "ladies" in favour of "women" during the summer of 2021.

Loena Hendrickx made history as the first skater from Belgium to win a medal in the women's event at the World Championships.

The Russian doping scandal that came to a head at the 2022 Olympic Games in Beijing was major news in the figure skating community, as was Russia's invasion of Ukraine. The ISU released a communication stating, "The ISU Council reiterates its solidarity with all those affected by the conflict in Ukraine and our thoughts are with the entire Ukrainian people and country... Until further notice, no Skaters belonging to the ISU Members in Russia... and Belarus... shall be invited or allowed to participate in International ice skating Competitions including ISU Championships and other ISU Events."

Ukrainian skaters protested the unlawful invasion of their country. Ivan Shmuratko and Alexandra Nazarova and Maxim Nikitin chose to wear the colors of the Ukrainian flag instead of traditional costumes. The ISU rejected Nazarova and Nikitin's rhythm dance, which featured a short sample of a speech by Ukrainian President Volodymyr Zelenskyy, on the grounds that the snippet from the speech, which called for peace, was "propaganda". The ISU insisted that Nazarova and Nikitin remove the speech from their music. This decision was appealed by the President of the Ukrainian Figure Skating Federation, on the basis that this decision violated the ISU's Code of Ethics. Ultimately, Nazarova and Nikitin withdrew prior to the free dance, believing that their upbeat program was inappropriate, given their circumstances.

The pairs free skate was interrupted when American skater Ashley Cain-Gribble took a very serious fall. Cain-Gribble was removed from the ice on a stretcher and hospitalized, forcing she and partner Timothy LeDuc to withdraw from the competition.

Gabriella Papadakis and Guillaume Cizeron set a record for the highest overall score awarded in the ice dance event at the World Championships under the IJS System after the 2018/2019 season (229.82).

Simon Reed, who was providing commentary for the ISU's live feed of the competition, was overheard on a hot mic referring to Meagan Duhamel, a two-time World Champion in pair skating, as "that bitch from Canada," while his co-host Nicky Slater could be heard laughing in the background. Duhamel had criticized the Reed and Slater's commentary on social media the day prior. Reed's comment went viral and consequently, the ISU decided to remove both Reed and Slater from their roles as commentators for the remainder of the competition, as well as for any future ISU events. The ISU stated, "There is no place for harassing and abusive language or remarks and behaviour in sport and our society."

Sources: NBC Sports, February 6 and March 24, 2022; ISU Statement on the Ukrainian crisis - Participation in international competitions of Skaters and Officials from Russia and Belarus, March 1, 2022; BBC, March 24, 2022; CBC Sports, March 24, 2022; New York Post, March 25, 2022; Daily Mail, March 25, 2022; Appeal to ISU, Ukrainian Figure Skating Federation, March 26, 2022; Europe on Ice, April 1, 2022; Skating magazine, May 2022; Entries, 2022 World Figure Skating Championships; Protocol, 2022 World Figure Skating Championships; ISU Highest Total Scores Statistics

2023 WORLD FIGURE SKATING CHAMPIONSHIPS
Saitama, Japan, March 22-26, 2023

World Men's Figure Skating Championships:

	SP	FS
1. Shoma Uno (JPN)	1	1
2. Jun-hwan Cha (KOR)	3	2
3. Ilia Malinin (USA)	2	3
4. Kévin Aymoz (FRA)	5	4
5. Jason Brown (USA)	6	5
6. Kazuki Tomono (JPN)	7	6
7. Keegan Messing (CAN)	**4**	**11**
8. Lukas Britschgi (SUI)	9	9
9. Matteo Rizzo (ITA)	13	7
10. Adam Siao Him Fa (FRA)	12	8
11. Vladimir Litvintsev (AZE)	10	10
12. Daniel Grassl (ITA)	8	14
13. Deniss Vasiļjevs (LAT)	11	13
14. Mikhail Shaidorov (KAZ)	18	12
15. Sōta Yamamoto (JPN)	17	15
16. Mark Gorodnitsky (ISR)	14	16
17. Mihhail Selevko (EST)	15	17
18. Andreas Nordebäck (SWE)	20	18
19. Nikita Starostin (GER)	16	19
20. Morisi Kvitelashvili (GEO)	21	20
21. Andrew Torgashev (USA)	22	21
22. Boyang Jin (CHN)	19	23
23. Adam Hagara (SVK)	24	22
24. Maurizio Zandron (AUT)	23	24
25. Kyrylo Marsak (UKR)	25	-
26. Conrad Orzel (CAN)	**26**	**-**
27. Tomàs-Llorenç Guarino Sabaté (ESP)	27	-
28. Burak Demirboğa (TUR)	28	-
29. Nika Egadze (GEO)	29	-
30. Alexander Zlatkov (BUL)	30	-
31. Jari Kessler (CRO)	31	-
32. Graham Newberry (GRB)	32	-
33. Vladimir Samoilov (POL)	33	-

34. Georgii Reshtenko (CZE)	34	-
WD. Aleksandr Vlasenko (HUN)	-	-

World Women's Figure Skating Championships:

	SP	FS
1. Kaori Sakamoto (JPN)	1	2
2. Hae-in Lee (KOR)	2	1
3. Loena Hendrickx (BEL)	5	4
4. Isabeau Levito (USA)	4	5
5. Mai Mihara (JPN)	3	6
6. Chae-yeon Kim (KOR)	12	3
7. Nicole Schott (GER)	7	9
8. Kimmy Repond (SUI)	13	8
9. Niina Petrõkina (EST)	6	12
10. Rinka Watanabe (JPN)	15	7
11. Nina Pinzarrone (BEL)	14	10
12. Amber Glenn (USA)	10	14
13. Madeline Schizas (CAN)	**16**	**11**
14. Anastasiia Gubanova (GEO)	11	15
15. Bradie Tennell (USA)	8	16
16. Ekaterina Kurakova (POL)	9	17
17. Lara Naki Gutmann (ITA)	23	13
18. Ye-lim Kim (KOR)	17	19
19. Olga Mikutina (AUT)	20	18
20. Julia Sauter (ROM)	22	20
21. Janna Jyrkinen (FIN)	21	21
22. Lindsay van Zundert (NED)	19	22
23. Sofja Stepčenko (LAT)	18	24
24. Alexandra Feigin (BUL)	24	23
25. Lorine Schild (FRA)	25	-
26. Jade Hovine (BEL)	26	-
27. Kristen Spours (GRB)	27	-
28. Ema Doboszová (SVK)	28	-
29. Kristina Isaev (GER)	29	-
30. Anastasia Gracheva (MDA)	30	-
31. Marilena Kitromilis (CYP)	31	-
32. Eliška Březinová (CZE)	32	-
33. Daša Grm (SLO)	33	-

34. Júlia Láng (HUN) — 34 — -
35. Mia Caroline Risa Gomez (NOR) — 35 — -

World Pairs Skating Championships:

	SP	FS
1. Riku Miura/Ryuichi Kihara (JPN)	1	2
2. Alexa Scimeca Knierim/Brandon Frazier (USA)	2	1
3. Sara Conti/Niccolò Macii (ITA)	3	3
4. D. Stellato-Dudek/M. Deschamps (CAN)	**4**	**6**
5. Emily Chan/Spencer Akira Howe (USA)	5	8
6. Lia Pereira/Trennt Michaud (CAN)	**6**	**4**
7. Maria Pavlova/Alexei Sviatchenko (HUN)	8	7
8. A. Golubeva/H. Giotopoulos Moore (AUS)	11	5
9. Annika Hocke/Robert Kunkel (GER)	15	9
10. Alisa Efimova/Ruben Blommaert (GER)	7	10
11. Brooke McIntosh/Benjamin Mimar (CAN)	**10**	**11**
12. Ellie Kam/Danny O'Shea (USA)	9	13
13. Daria Danilova/Michel Tsiba (NED)	12	12
14. Camille Kovalev/Pavel Kovalev (FRA)	13	14
15. Oxana Vouillamoz/Flavien Giniaux (FRA)	16	15
16. Anastasia Vaipan-Law/Luke Digby (GRB)	17	16
17. Siyang Zhang/Yongchao Yang (CHN)	20	17
18. Isabella Gamez/Aleksandr Korovin (PHI)	19	18
19. Karina Safina/Luka Berulava (GEO)	14	20
20. Nika Osipova/Dmitry Epstein (NED)	18	19
21. Federica Simoli/Alessandro Zarbo (CZE)	21	-
22. Violetta Sierova/Ivan Khobta (UKR)	22	-
23. Lydia Smart/Harry Mattick (GRB)	23	-

World Ice Dancing Championships:

	RD	FD
1. Madison Chock/Evan Bates (USA)	1	1
2. Charlène Guignard/Marco Fabbri (ITA)	2	2
3. Piper Gilles/Paul Poirier (CAN)	**3**	**3**
4. Lilah Fear/Lewis Gibson (GRB)	4	5
5. L. Fournier Beaudry/N. Sørensen (CAN)	**5**	**4**
6. Caroline Green/Michael Parsons (USA)	6	6
7. Allison Reed/Saulius Ambrulevičius (LIT)	7	7

8. Natálie Taschlerová/Filip Taschler (CZE)	9	8
9. Juulia Turkkila/Matthias Versluis (FIN)	8	9
10. C. Carreira/A. Ponomarenko (USA)	10	11
11. Kana Muramoto/Daisuke Takahashi (JPN)	11	10
12. Evgenia Lopareva/Geoffrey Brissaud (FRA)	12	13
13. Maria Kazakova/Georgy Reviya (GEO)	14	12
14. Loïcia Demougeot/Théo Le Mercier (FRA)	13	14
15. J. Janse van Rensburg/B. Steffan (GER)	15	16
16. Holly Harris/Jason Chan (AUS)	16	15
17. M. Nosovitskaya/M. Nosovitskiy (ISR)	17	18
18. Victoria Manni/Carlo Röthlisberger (ITA)	18	17
19. Mariia Holubtsova/Kyryl Bielobrov (UKR)	19	19
20. Mariia Ignateva/Danijil Szemko (HUN)	20	20
21. Marie Dupayage/Thomas Nabais (FRA)	21	-
22. A. Polibina/P. Golovishnikov (POL)	22	-
23. Anna Šimová/Kirill Aksenov (SVK)	23	-
24. C. Lafond-Fournier/R. Kang In Kam (NZL)	24	-
25. Xizi Chen/Jianing Xing (CHN)	25	-
26. Paulina Ramanauskaitė/Deividas Kizala (LIT)	26	-
27. Aurelija Ipolito/Luke Russell (KAT)	27	-
28. S. Mazingue/M.J. Gaidajenko (EST)	28	-
29. A. Carhart/O. Kolosovskyi (AZE)	29	-
30. Sofía Val/Asaf Kazimov (ESP)	30	-
31. Chelsea Verhaegh/Sherim van Geffen (NED)	31	-
32. Olivia Josephine Shilling/Leo Baeten (BEL)	32	-
33. Gaukhar Nauryzova/Boyisangur Datiev (KAZ)	33	-
WD. Kaitlin Hawayek/Jean-Luc Baker (USA)	-	-

Riku Miura and Ryuichi Kihara made history as the first pair from Japan to win a gold medal at the World Figure Skating Championships. Sara Conti and Niccolò Macii made history as the first Italian pair to win a medal at the World Championships.

Kaori Sakamoto became the first Japanese skater to win back-to-back World titles in the women's event. Anastasia Gracheva made history as the first skater to represent Moldova at the World Figure Skating Championships.

Sources: CBC Sports, March 23, 2023; Entries, 2023 World Figure Skating Championships; Protocol, 2023 World Figure Skating Championships

Ilia Malinin, World Champion 2024 and 2025. Eric Canha / Cal Sport Media / Alamy Stock Photo.

THE NEW NORMAL

2024 WORLD FIGURE SKATING CHAMPIONSHIPS
Montreal, Canada, March 18-24, 2024

World Men's Figure Skating Championships:

	SP	FS
1. Ilia Malinin (USA)	3	1
2. Yuma Kagiyama (JPN)	2	3
3. Adam Siao Him Fa (FRA)	19	2
4. Shoma Uno (JPN)	1	6
5. Jason Brown (USA)	4	5
6. Lukas Britschgi (SUI)	5	4
7. Deniss Vasiļjevs (LAT)	8	8
8. Kao Miura (JPN)	10	7
9. Nikolaj Memola (ITA)	6	12
10. Jun-hwan Cha (KOR)	9	11
11. Aleksandr Selevko (EST)	12	9
12. Mark Gorodnitsky (ISR)	14	10
13. Nika Egadze (GEO)	7	15
14. Mikhail Shaidorov (KAZ)	16	13
15. Donovan Carrillo (MEX)	15	14
16. Gabriele Frangipani (ITA)	13	17
17. Wesley Chiu (CAN)	**18**	**17**
18. Hyun-gyeom Kim (KOR)	21	18
19. Roman Sadovsky (CAN)	**11**	**22**
20. Camden Pulkinen (USA)	17	20
21. Luc Economides (FRA)	22	19
22. Semen Daniliants (ARM)	23	21
23. Andreas Nordebäck (SWE)	20	23
24. Si-hyeong Lee (KOR)	24	24
25. Vladimir Litvintsev (AZE)	25	-
26. Davide Lewton Brain (MON)	26	-
27. Maurizio Zandron (AUT)	27	-
28. Tomàs-Llorenç Guarino Sabaté (ESP)	28	-
29. Jari Kessler (CRO)	29	-

30. Burak Demirboğa (TUR)	30	-
31. Vladimir Samoilov (POL)	31	-
32. Nikita Starostin (GER)	32	-
33. Ivan Shmuratko (UKR)	33	-
34. Valtter Virtanen (FIN)	34	-
35. Adam Hagara (SVK)	35	-
36. Georgii Reshtenko (CZE)	36	-
37. Alexander Zlatkov (BUL)	37	-
38. Edward Appleby (GRB)	38	-
39. Boyang Jin (CHN)	39	-
40. Aleksandr Vlasenko (HUN)	40	-
WD. Kévin Aymoz (FRA)	-	-
WD. Lev Vinokur (ISR)	-	-

World Women's Figure Skating Championships:

	SP	FS
1. Kaori Sakamoto (JPN)	4	1
2. Isabeau Levito (USA)	2	2
3. Chae-yeon Kim (KOR)	6	3
4. Loena Hendrickx (BEL)	1	8
5. Kimmy Repond (SUI)	12	4
6. Hae-in Lee (KOR)	3	12
7. Mone Chiba (JPN)	13	5
8. Hana Yoshida (JPN)	8	6
9. Livia Kaiser (SUI)	10	9
10. Amber Glenn (USA)	9	11
11. Ekaterina Kurakova (POL)	14	10
12. Young You (KOR)	5	14
13. Anastasiia Gubanova (GEO)	20	7
14. Olga Mikutina (AUT)	16	13
15. Nina Pinzarrone (BEL)	11	16
16. Niina Petrōkina (EST)	7	18
17. Lorine Schild (FRA)	18	15
18. Madeline Schizas (CAN)	**17**	**17**
19. Josefin Taljegård (SWE)	15	20
20. Sarina Joos (ITA)	19	19
21. Nataly Langerbaur (EST)	24	21
22. Tzu-Han Ting (TPE)	22	22

23. Mia Risa Gomez (NOR)	23	23
24. Nella Pelkonen (FIN)	21	24
25. Nina Povey (GRB)	25	-
26. Alexandra Feigin (BUL)	26	-
27. Julia Sauter (ROM)	27	-
28. Eliška Březinová (CZE)	28	-
29. Kristina Isaev (GER)	29	-
30. Vanesa Šelmeková (SVK)	30	-
31. Sofja Stepčenko (LAT)	31	-
32. Mariia Seniuk (ISR)	32	-
33. Anastasia Gracheva (MDA)	33	-
34. Anastasia Gozhva (UKR)	34	-
35. Meda Variakojytė (LIT)	35	-
WD. Léa Serna (FRA)	-	-

World Pairs Skating Championships:

	SP	FS
1. D. Stellato-Dudek/M. Deschamps (CAN)	**1**	**2**
2. Riku Miura/Ryuichi Kihara (JPN)	2	1
3. Minerva Fabienne Hase/Nikita Volodin (GER)	4	3
4. Maria Pavlova/Alexei Sviatchenko (HUN)	6	4
5. Annika Hocke/Robert Kunkel (GER)	7	5
6. Sara Conti/Niccolò Macii (ITA)	3	6
7. Anastasiia Metelkina/Luka Berulava (GEO)	5	10
8. Lia Pereira/Trennt Michaud (CAN)	**9**	**7**
9. Lucrezia Beccari/Matteo Guarise (ITA)	8	9
10. A. Golubeva/H. Giotopoulos Moore (AUS)	11	8
11. Ellie Kam/Danny O'Shea (USA)	10	11
12. Emily Chan/Spencer Akira Howe (USA)	12	13
13. V. Plazas/M. Fernandez (USA)	13	14
14. Daria Danilova/Michel Tsiba (NED)	17	12
15. Kelly Ann Laurin/Loucas Éthier (CAN)	**14**	**15**
16. Cheng Peng/Lei Wang (CHN)	15	16
17. Sofiia Holichenko/Artem Darenskyi (UKR)	16	18
18. Milania Väänänen/Filippo Clerici (FIN)	19	17
19. Ioulia Chtchetinina/Michał Woźniak (POL)	18	19
20. Anastasia Vaipan-Law/Luke Digby (GRB)	20	20
21. Isabella Gamez/Alexander Korovin (PHI)	21	-

22. Sophia Schaller/Livio Mayr (AUT) — 22 / -
23. Greta Crafoord/John Crafoord (SWE) — 23 / -
24. Federica Simioli/Alessandro Zarbo (CZE) — 24 / -
WD. Camille Kovalev/Pavel Kovalev (FRA) — - / -

World Ice Dancing Championships:

	RD	FD
1. Madison Chock/Evan Bates (USA)	1	2
2. Piper Gilles/Paul Poirier (CAN)	**3**	**1**
3. Charlène Guignard/Marco Fabbri (ITA)	2	3
4. Lilah Fear/Lewis Gibson (GRB)	4	4
5. Marjorie Lajoie/Zachary Lagha (CAN)	**5**	**5**
6. Allison Reed/Saulius Ambrulevičius (LIT)	6	9
7. C. Carreira/A. Ponomarenko (USA)	8	7
8. Evgenia Lopareva/Geoffrey Brissaud (FRA)	7	8
9. L. Fournier Beaudry/N. Sørensen (CAN)	**10**	**6**
10. Juulia Turkkila/Matthias Versluis (FIN)	9	10
11. Loïcia Demougeot/Théo le Mercier (FRA)	11	13
12. Diana Davis/Gleb Smolkin (GEO)	12	14
13. Kateřina Mrázková/Daniel Mrázek (CZE)	13	11
14. Hannah Lim/Ye Quan (KOR)	14	12
15. Natálie Taschlerová/Filip Taschler (CZE)	18	15
16. Yuka Orihara/Juho Pirinen (FIN)	17	16
17. Holly Harris/Jason Chan (AUS)	16	19
18. Misato Komatsubara/Tim Koleto (JPN)	20	17
19. Olivia Smart/Tim Dieck (ESP)	15	20
20. Carolane Soucisse/Shane Firus (IRL)	19	18
21. Phebe Bekker/James Hernandez (GRB)	21	-
22. J. Janse van Rensburg/B. Steffan (GER)	22	-
23. Emily Bratti/Ian Somerville (USA)	23	-
24. M. Ignateva/D. Leonyidovics Szemko (HUN)	24	-
25. Victoria Manni/Carlo Röthlisberger (ITA)	25	-
26. Mariia Holubtsova/Kyryl Bielobrov (UKR)	26	-
27. Anna Šimová/Kiril Aksenov (SVK)	27	-
28. Milla Ruud Reitan/Nikolaj Majorov (SWE)	28	-
29. M. Nosovitskaya/M. Nosovitskiy (ISR)	29	-
30. Xizi Chen/Jianing Xing (CHN)	30	-
31. P. Ramanauskaitė/D. Kizala (LIT)	31	-

32. Gina Zehnder/Beda Leon Sieber (SUI)	32	-
33. S. Mazingue/M.J. Gaidajenko (EST)	33	-
34. Olivia Oliver/Filip Bojanowski (POL)	34	-
35. Hanna Jakucs/Alessio Galli (NED)	35	-
36. A. Carhart/O. Kolosovskyi (AZE)	36	-
WD. Shiyue Wang/Xinyu Liu (CHN)	-	-

At the age of 40, Deanna Stellato-Dudek achieved the distinction of being the oldest woman to win a gold medal at the World Figure Skating Championships, with partner Maxime Deschamps. Her triumph was especially noteworthy as she had previously earned a medal in the ladies event at the 2000 World Junior Championships and retired from the sport in 2001. She made her return to competitive skating as a pairs skater in 2016. Following her victory, Stellato-Dudek told reporters, "40 is the new 20. It's something I carry with pride. I'm very proud of it. I hope a lot of athletes stay around a lot longer. I hope it encourages people to not stop before they've reached their potential."

Ilia Malinin set a record for the highest overall score awarded in the men's event at the World Championships under the IJS System after the 2018/2019 season (333.76). Malinin also made history as the first skater to land six quadruple jumps with positive GOEs in his winning free skate ((Salchow, toe-loop, loop, two Lutzes and Axel). His quadruple Axel was the first ever performed at the World Championships.

Adam Siao Him Fa won the bronze medal in the men's event, after placing nineteenth in the short program, in the largest climb in the standings in the history of the World Championships.

Sources: CBC Sports, March 21, 2024; Entries, 2024 World Figure Skating Championships; Protocol, 2024 World Figure Skating Championships; ISU Highest Total Scores Statistics

2025 WORLD FIGURE SKATING CHAMPIONSHIPS
Boston, United States, March 26-30, 2025

World Men's Figure Skating Championships:

	SP	FS
1. Ilia Malinin (USA)	1	1
2. Mikhail Shaidorov (KAZ)	3	2
3. Yuma Kagiyama (JPN)	2	10
4. Adam Siao Him Fa (FRA)	9	3
5. Kévin Aymoz (FRA)	4	7
6. Shun Sato (JPN)	5	6
7. Jun-hwan Cha (KOR)	10	5
8. Jason Brown (USA)	12	4
9. Nika Egadze (GEO)	6	8
10. Nikolaj Memola (ITA)	7	11
11. Deniss Vasiļjevs (LAT)	16	9
12. Lukas Britschgi (SUI)	11	14
13. Daniel Grassl (ITA)	14	12
14. Roman Sadovsky (CAN)	**15**	**13**
15. Vladimir Litvintsev (AZE)	13	17
16. Adam Hagara (SVK)	18	15
17. Andreas Nordebäck (SWE)	17	16
18. Daiwei Dai (CHN)	21	18
19. Mihhail Selevko (EST)	19	21
20. Tomàs-Llorenç Guarino Sabaté (ESP)	22	20
21. Tatsuya Tsuboi (JPN)	24	19
22. Andrew Torgashev (USA)	8	23
23. Vladimir Samoilov (POL)	20	22
24. Fedir Kulish (LAT)	23	24
25. Lev Vinokur (ISR)	25	-
26. Hyun-gyeom Kim (KOR)	26	-
27. Donovan Carrillo (MEX)	27	-
28. Nikita Starostin (GER)	28	-
29. Aleksandr Vlasenko (HUN)	29	-
30. Yu-Hsiang Li (TPE)	30	-
31. Georgii Reshtenko (CZE)	31	-
32. Edward Appleby (GRB)	32	-
33. Kyrylo Marsak (UKR)	33	-
34. Jari Kessler (CRO)	34	-
35. Maurizio Zandron (AUT)	35	-
36. Alexander Zlatkov (BUL)	36	-

37. Semen Daniliants (ARM) 37 -
38. Burak Demirboğa (TUR) 38 -
39. Davide Lewton Brain (MON) 39 -
WD. Mark Gorodnitsky (ISR) - -

World Women's Figure Skating Championships:

	SP	FS
1. Alysa Liu (USA)	1	1
2. Kaori Sakamoto (JPN)	5	2
3. Mone Chiba (JPN)	2	3
4. Isabeau Levito (USA)	3	5
5. Amber Glenn (USA)	9	4
6. Wakaba Higuchi (JPN)	4	6
7. Nina Pinzarrone (BEL)	8	7
8. Niina Petrõkina. (EST)	12	8
9. Hae-in Lee (KOR)	7	10
10. Chae-yeon Kim (KOR)	11	9
11. Madeline Schizas (CAN)	**6**	**11**
12. Kimmy Repond (SUI)	10	15
13. Lara Naki Gutmann (ITA)	14	12
14. Sofia Samodelkina (KAZ)	13	13
15. Lorine Schild (FRA)	15	14
16. Mariia Seniuk (ISR)	19	16
17. Olga Mikutina (AUT)	17	19
18. Linnea Ceder (FIN)	20	17
19. Julia Sauter (ROM)	16	20
20. Ekaterina Kurakova (POL)	21	18
21. Alexandra Feigin (BUL)	18	21
22. Kristen Spours (GRB)	22	22
23. Livia Kaiser (SUI)	23	23
24. Meda Variakojytė (LIT)	24	24
25. Nargiz Süleymanova (AZE)	25	-
26. Vanesa Šelmeková (SVK)	26	-
27. Xiangyi An (CHN)	27	-
28. Anastasiia Gubanova (GEO)	28	-
29. Mia Risa Gomez (NOR)	29	-
30. Sofja Stepčenko (LAT)	30	-
31. Yun Ah-sun (KOR)	31	-

32. Julija Lovrenčič (SLO) 32 -
33. Anastasia Gozhva (UKR) 33 -

World Pairs Skating Championships:

	SP	FS
1. Riku Miura/Ryuichi Kihara (JPN)	1	2
2. Minerva Fabienne Hase/Nikita Volodin (GER)	3	1
3. Sara Conti/Niccolò Macii (ITA)	2	3
4. Anastasiia Metelkina/Luka Berulava (GEO)	4	6
5. D. Stellato-Dudek/M. Deschamps (CAN)	**7**	**5**
6. Alisa Efimova/Misha Mitrofanov (USA)	9	4
7. Ellie Kam/Danny O'Shea (USA)	5	7
8. Maria Pavlova/Alexei Sviatchenko (HUN)	6	8
9. A. Golubeva/H. Giotopoulos Moore (AUS)	8	9
10. Ekaterina Geynish/Dmitrii Chigirev (UZB)	11	10
11. Lia Pereira/Trennt Michaud (CAN)	**10**	**13**
12. Anastasia Vaipan-Law/Luke Digby (GRB)	13	11
13. Rebecca Ghilardi/Filippo Ambrosini (ITA)	14	14
14. Ioulia Chtchetinina/Michał Woźniak (POL)	19	12
15. Daria Danilova/Michel Tsiba (NED)	15	16
16. Kelly Ann Laurin/Loucas Éthier (CAN)	**12**	**18**
17. Sofiia Holichenko/Artem Darenskyi (UKR)	17	17
18. Annika Hocke/Robert Kunkel (GER)	20	15
19. Milania Väänänen/Filippo Clerici (FIN)	16	20
20. Oxana Vouillamoz/Tom Bouvart (SUI)	18	19
21. Camille Kovalev/Pavel Kovalev (FRA)	21	-
22. Yuna Nagaoka/Sumitada Moriguchi (JPN)	22	-
23. Gabriella Izzo/Luc Maierhofer (AUT)	23	-

World Ice Dancing Championships:

	RD	FD
1. Madison Chock/Evan Bates (USA)	1	1
2. Piper Gilles/Paul Poirier (CAN)	**2**	**2**
3. Lilah Fear/Lewis Gibson (GRB)	3	6
4. Charlène Guignard/Marco Fabbri (ITA)	4	4
5. C. Carreira/A. Ponomarenko (USA)	6	5
6. Olivia Smart/Tim Dieck (ESP)	8	3
7. Marjorie Lajoie/Zachary Lagha (CAN)	**5**	**8**

8. Evgeniia Lopareva/Geoffrey Brissaud (FRA)	9	9
9. Caroline Green/Michael Parsons (USA)	7	11
10. Diana Davis/Gleb Smolkin (GEO)	14	10
11. Juulia Turkkila/Matthias Versluis (FIN)	20	7
12. Kateřina Mrázková/Daniel Mrázek (CZE)	10	12
13. Natálie Taschlerová/Filip Taschler (CZE)	13	13
14. Yuka Orihara/Juho Pirinen (FIN)	11	14
15. Loïcia Demougeot/Théo Le Mercier (FRA)	15	15
16. J. Janse van Rensburg/B. Steffan (GER)	12	17
17. Phebe Bekker/James Hernandez (GRB)	17	16
18. Hannah Lim/Ye Quan (KOR)	16	18
19. Holly Harris/Jason Chan (AUS)	18	19
20. Alicia Fabbri/Paul Ayer (CAN)	**19**	**20**
21. Allison Reed/Saulius Ambrulevičius (LIT)	21	-
22. Utana Yoshida/Masaya Morita (JPN)	22	-
23. Victoria Manni/Carlo Röthlisberger (ITA)	23	-
24. M. Ignateva/D.L. Szemko (HUN)	24	-
25. Milla Ruud Reitan/Nikolaj Majorov (SWE)	25	-
26. Elizabeth Tkachenko/Alexei Kiliakov (ISR)	26	-
27. Mária Sofia Pucherová/Nikita Lysak (SVK)	27	-
28. Carolane Soucisse/Shane Firus (IRL)	28	-
29. Zoe Larson/Andrii Kapran (UKR)	29	-
30. Gina Zehnder/Beda Leon Sieber (SUI)	30	-
31. Ren Junfei/Xing Jianing (CHN)	31	-
32. Chelsea Verhaegh/Sherim van Geffen (NED)	32	-
33. Samantha Ritter/Daniel Brykalov (AZE)	33	-
34. Sofiia Dovhal/Wiktor Kulesza (POL)	34	-
35. Katarina DelCamp/Berk Akalın (TUR)	35	-
36. A. Kudryavtseva/I. Karankevich (CYP)	36	-
WD. P. Ramanauskaitė/D. Kizala (LIT)	-	-
WD. Shira Ichilov/Dmytriy Kravchenko (ISR)	-	-

Lilah Fear and Lewis Gibson won Great Britain's first medal at the World Figure Skating Championships in over forty years.

Ilia Malinin made history the first skater to successfully land six different types of quadruple jumps (Salchow, toe-loop, loop, flip, Lutz and Axel) in a single program at the World Championships.

Mikhail Shaidorov made history as the first skater to land the difficult triple Axel/Euler/quadruple Salchow combination at the World Championships.

Sources: Entries, 2025 World Figure Skating Championships; Protocol, 2025 World Figure Skating Championships

APPRECIATION

This book would not have come to fruition without generous donations of materials to the Skate Guard Collections throughout the years. A heartfelt and particularly special thank you to the following individuals for their unique contributions:

Sandra Bezic
Yvonne Butorac
Karen Cover, World Figure Skating Museum & Hall of Fame
Paul Dean
Matthias Hampe
Phil Hayes, British Ice Skating Historian
Elaine Hooper, Former British Ice Skating Historian
Ingrid Hunnewell
PJ Kwong
Rachel Renton
Troy Schwindt, "Skating" magazine, U.S. Figure Skating
Ken Shelley
Pauliina Vuorinen, The National Library of Finland
Benjamin T. Wright†

I am also grateful to Stefan Prodanovic, who created the charming cover for this book. Stefan also designed the cover for my book "Sequins, Scandals & Salchows: Figure Skating in the 1980s," and it was a delight to collaborate with him once more on this project.

AUTHOR'S NOTE

I sincerely hope you found "A Complete History of the World Figure Skating Championships" to be an informative and valuable resource.

Reviews are vital for the success of all books, but they are especially crucial for those that are independently published.

I have a small request to make. Would you mind taking a few moments to leave a brief review on the retailer's website where you purchased your copy, as well as on popular book review sites?

I would also be incredibly grateful if you could take a moment to visit your local library's website and complete a short 'Suggest a Purchase' form.

Thank you for your support in helping this significant history reach a wider audience.

BOOKS BY THIS AUTHOR

A Complete History of the European Figure Skating Championships

A Complete History of the World Figure Skating Championships.

Barbara Ann Scott: Queen of the Ice

Sequins, Scandals & Salchows: Figure Skating in the 1980s

Jackson Haines: The Skating King

Technical Merit: A History of Figure Skating Jumps

A Bibliography of Figure Skating

The Almanac of Canadian Figure Skating